University of Chester

CHESTER CAMPUS
LIBRARY
01244 392738

This book is to be returned on or before the last date stamped below. Overdue charges will be incurred by the late return of books.

CATHOLICS AND SHI'A IN DIALOGUE: STUDIES IN THEOLOGY AND SPIRITUALITY

edited by
Anthony O'Mahony, Wulstan Peterburs
and
Mohammad Ali Shomali

MELISENDE

*Catholics and Shi'a
in dialogue:
Studies in theology and spirituality*
edited by
Anthony O'Mahony, Wulstan Peterburs and Mohammad Ali Shomali

First published 2004
by Melisende
an imprint of
Fox Communications and Publications
39 Chelmsford Road
London E18 2PW
Tel: 020 8498 9768
Fax: 020 8504 2558
e-mail: melisende@btinternet.com
www.melisende.com

ISBN 1 901764 37 0

Edited by Leonard Harrow
Printed in England at the Cromwell Press, Trowbridge, England

CONTENTS

The Catholic Shi'a Encounter: Prayer and Spirituality

The Catholic Shi'a Encounter: Meeting the Challenges

Afterword

CONTRIBUTORS

Catholic

Archbishop Michael L Fitzgerald MAfr, President of the Pontifical Council for Interreligious Dialogue, was born in Walsall (UK) in 1937. Ordained priest as a member of the Society of the Missionaries of Africa (White Fathers) in 1961, he obtained his doctorate in theology from the Pontifical Gregorian University (1965) and a BA Hons in Arabic from the School of Oriental and African Studies, London University (1968). After teaching at Makerere University, Kampala, Uganda, and at the Pontifical Institute of Arabic and Islamic Studies, Rome, there followed two years of pastoral work in Sudan. After a period on the General Council of the Missionaries of Africa 1980-1986, there came in 1987 an appointment as Secretary of the Secretariat for Non-Christians, now Pontifical Council for Interreligious Dialogue. In 1991 Fr Fitzgerald was appointed titular bishop of Nepte and was consecrated by Pope John Paul II on 6 January 1992. On 1 October 2002 he was appointed President of the Pontifical Council for Interreligious Dialogue and was raised to the rank of archbishop. He is author with R Caspar of *Signs of Dialogue. Christian Encounter with Muslims* (1992) and of numerous articles in *Concilium, Islamochristiana, Pro Dialogo, Spiritus*.

Rt Revd Dom Timothy Wright OSB is the Abbot of Ampleforth Abbey. He read geography at St Benet's Hall, Oxford, and subsequently took a theology degree at the University of London. He began full-time teaching at Ampleforth College in 1972, becoming Head of Religious Studies. As Head of Department he was involved in developing new religious studies syllabuses at GCSE and A level with several examination boards. He was a Housemaster and Deputy Headmaster before being elected Abbot in March 1997. As Abbot he has been involved in numerous ecumenical activities, especially in Yorkshire, and in 2002 co-authored *Doing Business with Benedict* on the application of the Rule of St Benedict to modern business practice. He has spoken on spirituality and theology at numerous conferences and gatherings, and in 2002 was invited to visit the Imam Khomeini Institute for Education and Research in Qum, Iran, where he spoke on Benedictine monasticism and spirituality, and again in 2004 on the right role of conscience within the Catholic theological tradition.

Revd Justo Lacunza Balda MAfr, Director of the Pontifical Institute for Arabic and Islamic Studies (PISAI), Rome, was born in Pamplona, Spain, and is a priest of the Missionaries of Africa. Having studied at PISAI, he completed a doctorate in African Languages and Cultures at the School of Oriental and African Studies in London, specializing in Islam and the Swahili language and culture. From 1989 he was a professor at PISAI, until being appointed Rector of the Institute in 2000. His publications include *Islam: Aspetti e immagini del mondo musulmano oggi* (2003), and numerous contributions to scholarly collections on Islam in Africa and to PISAI's own reviews *Encounter: Documents in Muslim-Christian Understanding* and *Islamochristiana.*

Revd John McDade SJ, Principal of Heythrop College, University of London, is a Jesuit priest and theologian. After doctoral studies in Christology at the University of Edinburgh, he has been on the staff of Heythrop College since 1985, and has been Principal since 1999, teaching Christology, Trinitarian Theology and Christian-Jewish Relations. His research interest is French 17th-century religious thought. He is also a former editor of the Jesuit journal *The Month* (London).

Revd Chris Clohessy, of the Pontifical Institute for Arabic and Islamic Studies (PISAI), was born and educated in South Africa, being ordained to the priesthood in Cape Town in 1988, after which he worked in a number of parishes before moving to Rome to complete a Licentiate in Arabic and Islamic Studies at PISAI. Having graduated in 2001, he is now a member of the staff of PISAI, teaching Shi'a Islam and researching a doctorate about Fatima, daughter of Muhammad, in the light of Catholic Mariology. He is editor of the College's English language journal, *Encounter: Documents in Muslim-Christian Understanding*; and has published a number of papers in Rome including: 'Islam in South Africa' (1998), 'Glimpses along a Sufi Path' (2000), 'Karbala', the Face of Islam Flushed' (2000) and 'The Gospel of Barnabas: A Précis' (2002).

Sr Catherine Cowley ra, is a Sister of the Assumption and a lecturer in theology at Heythrop College, University of London. She has a specialist interest in social ethics and is a member of the Institute for Religion and Public Life. She has recently published 'Christian Ethics and the Global Economy', in *World Christianity: Politics, Theology and Dialogues* (2004).

Revd Michael Kirwan SJ, is a priest in the Society of Jesus and lectures in Systematic and Pastoral Theology at Heythrop College, University of London. His principle interest is in Political and Liberation Theologies, with special attention to the theme of religion and violence in the modern world. His publications include 'The Struggles of Perpetua: Vision, Narrative and Meaning of Martyrdom' in *Passion For Critique: Essays in Honour of F J Laishley* (1997); 'Millenial Appetites and Refusal of Somoatocracy' in *Faith in the Millenium* (2001); 'The Limits of Interpretation: the Gadamer-Habermas Conversation' in *Philosophical Hermeneutics and Biblical Exegesis* (2002); 'Current Theological themes in World Christianity', in *World Christianity: Politics, Theology and Dialogues*, edited with A O'Mahony (2004); and *Discovering Girard* (2004).

Revd Ian Latham LBJ, of the Little Brothers of Jesus, has studied in France and lived for many years in Asia and the Middle East. He now lives in a community of followers of Charles de Foucauld in Peckham, London. He has made a number of special studies on Catholic encounter with Islam, including Louis Massignon in Iraq, and recently published 'Charles de Foucauld (1858-1916): Silent witness for Jesus in the face of Islam' in *Catholics and Interreligious Dialogue: Studies in Monasticism, Theology and Spirituality* (2004).

Sr Mary Mills SHCJ, is a member of the Society of the Holy Child Jesus. She is a very experienced educationalist, having taught first in secondary schools and then in higher education. She has lectured in biblical studies at seminaries in England and in St Mary's College, University of Surrey, and Heythrop College, University of London; and is currently Head of Theology at Newman College, University of Birmingham. Her research interests are in the links between biblical books and the contemporary study of literature, and has published a number of books in biblical studies, including *Reading Ecclesiastes* (2003).

Anthony O'Mahony, Director of Research at the Centre for Christianity and Interreligious Dialogue at Heythrop College, has a specialist interest in Eastern Christianity, theology and politics and Christian–Muslim relations. His publications include *Palestinian Christians: Religion, Politics and Society in the Holy Land* (1999); with Atauallah Siddiqui, *Christians and Muslims in the Commonwealth* (2001); *The Christian Communities in Jerusalem and the Holy Land: Studies in History, Religion and Politics* (2003); with Michael Kirwan SJ, *World Christianity: Politics, Theology and Dialogues* (2004); *Christianity in the Middle East: Studies in Modern History, Theology and Politics* (2004); *Eastern Christianity: Studies in Modern History, Religion and Politics* (2004); with Peter Bowe, OSB, *Catholics and Interreligious Dialogue: Studies in Monasticism, Theology and Spirituality* (2004).

Revd Dom Wulstan Peterburs OSB is a monk of Ampleforth Abbey where he is the Master of Studies and Head of the Department of Christian Theology at Ampleforth College. He holds both a bachelor's degree in Theology and a doctorate on 'Newman, Vatican II and ARCIC' from the University of Durham. His main publications have been in the field of Newman studies and he has undertaken research in Moral Theology, also teaching the Christian Ethics component of a MA in Theology offered at Ampleforth. He is a member of the British Association of the Teachers of Moral Theology and of the Monastic Interfaith Dialogue. In 2002 he was invited to speak on the nature and exercise of authority in the Catholic Church at the Imam Khomeini Institute for Education and Research in Qum, Iran, and has spoken in Britain at a number of conferences on topics ranging from spirituality to theology and ethics.

Patrick Riordan SJ is a Jesuit priest and an Associate Director of the Heythrop Institute for Religion, Ethics and Public Life. He teaches political philosophy in the undergraduate programmes, and topics from political philosophy in the MA in Christian Ethics and Society, at Heythrop College, University of London. His main areas of research are 'Religion in Public Life', on which he has recently published an article in *The Heythrop Journal*, 'Citizenship' (recent articles in *Administration*) and the 'Common Good', on which he is writing a book. His published books include *Philosophical Perspectives on People Power* (2001), and *A Politics of the Common Good* (1996).

Shi'a

Ayatollah Misbah Yazdi is the President of Imam Khomeini Education and Research Institute and a member of the Council of Experts (*Majlis-i Khubrigān-i Rahbañ*) in Iran. He has written widely on Islamic philosophy, spirituality and thought as well as Qur'anic exegesis. His publications include: *Philosophical Instructions* (1999), *Rah Tūshah* (1996), *Sharḥ-i Asfār al-Arbi'ah* (1996), *Rāhiyyān-i Kūy-i Dūst* (1995), *Tarjumah va Sharḥ-i Burhān-i Shifā* (1994), *Akhlāq dar Qur'ān* (1993), *Amūzish-i 'Aqā'id* (1991), *Ḥukūmat-i Islamī va Wilāyat-i Faqīh* (1990), *Ma'ārif-i Qur'ān* (1989), *Jāmi'ah va Tārīkh az Dīdgāh-i Qur'ān* (1989) and *Ta'līqat-un 'alā Nihāyat al-Ḥikmah* (1985).

Ayatollah Muhsin Araki is the Director of Islamic Centre of England (London) and a member of the Council of Experts *(Majlis-i Khubrigān-i Rahbañ)* in Iran. His publications include: *Introduction to Islamic Mysticism* (2001), *Foundations of Islamic Government* (2000), *Contemporary Islamic Awakening—Phases and Pioneers* (2000), *Ma'ālim al-Fikr al-Uṣūlī al-Jadīd* (1999) and *Islamic Epistemology* (1999).

Hujjat al-Islam Saied Reza Ameli, PhD, is a lecturer in the Sociology of Mass Media, Department of Communications at the University of Tehran. He is the author of *Globalization, Americanization and British Muslim Identity* (2002)

Hujjat al-Islam Mahmud Mohammadi Araghi is the Head of the Organization for Islamic Culture and Relations, a Member of the High Council for Cultural Affairs and Member of the High Council of the Representatives of the Supreme Leader in Universities, Iran. He has completed advanced studies in Islamic philosophy and the Qur'anic sciences and has taught in different universities and published numerous articles on Islamic studies. Among his books is *Shinākht-i Qur'ān* ('Knowing the Qur'an').

Hujjat al-Islam Mahmood Taghizadeh Davari, PhD, is a lecturer in and the Head of the Department of Sociology at the Imam Khomeini Education and Research Institute and Founding Director of the Institute of Shi'ite Studies, Qum.

Hujjat al-Islam Mohammad Ali Shomali, PhD, is a lecturer in and Head of the Department of Religion at the Imam Khomeini Education and Research Institute, Qum. His publications include: *Self-Knowledge* (1996), *Ethical Relativism:An Analysis of the Foundations of Morality* (2002), *Discovering Shi'a Islam* (2003), *Shi'a Islam: Origins, Faith and Practices* (2003) and *Principles of Jurisprudence: An Introduction to Methodology of Fiqh* (forthcoming).

Hujjat al-Islam Mohammad Jafar Elmi, PhD, is the Principal of the Islamic College for Advanced Studies, London. His PhD is on hermeneutics of the Qur'an.

Mohammad Fanaei Eshkervari, PhD, is a lecturer at the Imam Khomeini Education and Research Institute, Qum. His publications include: *Ma'qūl-i Thānī* (1996), *'Ilm-i Ḥuḍūrī* (1996), *Dānish-i Islāmī va Dānishgāh-i Islāmī* (1998), *Manzilat-i Zan dar Andīsha-yi Islāmī* (1998) and *Ta'ahhud bi Ḥaqīqat* (1999).

Mahnaz Heydarpoor is a lecturer at Jami'at al-Zahra, Qum. Her publications include *Love in Christianity and Islam: A Contribution to Religious Ethics* (2002).

Muhsin Javadi, PhD, is a lecturer at the University of Qum, where he is also the Director of International Relations. His publications include: *Mas'alah-yi Bāyad va Hast* ('The Is/Ought Problem') (1996), *Dar Āmadī Bar Khudāshināsī-yi Falsafī* ('An Introduction to Philosophical Theology') (1996), *Naẓarīya-yi Imān* ('A Theory of Faith') (1998) and co-author of *Ma'ārif-i Islāmī* ('Islamic Doctrines') (2000).

Reza Shah Kazemi, PhD, is a research associate at the Institute of Ismaili Studies, London. He has authored and translated several works, including *Paths of Transcendence: Shankara, Ibn Arabi and Meister Eckhart on Transcendent Spiritual realization* (2004), and *Doctrines of Shi'a Islam* (2001).

Morteza Sanei, is a postgraduate student in the Department of Religion at the Imam Khomeini Education and Research Institute, Qum.

Mohammad Soori, is a postgraduate student in the Department of Religion at the Imam Khomeini Education and Research Institute, Qum.

PREFACE
John McDade

The papers collected in this volume are the fruit, not simply of the conversations between Catholic and Shi'a scholars during their meetings in 2003, but also of the present context of respectful relations between the Christian and Islamic traditions. That these conversations happen at all is a wonderful thing; that they are so fruitful is surely a divine blessing. Scholars from both traditions now realise that dialogue among believers is a service of truth and that it is God's will that his worshippers should foster peace among themselves. Cardinal Joseph Ratzinger identifies one of the conditions of genuine dialogue:

> What is required is reverence for the other's belief, along with the willingness to seek truth in what I find alien—a truth that concerns me and that can correct me and lead me further. I must be willing to let my narrow understanding of truth be broken open, to learn my own beliefs better by understanding the other, and in this way to let myself be furthered on the path to God, who is greater. Among the religions we encounter people who through their religion have heard of God and try to live in relation to him. We are not saying something completely unknown to the other, but disclosing the hidden depth of what he already touches in his own belief. [1]

This is surely correct: a reverence for another tradition leads to a generosity of mind and heart that is ready to recognise truth in what is different; a willingness to believe that God is already active within this other tradition alters the way we speak to one another and so we can no

---

[1] J Ratzinger, 'Interreligious Dialogue and Jewish-Christian Relations', *Communio: International Catholic Review*, Vol. 25 (1998), 40-1.

longer utter mutual condemnations because how we deal with one another is a significant moment in our journey towards God and blessedness.

Genuine dialogue puts us in touch with the divine depths not only of another tradition but also of our own tradition. And surely one of the signs of genuine dialogue is when both parties come away from their conversations aware that their contact with God's action in another religious tradition brings them closer to God's action in their own tradition. I do not come away from this Catholic-Shi'a dialogue feeling less of a Catholic; instead, I am enriched in my Catholic faith by knowing that there is a refraction of God's Word in the lives of faithful Muslims. In the submission to the all powerful and merciful God enacted in Islam, Christians can see key features of Christian discipleship: obedience, faith, prayer, trust and righteous living. It is open to Muslims to see enacted in the lives of Christians a pattern of faithfulness which they can recognise from their own tradition.

This mutuality is not a new thing: in ways that we should make our own today, Pope Gregory VII in 1076 wrote to al-Nasir, the Muslim ruler of Bijaya in North Africa:

> Almighty God, who wishes that all should be saved and none lost, approves nothing in so much as that after loving Him one should love his fellow man, and that one should not do to others, what one does not want done to oneself. You and we owe this charity to ourselves especially because we believe in and confess one God, admittedly, in a different way, and daily praise and venerate him, the creator of the world and ruler of this world.

Examples like this of respectful relations between Catholics and Muslims are to be treasured for they show us that what we are doing now retrieves the best in our history. I hope that this volume of papers from the Catholic-Shi'a Conference at Heythrop College, University of London, and Ampleforth Abbey, will be read fruitfully by both Christians and Muslims.

INTRODUCTION

This book represents the deliberations of a conference entitled 'A Catholic-Shi'a Engagement: Sharing our Spiritual and Theological Resources in the Face of Contemporary Challenges', which met at Heythrop College in the University of London and at Ampleforth Abbey from 5-10 July 2003. The conference was the result of contacts between monks of Ampleforth Abbey and scholars of the Imam Khomeini Education and Research Institute in Qum, Iran, which grew to include Heythrop College as plans for a theological encounter began to develop. Ultimately, the conference included representatives from a number of institutions, including the Pontifical Institute for Arabic and Islamic Studies in Rome and the Islamic College of Advanced Studies in London. This led to the conference being described as 'the first major British encounter' of Catholic theologians with Shi'a scholars.[1]

The aim of this unique conference was to study how the Catholic Christian tradition and Shi'a Islam can bring their spiritual and theological resources to bear on some of the most critical of contemporary issues. This dialogue between Catholicism and Shi'a Islam is based on the conviction that the high regard in which both traditions hold prayer and contemplation forms a strong unifying element between the two traditions, and is thus a suitable context for a consideration of both shared mutualties and differences, thus allowing Catholics and Shi'a jointly to strengthen their response to contemporary challenges. A major feature of the conference was the fact that the plans for it grew out of an already existing friendship between the Catholic and Shi'a organisers, and this

---

[1] *The Tablet*, 19 July 2003, 13. The conference was also reported under the title of a 'Catholic-Shia Engagement (5-10 July 2003)' in the journal of the Pontifical Institute for Arabic and Islamic Studies, *Islamochristiana*, 29, 2003, 238-9; and in her bulletin entitled 'Relating to the Muslim Community: the Role of the CCJ', Sister Margaret Shepherd, Director of the Council of Christians and Jews, commented that the conference had been 'very successful' and 'advocate[d] a similar course of action for [dialogue among] Christians, Jews and Muslims.'

helped to contribute to an atmosphere of trust and understanding, which was further enhanced by opportunities for informal exchanges among the participants, the sharing of meals and some smaller group discussions. Furthermore, for some the conference became a genuinely spiritual experience, as during the three-day Ampleforth stage the presence of a praying monastic community, in whose prayer the participants were able to join, provided the backdrop to the conference's deliberations. It is very much hoped that the publication of this volume will help to contribute to a growing understanding on a variety of levels between Catholics and Shi'a.[2]

The papers in this volume are the work of individual contributors to this Catholic-Shi'a engagement, and so reflect their own personal standpoint within their respective traditions. Thus the papers stand on their own and the reader is invited to enter the dialogue, seeking to understand the faith and the positions of their dialogue-partners as they themselves understand them, and without imposing a preconceived framework upon them. Such an approach is not only mutually enriching, but allows for a genuine and substantial dialogue that enables the pursuit of truth and harmony, without glossing over important and irreconcilable differences.[3]

In this volume, the task of dialogue has been set against the historical and theological background in which contemporary Catholic-Shi'a relations are necessarily situated. Thus, providing the book's

---

[2] In furtherance of this dialogue, in April 2004 the Abbot of Ampleforth, Timothy Wright OSB, made a visit to Qum, accompanied by Fr Bonaventure Knollys OSB, also of Ampleforth, and Fr Michael Barnes SJ and Anthony O'Mahony of Heythrop College. The Abbot's account of this visit, during which plans were laid for a further Catholic-Shi'a engagement to be held at Heythrop College and Ampleforth Abbey in July 2005, was published as, 'Can Catholics and Muslims ever get along?' in the *Catholic Herald*, 28 May 2004. During the 2004 visit, the four Catholic participants lectured in Qum on the following themes: the right role of freedom of conscience, the way to God exemplified in the 'Spiritual Exercises' of St Ignatius, a detailed presentation of Jean-Pierre de Caussade's 'Abandonment to Divine Providence', and a detailed presentation on themes of shared interest to the Catholic and Shi'a tradition, the role of Mary and Fatima, the understanding of redemptive suffering and the contrasting attitudes of the Catholic Church and Shi'a Islam to the state and its role as lawmaker.

[3] In this spirit the editors have chosen not to revise significantly the English of the papers contributed by non-native English speakers, as it was felt this would be a disservice to the authors, whose distinctive voices and emphases would be lost. The texts have been amended to some extent to make them easier to read. The editors have also retained the transliteration systems—where used—as presented by the contributors.

immediate context, Wulstan Peterburs reflects briefly on the visit that he and Abbot Timothy Wright of Ampleforth made to Qum in April 2002, and then discusses some Catholic theological principles and spiritual values that lie at the heart of interreligious dialogue. Thereafter, in the first section of the book, consideration is given to how Catholics and Shi'a have engaged with each other over many centuries, and how both traditions have sought to understand and evaluate each other's fundamental beliefs and practices. Archbishop Michael L Fitzgerald, the President of the Pontifical Council for Interreligious Dialogue, comments on one particular, albeit little known, way in which Jesus has been perceived in Shi'a Islam, whilst Ayatollah Misbah Yazdi, the President of the Imam Khomeini Institute, reflects on the role of Muslim and Christian scholars in engaging with contemporary challenges to faith. Justo Lacunza Balda of the Pontifical Institute for Arabic and Islamic Studies in Rome takes a close look at the specificities of the Catholic-Shi'a engagement, and noting the importance of this dialogue, highlights some significant challenges facing the contemporary Christian-Muslim encounter, whilst Anthony O'Mahony takes an overview of the theological challenges which emerge from it. Mohammad Ali Shomali, emphasising the close links between Christians and Muslims, discusses from a Shi'a perspective the place of Mary, Jesus and Christianity in Islam, and Chris Clohessy complements this discussion by looking at how both Mary and Fatima are revered in the Catholic and Shi'a traditions. After this, O'Mahony unfolds one of the most interesting moments of Catholic-Shi'a encounter in the life and work of the Catholic scholar, priest, mystic and political thinker, Louis Massignon.

A central theme of this book is the question of how a person's spirituality should inform the way in which they live their life. Thus, in the book's second section, consideration is given to the remembrance of God in both the Catholic and Shi'a spiritual traditions, the value and necessity of prayer in uniting the believer to God and in forming their character. So, Ayatollah Mushin Araki undertakes a wide-ranging reflection on the remembrance of God; Reza Shah Kazemi follows this reflection with a detailed commentary on the principle and practice of the remembrance of God in the Muslim tradition; and Wulstan Peterburs looks at the remembrance of God as a distinctive aspect of Christian prayer and monastic spirituality, which some might regard as a possible bridge for contemporary dialogue between the two traditions. Given that contemplation and prayer are key to understanding the internal vitality and external face of both Catholicism and Shi'a Islam, Mahnaz Heydarpoor looks at contemplation in Islamic spirituality; Ian Latham discusses Christian prayer; and Mohammad Fanaei Eshkevari considers both the concept of prayer and the notion of contemplation in Islamic spirituality.

Although the idea of the 'Word of God' is understood differently in Christianity and Islam, their shared monotheistic heritage provides much common ground between the two faiths, and allows attention to be turned to the Catholic and Shi'a understandings of God's presence and action in the world. This includes some discussion of the Qur'anic principle of the word of God, the Catholic understanding of revelation, and belief in Christ's sacramental presence among people. This theme of God's presence in the world is further developed around Abraham, sacred in both traditions, as a model of faith for both Catholics and Shi'a: the discussion has a particular reference to the way in which the Abrahamic narratives have been interpreted, along with some consideration of humankind's free response to God's offer of salvation. So, Michael Kirwan provides a Catholic theological perspective on the word of God and idea of sacrament; Mohammad Jafar Elmi follows this with a Shi'a perspective on the word of God and revelation; and John McDade engages with the fundamental understanding that 'in Christ we die', a reflection on sacrifice and human life. A Shi'a perspective on Abraham as a 'man of faith' is offered by Morteza Sanei and Mohammad Soori, and Mary Mills offers a Catholic view.

Turning to practical themes, in its final section, this book examines the implications of the attempt to 'privatise' religion and morality, and the negative effects of this upon civil society and culture in general. Such 'privatisation' clearly results in significant challenges and difficulties for religious believers, who through their faith seek to enliven and inform society with a centuries-old, rooted tradition. Accordingly, this book discusses the ways in which both Catholics and Shi'a might seek to meet these challenges, and considers possibilities for co-operation in morality and social action. Saied Reza Ameli, looks at the question of globalisation and the power of religion; Patrick Riordan undertakes a Catholic theological and political reading of the Church; and Muhsin Javadi provides a Shi'a perspective on the challenges that the contemporary world poses to the question of certainty in faith and knowledge. Catherine

Cowley engages with a Christian understanding of work, culture and society; Mohammad Ali Shomali considers the value of life in Islam, whilst in relation to the family, Mahmood Taghizadeh Davari discusses religious socialization in contemporary Iran; and Huj Mahmud Mohammadi Araghi presents a Shi'a perspective on a culture of peace and dialogue. Finally, Abbot Timothy Wright of Ampleforth, in a wide-ranging reflection for a future agenda, draws together the wisdom and knowledge which the conference participants brought to its deliberations.

Overall, this volume attempts to draw upon the deep reservoir of shared Catholic and Shi'a spiritual resources, so as to engage with the world and to challenge our contemporary culture and society. Today we are witnessing a worldwide religious revival, and a pressing question for religious traditions is how best to resource and channel this thirst for God. This book brings together theologians, scholars and religious leaders from both the Catholic and Shi'a traditions, who recognise this challenge, and in so doing seeks to offer a lead.

A word of thanks: a conference of this nature could not have happened unless supported and encouraged by many others. We would particularly like to thank our respective institutes of Ampleforth Abbey, Heythrop College, University of London, and the Imam Khomeini Education and Research Institute in Qum. Several private donors who wish to remain anonymous have supported the conference, and to them we extend a special thank you. We would like to thank the Altajir World of Islam Trust, and its Director, Alistair Duncan, for their enthusiastic and generous support and especially for enabling the publication of the conference proceedings. In addition, the editors owe a significant debt of gratitude to the publisher Leonard Harrow of Melisende for his expert and committed work and to Patricia Hardcastle for her patient and accurate proof reading of the text of the book.

Anthony O'Mahony
Wulstan Peterburs OSB
Mohammad Ali Shomali

11 July 2003
The Feast of St Benedict

VISITING IRAN:
OBSERVATIONS AND SOME CATHOLIC
THEOLOGICAL PRINCIPLES OF DIALOGUE
WITH ISLAM[1]
Wulstan Peterburs

In April 2002, Abbot Timothy Wright and I, both Benedictine monks of Ampleforth Abbey in Yorkshire, visited Iran for a week. The trip was the result of an invitation from Dr Mohammad Ali Shomali who had visited Ampleforth a number of times during 2000-2001, giving three talks to the monastic community on Islam and Islamic spirituality and mysticism in the summer of 2001. Dr Shomali is the Head of the Department of Religious Studies at the Imam Khomeini Institute for Education and Research in Qum, the leading seminary city for Shi'a Islam: there are about 35,000 clerical students in Qum. Abbot Timothy and I were invited to give three talks each on Catholic theology and monastic spirituality, and Dr Shomali arranged a variety of visits and meetings with leading scholars and clerics to discuss matters of mutual interest. One of our last meetings was with Ayatollah Misbah, the President of the Imam Khomeini Institute, and one of the seventy-two ayatollahs who elect and supervise the Iranian Supreme Leader, the country's political head.

During our visit we led two seminars. Each was attended by about eighty students and staff and lasted about three and a half hours, rather than the scheduled two. We also gave a public lecture to an audience of about one hundred and fifty. The pattern of these meetings was that I spoke first, offering a theological paper which Abbot Timothy then complemented with an explanation of how this formed a basis for some aspect of monastic life and spirituality.

At the first seminar I discussed Vatican II's teaching in the 'Dogmatic Constitution on Divine Revelation', *Dei Verbum*, noting revelation's Christological and Trinitarian character, and explaining the Catholic understanding of the relationship of scripture and tradition. Abbot Timothy took up this theme starting with St Benedict's maxim

---

[1] This is a slightly revised version of a paper entitled, 'Visiting Iran: Observations and Some Theological principles of Catholic-Muslim Dialogue', which originally appeared in the *Ampleforth Journal*, Autumn 2002, Vol. 107, 29-37.

that the monk should prefer nothing to the love of Christ, and proceeded to outline the nature of the monastic life and calling, commenting on how the *Rule of St Benedict* is lived today. I began the second seminar by explaining how the Catholic understanding of revelation gives rise to a particular notion of the Church, and with reference to Vatican II's 'Dogmatic Constitution on the Church', *Lumen Gentium*, treated of her as the 'Body of Christ' and the 'People of God', before examining the roles of the laity and the hierarchy, and discussing the Church's teaching authority, particularly the concept of infallibility. Abbot Timothy followed this with a paper on the exercise of authority by an abbot in a monastic community, covering St Benedict's teaching on an abbot's responsibilities both to God and to his monks, service of others and monastic obedience. In the public lecture, we had been asked to address the question of the role of the Church in contemporary Western society and the particular place of the monastery. I spoke of the Church's understanding of, and relationship to, contemporary society in Vatican II's 'Pastoral Constitution on the Church in the Modern World', *Gaudium et Spes*, and in particular of her relationship to other Christians and to the members of non-Christian religions, especially Islam, as found in *Lumen Gentium* and the council's 'Decree on the Relations of the Church to non-Christian Religions', *Nostra Aetate*. Abbot Timothy considered how, within this broader context, a monastic community seeks to form its members spiritually and how the influence of this goes beyond the boundaries of the cloister into the lives of others as a force for good, whether through education, spiritual direction, or personal example.

We found that we had much in common with our hosts when speaking in general terms of a spirituality founded on regular times of formal prayer and the offering of oneself to God. We agreed that the type of culture and society that emerges from such a foundation is significantly different from the materialism of the West, but it was also noted, that whilst Iran seems to be a genuinely religious country, it is not immune from a number of damaging influences spread, for example, through the internet and satellite television. In the light of this challenge, we agreed that there was much scope for collaboration between Christians and Muslims in seeking to influence society for the better: the genuine openness that we encountered in discussions with our hosts and their willingness to examine a variety of ideas seem to provide some grounds for hope in this matter.

But there are, of course, a number of major differences between Christians and Muslims. In particular, along with a lack of belief in the central Christian doctrines of the Incarnation, Redemption in Christ, and the Trinity, Islamic thought seems to lack the notion of sacrament, and appears not to understand the Christian idea of community; and the idea of religious/priestly celibacy met with incomprehension. Accordingly, it was agreed that in order to increase mutual understanding and co-operation a careful examination of theological differences, including particularly ideas about the nature and transmission of revelation, would have to form a part of any continuing dialogue. There is also the question of how the Christian claim to the uniqueness of God's self-revelation in Christ and the obligation to evangelism are to be reconciled with dialogue with Islam, a religion that does indeed honour Jesus, though not in any sense as divine, and in viewing him through its own prism, abrogates the new covenant sealed in his blood.

The theological basis for the Catholic Church's dialogue with non-Christian religions, and thus with Islam, was set down by the Second Vatican Council, in particular in *Lumen Gentium* and *Nostra Aetate*. It is helpful, however, to consider this teaching within the context of what the Council taught about the Church herself, her place in the modern world, and her relationship to other Christians.

As the English title of the document implies, it was in the 'Pastoral Constitution on the Church in the Modern World' that the Council outlined the principles that should guide the Church's involvement in the affairs of contemporary society. This document marked a significant change of attitude within the Catholic Church towards the world outside, injecting a note of optimism to replace the bitter scepticism that had dominated much of nineteenth and early 20th-century thinking. The constitution, however, should not be read as a ringing endorsement of the modern materialist world, but as an acknowledgement that good is to be found in it, and that this is to be nurtured and encouraged through the bringing to it of Christian values. The Council was well aware of humanity's sinful nature, but it also taught that humankind has been redeemed in Christ, and that this provides a reason for hope. The opening paragraph of the document sets the tone:

> The joy and hope, the grief and anguish of the men of our time, especially of those who are poor or afflicted in any

way, are the joy and hope, the grief and anguish of the
followers of Christ as well. Nothing that is genuinely human
fails to find an echo in their hearts. For theirs is a community
composed of men, of men who, united in Christ and guided
by the Holy Spirit, press onwards towards the Kingdom of
the Father and are bearers of a message of salvation intended
for all men. That is why Christians cherish a feeling of deep
solidarity with the human race and its history.[2]

This openness to the world is reflected in the Council's teaching
about non-Catholic Christians, the adherents of non-Christian religions,
especially Jews and Muslims, and about religious liberty. In examining
these issues, however, it is necessary to be clear that the Catholic Church
approaches them from a position of faith in Jesus Christ as the redeemer
of all humanity. This means that for Catholics the best, or surest way, to
eternal life with God in heaven is through Christ and his Church,
especially as manifested in the Catholic Church: as the Council taught,
the 'fullness of the means of salvation'[3] is to be found only within the
Catholic Church. That said, the Council used the expression 'subsists in'[4]
to indicate that these means may not be always fully realised, and
recognised, in conformity with Catholic tradition that the Church,
although holy, is also in need of purification.[5] In other words, the Catholic
Church does not claim impeccability for herself or her members, and
recognises that some, if not all, of the 'means of salvation' exist outside
her visible boundaries. It follows, then, that the Catholic Church does
not reject other Christians or the adherents of other religions. Indeed,
she gladly acknowledges that there is much that is good and holy outside
her confines, and seeks dialogue with non-Christians, as well as with
non-Catholic Christians, seeing in this both a theological and a moral
necessity. As Vatican II taught in *Lumen Gentium*:

All men are called to this catholic unity which prefigures
and promotes universal peace. And in different ways to it

---

[2] *Gaudium et Spes*, 1. All quotations from the documents of the Second Vatican Council are
taken from ed. A Flannery, *Vatican Council II: Volume 1 The Conciliar and Postconciliar Documents*,
New York, 1998.

[3] Decree on Ecumenism, *Unitatis Redintegratio*, 3.

[4] *Lumen Gentium*, 8.

[5] *Lumen Gentium*, 8.

belong, or are related: the Catholic faithful, others who believe in Christ, and finally all mankind, called by God's grace to salvation.[6]

This sentence announces the theme of articles 14-16 of *Lumen Gentium* which treat of the Church, non-Catholic Christians and non-Christians.

Article 14 discusses the 'Catholic faithful', stressing the Catholic belief in the incorporation of the believer through baptism and faith into the Church for salvation. It emphasises that 'fully incorporated into the Church are those who, possessing the Spirit of Christ, accept all the means of salvation given to the Church together with her entire organisation, and who—by the bonds constituted by the profession of faith, the sacraments, ecclesiastical government, and communion—are joined in the visible structure of the Church of Christ, who rules through her Supreme Pontiff and the bishops.'[7] Such membership of the Church does not, however, guarantee salvation if one does not persevere in love. A person who does not, 'remains indeed in the bosom of the Church, but "in body" not "in heart."'[8] Thus full membership is on two levels—the spiritual and the visible. Indeed, those who do not respond to the graces thus offered them will be judged all the more severely. Catechumens, those who are preparing for baptism, come very close to this full incorporation into the Church due to their desire to be part of her. They are therefore described as 'joined to her' and 'mother Church embraces them as her own.'[9]

Article 15 is a treatment of the relationship of non-Catholic Christians to the Catholic Church. The most important of the links between these two is baptism, but they are also united, though imperfectly, through the episcopate, the sacrament of the Eucharist and the 'many who hold sacred Scripture in honour as a rule of faith and of life, who have a sincere religious zeal, who lovingly believe in God the Father Almighty and in Christ, the Son of God and the Saviour.'[10] Although the 'Decree on Ecumenism' emphasises that the Catholic Church regards herself as more closely joined to some bodies of Christians than to others, the

---

[6]   *Lumen Gentium,* 13.
[7]   *Lumen Gentium,* 14.
[8]   *Lumen Gentium,* 14.
[9]   *Lumen Gentium,* 14.
[10] *Lumen Gentium,* 15.

council recognised that all non-Catholic Christians are joined to the Catholic Church in a real way (that is, spiritually), and that their churches and ecclesial communities are a means of salvation for their members.[11]

Article 16 teaches that the adherents of non-Christian religions are also part of the 'People of God': 'the plan of salvation also includes those who acknowledge the Creator,'[12] particularly Jews, to whom God's revelation was first made known, and which Christians believe was fulfilled in Christ; and Muslims, who share the faith of Abraham, and as the council declares:

> together with us they adore the one, merciful God, mankind's judge on the last day.[13]

Furthermore, the council noted that God is not:

> remote from those who in shadows and images seek the unknown God, since He gives to men life and breath and all things.[14]

So, the Council taught that the members of non-Christian religions can be saved, that is, come to eternal life with God in heaven, and in harmony with this teaching the council affirmed, in *Nostra Aetate*, that:

> The Catholic Church rejects nothing of what is true and holy in these religions. She has a high regard for the manner of life and conduct, the precepts and doctrines which, although differing in many ways from her own teaching, nevertheless often reflect a ray of that truth which enlightens all men.[15]

However, given the Christian claim about the uniqueness of God's revelation in Christ, the Council also stressed the Christian duty

---

[11] *Unitatis Redintegratio,* 3 and 13; cf *Lumen Gentium,* 15.

[12] *Lumen Gentium,* 16.

[13] *Lumen Gentium,* 16.

[14] *Lumen Gentium,* 16.

[15] *Nostra Aetate,* 2.

of proclaiming the Gospel. Thus, the Council emphasised that the Church, which was willed by God, and instituted by Christ, is both the necessary sign and instrument of the salvation of all people.[16] Christ is at the centre of the Church, the 'universal sacrament of salvation',[17] which was established by his 'preaching the good news, that is, the coming of God's Kingdom'.[18] But the centrality of Christ and the importance of the Church for the salvation of all people do not legitimise proselytism or any attempts to force conversions to Christianity. Indeed, the council taught in the 'Declaration on Religious Liberty', *Dignitatis Humanae*, that as all people have a duty freely to seek the truth and to submit to it, such aggressive practices are a violation of a fundamental human right to religious liberty:

> The Vatican Council declares that the human person has a right to religious freedom. Freedom of this kind means that all men should be free from coercion on the part of individuals, social groups and every human power so that, within due limits, nobody is forced to act against his convictions, nor is anyone to be restrained from acting in accordance with his convictions in religious matters in private or in public, alone or in associations with others. The Council further declares that the right to religious freedom is based on the very dignity of the human person as known through the revealed word of God and by reason itself.[19]

Accordingly:

> The Church ... urges her sons to enter with prudence and charity into discussion and collaboration with members of other religions. Let Christians, while witnessing to their own faith and way of life, acknowledge, preserve and

---

[16] Cf. *Lumen Gentium*, 1 and 14. This teaching was repeated by the Congregation for the Doctrine of the Faith in its *Declaration 'Dominus Iesus' on the Unicity and Salvific Universality of Jesus Christ and the Church*, Vatican City, 2000, 5, 12 and 16-17.

[17] *Lumen Gentium*, 48.

[18] *Lumen Gentium*, 5.

[19] *Dignitatis Humanae*, 2.

encourage the spiritual and moral truths found among non-Christians, also their social life and culture.[20]

Of Islam, the Council declared:

> The Church has ... a high regard for the Muslims. They worship God, who is one, living and subsistent, merciful and almighty, the Creator of heaven and earth, who has also spoken to men. They strive to submit themselves without reserve to the decrees of God, just as Abraham submitted himself to God's plan, to whose faith Muslims eagerly link their own. Although not acknowledging him as God, they venerate Jesus as a prophet, his virgin mother they also honour, and even at times devoutly invoke. Further, they await the day of judgement and the reward of God following the resurrection of the dead. For this reason they highly esteem an upright life and worship God, especially by way of prayer, alms-deeds and fasting.[21]

The Council then noted that:

> Over the centuries many quarrels and dissensions have arisen between Christians and Muslims. The sacred Council now pleads with all to forget the past, and urges that a sincere effort be made to achieve mutual understanding; for the benefit of all men, let them together preserve and promote peace, liberty, social justice and moral values.[22]

As regards those who do not have any explicit knowledge of God, the Council, in the spirit of optimism that so characterised its proceedings, considered that salvation is also open to those who 'strive to lead a good life. Whatever good or truth is found amongst them is considered by the Church to be a preparation for the Gospel, and given by Him who enlightens all men that they may at length have life.'[23] In

---

[20] *Nostra Aetate*, 2.

[21] *Nostra Aetate*, 3.

[22] *Nostra Aetate*, 3.

[23] *Lumen Gentium*, 16.

other words, God's universal saving will underlies every truly human, genuine attempt to find the source of Goodness and Truth, and God will not ultimately hide Himself from those who seek Him, even if obscurely. Such hopefulness about the future of humanity, however, does not apply to those who have deliberately rejected God.

So, the Second Vatican Council marked a decisive shift in emphasis in the Church's view of herself and her relationship to others. The Council did not teach, as had previously been taught, in for example Pius XII's encyclical *Mystici Corporis* (1943), that a perfect equivalence exists between the Roman Catholic Church and the Church of Christ. Rather, the Council opened up the Church to discussion and co-operation with others: the imperfect communion that exists among all Christians was acknowledged, as was the goodness and the truth found among non-Christians. The teaching of the Council is normative for Catholics and sets, and will continue to set for the foreseeable future, the agenda for those actively involved in the life of the Catholic Church and her dialogue with those outside her visible boundaries.

In accordance with the teaching of the Council, the Catholic Church has since the 1960s been actively involved in dialogue with the adherents of the world's major non-Christian religions. In 1964 Pope Paul VI established the Secretariat for Non-Christians, which was renamed the Pontifical Council for Interreligious Dialogue (PCID) in 1988, and so, in the same way as there is a formal institutional structure within the Roman Curia for co-ordinating the dialogue with non-Catholic Christians, there is a body with responsibility for dialogue with non-Christian religions. This interreligious dialogue, however, does not have quite the same structures or purpose of unity as the dialogue with other Christians. The work of the PCID, headed by Archbishop Michael L Fitzgerald, is to promote mutual understanding, respect and collaboration between Catholics and the followers of other religious traditions; to encourage the study of religions; and to promote the formation of persons dedicated to dialogue; it does not seek a unity of believers, such as is pursued by the Anglican-Roman Catholic International Commission.[24]

So the work of the PCID is to promote a two-way communication between the Catholic Church and the members of the

---

[24] Christian-Jewish relations are dealt with by the Pontifical Council for Promoting Christian Unity.

other major world religions. This dialogue implies speaking and listening, giving and receiving, for mutual growth and enrichment, and includes witnessing to one's own faith, as well as an openness to that of the other. This dialogue is not a betrayal of the mission of the Church, but nor is it, as Pope John Paul II explained in his encyclical *Redemptoris Missio* (1990), a new method of seeking to win converts to Christianity.

In these times, when the question of Islam and politics is especially fraught, it is worth remembering that the PCID, without closing its eyes to political realities, restricts itself to religious questions. It pursues its mission by receiving visits from religious leaders and engaging them in dialogue. The President and the Secretary visit local Churches to learn more about their situation and to meet the leaders of the non-Christian religions in that place. It organises bilateral and multilateral meetings at regional, national and international level, and normally publishes the 'Acts' of these dialogue meetings; an Interreligious Dialogue Directory has also been published. There is a special commission for relations with Muslims, and the PCID has set up a foundation to provide grants for members of other religions who wish to study Christianity. In all this, the PCID maintains an ongoing relationship with the corresponding office in the World Council of Churches

So as to state more clearly the nature of its work, and to establish guidelines for those involved in interreligious dialogue, the PCID in 1991 issued a document entitled *Dialogue and Proclamation: Reflection and Orientations on Interreligious Dialogue and the Proclamation of the Gospel of Jesus Christ*. Based on *Lumen Gentium* and *Nostra Aetate*, but developing the teaching of these documents, *Dialogue and Proclamation* discusses the Church's mission of dialogue with non-Christians, whilst at the same time proclaiming unambiguously the saving truth of Jesus Christ. It is noted that although 'dialogue is treated first, this is not because it has any priority over proclamation. It is simply due to the fact that dialogue is the primary concern of the Pontifical Council for Interreligious Dialogue which initiated the preparation of the document.'[25] In the words of John Paul II, 'Just as interreligious dialogue is one element in the mission of the Church, the proclamation of God's saving work in Our Lord Jesus

---

[25] Pontifical Council for Interreligious Dialogue, *Dialogue and Proclamation: Reflection and Orientations on Interreligious Dialogue and the Proclamation of the Gospel of Jesus Christ*, Vatican City, 1991, 3.

Christ is another ... There can be no question of choosing one and ignoring or rejecting the other.'[26]

By 'proclamation', the PCID means:

> the communication of the Gospel message, the mystery of salvation realised by God for all in Jesus Christ by the power of the Spirit. It is an invitation to a commitment of faith in Jesus Christ and to entry through baptism into the community of believers which is the Church.[27]

Thus for those engaged in interreligious dialogue there can be no weakening of, or deviation from, Jesus' command, 'Go, therefore, make disciples of all nations; baptise them in the name of the Father and of the Son and of the Holy Spirit.'[28] It is, rather, that in the current situation of religious plurality, there is a need for 'positive and constructive interreligious relations with individuals and communities of other faiths which are directed at mutual understanding and enrichment, in obedience to truth and respect for freedom. It includes both witness and the exploration of respective religious convictions.'[29]

Dialogue and Proclamation reaffirms that the Catholic Church's dialogue with the world's non-Christian religions is based on the theological premise that:

> all men and women who are saved share, though differently, in the same mystery of salvation in Jesus Christ through his Spirit. Christians know this through their faith, while others remain unaware that Jesus Christ is the source of their salvation. The mystery of salvation reaches out to them, in a way known to God, through the invisible action of the Spirit of Christ. Concretely, it will be in the sincere practice of what is good in their own religious traditions and by following the dictates of their own conscience that the members of other religions respond positively to God's

---

[26] Cited in *Dialogue & Proclamation*, 6.

[27] *Dialogue & Proclamation*, 10.

[28] Matthew 28: 19.

[29] *Dialogue & Proclamation*, 9.

invitation and receive salvation in Jesus Christ, even while they do not acknowledge him as their saviour.[30]

Interreligious dialogue, as outlined in the PCID's 1984 document, *The Attitude of the Church Towards the Followers of Other Religions: Reflections and Orientations on Dialogue and Mission*, takes four forms: first, the *dialogue of life*, where people strive to live in an open and neighbourly spirit, sharing their joys and sorrows, their human problems and preoccupations; second, the *dialogue of action*, in which Christians and others collaborate for the integral development and liberation of people; third, the *dialogue of theological exchange*, where specialists seek to deepen their understanding of their respective religious heritages, and to appreciate each other's spiritual values; and fourth, the *dialogue of religious experience*, where persons, rooted in their own religious traditions, share their spiritual riches, for instance with regard to prayer and contemplation, faith and ways of searching for God or the Absolute.[31] There is no particular order of priority among these forms of dialogue, and the PCID notes that it is important that interreligious dialogue should not come to be seen as the preserve of specialists, 'a sort of luxury item in the Church's mission'; it is rather the obligation of all believers.[32]

Whilst it is, of course, central to interreligious dialogue that the dialogue partners should not lay aside their own religious convictions, it is also true that Catholics engaged in dialogue with Muslims should remember that God has 'manifested himself in some way to the followers of other religious traditions',[33] and seek to understand Islam as Muslims themselves understand it. The same attitude is required of Muslims who should try to understand Catholicism as Catholics understand it, so that genuine mutualities and differences can be examined positively, and used to increase co-operation. In other words:

Dialogue requires, on the part of Christians as well as the followers of other traditions, a balanced attitude. They should

---

[30] *Dialogue & Proclamation*, 29; cf. Vatican II's 'Decree on the Church's Missionary Activity', *Ad Gentes*, 3, 9 and 11.

[31] Pontifical Council for Interreligious Dialogue, *The Attitude of the Church Towards the Followers of Other Religions: Reflections and Orientations on Dialogue and Mission*, Vatican City, 1984, 28-35.

[32] *Dialogue & Proclamation*, 43.

[33] *Dialogue & Proclamation*, 48.

be neither ingenuous nor overly critical, but open and receptive. Unselfishness and impartiality, acceptance of differences and of possible contradictions [is necessary] ... The will to engage together in commitment to the truth and the readiness to allow oneself to be transformed by the encounter are other dispositions required.[34]

While keeping their identity intact, Christians must be prepared to learn and to receive from and through others the positive values of their traditions. Through dialogue they can be moved to give up ingrained prejudices, to revise preconceived ideas, and even sometimes to allow the understanding of their faith to be purified.[35]

If Christians cultivate such openness and allow themselves to be tested, they will be able to gather the fruits of dialogue. They will discover with admiration all that God's action through Jesus Christ in his Spirit has accomplished and continues to accomplish in the world and in the whole of humankind. Far from weakening their own faith, true dialogue will deepen it. They will become increasingly aware of their Christian identity and perceive more clearly the distinctive elements of the Christian message. Their faith will gain new dimensions as they discover the active presence of the mystery of Jesus Christ beyond the visible boundaries of the Church and of the Christian fold.[36]

What this approach to interreligious dialogue might mean in terms of the Christian believer's faith-commitment was described by Cardinal Francis Arinze when, in March 1999 as the then President of the PCID, he wrote to the Presidents of the Bishops' Conferences about the need to ground such work in a sound spirituality:

Catholics and other Christians engaged in ... interreligious dialogue are becoming more and more convinced of the

---

[34] *Dialogue & Proclamation*, 47.
[35] *Dialogue & Proclamation*, 49.
[36] *Dialogue & Proclamation*, 50.

need of a sound Christian spirituality to uphold their efforts.
The Christian who meets other believers is not involved in
an activity which is marginal to his or her faith. Rather it is
something which arises from the demands of that faith and
should be nourished by faith.

Arinze noted that God, who is Trinity, reveals Himself to
mankind so as 'to restore communion between humanity and God, to
communicate divine life to people and finally to bring them to the eternal
vision of God', and that this 'Trinitarian mystery of love and communion
is the eminent model for human relations and the foundation of dialogue.'
Furthermore, because the 'Incarnation is the supreme manifestation of
God's saving will ... When Christians meet other believers, they are
called to have the mind of Christ, to follow his footsteps.' Moreover, they
must be 'open to the action of the Spirit', ready to do God's will, because
'the more the partners in interreligious dialogue 'seek the face of God'
(cf. Ps 27:8), the nearer they will come to each other and the better
chance they will have of understanding each other. It can be seen, therefore,
that interreligious dialogue is a deeply religious activity.'

Arinze continued that although the Catholic Church
acknowledges that God gives His 'grace outside the visible boundaries of
the Church (cf. *Lumen Gentium* 16 and John Paul II's encyclical *Redemptor
Hominis* [1979] 10)', the Catholic Christian meets other believers, in all
humility, as 'a witness to Jesus Christ ... the one and only Saviour of all
humanity', and as a member of the Church within which 'the fullness of
the means of salvation (*Lumen Gentium* 8)' is to be found. He noted that,
'interreligious dialogue, when conducted in this vision of faith, in no
way leads to religious relativism.'

Arinze further explained that this interreligious dialogue
'presupposes conversion in the sense of the return of the heart to God
in love and obedience to His will' and 'the spirituality which is to
animate and uphold ... [such dialogue] is one which is lived out in
faith, hope and charity:' faith in the one God; hope that dialogue will
lead humanity along the path to the Kingdom; and charity in freely
sharing God's love with other believers. For the Christian, then,
'interreligious activity flows out of the heart of the Christian faith,'
and requires the nourishment of prayer that 'links the Christian with
the goodness and power of God without whom we can do nothing (cf.

Jn. 15:5) ... [and sacrifice which] strengthens prayer and promotes communion with others.'[37]

This willingness of the Catholic Church to enter into, and indeed the perceived necessity of, dialogue with the followers of the world's non-Christian religions was realised in Pope John Paul II's invitation to the leaders of these religions to join him at Assisi in a 'Day of Prayer for Peace' on 27 October 1986, an invitation again issued with some urgency after the terrorist attacks in the United States on 11 September 2001.

In 1986 the Pope spoke of the 'the fundamental unity of the human race, in its origin and its destiny, and the role of the Church as an effective sign of this unity',[38] and in 2001 he repeated the teaching of his social encyclical *Centesimus Annus* (1991), that:

> In the climate of increased cultural and religious pluralism
> which is expected to mark the society of the new millennium,
> it is obvious that ... [interreligious] dialogue will be especially
> important in establishing a sure basis for peace and warding
> off the dread spectre of those wars of religion which have
> so often bloodied human history.[39]

In his 'Reflections' on the 'Day of Prayer at Assisi' on 24 January 2002, Cardinal Arinze noted that the road to peace 'is marked by the acceptance of the fact of the interdependence between peoples when it is freely accepted and generously lived. Then the moral virtue of solidarity is generated. People learn to accept one another, not as enemies or threats, but as co-pilgrims in the journey of life.' Furthermore, the 'message of love and self-sacrifice which Jesus Christ, the Son of God made man, brought into the world is meant for all peoples, languages, cultures and religions. Christ chose to be born in Palestine ... But the religion he established is for all nations. He came 'to gather together into one the scattered children of God.' (Jn. 11: 52)[40]

---

[37] All quotations are taken from F Arinze, *The Spirituality of Interreligious Dialogue*, Vatican City, 1999.

[38] Cited in *Dialogue & Proclamation*, 5.

[39] The Apostolic Letter, *Novo Millennio Ineunte*, of His Holiness Pope John Paul II to the Bishops, Clergy and Lay Faithful at the Close of the Great Jubilee of the Year 2000, Vatican City, 2001, 55.

[40] *Reflections by Cardinal Francis Arinze on the Day of Prayer at Assisi, 24 January 2002*, Vatican City, 2002.

The Catholic Church, then, is committed to dialogue with those outside her visible boundaries. In a significant modification of the then current neo-scholastic orthodoxy, the fathers of the Second Vatican Council gave a renewed impetus to the Church's involvement with the contemporary world, recognising indeed the need for conversion and grace, but also acknowledging the good to be found in it. Vital to the Church's existence and mission is the proclamation of the gospel as a means of establishing the kingdom of God on earth. But also central to the Church's task is dialogue with other Christians and the adherents of the world's non-Christian religions. The origin and goal of the whole of humanity lie in God, as revealed in Christ, and the good that is found outside the Church comes from Him. Through dialogue and proclamation the Church seeks the will of God and the eternal salvation of all.

A REFLECTION ON JESUS IN A SHĪ'ITE COMMENTARY [1]

Michael L Fitzgerald

Introduction

Fr Maurice Borrmans of the Pontifical Institute for Arabic Studies and Islam in a collection of articles published under the title *Islam e Cristianesimo. Le vie del dialogo* in Milan by Edizioni Paoline in 1996, included two chapters concerned with the way Jesus is presented in the Qur'ān and understood in Qur'ān commentary. One discusses the Muslim attitude to the mystery of the Cross; the other looks at the figure of Mary. The first of these chapters does contain some references to Shī'ite positions, [2] yet it could be said that more attention needs to be paid to the Shī'ite understanding of the Qur'ān. The present essay is a modest contribution in this direction.

This paper has a limited scope. It examines one Shī'ite commentary to see whether it provides any material on the figure of Jesus which would differ from the normal Sunnī commentaries. The commentary chosen is that of Mir Ahmed Ali, a popular work based on Shī'ī sources.[3] The method followed here is simple. The two main passages of the Qur'ān which deal with Jesus will be examined and significant

---

[1] A version of this article has also appeared in *Recueil d'articles offert a Muarice Borrmans par ses collègues et amis*, Pontificio Istituto di Studi Arabi e d'Islamistica (PISAI) Rome, 1996, Collection 'Studi arabo-islamici del PISAI', no. 8; and *Encounter, Documents for Muslim-Christian Understanding*, The Pontifical Institute for Arabic Studies and Islam, no. 229, November 1996.

[2] M Borrmans, *Islam e Cristianesimo. Le vie del dialogo*, Edizioni Paoline, Milan, 1993, 61, notes 11, 14; 71. For a more extensive treatment, see Roger Arnaldez, *Jésus dans la pensée musulmane*, Desclée, Paris, 1988, 185-226; Neal Robinson, *Christ in Islam and Christianity*, Macmillan, London, 1991, 167-77.

[3] SV Mir Ahmed Ali, *The Holy Qur'ān (With English Translation of the Arabic Text and Commentary according to the Version of the Holy Ahl al-Bayt)*, Muhammad Khaleel Shirazi, Karachi, 1964. For further information on this work see Michael L Fitzgerald, 'Shī'ite Understanding of the Qur'ān', eds. Ludwig Hagemann and Ernst Pulsfort, *'Ihr alle aber seid Brüder'* (Festschrift für A Th. Khoury), Echter Verlag, Würzburg, 1990, 153-166, particularly 154-155. This article also appeared in *Encounter*, n. 178, October 1991.

features of the commentary on these passages will be presented. After that a number of isolated verses will be treated. Where appropriate, certain observations will be added. [4]

1 Sūrat Āl 'Imrān (3)

1.1 Verily, God did choose Adam and Noah and the descendants of Abraham and the descendants of 'Imrān above all the worlds. (3: 32)

The commentator notes that for Abraham and 'Imrān, as distinct from Adam and Noah, the family *(āl)* is mentioned, and it is this that is preferred above all the worlds. The *āl* indicates the 'spiritual quality' of posterity. Therefore what is to be understood here is the *ahl al-bayt*, referring 'only to the purest and the holiest members of the family. As the Holy Prophet and his divinely chosen issues *(sic)* or the Holy *ahl al-bayt* all belong to the posterity of Abraham, in the clear declaration made by this verse, the Holy Prophet and his Holy *ahl al-bayt* are the chosen ones of God who are naturally made superior to everyone in the human race as a whole' (n. 353, p. 272).

It might be thought at first that this understanding of the term *āl*, if it were to apply equally to 'Imrān, would extend to Jesus. There is, however, a doubt about the identity of 'Imrān. A marginal gloss on this passage understands the name to refer to the father of Moses. Later in the commentary Mir Ahmed Ali says it is more appropriate to understand it as referring to the father of Mary (n. 353, p. 276).

The commentator goes on to explain how the 'preference' is manifested. According to the Qur'ān there is a process of selection. There is a succession of prophets. In other words, prophets are followed by a lineage for a particular time. Thus there is a succession from Adam to Noah, and from Noah to Abraham. After Abraham the succession bifurcates: one line is that of Ishmael *(āl Ibrāhīm)*, and the other that of Isaac *(āl 'Imrān)*. The commentator then adds: 'The line of Āl 'Imrān ends with Jesus whose birth and disappearance is of unusual and of miraculous nature.' The line of Āl Ibrāhīm continues to 'Abd al-Muṭṭalib and then bifurcates again, through 'Abd Allāh to the Holy Prophet Muḥammad,

---

[4] The Qur'ān is cited according to the translation given by Mir Ahmed Ali. References to the commentary are given by note (n.) and page (p.). In both Qur'ānic text and commentary minor corrections, with regard to the transcription of proper names and punctuation, have been introduced.

and through Abū Ṭālib to 'Alī. 'These two channels are reunited through the Lady Fāṭima,' and the lineage of Āl Ibrāhīm continues with the eleven Holy Imāms, 'concluding in the Twelfth Imām, Muḥammad al-Mahdī, whose disappearance and reappearance are divinely designed to become the example of the House of Ishmael in the same way and manner as Jesus has been made to be an example of the House of Israel (cf. Q. 43, 59)' (n. 353, p. 274).

The passage concludes with the following remark. Both Jesus and al-Mahdī are to return at the end of the world, that is before the Day of Resurrection. Jesus will follow the Twelfth Imām—obedience is meant here—and all people will follow them both and none other.

The commentary on 3: 33 provides a further element in the process of selection. 'The choice of God in the seed of Abraham through Isaac stopped with Jesus and it did not continue any further, for Jesus was not given any posterity of his own, and it again started with the Holy Prophet Muḥammad who was a descendant of Abraham through his son Ishmael, and continued without any break in his family' (n. 354, p. 276).

The following verse (3: 34) mentions a vow made by the wife of 'Imrān (her name, Ḥanna, is added in the translation). The author of the commentary says that is possible that this vow of the grandmother explains why Jesus adopted an ascetic way of life (n. 355, p. 278).

The mother, having been delivered of her female child, commends her and her eventual offspring to God. The prayer is heard. 'The desire of Lady Ḥanna to dedicate a son to the service of the Temple was destined to be fulfilled in Jesus, associated with his miraculous birth as a clear sign of the omnipotent will of God which can act without any dependence upon any ordinary law of nature' (n. 357, p. 280).

Zachariah's prayer is also for a 'good offspring' (3: 37). The answer to his prayer is announced in the following verse:

1.2 Verily, God giveth thee the glad tidings of (a son) Yaḥyā (John) (who shall be) the confirmer of a Word from God (3: 38).

A marginal gloss explains that the 'Word' is Jesus. In the note, reference is made to Q. 4: 171 where Jesus is called God's Word. This is understood as referring to the 'immaculate virgin birth' of Jesus. Attention is called to the fact that in 3: 38 the indefinite form is used, *bi-kalimatin*. This is held to show that Jesus is not the only *kalima*, but just one such (n. 359, p. 282). John 'confirms this Word', in the sense that he was the first to believe in Jesus as a true apostle of God sent to revive the practice of the Mosaic Law.

In this last section of the commentary there is little that is specifically Shī'ite. Perhaps more distinctive is the parallel between Mary and Fāṭima. Just as the mother of Mary commended her to the Lord, so the Holy Prophet Muhammad commended Fāṭima to God for protection of herself and her progeny against Satan. These prayers were heard and Fāṭima became the 'Lady of Light' and the mother of Eleven Holy Imāms (n. 356, p. 279). Furthermore, just as Mary was nourished in the Temple with food provided by God, so Fāṭima was miraculously provided with food. The story is told of a time when the Prophet was hungry and so visited his daughter Fāṭima asking her to give him some food. She had none, but she went and prayed, and an empty vessel suddenly filled with fresh viands. The Prophet asked where the food had come from, and Fāṭima replied that it was from God who 'provides sustenance for whomsoever He will without any measure' (Q. 3: 36). 'The Holy Prophet said:"God be praised, He has made thee similar to Mary" ' (n. 357, p. 280).

1.3 And (recall O Our Apostle Muhammad) when said the Angels 'O Mary! Verily, God hath chosen thee and purified thee and chosen thee above the women of the worlds (3: 41).

The discussions on this verse are well known. Mir Ahmed Ali opts for the solution that Mary is above all women of her own time. He appeals to the authority of Muhammad who said that Mary was the most blessed of her own age, but Fāṭima is the most blessed of women of all ages. To back this up he appeals to Q. 33: 33 which establishes the purity of the *ahl al-bayt*. Fāṭima, being the only woman of the five people under the mantle, is obviously the most holy of women.

An objection is made. Mary is mentioned in the Qur'ān whereas Fāṭima is not; therefore surely Mary is superior to Fāṭima. The answer to this is that Mary is mentioned because it was necessary to defend her chastity. In the case of Fāṭima, her chastity was unquestionable, and her purity, both physical and spiritual, was recognized by both friends and foes (n. 363, p. 284).

In order to uphold the superiority of Fāṭima, the commentator draws attention to the words used about Mary in the verse. The first 'hath chosen thee' refers to her selection as a descendant of the prophets. 'Purified thee' means that Mary has been saved from fornication. The second 'chosen thee' refers to the selection of Mary for the birth of Jesus without a male partner. 'This shows that the distinction mentioned in the verse is in a restricted sense for a definite purpose and not general.' Fāṭima, on the other hand, is the daughter of the Last Prophet in the seed of Abraham. She is moreover 'the wife of an Imām who is next only to the Holy Prophet in all respects as of one and the same Divine Light: and the mother of Eleven Holy Imāms of the same grade and of the same Divine Light with the Last one through whom the Divine Will and Justice shall prevail on earth, and the son of Mary (Jesus) to follow him. In this distinction Fāṭima has no match at all' (n. 362, p. 285).[5]

1.4 Said she 'O My Lord! How can I have a son when hath not touched me (any) man? (3: 46)

Here the commentator upholds the virginity of Mary against the accusations of the Aḥmadiyya. He states that 'according to the Islamic tradition, Mary, the virgin mother of Jesus, did not meet any male before or after the birth of Jesus and she remained a virgin in the sense, till her departure from this world.' Reference is then made to 66: 12 where it is said that Mary 'guarded her chastity', and that the birth of Jesus was through the power of the Spirit. It is noted that 'the Aḥmadī view of Mary having children other than Jesus is based on the four canonical gospels which are unauthentic and a baseless folklore' (n. 367, p. 290). There are often such swipes at the Aḥmadiyya and also against Christians in the commentary.

---

[5] On the privileges of Fāṭima, see L Veccia Vaglieri, 'Fāṭima' in *Encyclopaedia of Islam* (2nd ed.); see also Jane Damen McAuliffe, 'Chosen of all Women. Mary and Fāṭima in Qur'ānic Exegesis', *Islamochristiana* 7 (1981), 19-28, in which *tafsīr* of three Shī'ī authors is considered.

1.5 And He will teach him the Book and the Wisdom, and the Torah and the Evangel (3: 47)

A marginal gloss states that this verse indicates that the Apostles are taught by God himself and not by any one else. The commentary expands on this. Jesus was sent into the world with knowledge which was not acquired but given to him. If this is true of Jesus, the forerunner of the Prophet, what about the Holy Prophet himself, asks Mir Ahmed Ali. Muḥammad was designated by Jesus as the 'Holy Ghost, the Comforter, the Spirit of Truth' (the usual reference is made to Dt 18: 15, 18–19 which foretells the coming of a prophet). He could therefore not be ignorant like ordinary people. According to the Qur'ān, Muḥammad was taught by a beneficent God and was designated as Man, i.e. the Perfect Man (Q. 55: 1-4). Jesus is presented as *muta'allim*, as one taught the Book of Wisdom by Divine Agency, and then sent to the children of Israel. The Last Prophet is *ummī*, sent to all who are born of woman.[6] His mission is therefore not limited, but extends to all, including those prophets who, like Jesus, had a limited mission (n. 368, p. 290).

Two things here would seem to be worthy of note as reflecting the Shī'ite position. One is the belief in a body of knowledge which is passed down from one prophet to the next and which is also the prerogative of the Imāms.[7] The second is the exaltation of Muḥammad as the Perfect Man. This doctrine is to be found in Sūfī writings which are close to the Shī'ī spirit.[8]

The next verse (3: 48) refers to Jesus' miracles. Here we have the signs of the usual twofold argument, against the Aḥmadiyya and against the Christians. The Aḥmadiyya would like to explain away all the miracles. Yet it is God the Absolute who is the ultimate agent; he merely allows actions to be attributed to secondary agencies. It is therefore not blasphemy for Jesus to say: 'I bring the dead to life', with God's permission. God has given curative power to honey (cf. Q. 16: 68). What wonder is

---

[6] The word *ummī* is usually interpreted as meaning 'illiterate', thus preparing for the miracle of the Qur'ān; cf. Anne-Marie Schimmel, 'Muḥammad: In Popular Piety', *Encyclopaedia of Islam* (2nd ed.), 377.

[7] Cf. T Fahd, 'Djafr', in *Encyclopaedia of Islam* (2nd ed.); see also Muḥammad Riḍā Al-Muẓaffar, *'Aqā'id al-Imāmiyya*, Arabic text and French translation in *Etudes Arabes*, 84-85 (1993), 120-123.

[8] Cf. R Arnaldez, 'al-Insān al-kāmil', in *Encyclopaedia of Islam* (2nd ed.).

there if curative property is given to dust coming from the grave of Ḥusayn? As for the Christians, their Scriptures are not complete, and they are distorted. For instance the 'miracle at Cana' is not fitting for an apostle of God. Jesus' words to Mary are unbecoming, and he certainly could not have supplied such 'nasty, demoralising stuff as wine'. The Holy Qur'ān thus defends Jesus. If it speaks about his miracles it is because he needed them, so that the mysterious circumstances of his birth might be confirmed. Muḥammad, on the other hand, had no need of miracles. The nobility of his birth as a descendant of Abraham was never in doubt. Furthermore, his character was well-proven since he was known as *al-amīn*. Finally the Qur'ān was given to him as a perpetual miracle. Yet 'whenever necessary, the Holy Prophet and his immediate successors, the Holy Imāms, could work any miracles, and they actually work such miracles as and when they deemed desirable' (n. 369, pp. 292-294).[9]

1.6 And when Jesus perceived disbelief on their part: said he, 'Who are (there) to be my helpers towards God?' (3.51)

Here a parallel is drawn with the event known as the *Da'wat 'Ashīra*. Muḥammad, feeling opposition to his message increasing, asked Quraysh who would be willing to help him. None responded except 'Alī. So Muḥammad declared 'Alī to be his Heir, his Brother, his Assistant, the Executor of his will, and his Successor after him (n. 371, p. 296). A cross-reference is given to Q. 11: 17, one of the verses in the Qur'ān where the term *imām* occurs. The commentary on this verse interprets it as a reference to 'Alī.[10] A further reference is made to Q. 3: 60 concerning the *mubāhala*, which will be dealt with below.

---

[9] Reference is given in the commentary on Q. 26: 214 to a miracle performed by Muḥammad with the help of 'Alī, when he fed forty guests with a few loaves and some meat and a cup of milk. Muḥammad was then accused of sorcery by Abū Lahab and the people left him so that he was unable to deliver his message. This was repeated three times. It ended with Muḥammad putting some of his saliva in 'Alī's mouth, taking his hand and declaring: 'Know ye all. This is my vizir, my heir, my khalīfa. Hear him, and obey him' (n. 1672, p. 1134 f.).

[10] For the details see Michael L Fitzgerald, *op. cit.*, 60-61.

1. 7 Recall (O Our Apostle Muḥammad!) when God said: 'O Jesus, I will take thee away and lift thee up unto Me. (3: 54)

In this verse the word *mutawaffi-ka* is examined closely. The marginal gloss understands it as meaning 'complete thy term'. Yet the exact meaning is disputed. If by the word is understood 'death', then the *nuzūl* of Jesus would mean his return to the world after his death. The possibility of 'a partial resurrection before the final or the total resurrection' is accepted on the authority of a Shī'ī author, Shaykh Ṣadūq.[11] If the term is taken to mean 'departure' other than death, then the return of Jesus would be a 're-appearance' and would be similar to that of the Twelfth Imām. There is however a difference. The Twelfth Imām is 'living on the earth (so) as to be its Centre to mediate between man and God'. Jesus, for his part, has been raised from his earthly station either to God (*illayya*) or to heaven. 'He is no more concerned with terrestrial affairs while the Twelfth Imām is alive on the earth and has sole charge of it'. At the reappearance of the two, Jesus will be the follower whereas the lead will be with Muḥammad al-Mahdī, the last Deputy of the Holy Prophet (n. 373, pp. 299-300).

1. 8 Verily, similitude of Jesus with God is as the similitude of Adam; He created him out of dust then said He unto him BE, and he became. (3.58)

This verse is understood to concern the dispute with the Christians of Najrān. They claimed that Muḥammad was disrespectful to Jesus since he called him a man. Muḥammad replied that there was no disrespect intended for the 'word of God communicated through the Chaste and pure Holy Lady Mary'. Asked whether any other man was born without a father, the reply came in the form of this verse. The commentator adds that the argument stands 'even if we put aside the view of the immediate creation of Adam from the earth and adhere to the evolutionary process of creation, because then the question will be shifted further, as to the creation of the first living cell from the unliving elements.' Divine intervention will be necessary (n. 376, p. 300).

A further purpose in this verse is discerned, namely to refute the Christian claim to the divinity of Jesus based on his virgin birth (*ibid.*). It

---

[11] I have not been able to identify this author.

might be observed that the virgin birth is not the basis for the Christian belief in the divinity of Jesus, but this is perhaps beside the point.

There follows a long commentary on 3: 60 (n. 378, pp. 302-308). This is one of the fundamental verses for the Shī'a since it establishes who are the *Ahl al-Bayt*. They are identified with the *Ahl al-kisā'*, [12] the People of the Mantle, that is Muḥammad, Fāṭima, 'Alī, Ḥasan and Ḥusayn. It will not be necessary to go into detail, since this teaching has little relevance to the Shī'ite view of Jesus. It is interesting to note, however, the answer to the question about the inclusion of small children (Ḥasan and Ḥusayn). Mir Ahmed Ali says that 'Alī was called while still a child, just as Jesus and John (the Baptist) were given *nubuwwa*, the *kitāb* and *ḥikma*, as children. The intellectual maturity required for the responsibility of prophethood is not usually found in babies, but there are exceptions following God's choice. Such are 'the chosen persons of the House of Abraham, of which John, Moses, Jesus, Muḥammad, 'Alī, Fāṭima, Ḥasan and Ḥusayn (are) the outstanding personalities' (p. 308). Though it is not said here, the same could apply to certain of the Imāms, including the Twelfth Imām, who inherited the imamate when they were still young children.

2 Sūrat Maryam (19)

This sūra starts off with the letters *kāf*, *hā'*, *yā'*, *'ayn* and *ṣād*. It is said that the true meaning of these mysterious letters is known to God and the Holy Prophet, and besides them to the Holy *Ahl al-Bayt*. The following is one of the explanations given:

> *kāf* stands for Karbalā';
> *hā'* for *halakat*, i.e. the annihilation of the Holy Family;
> *yā'* for Yazīd, the cause of the massacre;
> *'ayn* for *'atsh*, the thirst that was suffered;
> *ṣād* for *ṣabr*, the marvellous patience shown by Ḥusayn (n. 1309, p. 943).

---

[12] Cf. A S Tritton, 'Ahl al-kisā", *Encyclopaedia of Islam* (2nd ed.).

This explanation has been given in detail because it forms a good introduction to commentary on the sūra which contains many references to the events of Karbalā'. For instance, the same note traces a parallel between John (Yaḥyā) and Ḥusayn: 'like Yaḥyā Ḥusayn also was born in six months' (Luke's Gospel does not in fact say this; Elizabeth is six months pregnant when Mary goes to visit her, but the birth takes place afterwards); 'Ḥusayn's name was peculiar to him as was the name of Yaḥyā; Ḥusayn was also martyred for opposing the brute Yazīd's devilish life as was Yaḥyā for declaring what the King did was wrong.' It is remarked that Ḥusayn, during his journey to Karbalā', frequently remembered Yaḥyā (*ibid.*).

2.1 O Zachariah! Verily we give thee glad tidings of a son, his name shall be Yaḥya (John), and We gave not to any one before (him) that name!' (19: 7)

The last words of this verse are taken to mean 'We did not make any one like him'. This is then explained in detail. Yaḥyā neither sinned nor had any inclination to sin. He was not inclined to marry, nor did he in fact marry. He was born of a barren woman in advanced age, just as Jesus was born of a virgin (n. 131, p. 947). We see that the parallel with Jesus is made with regard to this third distinguishing mark of Yaḥyā, but not with regard to the first two where it might well have been also.

The commentary then continues to show the resemblance between Yaḥyā and Ḥusayn. The heavens mourned for both of them, as they did for none other. As Yaḥyā's head was handed over to a prostitute, so Ḥusayn's head was handed over to the sons of prostitutes (n. 1313, p. 948). Here it is added that Ḥusayn was well aware of what would happen to him at Karbalā'. He knew that he and his family would suffer torment and death. What he wanted was that 'his sacrifice should not take place unnoticed and go waste ineffective.' He succeeded in shaking the throne of the Tyrant 'and the heart of every Muslim in particular and humanity in general' (n. 1313, p. 949).[13]

---

[13] On the significance of the events of Karbalā' in the Shī'ī tradition, see the long quotation from a Shī'ī historian, S H M Jafri, in Moojan Momen, *An Introduction to Shī'ī Islam*, Yale UP, New Haven and London, 1985, 31-32.

2.2 (The Lord said unto Zachariah's son) 'O Yaḥyā! Hold thou the Book fast!' and We granted him wisdom (apostleship) while yet a child. (19: 12)

Here the commentary is similar to that on Q. 3: 45 which says that Jesus spoke in the cradle. Yaḥyā, while a young boy, was endowed with wisdom, understood to be a reference to the apostleship. This has the force of a divine model. Thus it is sheer ignorance to say that the Holy Prophet was ignorant and illiterate until the age of forty, and that he could not recognize the commission of apostleship but had to have it confirmed by a woman, i.e. Khadīja. It is also a wilful distortion to accept that Yaḥyā received Wisdom while a young boy, and yet to deny that 'Alī could embrace the faith at a young age, or to say that his allegiance to the Prophet had no value (n. 1317, pp. 950-951). It is obvious that the commentator is refuting the Sūnnis for whom 'Alī was too young to succeed the Prophet.

A further example is given of precocious wisdom. Someone expressed surprise at the wisdom of the eighth Imām, Al-Riḍā, who was at the time five years old. Aware of this astonishment, the Imām himself recited this verse about Yaḥyā. The commentator continues: 'The Holy Prophet and the chosen successors from their birth are gifted with the extraordinary power of receiving the Divine Blessings and expressing it (*sic*) to others and this is clearly asserted in the Qur'ān in the case of the Holy Prophet' (the reference indicated being the opening verses of Q. 55) (n. 1317, pp. 951-952).

There is a long commentary on this passage of Sūrat al-Raḥmān. In particular, on 55: 3 *He created man*, it is said that this could never refer to a sinner, a man of an ordinary order. 'When a quality is indefinitely mentioned, it means the perfect degree of it.' This means that the verse is really referring to the Prophet in his pre-physical state. 'The first thing God created was my Light,' the Prophet is reported to have said. This is the *nūr muḥammadī* which passed on through the lines of the prophets until it reached 'Abd al-Muṭṭalib. It then bifurcated, as has been seen, through 'Abd Allāh to Muḥammad, and through Abū Ṭālib to 'Alī. Thus the Prophet could say 'I and 'Alī are of one and the same light.' The two rays of light are united through the medium of Fāṭima, daughter of the Prophet, wife of 'Alī, and thus the light is transmitted to their offspring, the Eleven Holy Imāms (n. 2451, pp. 1598-1601).

46

2.3 And mention in the Book (Qur'ān) about Mary (also) when she withdrew from her family (in the house) eastward. (19: 16)

With regard to the word 'eastward' a cross-reference is given in the margin to Q. 28: 44. This verse speaks of Moses being on the 'western side' of Mt Sinai when he received the commandment (*amr*). Here the cross-reference is back to 19: 16! The commentary on the verse in Sūrat Maryam explains the significance of these directions. Jesus' mission deals more with the spiritual aspects of life, and thus is symbolized by the East, by the rising sun. Moses' mission, on the other hand, was mainly concerned with the temporal aspect of human life, and thus was symbolized by the West, the setting sun. When this is borne in mind, it is clear that Q. 24: 35, which contains the words 'neither Eastern nor Western', refers to the mission of the Last Apostle of God which combines both of these aspects (n. 1319, p. 955).

There is little of significance for this paper in the commentary on the following verses. A further criticism of the New Testament can be noted in the commentary on v. 22 which says that Mary retired with the son she had conceived 'to a remote place'. A marginal note states 'Not to a mean place like a manger as the Bible says' (p. 946).

2.4 He (Jesus miraculously) said: Verily I am a servant of God; He hath given me a Book (Evangel) and made me a Prophet! (19: 30)

Here Mir Ahmed Ali refers back to what was said in the commentary on v. 12 concerning the Wisdom given to Yaḥyā. He also sends the reader back to what has been said about Q. 13: 7 where it is affirmed that Muhammad is *a Warner and Guide unto every people*. The Holy Prophet is thus the universal guide for all nations and for all time. It is a law of divine mercy that for every nation there has been and there will be a guide. The guides following the Holy Prophet are the Holy Imāms. Here the objection is put as to how the Last Imām, the Mahdī, can be a guide since he is hidden, like 'Jesus and the Angels'. This is considered to be 'a childish question'. God is hidden, and yet he is the source of guidance. Muhammad lived only in Mecca, and yet it has been declared that he was the prophet for all people and for all times (n. 1117, pp. 800–806). Thus it is not necessary for the Guide to be visible. The original note concludes: 'As Jesus was from the very birth a believer in God and His devotee, the First Holy Imām, 'Alī ibn Abī Ṭālib, was born in the Holy Ka'ba and never in his life worshipped any one besides God and was the first to believe in the Holy Prophet' (n. 1327, p. 958).

2.5 And He hath made me blessed wherever I be and he hath enjoined on me prayer and poor-rate so long as I live. (19: 31)

The commentary here goes beyond the outward meaning of the words. The term ṣalāt does not refer only to formal prayers accompanied by physical movements. It means also a prayerful attitude, for 'the soul of an apostle would naturally be always in communion with the Almighty One who has sent the soul into the world with some particular purpose'. Similarly zakāt means not only the action of giving, but more especially 'purity of thought and conduct'. For 'the whole life of an apostle of God would naturally need to be ideally pure in word and action as a model to his followers' (n. 1328, p. 958). These annotations could be understood in connection with the privilege of *'isma* which is given to the Prophets and to the Imāms.[14]

2.6 This is Jesus, the son of Mary; (this is) a statement of the truth about which they dispute (19: 34)

On this final verse the marginal note states quite categorically: 'All about Jesus is that he is a created being, the outcome of the creative will and command of God'. It is so simple, and yet opinions about Jesus differ, as the Qur'ān itself notes: *Then did differ the sects among themselves* (19: 37). Mir Ahmed Ali comments: 'In several other verses such as 3: 19 the Qur'ān declares that the differences among the various groups of the people of the Book, *including the Muslims*, are based on the rebellious tendency against the unequivocal declarations of God' (n. 1331, p. 959). The emphasis is mine, since it is interesting to see first of all that Muslims are included among the People of the Book, and secondly that their

---

[14] Cf. W Madelung, ' 'Isma' in *Encyclopaedia of Islam* (2nd ed.); see also Muḥammad Riḍā Al-Muẓaffar, *'Aqā'id*, 120-121.

disagreements are taken into account. These may however not refer to Jesus at all; rather they could refer to the differences between Shī'a and Sunnīs as regards caliphate and imamate.

After having examined the main pericopes which deal with Jesus, attention can be paid briefly to isolated verses or passages in which Jesus is mentioned. As regards some of these Mir Ahmed Ali makes no comment, while on others there is little of significance.

3 Isolated Verses and Passages
3.1 Q. 2: 253

Q. 2: 253 speaks of the apostles of whom some are exalted above the others. Thus the 'personal excellence' of the prophets is graded. Mention is made in the verse of Moses (not explicitly, but as one to whom God spoke directly) and of Jesus, who was aided by the Holy Ghost. These two are singled out because they were both 'reformers'. Yet they both had to 'sing the praises of the Holy Prophet'. The usual references are indicated: Dt 18: 18-19; Acts 3: 22-25; Jn 14: 16-17, 15: 26, 16: 7-13. Their missions are limited, in particular that of Jesus, whereas the highest mission is reserved for the Last Prophet, Muhammad (n. 286, p. 222).

It seems strange that the words *bi-rūh al-qudūs* would be translated with the very Christian term 'Holy Ghost'. The commentator corrects any wrong impression by stating that prophets are inspired in various manners. Jesus was aided by the Holy Spirit, that is by the Archangel Gabriel (n. 287, p. 224).

3.2 Q. 4: 157-158

Given the place accorded to suffering in the Shī'ī outlook and devotion,[15] it might have been expected that there would be some significant reflection on the sufferings of Jesus. In fact the whole burden of the commentary on Q. 4: 157-158 is to refute the Christian belief in the death of Jesus on the cross. It is stated quite clearly that 'the doctrine of the crucifixion,

---

[15] M Borrmans mentions this in the chapter on the Cross referred to above (M Borrmans, *Islam e Cristianesimo*, 71).

the death or the resurrection of Jesus is of no value at all to the Muslims' (n. 634, p. 434).

The following verse (159) says that all the People of the Book will believe in Jesus. Here is how Mir Ahmed Ali understands this verse. 'Every one of the followers of the various scriptures will ultimately recognize Jesus when he descends from Heaven when the last Holy Imām Muḥammad al-Mahdī would have appeared. Jesus will live for forty years following Islam and the Islamic law and offer prayers led by the Last Holy Imām Muḥammad al-Mahdī, he would suffer death and the Muslims will conduct the funeral congregational prayers' (n. 636, p. 435). As has been seen before, Jesus is subordinate to the Mahdī.

The time of the second coming will be 'an age of perfect peace and security of life and justice will have its full play in the whole world.' It is interesting, in passing, to note the signs which the Indian, Mir Ahmed Ali, writing in the early 1950s, indicates for the coming of this reign of justice and peace: prohibition (i.e. of alcohol), the overcoming of the caste system, the opening of places of worship to all, widow marriage (instead of *sutee?*), anti-dowry agitation, unitarian belief about God, respect for all faiths and regard for all religious leaders, the proposal for One World Government (n. 636, p. 436). He concludes: the re-appearance of Jesus will be as the Holy Imāms have declared, all the People of the Book will believe in Jesus as well as the (Last) Holy Imām (*ibid.*).

3.3 Q. 4: 163

Q. 4: 163 gives a list of some of the prophets. The commentary observes that the Qur'ān upholds the truthfulness and the holiness of all the prophets, whereas 'the Holy Book of the Christian Church seems to hold brief exclusively on behalf of Jesus and decries other apostles of God like Noah, Abraham, David' (n. 640, p. 436). This is to conform to the doctrine of the sinlessness of the prophets, particularly developed among the Shī'a, as has been noted, with regard to *'isma*. More significant perhaps is the refutation of the criticism of the order in which the verse mentions the prophets. It is said that the order reflects the experience of Muḥammad. Thus Abraham's preaching and his persecution at the hands of Nimrod is paralleled by the Prophet's persecution by his people. Ishmael's abandonment is reflected in Muḥammad's helplessness after the death of his uncle and protector Abū Ṭālib. What trait is drawn from the life of Jesus? It is not one a Christian would think of immediately. He is said to have sought to storm Jerusalem, but he eventually escaped death at the hands of the Jews. Muḥammad, for his part, shows success in his mission even in Madina, and he clearly shows warlike designs. The Meccans, alarmed, try to kill him, but he escapes yet, like Job (mentioned next in the verse), loses everything, only to gain more than he had lost (n. 640, p. 437).

3.4 Q. 4: 171

Q. 4: 171, in which the People of the Book are told *overstep not in your religion*, gives rise to an interesting commentary. For the word translated by 'overstep' is from the root *gh-l-w*, from which comes the term *ghulāt*, or those who exaggerate in their beliefs. The opposite of *ghulw* is *taqṣīr*, or falling short. These two defects can occur with regard to Jesus. There is *ghulw* when Jesus is given the status of 'one of the Three in the Trinity', or when a finite being is considered the incarnation or the embodiment of the Absolute (this refers also to the Hindu belief in *avatars*). There is *taqṣīr* when the apostleship of Jesus is denied, as by the Jews. Yet the same defects can occur as regards 'Alī. The Nuṣayrīs, who are alleged to hold 'Alī as God, would be guilty of *ghulw*, whereas all who fail to recognize the status that God has granted to 'Alī can be taxed with *taqṣīr*. 'Alī is to be accepted with 'all the qualifications of excellence and infallibility, *Imāma* and *Wilāya*' (n. 643, pp. 438-439).

3.5 Q. 5: 78

In Q. 5: 78 we find the unbelievers from among the people of Israel cursed by David and Jesus on account of their disobedience. Though the Arabic for cursed is *lu'ina*, the commentator takes it as a reference to *tabarra'*. He does not explain this, but merely states that *tabarra'* is one of the articles of faith of 'Islam-Original', i.e. Shī'ism (n. 711, p. 502). In fact, *tabarra'* is the opposite of *wilāya*. Just as *wilāya* means to be directed towards God through being attached to the Imāms, so *tabarra'* consists in turning away from anything that is contrary to God, and so also from all enemies of the Imāms.

3.6 Q. 5: 111, 117

Q. 5: 111 speaks about the disciples receiving a revelation that they are to believe in Jesus. Here a long marginal note applies the verse to the case of Muḥammad. It is worth quoting in full:

> This shows that the first disciples of Jesus were under direct guidance through divine inspiration. This corroborates with what 'Alī ibn Abī Ṭālib says. When the Holy Prophet used to retire to Mt Hīra on the eve of his being commissioned (he) used to see the light of revelation and feel the good smell of the apostleship and the Holy Prophet said to me, 'O 'Alī, Thou seest what I see and heareth what I hear.' This indicates that if one of the Holy souls whose state of the excellence of the purity of mind are (*sic*) close to each other or one be sub-ordinate to the other the spiritual experience of the one reflects on the other (pp. 499, 501).

Despite the rather involved style, the message is clear. As was said in the commentary on 19: 12 (see above), Muḥammad and 'Alī are seen to be in close communion, so much so that they can be considered one.

A few verses later, in 5: 117, the word *tawaffayta-nī* occurs. Mir Ahmed Ali repeats what he has said about this verb (see the commentary on 3: 54 above). He adds the following reflection: 'It has been said that there will be nothing which has happened in the history of the older religions but will find a parallel in Islam'. The parallel that he draws here is between 'the continued life of Jesus, the last of the Israelite prophets', and 'the divinely continued life of Muḥammad ibn Ḥasan al-'Askarī al-Mahdī—the last of the Imāms of the Islamic faith' (n. 735, p. 509).

This idea is repeated very concisely in the commentary on 23: 50 where Jesus and Mary are constituted a sign. Mir Ahmed Ali is at pains to refute the Aḥmadī interpretation of this verse which would see in the mention of 'a refuge on a high land' a reference to Kashmir where

Jesus is said to have wandered and finally died. He says that, on the authority of the Fifth and Sixth Imāms, the place of refuge is identified with the 'fertile land on the banks of the Euphrates, in Iraq'. More importantly, he holds that there is no need to try to prove that Jesus was a mere mortal by inventing a story of his death. For, 'God the Omnipotent Lord wants him to be alive as His Sign to be presented along with His other Sign, the Last Imām' (n. 1551, p.1062).

3. 7 Q. 42: 13

Jesus is mentioned in Q. 42: 13 along with Noah, Abraham and Moses. It is a key verse in which Islam, as the religion established by God, is seen to be in succession to the religion enjoined on the previous prophets. So 'the religion preached by the Holy Prophet is based upon the same basic principles which were preached by Noah, Abraham, Moses and Jesus', namely 'the Unity of God and the righteousness of life disciplined by morals and ethics copying the divine attributes in the human character and conduct'. Yet there is a difference between Islam and other religions. Religions are not named by the first preachers, but by the followers after they have systematized them. So it is with Hinduism and Buddhism, Judaism and Christianity. 'But *Islam received its name from God Himself*' (underlined in the text). There is a cross-reference to Q. 5: 3 which reads 'This day have I perfected for you your religion, and have completed My favour on you and chosen for you ISLAM (to be) the Religion'. This is a fundamental verse for the Shī'a, since the 'completion' is taken as referring to the appointment of 'Alī as the first Imām, perfecting the structure of the religion by providing for its continuity.[16] Christianity, on the other hand, was not the complete definitive religion, since 'Jesus left this world only prophesying the advent of the *Spirit of Truth* to give the Whole Truth' (reference being made to Jn 16: 5-14) (n. 2190, pp. 1441-1443).

The same passage of the Gospel of John occurs in the commentary on Q. 61: 6 in which Jesus gives 'the glad tidings of an Apostle who shall

---

[16] For Mir Ahmed Ali's commentary on this verse see Michael L Fitzgerald, 'Shī'ite Understanding of the Qur'ān', *op. cit.*, 156-158.

come after me, his name being Aḥmad (i.e. Muḥammad)'. The long concludes with the following affirmation:

> 'Thus the very description of the 'Comforter' announces the 'Spirit of Truth' to be a man with the Holy Ghost actuating him, i.e. his soul would not be like an ordinary one but Holy, i.e. *the one purified by God* Himself which quality of the Holy Prophet Muḥammad and his *Ahl al-Bayt* is given in 33: 33. Naturally the one purified by God Himself could be nothing but the manifestation of the Spirit of Truth and the Divine holiness' (n. 2571, p. 1672).

Conclusion

The results of this investigation into Mir Ahmed Ali's commentary can be summarized briefly in a number of points.

1.   The commentator, although making considerable use of the Christian Scriptures, distances himself from them. He considers them to be unreliable documents. In elaborating on the verses that refer to Jesus he remains generally within the usual paradigms of Islam.

2.   Trouble is taken to refute the doctrine of the Aḥmadiyya on Jesus, particularly with regard to the reality of the crucifixion and Jesus' escape from death on the cross and subsequent death in Kashmir. This view is considered quite fantastic, but attention is paid to it, presumably on account of the Indian context in which the commentary is written.

3.   The persecution of Jesus, the opposition which leads up to the verse about the crucifixion (Q. 4: 157), is not brought into connection in any way with the opposition to the Third Imām, Ḥusayn. The parallel is drawn between Ḥusayn and John/Yaḥyā.

4.   The two main points of contact between Jesus and Shī'a doctrine are the privileges he receives while a young child and his return.

5.   The fact that Jesus (and John/Yaḥyā) are seen to be endowed with Wisdom from birth is connected with the divine election of the Prophets and the Imāms and the infused knowledge they possess.

6.   Jesus is seen to be a Sign connected with, but subordinate to, the Sign of the Last Imām who is to re-appear at the end of time.

It can perhaps be said that, in the final analysis, Mir Ahmed Ali is not interested so much in the figure of Jesus as in what he calls 'Islam-Original', that is in the Shī'ī version of Islam. It is this very often that he puts forward in his commentaries on the passages in the Qur'ān where Jesus is mentioned. Though, from a Christian's point of view, this may be a disappointment, it should not really be found surprising.

REFLECTIONS ON THE
ROLE OF MUSLIM AND CHRISTIAN
SCHOLARS IN THE FACE OF
CONTEMPORARY CHALLENGES

Ayatollah Misbah Yazdi

In this brief paper, I wish to explore the wider context in which both Muslims and Christians, especially Shi'a and Catholic scholars, can co-operate with each other to ensure and promote the prosperity and happiness of human beings with regard to the intellectual and crisis in values in this critical era. For this purpose, we should first take a brief glance at the disturbed situation of the globe along with man's moral and spiritual crises and his grave need for a rational world-view and a firm doctrinal system as well as proportionate moral and value systems. Then we will explore the wide range of possibilities open to the Abrahamic religions, especially Christianity and Islam. Then we will point to the positive factors which pave the way for these two divine religions— especially Catholic and Shi'a denominations—to co-operate and come closer, and finally we will bring our discussion to an end by putting an emphasis on the necessity of close and friendly co-operation between scholars of these two faiths as a common divine and human duty.

1

In the modern era, especially in the last century, there have been radical changes and developments which are still proceeding swiftly and seem to be so astonishing that they cannot be compared with the slow change and development that occurred in other times, as if a new world has come to existence and a new mankind has been created.

These changes and developments can be traced back to the development of the empirical sciences and the discovery of many secrets of nature which, in turn, contributed to the remarkable advances in various fields of technology and to the invention of so many astonishing instruments and tools that opened up new ways for many people to make fortunes, enjoy welfare and seek numerous sorts of pleasure and entertainment. This process is still going on so swiftly that it makes it impossible to predict exactly how man's life in the future will be.

These changes and developments have carried with them so many positive and favourable aspects to life that have motivated people to pursue this course of development as rapidly as possible, on the one hand, and have had some negative and undesirable aspects which have brought harmful consequences on the other. Among the positive aspects, the major one is that man can have easy access to material gifts and all means of welfare and a comfortable life which have never been available to such an extent, quantitatively and qualitatively, in the past. These changes, however, have brought about harmful effects which make masses of people feel that they lead a life of total misery or which have led to the decline in man's moral and spiritual standards.

Not only are poor and oppressed people captive in the fetters and chains of these harmful effects, but even rich people are also suffering from them to the extent that few people can be seen among them to feel completely at ease, living in peace and tranquillity, and be free of fear, agitation, anxiety and mental problems.

No doubt, there is a greedy and power-seeking minority in human society which is to be held responsible for much of this disturbance and crisis, since they have misused various achievements of natural sciences, manipulated and oppressed others, and committed many sorts of injustice and evil in order to secure for themselves more wealth and power. They have even chosen to satisfy their demonic carnal desires and physical needs at the expense of killing millions of people (the bloody massacre of innocent civilians) or subjecting them to various fatal diseases. They have launched bloody wars on purpose in the world, as we witnessed in the case of the two great world wars in the last century in which millions of innocent people were slaughtered.

Surprisingly enough, even though this rich minority possesses all the dangerous means of destroying all the residents on the planet, such as nuclear bombs, chemical weapons, etc., they still seek to make more and more various, destructive, dangerous and complicated weapons while they try to obstruct the way to other nations to gain access to conventional weapons even for defensive purposes.

2

The observation of this oppression, corruption and violence, and their unpleasant subsequences has led many youths to the conception that this miserable and painful condition is the necessary outcome of modern life and the bitter fruit of modern civilization imposed by historical determinism and therefore they think that there is no way out of this miserable unfortunate condition. Hence they may turn to drugs, alcoholic drinks and destructive entertainments and may even commit suicide. More regrettable is the fact that even these drugs and destructive entertainments have been made available to them by those profit-seekers who out of their greed provide them with disease-causing, mind-damaging and even deadly goods. Alas! Ignorance and lack of wisdom and, in fact, the eagerness to amass wealth and the struggle for power drive man to commit such disastrous crimes!

But do we suppose that this miserable condition is a matter of unavoidable—historical—determinism and that nobody should be held responsible or blamed for it? Are not the continuation of this situation and the emergence of a possibly more dangerous situation an unavoidable necessity? Is there not any way open to people to avoid it or, at least, decrease pain and misery?

There is no doubt that, as we observed earlier, man's greediness, lust for power, personal ambitions, carnal desires and arrogance, all in all, have contributed to the emergence of these miseries, crises and social corruption. However, it should be pointed out that, in spite of all appearances to the contrary, the way is not totally obstructed for man to avoid, increase or decrease them. Moreover, drawing people's attention to the harmful or fatal consequences of oppression, violence and corruption can be in one way or another effective in reducing them by taking preventive measures, such as setting up and executing laws, rules and regulations by those sympathetic who feel seriously responsible for the welfare and happiness of all mankind. However, the most effective and essential way is that people should be driven into a recognition that they themselves decide and determine to change or reform their situation and this aim cannot be fulfilled save through the change of man's attitudes or insights, or, in other words, through the change of his beliefs and values; and this is what the divine prophets were asked by God to carry out. In this way the divine laws *(shari'ahs)* took form and in this regard the Abrahamic religions are outstanding.

3

Human voluntary actions are usually performed through making a choice between several alternatives and, at least, with the preference given to the performance of the action rather than its omission. And, naturally, making a choice between two or more alternatives seems to be a sort of evaluation one makes in terms of certain widely established criteria (standards), though it may be the case that one is not totally cognizant of the standards in question. It is the sum-total of these standards (norms) that constitute the value system of an individual or group or society.

Value systems, whether or not one holds that they derive directly from certain beliefs about facts, without doubt do not comply with every doctrinal system.[1] Thus, it should be admitted that certain value systems are more compatible with certain dogmas and world-views than others.

The most important task of divine prophets was to present a rational and tenable world-view and doctrinal system as well as a moral or value system compatible with that world-view or doctrinal system. In other words, the prophets were asked by God to provide mankind with a true insight, to improve or correct their systems of thought, creeds and values, and to direct their desires, inclinations or tendencies in accordance with those true insights. To sum, up the prophets have come to invite human beings to a true value system.

We believe that the doctrinal system that all prophets have preached is this very monotheistic belief and divine world-view. We also believe that the value system accepted by all the divine prophets derives from those monotheistic beliefs or, at least, is in compliance with them and therefore leads mankind towards the station of approximation to God and everlasting happiness. These two systems, doctrinal system and value system, have best manifested themselves in Abrahamic religions.

---

[1] The relation between values and beliefs or 'Is–Ought Problem' is an important philosophical problem which needs to be addressed separately. What has been said above is the minimal relation that cannot be denied.

A careful study of the roots of current corruption and deviation and the underlying causes of crises and disasters shows that the most fundamental reason for all this is disorder in the value system, and, finally, in the doctrinal system of some people. To conclude, one can argue that the most promising way to put an end to all these problems is to follow the example of the prophets in correcting the value and doctrinal systems of the people.

Therefore, by following the prophets and making use of their teachings and their scientific and cultural heritage, their true followers can best help contemporary man as well as future generations, who will naturally be exposed to more threats. For this purpose, co-operation and the exchange of ideas and experiences among believers will certainly be very helpful.

4

The common intellectual and doctrinal grounds as well as the shared moral principles of all the Abrahamic religions can very well pave the way for co-operation in the efforts to strengthen the faith in the hearts of the young generation and to reform their moral and value standards.

Furthermore, Islam has a particularly high esteem for Christianity and this has provided a special opportunity for Muslim-Christian co-operation which can hardly be found among other religions. Denying calumny against the Virgin Maryam (Mary) (May God's peace be upon her!), introducing her as a perfect role model for all believers and righteous people, the existence of one complete chapter in the Qur'an under the name of Mary and about her status, praise of Christians in the Qur'an as a humble and truth-seeking people who, on hearing the divine verses, had tears of happiness rolling down their faces (5: 82) and introducing Christians as the best friends of Muslims, all give clear and remarkable indications that Islam has a high regard for Christianity and Christians. What gives great hope to Muslims, especially the Shi'a Muslims, is that according to Islamic *hadiths* when Imam al-Mahdi (the Twelfth Imam of the Shi'ite Muslims who is now protected by God in the state of occultation) arises with divine blessing, Jesus Christ will descend from heaven and will accompany him in prayer. They will establish divine law in the world and fill the world with justice and uproot any sort of oppression and injustice from the earth.

5

In view of the above mentioned points, the necessity of co-operation by Muslim and Christian scholars, especially the Shi'a and Catholics, for the establishment of a global movement against atheism, faithlessness, moral indulgence and any other sort of evil act becomes more urgent. The key to this great task is dialogue and mutual understanding.

A proper dialogue should play a significant role in the clarification of common ground and principles and provide the young generation with a rational and tenable doctrinal system as well as a proportionate value system. Naturally, avoiding prejudices, forgetting the regrettable memories of past events, the misconduct of some followers of each religion in the past on the one hand, and insistence upon rationalism and the use of rational arguments in preaching activities on the other, all contribute greatly to the success of this dialogue.

The present writer in numerous meetings with the Christian scholars, bishops, and even the Pope, has always insisted on the above points and has always received a warm welcome, and this has caused greater hope for the possibility and success of such co-operation. I should especially mention my happy memories of the sincere talks and meetings with the Bishop of Croatia (Zagreb), the Bishop of Naples, the Council of the Bishops in Mexico City and other bishops of the Latin-American countries. Furthermore, my numerous visits to different universities of the world, and constructive talks with their professors, students and governors, have all confirmed the existence of appropriate and prepared grounds for dialogue and co-operation in the battle against doctrinal deviations, behavioural corruption and for guiding the younger generation towards happiness in this world and hereafter, which definitely pleases God and will bring about His provision and support.

CONTEMPORARY CHALLENGES TO CATHOLIC-SHI'A ENGAGEMENT

Justo Lacunza Balda

Introduction

There is no doubt that we live in hard and difficult times. In spite of technological achievements, scientific developments and closer awareness of a global community, the signs of ill feelings and evident animosity between Christians and Muslims continue in many parts of the world. The rising tide of violence, conflict and war in many zones of today's community of nations, make me aware more than ever before of four personal ideas. I would like, here, to develop them succinctly, in order to understand some of the challenges that Christians and Muslims face today. They are: (1) violence and war, (2) reconciliation and peace, (3) dialogue and understanding, (4) religious freedom. These headings are the object of my personal choice, as I think that they represent in a fair way the areas of challenge, progress and debate for Muslims and Christians anywhere in the world today.

1 Violence and war

There is an urgent need today to deal with questions of violence and war in a way that is conducive to realistic and true solutions of society's problems. While conflicts continue to grow in number, and violence in many cases has become endemic, few authentic solutions are found to existing problems. One interesting and illuminating point is the fact that enormous natural and human resources are channelled towards maintaining what I call *the invisible culture of war*. War is considered to be the inevitable road to solve thorny problems and deal with complex questions, such as nuclear proliferation and weapons of mass destruction.

There is almost an obsession among the leaders of today's nations. They want to acquire the most sophisticated weapons, develop arms programmes in defence and stock their arsenals with the latest inventions for warfare. Meanwhile, millions of people starve to death, undergo violence in all its forms and continue to live in appalling conditions of poverty, deprivation and hardship. These are modern forms of human slavery, which cannot be hidden nor ignored. They are the shame of the contemporary world. Liberation means a decent human life and freedom means food and water. But one is profoundly shocked and very puzzled to see that even the open debate about war, considered by many as the only solution to society's problems, upsets many world leaders and disturbs their well-trimmed projects. In this way, the culture of war continues to take root and develop in our societies, and even to find its glamour in the world of fashion.

There was a time when news arrived at a time when probably conflicts were over. Things have changed drastically today. Instant communication, internet links, news agencies put on our doorstep events that happen thousands of miles away from the places where we live and work. It is difficult today to deal with the avalanche of news that comes through the media in every possible field, from science to religion, from sport to disease, from war to prospects of peace. The zones of conflict are dramatically increasing, while viable solutions for conflict resolution are slow to come. The causes of conflict are many and religion has become indirectly the object of debate and dialectics, if not of heated polemics and open confrontation.

Christians and Muslims are facing a big challenge in questions related to war and violence. Such challenges can be seen at three different levels of action:

> a. The interpretation of sacred texts must help to clear any doubts that there might be to place the foundation of war and aggression on the scriptural data offered by the sacred books. It is unacceptable to believe that sacred texts can be brought forward to prove that the use of violence to defend, propagate or cement religion has its foundational bases in texts considered to be revealed. There is always a danger that man's human vision becomes the centre of the wheel around which every action must turn and orbit, including the Supreme Divinity.
>
> b. Christian and Muslim leaders cannot adopt an attitude

of passivity in the face of war and violence, fearing that they might enter the arena of politics, and therefore remain on the fringes, as mere spectators of what is happening in the world. There are people who base their violent actions on sacred texts and refer to past history when making proposals for action against those who do not share the same faith.

c. There is a danger that the debate around war and violence takes a political bent. Therefore, society at large is supposed to accept what their leaders say, propose and do. Christians and Muslims can play a vital role here, stressing the fact that war and violence are not *political questions*, but rather *human issues*. Any concerted action in Muslim-Christian perception must underline this aspect, bringing together the efforts of both communities for the good of society.

2 Reconciliation and peace

Religions must play a role at the forefront of offering avenues of true reconciliation and sound peace. There are too many energies wasted in the world, in trying to explore the mysteries of a particular faith, not with the desire of searching and finding common grounds, but with the aim of proving how wrong others' doctrinal positions are.

Exploring the mysteries of God certainly draws together believers of different faith traditions. One of the major problems in reconciliation and peace is the belief that we are very smart and terribly intelligent. Therefore, we will be able to build peace and reconciliation with our own forces. But we fail again and again, because we trust too much in our own plans and not enough in the inspiration that comes constantly from above. It is simply impossible to offer reconciliation and peace when we are at odds with each other, feel that the other is the enemy to be fought and not the brother/sister with whom to build this world together.

Reconciliation seems a strange word today and yet, there is no progress without reconciliation and no well-being without peace with each other. Reconciliation is not only a religious term, it is also a human term that covers a wide range of human activities. Making peace with others is not a defeat, but a victory. Peace is not a sign of weakness, but a sign of being human and a beacon of humanity. We live in a world where political power, economic wealth and military force often dictate conditions for peace. That might be necessary at times, but peace cannot blossom unless it is born in the hearts of men and women. They are the real actors and the true protagonists of peace.

It is interesting to notice how modern language influences the perception of other people's faith history. The search for reconciliation and peace leads to explore the history, religion and culture of peoples. It is in a human framework where reconciliation grows and where peace develops. Knowledge and understanding of the other becomes a fundamental part of building peace together.

Christians and Muslims are, perhaps, confronted today with the greatest challenge of all times, that of reconciliation and peace with each other. There are certainly many ways to work together in that direction. I can only suggest three ways:

a. It is important to watch the language we use when speaking of other faiths, other religions and other cultures. We often forget that behind the Christian and Muslim faiths are men and women who draw from them inspiration and comfort for their lives. Therefore, language can be conducive to reconciliation and can promote peace among Christian and Muslim believers.

b. We know that Muslim communities are divided and we are aware that the Churches are divided. The process of peace and reconciliation cannot forget those who share the same faith vision, be they Christian or Muslim. Therefore, there is a need to further the progress of reconciliation and peace within our own Christian and Muslim communities.

c. Reconciliation and peace are not for the hereafter, they are for the here and now. It is, therefore, vital that Christians and Muslims fully respect each other's religious and cultural identities in the place where they live. There are too many acts of aggression and too many people have been killed because of hatred between Christians and Muslims. It is time to show the true face of our respective faiths and, only in that way, will peace and reconciliation flourish. This will lead to better life conditions.

3 Dialogue and understanding

Terms such as dialogue and understanding between Christians and Muslims seem to be out of place and completely irrelevant in the minds of many people. But here we need to look more closely at human reality in order to draw inspiration from life. A human person is essentially 'a communication unit'. Right from its birth a human person is fundamentally communicating its very self through gestures, sounds, music, words, ideas, concepts, art, architecture, writing. These are some of the many aspects of this 'communicating unit', that represents each human being.

Love and tenderness are communicated to others and so are hatred and violence. Therefore, dialogue and understanding are not the invention of our times, but rather the awareness of something that it is hidden within us. The process of learning and education in man's life is a continuous process of dialogue and understanding within us. Then we are prepared and ready to dialogue with others, understand who they are, what and how they believe. In other words, we will be able to 'dialogue' without fear and to understand without prejudice.

There are those who do not favour dialogue between people of different religious and cultural traditions, but fail to offer other ways which lead to peace, freedom, dignity and prosperity. One asks oneself: how is it possible to live without seeking to understand the framework of somebody else's faith, culture and religion?

There are many ways, which one could take to walk on the road of dialogue and understanding. I would like to suggest three major ways, which can help to foster dialogue and understanding between Christians and Muslims:

a. Simple curiosity and genuine interest of each other's faith are the first steps that can help Christians and Muslims to dialogue and understand each other. It is quite possible that Muslims see a church building and never ask themselves:

what does such a building represent for Christians? On the other hand, Christians might see a mosque in their neighbourhood and never ask themselves: what is the place of the mosque in Muslim life?

b. Believers of different traditions build their own cultural and religious identities not only around credo formulas, doctrinal precepts and legal injunctions. There are other ingredients that give strength to peoples' identities, such as food and drink, festivals and gatherings, rituals, colours and buildings. They are the screen on which believers show their religion with a human face.

c. Christians and Muslims need to have leaders, who know not only their own faith, but also that of their partners in dialogue. Knowledge in depth is necessary if progress is going to be made at all in dialogue and understanding. These are not an aim in itself, but rather a means to live in a better way.

4 Religious freedom

The complex term globalisation has drawn peoples, communities and nations closer together. Looking at the faces of the people in any of the cities and towns of our societies, we realise that cultural diversity and religious pluralism are two fundamental trademarks of our human societies. Yet, when we come to the question of religious freedom, we get stuck somewhere and fear that creating the space for genuine religious freedom will be detrimental to the majority religion of a country. Those who do not seem to agree fundamentally with religious freedom will use basically three major arguments:

a. Tradition carries weight, marks the history of a nation and shows the way of the future. The defenders of tradition argue that they have the responsibility of preserving the religious identity of their societies by all the means at their disposal. Therefore, the majority religion needs to prevail, because religious freedom is a foreign concept and other faiths need to be kept under control.

b. There are those who are against religious freedom,

arguing that it might endanger the home faith. Therefore, religious freedom has no place in their minds and cannot be tolerated, because eventually it will go against the faith of those who are citizens of the country.

c. There is another argument that is brought forward and it is the reference to the content of the constitution. There is simply no place for religious freedom within the framework of the country's constitutional order. Therefore, those who happen to be of a different religion will not enjoy the benefits of religious freedom.

The complex, and at the same time simple, question of religious freedom needs to be discussed openly by Christians and Muslims. In my personal opinion it is the most essential question that Christians and Muslims need to debate today. There are three major reasons, which seem to me relevant and important in this respect:

a. Pluralism and diversity anywhere in the world require today that a person be given the possibility of expressing freely his/her religion, if necessary within the framework of a community. Religious freedom cannot be regarded with contempt, as something that can be denied to an individual. One hopes that the world will eventually move towards avoiding any form of religious racism.

b. Democratic freedoms cannot leave room for apathy, ignorance or hatred in matters of religious freedom. The state must guarantee that there is religious freedom in the country for all those who live within its national boundaries. Religious freedom is a sacrosanct right of the individual, no matter what religion he/she belongs to, and no matter where he/she lives.

c. Religious freedom is a great challenge to a religion, particularly to the way sacred texts are understood and interpreted. Religious freedom helps, and hopefully will force, religious leaders to discuss and debate among themselves the meaning of their faith in the context of religious diversity and pluralism of faith traditions.

There are many other aspects that can be taken into consideration and study when looking at the way Muslims and Christians interact. My choice of the above areas has been led by three principal ideas: (1) conflicting interests among Christian and Muslims; (2) the possibility of real progress to bring relations between Christians and Muslims into the open and beyond the classroom debate; (3) to take relations between Christians and Muslims away from the narrow approach of political discourse in the name of religion.

INTERRELIGIOUS DIALOGUE, MUSLIM-CHRISTIAN RELATIONS AND CATHOLIC-SHI'A ENGAGEMENT

Anthony O'Mahony

I have been on my guard
not to condemn the unfamiliar.
For it is easy to miss.
At the turn of a civilization.[1]

This paper has three aims: one to reflect on implications for Christianity in its relations with other faiths; to reflect on the specificity of Christian-Muslim encounter; and finally to look at some of the possible areas of engagement between Catholicism and Shi'a Islam.

Christianity and interreligious dialogue

Never before has history known so many frontiers as in our contemporary world, and at no period has there been such a frequent violation of frontiers as happens today. It would seem that the establishment and removal of frontiers is the order of the day. This contradictory process is a window into the plight of humanity in these times: a dialectical tension between demarcation of particular identities and crossing over to the other shore. If the consolidation of frontiers is characterized as ethnicity, tribalism, nationalism, and a certain type of religious fundamentalism; the crossing of them is known as a global awareness, the encountering of cultures, trans-nationalism and the expression of world religiosity.[2]

We are struck by the ambiguity of the phenomenon of frontier crossing. Crossing over could mean a march of aggression that infringes

---

[1] From the poem *The Sleeping Lord*, by David Jones (1895-1974), Anglo-Welsh Christian poet and artist.

[2] Felix Wilfred, 'The Art of Negotiating the Frontiers', *Concilium: Frontier violations: the Beginnings of new identities*, no. 2 (1999), vii-xiii. Several Muslim-Christian frontiers have been outlined in 'Asia and Africa and the Mediterranean' by M Marion, 'Les sept frontières chrétiennes devant l'Islam', *Esprit*, 116 (1986), no. 10, 39-59.

upon the freedom and autonomy of the realm invaded. It could be overt and violent, as when a power intrudes into the territory—physical, cultural, spiritual—of the other; or it could be covert and subtle, nevertheless destructive, as in the transnationalization of capital and homogenisation of cultures. A sense of ambiguity marks the affirmation and negation of frontiers.[3]

However, the violation of frontiers is also often a matter of creativity. This aspect can offer great hope for the emergence of refreshing new identities and encounters and the envisioning of alternatives. To be able to cross over, one has to locate oneself at the frontier or at the edges of the present identity. To position oneself at the frontier is to adopt a very advantageous standpoint inasmuch as one can assess one's identity in a creative and critical way. There is a great epistemological potential in being positioned on the outer edge, where the view of things is bound to be quite different from the centre where one may not understand what it means to come face-to-face with another spiritual identity or religious territory.

It is important to note that the crossing of frontiers and the birth of the new are a sheer necessity for all life in history. The reality or the search for authentic renewal from within tradition pushes the bounds of the framework in which it was set up and forces the crossing of frontiers and the expansion of the frame. A re-mapping of the territory and a re-drawing of the frontiers follow it—tradition is an ever-emerging source of theological creativity, rooted identity, and wise compassion.

'Always be ready to make a defence to anyone who asks for a reason for the hope that is in you, and make it with modesty and respect' (1Peter 3: 15-16). Since the Middle Ages, this biblical text has been considered to state the fundamental charge given to the theologian. One could say that four fundamental features of theology thus appear: it is an articulation of the grounds of one's hope; it arises as a response to questions about the way Christians live their lives; the norm for that hope and practice in Jesus Christ; and reasons may be given for that hopeful practice, whether those addressed are fellow Christians or others. Taking the text

---

[3] Claude Geffré, 'Chrsitianity and Culture, *International Review of Mission*, Vol. 84 (1995), 17-32; Claude Geffré, 'Mission Issues in the Contemporary Context of Multifaith Situations', *International Review of Mission*, Vol. 86 (1997), 407-409. See also Geffré's theological 'autobiography' which sets out these tasks for Christian theology, *Claude Geffré entretiens avec Gwendoline Jarczyk—Profession Théologien. Quelle pensée chrétienne pour le XXIe siècle?*, Albin Michel, Paris, 1999.

of First Peter as a fundamental challenge, theology may be thus conceived as a mediation of the Christian gospel within a cultural context. Addressing two not entirely distinct audiences, those who have already accepted the gospel and those who have not, theology faces two tasks, one primarily *ecclesial* and the other primarily *cultural*. How these tasks are conceived and interrelated is a basic question for the conception of theology. For most of the Catholic tradition both dimensions and roles of theology have been visible.[4]

Crossing, however, is not simply an external event. It is also a spiritual experience. This 'journey as an enriching spiritual endeavour' has been taken up by the American Catholic theologian, David Burrell who writes:

> We are invited, in our time, on a voyage of discovery stripped of colonizing pretensions: an invitation to explore the other on the way to discovering ourselves. The world into which we have been thrust asks nothing less of us; those of us intent on discovering our individual vocations cannot proceed except as partners in such a variegated community. And as that journey enters the domain of faith, our community must needs assume interfaith dimension. What once were boundaries have become frontiers, which beckon to be broached, as we seek to understand where we stand by expanding or minds and hearts to embrace the other. Put in this fashion, our inner journey can neither be syncretic nor procrustean: assimilating or appropriating. What is rather called for is mutuality of understanding and of appreciation, a critical perception which is already incipiently self-critical. Rather than reach for commonality, we are invited to expand our horizons in the face of diversity. The goal is not an expanded scheme, but an enriched inquirer: discovery of one's own faith in encountering the faith of another.[5]

---

[4] Joseph A Komonchak, 'Defending Our Hope: On the Fundamental Tasks of Theology', eds. Leo J O'Donovan and T Howland Sanks, *Faithful Witness: Foundations of Theology for Today's Church*, Geoffrey Chapman, London, 1989, 14-26.

[5] David Burrell writes in the preface to Roger Arnaldez, *Three Messengers for One God*, University of Notre Dame Press, Notre Dame, Indiana, 1994, vii.

Felix Wilfred has observed several distinct moments in the early history of Christianity when identity recorded itself as a shift in its self-understanding. Thus Christianity has re-drawn its own frontiers several times. This has always been a critical act at crucial times. The first crisis is connected with the times when disciples of Jesus stood on the crossroads of forging their identity either as a 'sect' within Judaism, with strict Jewish membership and following its customs and traditions, or opening up the way of Jesus beyond ethnic frontiers.[6] What was achieved after many struggles was in fact a frontier-moving act. The widening of the circumference of the group led to the widening of its identity. If the first re-drawing of frontiers was thus a matter of *ethnos*—overcoming the tendency of a reduction of Christianity within ethnic bounds, the second frontier-moving act had to do with the *chronos*: against the apocalyptic background of the imminent expectation of the Risen Christ, Christian discipleship was viewed as a matter for a brief period. A realization of the delayed *parousia* pushed back the temporal frontiers of Christianity with very significant consequences. It paved the way not only for the consolidation of ecclesial structures providing for an indeterminate period, but also for shaping the Christian identity anew.

Today we are witnessing a further shift or moment in Christian history which witnesses to profound deepening or self-understanding in relation to other religious traditions. This not only engages the Christian tradition in a reassessment of its own Trinitarian unity, at present a Church which is a 'fractured oneness' or how it understands itself from within, but also how others bear witness to the Christian tradition from without.

This is of particular importance in the relationship between Christianity and Islam, as here in this encounter the Muslim tradition grasps within itself a particular understanding and interpretation of Judaism and Christianity.[7] It is thus linked into the Jewish-Christian

---

[6] Although, one should note the particular relationship between Judaism and Christianity. See Bruce Marshall, 'Christ and the cultures: The Jewish People and Christian Theology', *The Cambridge Companion to Christian Doctrine*, ed. Colin E Gunton, Cambridge University Press, Cambridge, 81-100. For the continuing debate regarding the relationship between Christianity and Judaism in Catholic thought see the interaction between the thought of Thomas Aquinas and Judaism: Matthew Levering, *Christ's Fulfillment of Torah and Temple*, University Press of Notre Dame, Notre Dame, Indiana, 2002; Henk Schoot and Pim Valkenberg, 'Thomas Aquinas and Judaism', *Modern Theology*, 20, no. 1, 2004, 51-70.

[7] David Marshall, 'Christianity in the Qur'an', in ed. Lloyd Ridgeon, *Islamic Interpretations of Christianity*, Curzon, Richmond, 2001, 3-29.

Other, and it is on a certain level held hostage by this relationship. Christian theologians are now becoming aware of a Christian identity within Islam, and of what that says to the Christian tradition.[8]

Christianity was born into a religiously plural world and has remained in one ever since. At different times in its history it has been especially sensitive to this context. The mandate to go preach the gospel to the corners of the earth as well as its own socio-economic political position has resulted in a complex range of relations and response to other religions. In the modern period Christians cannot ignore the existence of other religions. Global communications, extensive travel, migration, colonialism, and international trade are all factors that have brought the religions closer to each other in both destructive and creative ways. [9]

Christians cannot ignore the existence of other religions. Furthermore, with the awareness of their existence a host of theological, philosophical, methodological and practical questions are raised. Should,

---

[8] Kenneth Cragg, 'Islam and Other Faiths', *Studia Missionalia*, 42, 1993, 257-270.

[9] For a distinctive Catholic theological response to the question of the Christian encounter with other faiths, the work of Gavin D'Costa has had a distinct and important contribution to a Christian theological response to other faiths; see *Theology and Religious Pluralism Trinity*, Basil Blackwell, Oxford, 1986; 'Theology of Religions', *The Modern Theologians*, ed. David F Ford, Basil Blackwell, Oxford, 1997, 626-644; *The Trinity and the Meeting of Religions*, T & T Clark, Edinburgh, 2000; *Sexing the Trinity*, SCM Press, London, 2000. D'Costa has been concerned with the practices of other faiths, and although he continues to use the word 'religion' he is more than aware that the concept has a genealogy. Modernity constructed a discourse on religions, then turned to the study of religions and, more recently, the comparison of religions. D'Costa's work challenges this construction and seeks to further dialogue between world faiths in a way that accepts and works with some of the categories forged by modernity; see 'Postmodernity and Religious Plurality: Is a Common Global Ethic Possible or Desirable?', *The Blackwell Companion to Postmodern Theology*, ed. Graham Ward, Basil Blackwell, Oxford, 2001, 131-143. D'Costa continues to appeal to tradition-based reasoning. At the centre of his challenge to these universalist methods which continue to work with an uncritical understanding of the term 'religion', is his appeal to the specific differences between faiths. D'Costa is keen to demonstrate that a religion is not simply a set of ideas, but a complex living practice in which beliefs are continually formed and transformed in a dialogue with its traditions, its institutions, and its cultural contexts. We can understand the distinctiveness of D'Costa's approach if we examine the debate that took place between 1987 and 1990 on Christianity and pluralism. In 1987 the liberal thinkers John Hick and Paul Knitter published a collection of essays entitled *The Myth of Christian Uniqueness*. D'Costa responded with *Christian Uniqueness Reconsidered: The Myth of a Pluralistic Theology of Religions*, (Orbis, Maryknoll, 1990), which posited Christology and Trinitarian theology as the two distinctive differences of the Christian faith.

for example, Buddhist meditation be used in Christian prayer and practice? How should religious education be taught? What kind of social and political co-operation or opposition is appropriate with people of other faiths? There are also fundamental theological issues at stake. If salvation is possible outside Christ/Christianity, is the uniqueness of Christ and the universal mission of the Church called into question? Or if salvation is not possible outside Christ/Christianity, is it credible that a loving God would consign the majority of humankind to perdition, often through no fault of their own? Can Christians learn from other faiths? Can they be enriched rather than diluted or polluted from this encounter? Clearly, other religious traditions in varying degrees have also undergone their own self-questioning in the light of religious multiplicity, but that is another question.[10]

The theologian John Renard once told a story to convey a warning. Once upon a time an itinerant grammarian came to a body of water and enlisted the services of a boatman to ferry him across. As they made their way, the grammarian asked the boatman, 'Do you know the science of grammar?' The humble boatman thought for a moment and admitted somewhat dejectedly that he did not. Not much later, a growing

---

[10] The development of a Christian theology for the religious Other is an important area of exploration. For some time now the debate in the Christian theology of religions has centred on the question of the possibility of salvation for non-Christians. The answers to this question have often been placed in a threefold typology: exclusivism, inclusivism or pluralism. Exclusivists generally maintain that salvation is conditional on an explicit confession of faith in Jesus Christ, hence non-Christians are lost. Pluralists, on the other hand, maintain that salvation can be found in different religions in various ways, and that Christianity is one among many paths to the divine reality. Inclusivists agree that non-Christians may be saved, and if they are it may be through, rather than despite, their religion. Inclusivists differ from pluralists in believing that Christ is the constitutive cause of all salvation, even, therefore, the salavation of a non-Christian. However, see the important corrective to this scheme in the work of the American Dominican theologian J A DiNoia's main work, *The Diversity of Religions: A Christian Perspective*, Catholic University of America Press, Washington, 1992; and further his various papers on theme of theology and the religious other: 'Philosophical Theology in the Perspective of Religious Diversity', *Theological Studies*, Vol. 1988, 401-416; 'Pluralist Theology of Religions: Pluralistic or Non-Pluralistic?, *Christian Uniqueness Reconsidered*, ed. Gavin D'Costa, Orbis, Maryknoll, 1990, 119-134; 'The Doctrine of a Religious Community about Other Religions', *Religious Studies*, 19, 1982-83, 293-307; 'Implicit Faith, General Revelation and the State of Non-Christians', *The Thomist*, 47, 1983, 209-241; 'Varieties of Religious Aims: Beyond Exclusiveness and Pluralism', *Theology and Dialogue*, ed. Bruce Marshall, University of Notre Dame Press, Notre Dame, Indiana, 1991, 247-272.

storm began to imperil the small vessel. Said the boatman to the grammarian, 'Do you know the science of swimming?'[11]

Thus we are reminded that at the beginning of the new millennium too much of our theological activity remains shockingly introverted. Instead of allowing an inherent energy to launch us into the larger reality of global religiosity, we insist on protecting our theology from the threat of contamination. If we continue to resist serious engagement with other theological traditions, our theology may prove as useful as grammar in a typhoon. One of the most important tasks of theology today is to develop strategies for determining how to enter into the meaning system of another tradition, not merely as a temporary member of that tradition, but in such a way as to see how they bear upon one another.[12]

The concern for an understanding of the 'Other'—seeing the relationship of the one to the many, struggling with the questions of identity and difference, unity and diversity—has been a serious preoccupation of post-modern philosophy. In a somewhat different though not unrelated arena, contemporary Christian theologians have been increasingly aware of the necessity of formulating a theology, or set of theologies, that takes serious account of the 'otherness' as it is reflected in the existence of a great variety of forms of human religiosity.[13] The French Dominican theologian, Claude Geffré, suggests that there is a risk involved in the work of theology. Since theology is a hermeneutical task 'from beginning to end', it involves 'the risk of distortion and error', but unless theology is willing to take that risk by presenting a creative interpretation of Christianity, it runs the no less serious risk of 'simply handing on a dead past'. Thus Christian theology draws upon two axes:

---

[11] John Renard, 'Islam and Christian Theologians', *The Catholic Theological Society of America: Proceedings*, 48 (1993), 41-54, 41.

[12] Emilio Platti, of the Dominican Institute for Oriental Studies in Cairo, has two interesting accounts of how this might be done in relation to the Muslim-Christian encounter: 'Risques respectifs du souci de fidelité dans l'Islam et dans le christianisme', *Christianisme, Judaisme et Islam: Fidelité et ouverture* (sous la direction de Joseph Doré), Editions du Cerf, Paris, 1999, 223-242 and 'Islam et Occident: "Choc de theologies"?', *Melanges Institut Dominicain d' etudes orientales du Caire*, 24 (2000), 347-379.

[13] See the work of the two Jesuit scholars: Jacques Dupuis SJ, *Toward a Christian Theology of Religious Pluralism*, Orbis, Maryknoll, 1997; Michael Barnes SJ, *Theology and the Dialogue of Religions*, Cambridge University Press, Cambridge, 2002. See also Gerald O'Collins SJ, 'Christ and the Religions', *Gregorianum*, 84, 2003, 347-362.

ressourcement—reaffirmation of Christian identity by appeal to its ancient sources; and *aggiornamento*—renewal through the modernization of Christian thought and institutions.

These observations find an echo in the thought of the Irish-American writer and political scientist David Walsh:

> Even the discovery of God does not lift us out of this world. For as long as he wills it we must remain in this life to work out as best we can the meaning and direction we must follow within it. The light of transcendent illumination is a piercing beam from beyond, but it does not illuminate the surrounding area. The mystery of the whole remains. The difficulty of articulating the consequences of revelation for the modern secular world is evident in the confusion concerning the relationship between religion and politics.[14]

As we have now embarked on the third millennium, the major challenges for the mission of the Christian Churches, and a reality for all mainstream religious traditions, is not only atheism and religious indifference, but what amounts to a religious explosion and the proliferation of beliefs of all kinds. As we survey the religious supermarket, it is important to make the necessary distinctions between 'sects' in the strict sense of the term, the New Age, with its nebulous esoteric and mystical currents, and the increased vitality of the great non-Christian religions. The religious 'come-back' is a typical symptom of our post-modern age. It coincides with the death of ideologies, and is a reaction to the failure of modernity to keep its promises in the face of secularization and the anxiety caused by meaninglessness. It is part of the great movement of the *re-enchantment* of the world, of humanity, and even of God. With regard to the urgency for mission, the most formidable challenge for the Christian faith is the historical experience of a plurality of religious faiths.[15]

One observer has recently commented:

---

[14] David Walsh, *Guarded by Mystery. Meaning in a Postmodern Age*, Catholic University of America Press, Washington DC, 1999, 98-99.

[15] Terrence W Tilley, ' "Christianity and the World Religions": A Recent Vatican Document', *Theological Studies*, 60, 1999, 318-337; James Frederick, 'The Catholic Church and the Other Religious Paths: Rejecting Nothing That is True and Holy', *Theological Studies*, Vol. 64, 2003, 225-254; James L Fredericks, *Faith among Faiths: Christian Theology and Non-Christian Religions*, Paulist Press, Mahwah, New York, 1999.

The Western culture of modernity and the institutions of international society embedded in it are being challenged by the global resurgence of religion and cultural pluralism in international relations. As a result of this large-scale religious change international society is becoming a genuinely multicultural international society for the first time. A new approach to international order is required which overcomes the 'Westphalian presumption' in international relations. This is the notion that religious and cultural pluralism can be accommodated in international society, but must be privatized, marginalized, or even overcome—by an ethic of cosmopolitanism—if there is to be international order.[16]

A vital component of our contemporary situation is the growth of a certain awareness among the world's religious communities of the Other. The engagement between the religions has been characterized by two points of orientation; one of fear and one of hope, both elements poised between, on the one hand, conflict and on the other, a deepening realization of the necessity and possibility of dialogue. The re-discovery of the 'virtue of compassion' might be one of the principal themes in this encounter: Anthony H Johns, the Australian Christian Islamicist, has asked 'How can one re-discover what has never yet been fully realized ... such a compassion, in its fullness, is at best, something only dreamt of; or like the lost chord, is heard but once, and then vanishes into silence. Yet the memory of its haunting beauty has such power that it compels all who have ever heard it, to search to recover it, without ceasing.' One might say that the history of ecumenism and interreligious dialogue will be the history of growth and development of this awareness and of actions inspired by it, and of changes brought about in this directly in relation to this creative virtue of engagement. However, this does not allow for some sort of neutral position *vis-à-vis* one's own religious identity and the Other. Those who adopt a theoretical, privileged position outside

---

[16] Scott M Thomas, 'Taking Religious and Cultural Pluralism Seriously: The Global Resurgence of Religion and the Transformation of International Society', *Millennium: Journal of International Relations*, 29, no.3, 2000, 815-841. See also by the same author: 'Religious resurgence, postmodernism and world politics', *Religion and Global Order*, ed. John L Esposito and Michael Watson, University of Wales Press, Cardiff, 2000, 38-65.

any specific faith community, and elaborate a general structure of religious 'truth' that can provide a space for every religious tradition, but which nobody believes in, will not satisfy.[17]

Thus any dialogue requires respect for the dialogue partners and interest in their beliefs—especially if those beliefs are culturally and religiously different from our own. At the same time we must retain our own cultural and religious identity. Lack of commitment under the pretext of openness leads to no real dialogue, or to sham agreements. We cannot put our faith in parentheses to connect with another's faith.[18]

This is particularly true with regard to Christian-Muslim encounters, when what is at issue is not only the identity of each tradition, but the future character of an engagement which encompasses approximately one half of humanity.[19] Christian-Muslim relations in all their multi-faceted complexity, religious in the strict sense, cultural, societal, economic, political, are fundamentally an encounter of believers called to give, through life and word, a witness. In these two living traditions is the giving of a witness in and of faith. Members of these two traditions know themselves to be called in faith to witness faith. The meeting of these two distinct overall witnesses, Christian and Muslim, is lived in countless concrete practical ways and adaptations and, hence, produces an endless number of encounters, both by individuals and by groups.[20]

---

[17] Georges Cottier, 'Jésus, l'Eglise, le salut des non-chrétiens et la place des religions', *Studia Missionalia*, 50, 2001, 159-177; Charles Morerod, 'La relation entre les religions selon John Hick', *Nova et Vetra*, 75, 2000, 35-62; Geneviève Comeau, 'La christologie à la rencontre de la thélogie des religions', *Études*, no. 3931, 2000, 57-65.

[18] Cl. Geffré, 'La portée théologique du dialogue islamo-chrétien', *Islamochristiana*, 18 (1992), 1-23; 'La théologie des religions non-chrétiennes vingt ans après Vatican II', *Islamochristiana*, 11 (1985), 115-133; 'Théologie chrétienne et dialogue interreligieux', *Revue de l'Institut Catholique de Paris*, 38, 1991, 63-82; 'Un salut au pluriel', *Lumière et vie*, no. 250, 2001, 21-38; 'Les déplacements de la vérité dans la théologie contemporaine', *Communion et reunion— Mélanges Jean-Marie Roger Tillard*, eds. Gillian R Evans and Michel Gourgues, Leuven University Press, Leuven, 1995, 309-321; 'Le pluralisme religieux et l'indifférentisme, ou le vrai défi de la théologie chrétienne', *Revue théologique de Louvain*, 31, 2000, 3-32; 'La vérité du christianisme à l'âge du pluralisme religieux', *Angelicum*, 74, 1997, 171-192.

[19] Thomas Michel, 'Christian-Muslim dialogue in a changing world', *Theology Digest*, 39, 1992, 303-320.

[20] Jacques Waardenburg, 'Critical Issues in Muslim-Christian Relations: theoretical, practical, dialogical, scholarly', *Islam and Christian Muslim Relations*, 8, no. 1, 1997, 9-26, and Thomas Michel, 'Social and religious factors affecting Muslim-Christian relations', *Islam and Christian Muslim Relations*, 8, no. 1, 1997, 53-66.

The Jesuit Islamicist, Christian Troll has imaginatively reminded us that the Franco-Algerian Jesuit Henri Sanson[21] suggested that we should reflect on our Christian vocation towards Muslims 'in the mirror of Islam', that is, taking into account at every step the missionary vocation which our Muslim partners, in faith, know themselves to be charged with. We shall then reflect on our mission to Islam in the light of that of Islam, i.e. the Muslims' consciousness to be called by God, individually and collectively, to witness the Truth, to proclaim it, to establish the true religion and to invite all and everyone to membership in the *umma muslima*. This encounter with Islam as a missionary religion will lead us to greater precision in the grasp of the distinctive features of our Christian missionary vocation and message, and of appropriate ways to respond to them today. For Islam is more than a social and political, a religious and humanitarian, phenomenon; it is rather a challenge to the growth of the Church. It is ultimately a theological issue as the heart of the *missio Dei*.[22]

There is a context to this engagement. The Muslim and Christian worlds have known violent confrontations. Muslim conquests which brought parts of the Christian world under Muslim domination; the Crusades still vividly remembered today; the expansion of the Turkish Ottoman empire with its threat to Christian centres; the massacre and genocide of Armenian and Syriac Christians in the Middle East; European colonialism; the continuing difficult situations in which Christians find themselves in dominant Muslim societies; the violent drama of 11 September 2001 in New York.[23] It would be petty to try to figure out who is more guilty in these conflicts. History should make us all a little

---

[21] Henri Sanson, *Dialogue interieur avec l'Islam*, Centurion, Paris, 1990.

[22] Christian W Troll, 'Witness Meets Witness: The Church's Mission in the Context of the Worldwide Encounter of Christian and Muslim Believers Today', *Encounter*, Vol. 4, no.1 (1998), 15-34.

[23] Since the events of September 11 2001 there have been a increasing number of reflections on Christian-Muslim encounters see: Stanley L Jaki, 'Myopia about Islam, with an eye on Chesterbelloc', *The Chesterton Review*, 28, 2002, 485-502; Stratford Caldecott, 'The Mystery of Islam: Further Reflections', 28, 2002, 521-530; Roch Kereszty, 'The Word of God: A Catholic Perspective in Dialogue with Judaism and Islam', *Communio*, 28, 2001, 568-580; David Novak, 'Pluralism and Interreligious Dialogue. Reply to Roch Kereszty', Mahmoud M Ayoub, 'The Word of God in Islam: Some Personal Reflections', Roch Kereszty; 'Brothers in a Strange Land: A Response to the Responses', all to be found in *Communio*, 29, 2002, 172-184; R Kereszty, 'Toward a Christian Theology of Inter-religious Dialogue', *Communio*, 29, 2002, 579-97; Wilfried Dettling, 'Encounter and the Risk of Change: Religious Experience and Christian-Muslim Dialogue', *The Way Supplement*, no. 104, 2002, 67-74; Thomas Hughson, 'September 11 and Christian Spirituality in the United

more humble. The weight of this history may be why few approach Islam without strong feelings one way or the other. To quote a sage: 'We cannot change the past, but we do have a responsibility of how it is remembered.'

Christian theology of religions is an area within systematic theology that has lately undergone considerable development. The area has taken on greater definition in recent years as Christian communities throughout the world come to grips with a heightened awareness of other religious traditions, and with a growing desire on the part of Christians to pursue interreligious dialogue and other forms of positive engagement with Jews, Muslims, Hindus, Buddhists, and others.[24] Theologians practising this sub-speciality address such questions as these: Are any of the teachings of other religious traditions true? How should judgments about this issue proceed? Do other religions point their adherents in the right direction? Can Jews, Muslims, Hindus, and Buddhists be saved? Can they be saved by following the teachings of their religions? How should Christians relate to Jews, Muslims, Hindus, Buddhists and others? Should they attempt to persuade non-Christians to become Christians? Should they engage in dialogue with the adherents of other religions? What purposes does such interreligious dialogue serve?[25] Drawing upon a long and substantial tradition of inquiry about these issues within Christian doctrine and theology, the agenda of the theology of religions has taken on an increasingly systematic shape as more and more theologians within the Christian Churches turn their attention to these questions.

As has been observed by the Jesuit theologian and scholar of Islam, Patrick Ryan, on the Christian encounter with other religious

---

States', *The Way*, 42, 2003, 85-97; Peter Riddell, 'Christian-Muslim dialogue: a challenge for the new millennium', *St Mark's Review*, no. 184, 2001, 3-13; P Riddell, 'Islamic Perspectives on Globalisation', *St Mark's Review*, no. 192, 2003, 10-17; A O'Mahony, 'Reflections on the Encounter between Christianity and Islam', *Encounter: Documents for Muslim-Christian Understanding*, no. 302, 2004, 1-9, no. 303, 2004, 1-7; A O'Mahony, 'Islam face-à-face Christianity', *The Way Supplement*, no. 104, 2002, 75-85.

[24] For an example of the Catholic-Buddhist encounter see, Paul Williams, *The Unexpected Way: On Converting from Buddhism to Catholicism*, T & T Clark, Edinburgh, 2002; P Williams, 'Aquinas Meets the Buddhists: Prolegomenon to an Authenticity Thomas-ist Basis for Dialogue', *Modern Theology*, 20, 2004, 91-122.

[25] J A DiNoia takes a interesting reading of reformed theologian Karl Barth, 'Religion and the religions', *The Cambridge Companion to Karl Barth*, ed. John Webster, Cambridge University Press, Cambridge, 2000, 243-257.

traditions there is an important sense in which the Christian tradition has to become more *catholic*, in the root sense of the word: embracing the whole of human experience. Christianity in the future will face two major challenges, each of which has theological and philosophical implications. The first of these challenges is polycentrism of intellect and the second one could be summed up under the heading of the unity of humankind. Augustine in the first millennium of the Christian era and Aquinas in the second led the honourable procession of Christian intellectuals of those two millennia who retrieved the thought of Plato and Aristotle, the fountainheads of philosophical speculation in the millennium before Christ. These two Doctors of the Church transformed Greek thought in terms of their own respective grasps, not only on that philosophy, but also on the cumulative Judeo-Christian traditions of faith and hope and love.[26]

As we start the third millennium, it might be suggested that those who would follow Augustine and Aquinas[27] over the next thousand years would have a task somewhat similar to that of their intellectual ancestors. But they will have to retrieve from many more non-Christian intellectual

---

[26] Patrick J Ryan, 'Sailing Beyond the Horizon: Challenges for the Third Millennium', *America*, May 23, 1998, 14-28. See also his 'Is Dialogue Possible with Muslims?', *America*, 31 December, 1994, 13-17; 'The Monotheism of the Excluded: Towards an Understanding of Islam', *The Month*, 16, no. 8 (1983), 264-267 and 'Creative Misunderstanding and the Possibility of Jewish-Christian-Muslim Trialogue', *The Month*, 31, no. 7 (1998), 267-274. See also Thomas F O'Meara, 'Tarzan, Las Casas, and Rahner: Aquinas's theology of wider grace', *Theology Digest*, 45 (1998), 319-327.

[27] However, as J A DiNoia has reminded us Aquinas also has something to contribute to Christian theology's encounter with the alternative systems of belief and practice embodied in the world's major religious traditions. Thus, Aquinas's theology of the triune God and to introduce a concrete illustration, philosophical argument would be needed in conversation between Buddhists and Christians. Segments of the Buddhist community seem to be non-theistic in their doctrines, and their canonical and commentatorial literatures possess highly subtle explanations for the prevalence of theistic beliefs in other religious traditions. Presumably, in conversations with Buddhists, Christians would need to invoke patterns of argument analogous to those sketched by Aquinas in the Prima Pars of the *Summa* (and elsewhere). A readiness to advance such arguments would be a way of taking Buddhist objections to theistic beliefs seriously. Given the empirical bent of Buddhist patterns of reflection and argument, there would be considerable scope here for empirically based discussions such as those elaborated in the Five Ways and similar arguments. Patterns of argument appealing to objective states of affairs would have an important role in the religiously pluralistic environment of some current theology. Only these kinds of arguments presuppose a field broad enough to sustain interreligious conversations. The issue can be joined in a common logical field, so to speak, where rival particularistic claims to universality would be taken seriously and debated. The readiness

and faith traditions of all the past century's new ways of thinking about the experience of Christian revelation. They will also have to do philosophy and theology and work out an ethics that borrow categories from broader perspectives. One most notable dimension is the interreligious encounter. One could be tempted to say that the future of theology depends upon a more intensive 'inter-penetration' of systematic theology and the history of religions. Some do not hesitate to speak of a new planetary ecumenism. We must agree with them inasmuch as the dialogue between religions coincides with the keener awareness of the unity of the human family and a more acute sense of the common responsibility of religions for the future of humankind and its environment.

But it would be absurd to think that the new 'dialogue' makes Christian ecumenism in the primary sense obsolete or secondary. The ecumenical dialogue within the Christian community which began to take shape in the early decades of the 20th century and which started to mature after the Second World War has shattered a certain type of absolutism and has generally promoted the dialogue of the Church, first with the other two monotheistic religions, and then with the great Eastern religions.

The theology of religions has become an important chapter in Christian theology. But it has taken time to understand that frank and open dialogue does not necessarily lead to false 'ecumenism', that is, to religious indifferentism. A widespread consensus exists today among theologians that a certain type of exclusive model for understanding Christianity cannot be sustained in its totality or for whom Christianity is the only source of grace. However, on the other hand, it is not enough to adopt an inclusive religious model—Christ fulfils everything that is good, true, and holy in other religions—to believe that we have thereby demystified the absolute character of Christianity as an historical religion. Indeed, a fundamental tension remains between the demands of equality

---

to advance arguments would make it possible for a true meeting of minds, though not necessarily agreement, to occur. It seems clear that, in order to rise to the occasion, logically speaking, appeals to history, narratives, texts, personal experiences, and the like would need to be combined with philosophical arguments having features of objective states of affairs as their context. Aquinas's incorporation of such arguments in his theology provides a model for Christian engagement in interreligious conversation. Cf. 'Thomism After Thomism: Aquinas and the Future of Theology', *The Future of Thomism*, eds. Deal W Hudson and Dennis Wm Moran, University of Notre Dame Press, Notre Dame, Indiana, 1992, 231-245.

and reciprocity inherent in true dialogue and the legitimate claim of Christianity to be the religion of the absolute and definitive manifestation of God in Jesus Christ. If Jesus himself is only one mediator among others and not God's decisive manifestation for all men and women, then we can seriously question whether we have not already discarded the faith inherited from the apostles.[28]

For religions as well as cultures, globalization presents a double reef or dialectic: it can only lead to destructive syncretism but also to fundamentalist reactions.[29] It should be able, nevertheless, to favour an interreligious engagement on a planetary scale, without falling into the myth of world religion. Each religion, faithful to its proper identity, can witness to the universal search of the Ultimate or Last Reality, which no religious system can exhaust. In other words, it is not at all certain that we yet possess an adequate theological response, which takes seriously the implications of interreligious dialogue without sacrificing Christian identity. In any event, it is not sufficient to go from Christocentrism to theocentrism as the adepts of a pluralistic theology of religions suggest. Every responsible Christian theology must maintain the normative character of Christology. Rather than adopting some general theocentrism, we must start at the very centre of the Christian message, that is, God's manifestation in the historical particularity of Jesus of Nazareth, and find there the justification for the dialectical nature of Christianity.

At one level it seems difficult to see how we can leave completely behind a certain inclusivism, that is, a theology of the *fulfilment* (to use a term present in Catholic theology since the Second Vatican Council) in Jesus Christ of all seeds of truth, goodness, and holiness contained in the religious experience of humankind. However it might be possible to reinterpret this notion of fulfilment in a non-possessive and non-totalizing sense. Rather than renouncing the confession of Jesus Christ, according to Claude Geffré, 'Christians must renounce all claims to absolute truth precisely because they confess Jesus Christ as absolute, that is, as

---

[28] My own reflections here owe much to the thought of the Claude Geffré: 'Pour un christianisme mondial', *Recherches de Sciences religieuses*, (1998), 53-75, who observes, 'La croix est le symbole d'une universalité qui est toujours liée au sacrifice d'une particularité pour renaître en figure d'universalité concrète, en figure de Christ' (p.64).

[29] Cl. Geffré, 'La rencontre du christianisisme et des cultures', *Reuve d'Ethique et de théologie morale. Le Supplement*, no. 192, 1995, 69-91.

eschatological fullness that will never be revealed in history.' Can we ever cease to ponder the paradox of Christianity as a non-absolute religion, which nonetheless attests to the final revelation? Might we not say that we need to remain equally removed from the hubris of dialectical theology on the one hand and neo-liberalism, with its readiness to relinquish the Christological norm for the sake of facilitating interreligious dialogue, on the other?

By virtue of the very demands of interreligious dialogue, are we ready to accept the historical particularity of Christianity? It would be an unwarranted pretension to claim that historical Christianity has been and will be able to encompass all the riches contained in the religious history of humankind, still less in history itself. But we must not confuse the particular character of Christianity as an historical religion with the particular character of Christ as mediator of the Absolute in history. The link between God's presence and the contingent event 'Jesus as the Christ' will always remain, in the eyes of other religions, as the scandal of the Christian claim. By confessing Jesus of Nazareth to be the Christ, the Church claims for Christianity a unique and unrivalled excellence.[30]

In an effort to facilitate dialogue with other religions, certain theologians are tempted today to downplay this extravagant 'allegation' made by Christianity. In the encounter between Christianity and Islam this downplaying of the Christian difference is problematic, as the Islamic tradition makes a direct connection between its own existence and the Christian claim to Christ as of God the incarnate one. Muslims, say, for instance, that to speak of Jesus' divinity is a 'manner of speech', that the incarnation is a 'metaphor' expressing his incomparable openness to God.[31] Or else they attempt to loosen the indissoluble link between the Christ of faith and the Jesus of history. The human Jesus would be only one historical manifestation, among others, of a transcendent and pre-

---

[30] Cl. Geffré, 'From the Theology of Religious Pluralism to an Interreligious Theology', eds. Daniel Kendall and Gerald O'Collins, *In Many and Diverse Ways—In Honor of Jacques Dupuis*, Orbis, Maryknoll, 2003,.45-59.

[31] Eric O Springsted in an interesting article on Christian encounters with other faiths, has suggested that the Incarnation may not in fact hinder dialogue but actually encourage it. Reflecting on the position of Simone Weil, he suggests that this central Christian doctrine may encourage dialogue if taken seriously as a value commitment constitutive of a way of life, and not just a position. In order to do so, he takes the example of Weil to show how she used the doctrine in practice and to show the theory of 'rootedness' she developed to explain that practice. See 'Conditions of Dialogue: John Hick and Simone Weil', *Journal of Religion*, 1992, 19-36.

existing Christ. In such a case, one may well wonder whether the uniqueness of Christianity is not jeopardized, in the sense that Jesus would only become one of the several historical realizations of the Absolute.

Thus, in order to firmly establish the dialogical character of Christianity, it is preferable to return to the very centre of Christian faith, that is, to the mystery of the incarnation itself in its most realistic and non-mythical meaning. The paradoxical character of Christianity originates in the paradox of the 'Logos made flesh'. There is, in the last analysis, only *one* genuine paradox in the Christian message—the appearance of that which conquers existence under the conditions of existence. Incarnation, redemption, justification are implied in this paradoxical event. In theology, paradox is not contrary to the demands of logical reason. Paradox does not result from logical contradiction, but from the fact that an event transcends all human expectations and possibilities. Thus for Christianity, to quote Paul Tillich, 'the Logos doctrine as the doctrine of identity of the absolutely concrete with the absolutely universal is not one theological doctrine among others; it is the only possible foundation of a Christian theology which claims to be *the* theology'. And again quoting Tillich, 'the paradox of the Christian message is that in *one* personal life, essential manhood has appeared under the conditions of existence without being conquered by them'.[32]

The Christological paradox is the foundation of the paradoxical condition of Christianity as a religion. Can we say that Christianity is based upon an original absence? And must we add that it is precisely this consciousness of a lack which is the condition of a relation to the other, the stranger, the difference? It is for this reason that dialogue with other religious experiences is written into the original vocation of Christianity. For each Christian, each community, and for Christianity as a whole, the goal is to be a sign of what is lacking.

Without having the pretension of installing a New World order, Christianity holds a prophetic and counter-cultural power against the risks of, not only dehumanization, but also fragmentation between persons and ethnic and religious communities. As a religion of incarnation, Christianity not only announces to every human being the gratuitous salvation of God, but it works in healing cultures and all creation. The

---

[32] Cl. Geffré, 'Paul Tillich et l'avenir de l'oecuménisme inter-religieux', *Revue des sciences philosophiques et théologiques*, 77, 1993, 3-22.

Church announces Jesus Christ as an event of universal salvation for all humanity, including those who belong to other religious traditions. But the witness of the Gospel must learn not to confuse the universality of the mystery of Christ with that of a Christianity understood as a historical religion inseparable from its Western form, and to maintain a distance between the Church as means of salvation and the Kingdom of God that does not cease to go beyond its frontiers, which at present can present themselves as borders.

Christian encounters with Islam

The Iraqi Jesuit, Paul Nwyia (1925-1980), grew up in the northern Iraq in a mixed Christian-Muslim village. Reflecting on his childhood, he remembered his first contacts with Muslims:

> Searching far back in my memory, I rediscovered my first impression of my contacts with Muslims. Those contacts were frequent, for many Muslim religious leaders used to visit my family. But despite the real friendship on which these relations were based, I had a strong feeling that, in the eyes of these Muslim friends, we were and remained *strangers*: people who because of their religion were fundamentally different. What awakened this feeling in me was the superior attitude which these friends adopted, an attitude that only their religion could justify. They regarded themselves as followers of the true religion and manifested this conviction with such self-satisfaction and such contempt for others that they were the living image of those whom the Gospel describes as men with pharisaical traits. Many of them were very brave and their attitude towards us was often only unconsciously superior, but we always remained strangers in relation to them. This fact did not bother them; on the contrary, it made them feel that they were all the more faithful to their religion.[33]

---

[33] Paul Nwyia, 'Pour mieux connaître l'Islam', *Lumen vitae*, 30 (1975), 159-171.

Even as a child, Nwyia was sensitive to the tensions between Christianity and Islam. Not only is Islam different from Christianity; it sees itself as positively abrogating Christianity. Muhammad is the 'seal of prophets'; the revelation accorded to him supersedes all that came before.

Christianity nevertheless has an important, if negative, role in Muslim self-understanding. Muslim writers have always been quick to claim that Islam's abrogation of Christianity mirrors the Christian abrogation of Judaism. A Christian might respond that this is unfair, since Christianity understands itself not as abolishing Judaism but fulfilling it. The Christian tradition continues to acknowledge Judaism as a source of its identity; it at least claims to be constantly revisiting Judaism, and it continues to use—in its own fashion—the Hebrew Scriptures. Islam, by contrast, sees itself as the restoration of what Judaism and Christianity would have been, had they not become corrupted, especially with regard to their Scriptures.[34]

Within the long history of polemics between Muslims and Christians, the most persistent Christian response to the assertion of abrogation has been a straightforward rejection of how Muslims understand Christianity. Christian apologists have repeatedly insisted that the qur'anic and post-qur'anic comprehension of Christian doctrine is seriously flawed. The conflict centres on three issues: the reality of Jesus' crucifixion and death; the doctrine of the incarnation; and the Christian understanding of God as Trinity. The qur'anic accounts of all three of these, as well as subsequent interpretations and elaborations, stand in sharp contrast with mainstream Christian self-understanding. Conversely, both Jews and Christians questioned Muhammad's prophetic status. This led Muslims to develop traditions of argument in vindication of Muhammad as prophet, and Christians in turn responded by articulating their own version of the 'signs of prophecy'.[35]

---

[34] Frederick Mathewson Denny, 'Corruption', in *Encyclopedia of the Qur'an*, ed. Jane Dammen McAuliffe, Brill, Leiden, 2001, 439-440. On the Qu'ran as Scripture and the qur'anic view of religion see the work of Guy Monnot, for example: 'Le corpus coranique', in *La formation des canons scripturarires*, ed. Michel Tardieu, Editions du Cerf, Paris, 1993, 61-73; and 'L'ideé de religion et son evolution dans le Coran', *The Notion of Religion in Comparative Research*, ed. Ugo Bianchi, 'L'Erma' di Brettschneider, Rome, 1994, 97-102.

[35] Jane Dammen McAuliffe, 'The Abrogation of Judaism and Christianity in Islam: A Christian Perspective', *Concilium*, 1994/3, 116-123, esp. 117-118; Sarah Strouwsma, 'The Signs of Prophecy: the Emergence and Early Development of a Theme in Arabic Theological Literature', *Harvard Theological Review*, 78, 1985, 101-114, esp. 114.

Muslims assert the superiority of the Qur'an by identifying it with the divine word (*Kalima*). This word is a divine attribute subsisting in God but distinct from God's essence. God is therefore the unique, total and exclusive cause of Scripture, and the Qur'an must be considered to be *uncreated*. Consequently Muhammad is simply the spokesman who hands on 'the supernatural dictation' he receives from God.

However, qualifications must be made. Though Islam claims that Judaism and Christianity are superseded as independent traditions, it nevertheless sees the revelations accorded to Moses, the *Tawrat*, and Jesus, the *Injil*, as something like proto-Qur'ans: compilations of God's direct verbal revelation to Moses and Jesus. Consequently, it matters greatly how reliably or unreliably these traditions have been transmitted. And Muslims claim that the Jewish and Christian Scriptures are, in their present form, both textually and semantically corrupt. What Jews and Christians now recognize as their scriptures does not coincide with the Qur'an, God's full and final revelation. Since God's word does not change, this lack of consonance must result from more or less intentional alteration or corruption of the text. When Muslim theologians and apologists speak of Jewish and Christian corruption, therefore, they rarely use it to justify a wholesale rejection of either the Hebrew Bible or the Christian Gospel.[36] Rather, they balance assertions about corruption with an insistence that both Testaments prefigure the advent of Muhammad and the success of his mission.

Christian accounts of Islam vary, but they nevertheless generally draw attention to how Islam is expressive of a kind of natural law, given with the creation. Louis Massignon, for example, writes as follows:

> The goal of Qur'anic revelation is not to expose or justify supernatural gifts so as to be ignorant of them, but, in recalling them to the name of God, to bring back to intelligent beings the temporal and eternal sanctions—natural religion—primitive law, the simple worship that God has

---

[36] David Thomas, 'The Bible in Early Muslim Anti-Christian Polemic', *Islam and Christian-Muslim Relations*, 7, 1996, 29-38; Jane Dammen McAuliffe, 'The Qur'anic Context of Muslim Biblical Scholarship', *Islam and Christian-Muslim Relations*, 7, 1996, 141-158.

prescribed for all time—that Adam, Abraham and the prophets have always practised in the same way'.[37]

Jacques Jomier, another great Catholic Islamicist, complements this account:

> Islam is a natural religion in which the religious instinct which is present in the heart of each person is protected by a way of life, with obligations and religious observations imposed in the name of One who is, for the Muslim, the Qur'an revelation. It is a patriarchal religion, spiritually pre-dating the biblical promise made by God to Abraham, but which conserves the episodes of the life of the Patriarch involving his struggle against his fathers' idols and his voluntary submission to God, even his sacrifice of his own son. Islam re-presents Abraham (Father of the Prophets) as its great ancestor.[38]

For Muslims, Islam is not simply God's final revelation but also God's first.[39] Both cosmically and individually, human beings are born in submission (*islam*) to God. An important Qur'anic passage vividly depicts the primordial covenant which God forged with the creation:

> 'When your Lord brought forth their own behalf, saying, 'Am I not your Lord?' they said, 'Most certainly; we have testified.'

The verse closes with God's explanation that he had forged this covenant with humankind lest 'you say on the Day of resurrection that 'of

---

[37] Louis Massignon, *Examen du 'Présent de l'Homme Lettré' par Abdallah ibn Torjoman*, Pontifical Institute of Arabic and Islamic Studies of Rome, Rome, 1992, (following the French translation published in *Revue de l'Histoire des Religions*, 1886, Vol. XII), with a preface by Daniel Massignon, introduction by Père Henri Cazelles and observations by Père Albert (M J) Lagrange. Collection 'Studi arabo-islamic del PISAI', No. 5, Rome, PISAI, 1992.

[38] Jacques Jomier, 'Le Coran et la Liturgie dans l'Islam', *La Maison-Dieu*, 190, 1992, 121-127, here 121.

[39] Guy Monnot, 'Ce que l'Islam n'est pas', *Communio* (French edition), 16, 1991, 28-41.

this we were unaware' (7: 172). Thus other religious identities are seen as conflicting with a fundamental state of *islam*, a primordial Muslim identity.

A saying ascribed to Muhammad runs as follows: 'Every child is born a Muslim, but his father makes him a Jew, Christian or Magian/Zoroastrian'. Like all humans, therefore, Moses and Jesus were Muslim. Further, as prophets, they were privileged with a special divine covenant:

> When We took their covenant from the prophets, from
> you [Muhammad] and from Noah, Abraham, Moses and
> Jesus, son of Mary, We took from them a binding covenant.
> (33: 7)

God sent these prophets and others to particular peoples so that they might remind their listeners of the primordial covenant, and summon them to *islam* (submission). While Judaism and Christianity tend to think of prophets as inspired, classic Islamic thought has functioned with what might be termed a 'doctrine of dictation', with the human agent being far more transparent. Prophets receive and transmit God's very words; Muslims revere Jesus, Moses, and their prophetic predecessors as faithful conduits of God's invariant message to humanity. Though Muslims do minimally recognise the importance of historical context, the Islamic notion of prophet-as-divine-mouthpiece is essentially atemporal. God's words and God's will can never change: the message conveyed by Abraham or Moses or Jesus or Muhammad has an inherent and inviolable continuity. Muslims believe that these earlier messages as originally proclaimed were perfectly consonant with the Qur'an. It was in order to account for the evident inconsistency between these texts in the forms now available that Muslim apologists and theologians developed a doctrine of scriptural corruption. And this doctrine supports a wider vision of Islam abrogating both Judaism and Christianity.

The historic break caused by Islam did not influence in the slightest the internal development of Christianity. One can study that development today as a completely autonomous whole, as though Islam did not exist. Christianity is wholly intelligible, to the extent to which it is intelligible at all, without any reference to Islam. By contrast, Islam is not so intelligible unless reference is made to Christianity.

Historically and theologically, however, Christianity inevitably challenges and disturbs Islam; and Islam inevitably challenges and disturbs

Christianity. Neither religion can ignore the other, happy in its own conviction and simplicity.

A Christian is disturbed and challenged by the Islamic refutation of Christianity: that the Holy Trinity is *shirk* (polytheistic blasphemy); that the crucifixion was only an apparition; that the stories about Christ and his mother in the Qur'an are the authentic ones, rather than those in the four Gospels. Similarly, a Muslim must be disturbed by what Christianity at least implies about Islam: that Christianity has not in fact been abrogated by Islam; that God became flesh in Jesus of Nazareth without ceasing to be God; that this same Jesus actually died and rose from the dead on the third day; that the Church, as a distinct historic body, makes absolute claims about itself. And this mutuality of disturbance is not confined to the order of theory: it expresses itself in the growth of distinct historic communities, with conflicting norms, laws and mores.

The central question is whether the Word of God is literally a word, or rather a living person. On this issue, Christianity and Islam frankly diverge, and all the other differences relate to this one. Whatever affinities between Christianity and Islam there may be, arising from their common links with Abraham, this question about the nature of revelation remains. Any dialogue which avoids it remains sentimental and superficial. The Qur'an has the highest respect for Christ and his mother, and speaks of him as a Word of God; nevertheless, the authoritative Muslim doctrine is that *the* Word of God is the Qur'an itself.

Paul Nwyia may have sensed the conflict between Islam and Christianity even as a child. But he was also aware, even then, that a Christian could not rest content with this situation. The passage quoted at the beginning continues as follows:

> One could easily have been tempted to react like them, to regard them as 'strangers', to transform the difference into indifference, or to meet their contempt with even deeper scorn. But this is precisely what my faith forbade me to do. To react thus would have meant doing away with the difference and, by that very fact, disowning my Christian identity. Hence I came to ask myself: 'How can I turn these strangers into the *neighbours* of which the Gospel speaks? How can I resist the temptation to react as they do, so that my way of seeing them may be different from

the way they look upon me?' I understood that to achieve this I would have to discover, beyond the image they projected of themselves, certain things in them or in their religion which could help me regard them as neighbours whom one must love.

This quest for understanding and for the love of neighbour led Nwyia to study and reflect on Islam throughout his life until his tragic death in 1980. Trained in France by Louis Massignon, Nywia became a widely renowned and celebrated scholar in the field of Islamic mysticism. His contributions included an edition of letters on spiritual direction by Ibn 'Abbad of Ronda, who was chiefly responsible for putting forward an understanding of Sufism as a spirituality available to all who put their trust in God. He also wrote on Islamic mysticism and Christianity, with special reference to the *Spiritual Exercises* of Ignatius of Loyola; and on the monastic character of early Muslim spiritual life.[40]

Nwyia reflected on the different ways in which Islam characterized the religious Other, and what these revealed about Muslim self-understanding. For Nwyia, Islam's relations with other faiths are shaped by the tension between two antagonistic principles: mutabilities and immutability, between the diverse, changing forms in which religious commitment is lived on the one hand, and the unchangingness of Allah on the other. This tension has been operative since Islam began; it reflects the complex attitude of Muhammad towards the religious Other: polytheists, Jews and Christians. Islam is faced with a crucial dilemma of how to find 'the synthesis between historical and spiritual truth'.[41]

Within the Qur'an, there are also discussions of how Muslims should relate to Christianity. These vary in tone from unequivocal rejection to ambivalent co-existence. We find both warnings to Muslims not to make friends with Christians, as well as more positive calls for

---

[40] See Nwyia's second edition of Ibn 'Abbad de Ronda, *Lettres de direction spirituelle (ar-Rasa'il as-sugrä)*, Dar el-Machreq, Beirut, 1974, and also the following from among his numerous academic studies: 'Ibn 'Abbad de Ronda et Jean de la Croix: à propos d'une hypothèse d'Asin Palacios', *Al-Andalus*, 22, 1957, 113-130; *Ibn-'Abbad de Ronda (1332-1390): un mystique prédicateur à la Qarawiyin de Fès*, Catholic Press, Beirut, 1961; *Exégèse coranique et langage mystique: nouvel essai sur le lexique technique des mystiques musulmans*, Dar el-Machreq, Beirut, 1970.

[41] Paul Nwyia, 'Mutabilités et immutabilité en Islam', *Recherches de sciences religieuses*, 63, 1975, 197-213.

interreligious understanding. A dictum in the Qur'an placed on Muhammad's lips, 'to you your religion and to me mine' (109: 6), can be interpreted in both these ways. It might suggest a gentle tolerance, honouring the diversities of culture and experience. Alternatively, it could be taken as expressing an exasperated weariness with the fact that the differences in belief and ritual can never be resolved.[42]

Christianity's encounter with Judaism following the *Shoah* raises questions touching very deeply on the core identity of the Christian. Similar questions arise from its encounter with Islam, particularly as regards mission. The Jesuit Islamicists, Henri Sanson and Christian Troll, have suggested that Christians should reflect on their missionary vocation towards Muslims 'in the mirror of Islam'. This means that we should take into account at every step the fact that our Muslim partners are convinced in faith that they have a missionary vocation towards us, that they too are called, individually and collectively, to witness to the Truth. Only in this light can we discern with any sensitivity what a Christian missionary vocation towards Islam might amount to, and how it might appropriately be lived out.[43]

There are also tensions within Islam that may serve as a stimulus for Muslims to move beyond the impasse I have been sketching out. The German scholar, Josef van Ess, has documented three forms that sceptical challenges have taken in Islamic tradition. The first of these is theoretical and philosophical: it draws on the sceptical tradition in Hellenism. The second arises from doctrinal tensions and difficulties internal to Islam. The third is generated by practical and political concerns.[44] Scepticism, says van Ess, 'is something like the salt in the soup'; it makes theology interesting. Dogmatic speculation, of the kind put forward by Islam's great systematic thinker, al-Ghazzali, is 'like a game of chess' that becomes interesting only when there is an opponent, 'when the devil is playing on the other side.'

Van Ess speculates that Islam might have improved had the sceptical tradition continued into more recent times. He brings out the

---

[42] Kenneth Cragg, 'Islam and Other Faiths', *Studia missionalia*, 42, 1993, 257-270, here 257.

[43] Henri Sanson: *Dialogue intérieur avec l'Islam*, Centurion, Paris, 1990; Christian W Troll, 'Witness Meets Witness: The Church's Mission in the Context of the Worldwide Encounter of Christian and Muslim Believers Today', *Vidyajyoti Journal of Theological Reflection*, 62/3, March 1998, 152-171, reprinted in *Encounters*, 4/1, March 1998, 15-34.

[44] Josef van Ess, 'Scepticism in Islamic Religious Thought', in *God and Man in Contemporary Islamic Thought*, ed. Charles Malik, American University of Beirut, Beirut, 1972, 83-98.

positive contribution made by scepticism to Islam. Islamic scepticism arose within the 'pluralistic outlook of a multiform society'. Islam was being challenged by the close proximity of other faith-systems, and was only one among many vigorous traditions: Christianity, Judaism, Zoroastrianism, Manichaeism, various forms of religious Hellenism. Scepticism was a stimulus to Islam's health and progress: 'Islam as well as Christianity ought to be glad about a time full of spiritual plurality, a time like ours.'

Contemporary pluralism is challenging Islam almost to breaking point. When it was more or less alone or apart, it did not need to ask fundamental questions about itself: it could take itself for granted. Where it was the dominant cultural and religious force, it could dismiss minority traditions out of hand. Today such attitudes are impossible. Today, Islam finds itself neither alone, nor apart, nor dominant. Moreover, like Christianity, it must also face the profound questions raised by modern intellectual discoveries, technological changes, and socio-economic globalization.

However, one factor that makes it difficult for Muslims to face these questions, and for non-Muslims to understand the world of Islam, is that there is nothing like the Church in Islam. There is no worldwide organization with a strong sense of its own historical continuity, speaking and teaching authoritatively about itself. For all its fragmentariness, there is a Christian Church; there is no such organized, unitary, historical tradition in the world of Islam. 'Christianity' means something more than the physical or cultural space occupied by Christians; it means primarily the Kingdom of Christ, manifest in his Body, the Church. The word 'Islam' can only mean the world of Muslims.

In this context, van Ess's observation about the positive role of scepticism may need to be qualified. Scepticism can act as 'the salt in the soup' only if the soup is there to be tasted, out of a definite, secure vessel. When 'the salt of doubt' is sprinkled over the Christian world, when 'the devil' tantalizes and undermines or even checkmates Christian thought, the Church can sooner or later address the issue in an ecumenical council, a forum where the matter is considered and then somehow settled by an authoritative pronouncement. There is no such possibility in Islam.

If a Muslim thinker or theologian or even a whole Islamic state seeks to move Islam forward by asking fundamental questions, the question arises whether the result is still authentically Muslim. Because there is no central teaching authority in Islam, there is no possible answer to this question. There is, therefore, a permanent ambiguity about the nature of Islam, although the situation is somewhat different in the Shi'a tradition. Nevertheless, Islam still needs to ask itself fundamental questions regarding its nature and origins. It cannot let these questions be asked only by people outside Islam; it needs to answer these questions for itself. Can it still be seriously and responsibly maintained that the Hebrew Scriptures have been falsified by the Jews and the Christians, and moreover that the original Gospel is lost, corrupted by the Christians? Islam is at a point when scepticism may be a creative force. Scepticism may help Muslims realise that the Jewish and Christian Scriptures—Scriptures which existed as we have them today long before Islam arose—are authentic. This may help Islam set about reconciling, in all truth and humility, the Qur'an with the Bible.[45]

The Muslim claim that Islam constitutes 'the essence of truth and religion' implies a sharp judgment on other religions. It is saying, for instance, that Christianity's true essence is found in Islam. But if that is so, then Christians ought to find themselves wholly at home in Islam. This is manifestly not the case. Perhaps Islam needs to ask itself some sceptical questions and move forward.

Several decades ago, the Lebanese Christian thinker Charles Malik, a former President of the General Assembly of the United Nations who helped draft the Universal Declaration of Human Rights, set out an agenda for ongoing Christian-Muslim encounter. The list of tasks that he gives is still worth reading.

One set of tasks centres round the sacred texts: how and why the Bible and the Qur'an were each formed; the intentions of the Bible and the intention of the Qur'an; the difference in their contents; why Muslims never read the Bible, whereas Christianity has fully incorporated the Old Testament into its theology and liturgy; how revelation is understood both in the foundational texts of the two religions and in subsequent tradition. Then there is the issue, already mentioned, about the word of God: in Christianity the Word is a person, while in Islam it is literally a word. A

---

[45] For further explorations of this theme, see the studies by Ronald L Nettler, 'Mohamed Talbi, "For Dialogue Between All Religions"', *Muslim-Jewish Encounters Intellectual Traditions and Modern Politics*, ed. Ronald L Nettler and Suha Taji-Farouki, Harwood Academic Press, Amsterdam, 1998, 171-199; and 'A Post-Colonial Encounter of Traditions: Muhammad Sa'id Al-Ashmawi on Islam and Judaism', *Medieval and Modern Perspectives on Muslim-Jewish Relations*, ed. Ronald L Nettler, Harwood Academic Press, Luxembourg, 1995, 174-185.

further set of issues centres on Muhammad's limited knowledge of Christianity. Must Muhammad's objectively deficient understanding be permanently binding on Islam, or can this knowledge be supplemented and corrected today by a fuller awareness of what Christianity is? It is worth noting, too, that the temporal and spiritual orders tend to be separated in Christian thought, whereas Islam makes no such separation.[46]

Malik's list, here quoted only selectively, brings home how wide the differences are between Christianity and Islam: a Christian committed to dialogue can only think of Jacque Maritain's dictum, *distinguer pour unir*. Moreover, these questions touch on the very identity of Islam, since Islam's self-understanding essentially refers to how it abrogates or supersedes Christianity. Even though, then, Islam may traditionally have set itself in confrontation with Christianity, it must face questions about its own identity that it cannot settle without involving authoritative representatives of Christianity. Perhaps, therefore, Islam's own internal tensions may lead it, eventually, to move forward. If so, the work of pioneers such as Paul Nwyia will not have been in vain.

Catholic Christianity and Shi'a Islam

In the two sections above, I have tried to set out what I think are some of the contours in the encounter between Christianity and other faiths; and to further understand that engagement within the particular nature of Christian–Muslim relations. The history of religious encounter between Christianity and Islam does not allow for any sentimentality. However, there are many areas of religious exploration for Christians and Muslims to pursue jointly, be they social, scientific, ethical, political, economic or ecological. There is much to commend this activity. What I want to do in this last section is to sketch out some of the areas of possible similarity and exploration between Catholic Christianity and Shi'a Islam.

What is Catholicism? Catholicism is a not a reality that stands by itself. The word *Catholic* is a qualification of *Christian*, and *Christian* is a qualification of *religious* and *religious* is a qualification of *human*. Catholicism is a configuration of values, which enjoy a normative character in discerning the Christian tradition as a whole. There has

[46] Charles Malik, 'Introduction', *God and Man in Contemporary Islamic Thought*, American University of Beirut, Beirut, 1972, 98-99.

been throughout Catholic history a drive toward rationality, the insistence that the divine mystery manifest in tradition and sacramental presence be, insofar as possible penetrated, defended, and explicated by the most acute rational reflection.

Catholicism is a rich and diverse reality. It is a Christian tradition, a way of life, and a community. That is to say, it is comprised of faith, theologies and doctrines, and is characterized by specific liturgical, ethical and spiritual orientations and behaviours; at the same time, it is a people, or cluster of peoples, with a particular history. These values include Catholicism's sense of sacramentality: God is present everywhere, the invisible in the visible, within us and within the whole created order; its principle of mediation, the divine is available to us as a transforming, healing, renewing power through the ordinary things of life: persons, communities, events, places, institutions, natural objects, etc; its sense of communion, we are radically social and so, too, is our relationship with God and God's with us; its drive toward rationality and its critical realism, reality is neither self-evident nor confined to the realm of ideas; its corresponding respect for history, for tradition, and for continuity, we are products of our past as well as shapers of our present and our future; its analogical imagination, the divine and the human are now more alike than unalike; its conviction that we can have as radical notion of sin as we like so long as our understanding and appreciation of grace is even more radical; its high regard for authority and order as well as conscience and freedom; indeed its fundamental openness to all truth and to every value—in a word, its *catholicity*.

The similarities in religious tradition between Catholic Christianity[47] and Shi'a Islam[48] have caught the attention of many

---

[47] An introduction to the Catholic tradition can be gained by reading the texts of the following modern theologians: Johann Adam Möhler (1796-1838), *Unity of the Church or The Principle of Catholicism. Presented in the Spirit of the Church Fathers of the First Three Centuries* (first published in 1825), ed. and trans. with an introduction by Peter C Erb, Catholic University of America Press, Washington DC, 1996; Karl Adam(1876-1966), *The Spirit of Catholicism* (first published in 1924), trans. Dom Justin McCann OSB, introduction by Robert A Kreig CSC, Collection 'Milestones in Catholic Theology', Crossroad Herder, New York, 1997; and Henri Cardinal de Lubac SJ (1896-1991), *Catholicism: Christ and the Common Destiny of Man*, (first published in 1937) trans. Lancelot C Sheppard and Sister Elizabeth Englund OCD, Ignatius Press, San Francisco, 1988.

[48] For Shi'a Islam see the work of Yann Richard, *L'Islam chi'ite*, Fayard, Paris, 1991, trans. Antonia Nevill as *Shi'ite Islam*, Basil Blackwell, Oxford, 1995; and *Le Shi'isme en Iran: Imam et Révolution*, Maisonneuve, Paris, 1980.

observers. Indeed, as part of the historical encounter between the two great faiths Christianity and Islam, Catholicism and Shi'ism have sought and engaged in dialogue with each other over the centuries.[49] Whilst similar religious and structural parallels between Catholic Christianity and Shi'a Islam have been noted, these religious systems have fundamental differences. Each has its own history and enduring and essential characteristics, although both traditions have certain characteristics that are strikingly similar; for example, the matter of the nature of religious authority in both traditions.[50]

Catholics believe in the primacy of Peter among the apostles, and in the primacy of his successor among the bishops. Religious authority for them is thus centralized and articulated in every age. Islam is divided into two dominant traditions: Sunni and Shi'a both locate religious authority differently. The Shi'i position, however, is that the community can only be infallible when it is led by the legitimate descendant of the Prophecy (i.e. of bringing new revelation). Various Shi'i sects have differing views as to which descendants of Muhammad led the community. The last of these was taken into occultation due to the harassment of the Sunnis, but even in his absence, he is the true leader of the community. He will reappear at the end of time along with the Messiah Jesus, in order to slay the Antichrist and usher in the triumph of true religion in the messianic age.

Among the several parallels that we may observe between Twelver Shi'ism and Catholicism, three are perhaps most telling: meditation upon the significance of the passion of an innocent victim who took upon himself the sins of the community and atoned for them; belief that God's grace is mediated through earthly and heavenly hierarchies; and faith in intercessors.

---

[49] The history of the encounter between Catholicism and Shi'a Islam has been richly documented, for example the Gospel in Persia: Roberto Gulbenkian, 'The Translation of the Four Gospels into Persian', *Les Cahiers de la Nouvelle Revue de science missionnaire*, Immensee, 1981; The interreligious encounter in the 17th century Iran—Francis Richard: 'Catholicisme et Islam Chiite au "Grand Siècle"': Autour de quelques documents concernant les Missions catholiques en Perse au XVIIème siècle', *Euntes Docete* (Rome), Vol. XXXIII, 1980, 339-403; and the martyrdom of the Georgian Catholic Queen in Iran: R Gulbenkian, 'Relation véritable du glorieux martyre de la reine Kétévan de Géorgie', *Bedi Kartlisa* (Paris), Vol. XL, 1982, 31-97.

[50] For a political-theological comparison between Catholic Christianity and Shi'a Islam see: James A Bill and John Aiden Williams, 'Shi'a Islam and Roman Catholicism: An Ecclesial and Political Analysis', *The Vatican, Islam and the Middle East*, ed. Kail C Ellis OSA, Syracuse University Press, New York, 1987, 69-105, 70.

In Sunni Islam as in Protestantism, by comparison, the dominant view is that only Muhammad (or Jesus) is the intercessor—or even that the intercessory function has now been performed, and that therefore each believer must now 'carry his own weight.' Shi'ism, in common with the *sufis* (the mystics of Islam), places great value on the model, the intercession, and the accessibility of the 'friends of God,' the saints.

In particular, both Catholicism and Shi'ism emphasize an overarching mother-figure as a leading intercessor, a pattern for women, a refuge for those in trouble, a radiant 'mother of sorrows' and hope for the sorrowing. Both emphasize the great value of martyrdom and of redemptive suffering, even to the extent that individual suffering can become part of a 'treasury of grace' upon which coreligionists can draw. And finally, each community believes and proclaims that it is led by a charismatic leader who is guided by God and hence preserved from error, and believes further that there is a religious hierarchy that shares his authority and upholds and diffuses his teaching. This enables that hierarchy to speak with great confidence and authority, upheld as it is by the accompanying belief that God would never leave the faithful without such an infallible guide through the complexities of its religion.

Mary, the mother of Christ, is a central figure and symbol for Catholic Christianity. Especially blessed and immaculately conceived, she was privileged to be the virginal mother of the *logos*, through whom the world was created—hence, truly *Theotokos*: Mother of God. As the mother of the prophet and promised Messiah, Mary is recognized as well in the Qur'an as 'purified' and 'chosen above all women' by God, who Himself ordained the virginal birth. The Virgin Mary is thus a sacred historical and theological link binding Christians and Muslims. Catholics and Orthodox Christians view her as mother of Christ the divine *logos*, and therefore the mother of God; Muslims consider her mother of the Messiah selected by God for this very special role.

The two American scholars James A Bill and John Alden Williams in their imaginative and at times magisterial account of the encounter between Catholicism and Shi'a Islam, make some very important observations.[51] The linking of the Catholic believer with God through

---

[51] James A Bill and John Alden Williams, *Roman Catholics and Shi'i Muslims: Prayer, Passion and Politics*, The University of North Carolina Press, Chapel Hill and London, 2002. See my review in *International Journal for the Study of the Christian Church* (Special Issue on Christian-Muslim relations), Vol. 3, no. 3, 2003, 107-110.

Mary is strikingly similar to the relationship that Shi'i Muslims hold with respect to the imams. The emanating chain of the imams links the divine and the human. Shi'is bind themselves directly and totally into this chain. The Catholic-Shi'i parallel here, however, is more than one between the Virgin Mary and the imams. Rather, it is one between Mary and Fatima, the daughter of the Prophet Muhammad, the wife of Imam Ali, and the mother of imams Husayn and Hasan.

Both Fatima and the Virgin Mary stand as female members of a central holy family; both are considered to be immaculate and impeccable; and both are emanating extensions of their fathers and sons. While Mary's personality is completely contained in that of her son Jesus, the figure of Fatima emanates forth from both her father Muhammad and her son Husayn. Mary and Fatima pass along the special grace derived directly from Christ and Muhammad, respectively, to Catholics and Shi'i Muslims. The important symbolism of a linking and emanating source is seen in the images of radiant light that dominate the stories of both the Virgin Mary and of Fatima. Fatima is usually referred to as *al-Zahra* ('The Shining One'); at the moment of her birth, light is said to have spread over the sky and the earth, to the west and to the east. According to Shi'i believers, Fatima, like Muhammad and Ali, received a special light from God and passed it along to all mankind. Mary is also believed to have emanated a special holy radiance, and is referred to in Catholic prayers as, variously, 'Morning Star', 'Our Light in Uncertainty', and 'Radiant Mother'.

Suffering and martyrdom are central themes in both Islam and Christianity. [52] These themes are most clearly stressed and fundamentally emphasized in Shi'ism and Catholicism, where they dominate both belief and practice. In both cases, there is a critically important redemptive aspect to this suffering. In Catholicism, the doctrine of redemption is sharply and formally defined as part of Church teaching; it stresses the great offence of sin to God, and the need to satisfy his justice—something man unaided by Christ could not accomplish. Although Shi'ism has no such formally defined doctrine of redemption, suffering clearly helps to cut a path through to salvation. This occurs not only through the suffering of the individual Muslim, but also through the assistance and intercession of the martyred imams.

---

[52] Emilio Platti OP, 'Le sacrifice en Islam', in *Le sacrifice dans les religions*, ed. M Neusch, Editions Beauchesne, Paris, 1994, 157-174.

Both Catholicism and Shi'ism view suffering in the context of intercession and salvation. Both Jesus Christ and Imam Husayn stand as central suffering figures, whose violent deaths at the hands of powerful temporal adversaries are revealed as pre-eminent, purifying, universal redemptive acts. Both deaths represented the climax of a terrible period of passion and suffering that helped cleanse the world of injustice, tyranny, and corruption, and opened the way to salvation. In their physical destruction and temporal defeat, both Christ and Husayn achieved major spiritual triumph and everlasting victory. In addition, their act of ultimate sacrifice spawned a long history of similar acts of martyrdom by Christians and Muslims alike. In Roman Catholicism and Shi'i Islam, these acts of martyrdom have been historically viewed as a form of blessed heroism that stands as continuing proof of the power of faith.

Again, James A Bill and John Alden Williams make some very important observations in their work *Roman Catholics and Shi'i Muslims: Prayer, Passion and Politics*. Both Catholicism and Shi'i Islam emphasize the central importance of sacred chains of saintly personalities who serve both as models and intercessors for the faithful. These individuals, whether saints or imams, are ultimately links to the Divine. In Catholicism, the saints 'who have put on Christ' have become images of Christ Himself; when Catholics devote themselves to these saints, they are held to connect themselves with Christ. In Shi'ism, the imams represent a chain, with each imam existing as the emanation of the ones before him. Ultimately, they are extensions of the spirit and personalities of Imam Husayn, Imam Ali, and the Prophet Muhammad, who was himself of course the receptacle for God's revelations. These sacred chains of saintly intermediaries are reinforced by a special spiritual strength that is the product of great suffering, travail, and pain. The chains have been fashioned and fired by the flames of suffering, and the major links are martyrs who consciously chose death and thus demonstrated the depth of their commitment. The stories of the suffering and death of Imam Husayn and his companions and the passion and death of Jesus Christ and his followers permeate the consciousness and beliefs of Shi'a and Catholics respectively. This reality of suffering and martyrdom both strengthens the power of these sacred chains of saints and deepens their appeal to the faithful, who seek to link themselves into these powerful systems of emanation. For Catholics and Shi'is alike believe that it is here that they are likely to find assistance in their quest for redemption and salvation.

Although neither Catholicism nor Shi'a Islam can be said to have simple, universally accepted models of politics and the state, there are certain accepted principles on these areas that are identifiable in the teachings of both faith systems. These include an emphasis upon normative foundations of political systems and the pre-eminence of divine and natural law over human, man–made law. The goal of the ideal state should be to further the moral and spiritual fulfilment of the human being and the human community. In short, the form of the state should be such that it assists men and women to pursue lives of a quality that will enable them to attain everlasting union with God. Within this general framework, both Shi'ism and Catholicism have historically indicated a willingness to accept and to live within a wide variety of specific political systems.

In conclusion, since Catholicism and Shi'ism bear certain important doctrinal, structural, and socio–political similarities, and since both face similar problems in the world today, they could do well to communicate with and to try to learn from each other. In this way, both religious traditions could increase their chances to meet successfully the challenges that they will inevitably confront. [53]

---

[53] Again one could do no better than see the work by James A Bill and John Alden Williams, *op. cit.*

MARY, JESUS AND CHRISTIANITY:
AN ISLAMIC PERSPECTIVE
Mohammad Ali Shomali

It is very difficult to write about people to whom one is personally attached. For me as someone who has been brought up in an Islamic culture, Mary and Jesus have always been two of those heroic figures whose lives are to be taken as great examples and role models. I remember that when I was growing up in Tehran I used to attend a local mosque for congregational prayers. Usually in mosques after congregational prayers, an individual recites some verses of the Qur'an or some supplications. As recommended in some *hadiths,* in our mosque the last two verses of the second chapter of the Qur'an were very frequently recited and for days and days I would listen to and reflect on them. The first of them reads as follows:

> The Messenger believes in that which has been revealed unto him from his Lord and (so do) the believers. Each one believes in God and His angels and His scriptures and His messengers—'We make no distinction between any of His messengers'—and they say: 'We hear, and we obey. (Grant us) Your forgiveness, our Lord. Unto You is the journeying.' (2: 285)

This verse, like many other verses of the Qur'an, puts great emphasis on the uniformity of the prophets, their scriptures, and their missions. It makes you think that you belong to a great community of faith including all believers throughout the history of mankind who have followed the same path. Therefore, for me all the champions of this path are very respected. Among them, some are more outstanding. Jesus was one of the five greatest prophets[1] and Mary was chosen above the women

---

[1] For example, see *Uṣūl al-Kāfī,* Vol 1, 175, *Hadith* 3. Elsewhere I have written: 'The Qur'an mentions twenty-five of the prophets and states that there were many more.(40: 78) Through the indications of *hadiths,* Muslims believe that there have been 124,000

of the world (3: 42) and introduced as an example for those who believe (66: 12). In this paper I will first try to address briefly some aspects of personalities of Mary and Jesus from an Islamic perspective and then I will refer to Muslim–Christian relations.

Maybe more than any other mother and child, Mary and Jesus were related and linked to each other. It is very interesting that in Chapter 21 of the Qur'an ('the Prophets') which is about the prophets, when it comes to Jesus the Qur'an talks about Mary and through her about Jesus and says:

> And (remember) her who guarded her chastity: We breathed
> into her of Our Spirit and We made her and her son *a sign*
> for all peoples. (21: 91)

The Qur'an here refers to Mary and her son as '*a* sign for all peoples.'[2] Why? A typical interpretation of this verse is given by 'Allamah Sayyid M H Tabataba'i who holds that the sign here is the birth of Jesus from Mary. Therefore, Jesus and Mary are two sides of the same sign. He adds that the fact that Mary is mentioned in the first place alongside the prophets (though she was not a prophet) and then she and her son are introduced as 'a sign' is a great honour for Mary.[3]

I think it is true that this birth was very special and definitely it can be considered as 'a sign' of God. As we know, the Qur'an confirms the virgin birth of Jesus as follows:

> 'O Mary, God gives you good news of a word from Him,
> whose name shall be the Messiah, Jesus son of Mary, honoured
> in this world and the Hereafter, and one of those brought
> near to God. He shall speak to the people from his cradle
> and in maturity, and shall be of the righteous.'

---

prophets. Amongst those mentioned in the Qur'an are Adam, Noah, Abraham, Ishmael, Isaac, Lot, Jacob, Joseph, Job, Moses, Aaron, Ezekiel, David, Solomon, Jonah, Zachariah, John the Baptist, Jesus and Muhammad. Among them, Noah, Abraham, Moses, Jesus and Muhammad had universal mission and brought new codes of law. They are called, *Ulū al-'Azm* meaning those of great determination.' (M A Shomali , *Discovering Shi'i Islam,* Jami'at al-Zahra, Qum, 2003, 43)

2   This does not mean that from another perspective each of them independently cannot be considered as a sign of God. For example, in the verse (19: 21) God says that He wishes to appoint Mary's son as a sign for mankind and a mercy.

3   See *Al-Mīzān fī Tafsīr al-Qur'ān,* Vol. 14, Isma'iliyan, Qum, 1972, 317.

She said: 'O my Lord! How shall I have a son when no man
has touched me?' He said: 'Even so; God creates what He
will. When He decrees a thing He says to it, 'Be!' and it is.'
(3: 43–47)

Certainly Jesus was born miraculously through the same power
which had brought Adam into being without a father:

Truly, the likeness of Jesus with God is as the likeness of
Adam. He created him of dust, and then said to him, 'Be!'
and he was. (3: 59)

However, the verse (21: 91) seems to refer to something more,
since it indicates that God 'made *her and her son* a sign' and not just the
birth. It is striking that elsewhere again the Qur'an refers to Mary and
Jesus as 'a sign':

And We made the son of Mary and his mother as a Sign: We
gave them both shelter on high ground affording rest and
security and furnished with springs. (23.50)

Mary and Jesus were very close to each other. It was not accidental
that Mary could have a son like Jesus. Therefore, let us see who Mary was.

Mary is the only woman who is mentioned by name in the
Qur'an. There is an entire chapter in the Qur'an entitled 'Maryam'. She
is mentioned 34 times in the Qur'an, much more than in the Bible.
Mary's birth was very special. Her parents, 'Imran (Joachim in Christian
tradition) and Hannah (Anne) were old and had no child for a long time
after their marriage. God revealed to Imran that they would be given a
blessed son who would be able to heal the ill, revive the dead, and be an
apostle for the people of Israel. Imran informed Hannah about this son
and therefore everyone was expecting a son.[4] When Hannah became
pregnant, she wanted to make her son a special devotee of God.[5] Let us
follow the story from the Qur'an:

---

[4] Ayatollah Nasir Makarim Shirazi, *Qiṣṣahā-yi Qur'ān*, Dar al-Kutub al-Islamiyyah, Tehran,
2001, 323.

[5] The Arabic term which is used in the Qur'an is *muḥarrar*, which means freed (from all
worldly affairs and especially dedicated to God's service).

Behold! The wife of Imran said: 'O my Lord! I do dedicate unto You what is in my womb for Your special service so accept this of me for You hear and know all things.'
When she was delivered she said: 'O my Lord! behold! I am delivered of a female child!' And God knew best what she brought forth, 'and nowise is the male like the female. I have named her Mary and I commend her and her offspring to Your protection from the Evil One the Rejected.'
Right graciously did her Lord accept her: He made her grow in purity and beauty; to the care of Zachariah was she assigned. Every time that he entered (her) chamber to see her he found her supplied with sustenance. He said: 'O Mary! whence (comes) this to you?' She said: 'From God: for God provides sustenance to whom He pleases without measure.'[6] (3: 35-37)

To me one of the interesting points in this story is that Imran and Hannah were told that they would have a son, the Messiah. Instead, they had Mary, the mother of that son. It is true that the son of one's daughter is sometimes considered as one's own son, but I think this is yet another indication of the close relationship between Mary and Jesus, as if Mary is the beginning of Jesus. It is also interesting that, to the surprise of many, if not all, Hannah's promise of making her son a devotee of God was accepted by God in Mary, and for the first time a girl was allowed to stay in the Temple.[7]

Not only Mary was born into a pious family, but she was also brought up under the care of the Prophet Zachariah in a pure and holy

---

[6] It was this statement of Mary that inspired old Zachariah to pray to God and ask for a child. Immediately after the above verses the Qur'an says:
There did Zakariya pray to his Lord saying: 'O my Lord! grant unto me from You a progeny that is pure; for You are He that hears prayer!'
While he was standing in prayer in the chamber the angels called unto him: 'God does give you glad tidings of Yaḥyā (John) witnessing the truth of a Word from God and (be besides) noble chaste and a Prophet of the (goodly) company of the righteous.'
He said: 'O my Lord! how shall I have a son seeing I am very old and my wife is barren?'
'Thus' was the answer 'God does accomplish what He wills.' (3: 38-40)

[7] Some exegetes of the Qur'an have said that a sign of God's acceptance of Mary was that she was freed from menstruation so that she did not have to leave the Temple. Cited in Makarim Shirazi, 324.

place such as the Temple.[8] She herself tried to attain purity and piety by serving God wholeheartedly. In what follows, I will try to refer quickly to some merits or achievements of Mary that have made her an example:

—Chastity[9]
—Obedience[10];
—Truthfulness[11];
—Being purified by God[12];
—Being chosen by God above all women[13];
—Being addressed by angels[14];
—Receiving food from God[15];
—Annunciation of Jesus.[16]

---

[8] According to Islamic tradition, Imran had died before the birth of Maryam.

[9] In addition to the verse (21: 91) that was mentioned before, one may refer to the following verse:

And God sets forth as an example to those who believe the wife of Pharaoh ...

And Mary the daughter of Imran who guarded her chastity; and We breathed into her (body) of Our spirit; and she testified faithfully to the truth of the words of her Lord and of His scriptures, and was of the obedient. (66: 11 and 12)

[10] 'She ... was of the obedient.' (cf. 66: 12)

[11] 'She Mary testified faithfully to the truth of the words of her Lord and of His scriptures' (*ibid.*)

'Christ the son of Mary was no more than an Apostle; many were the Apostles that passed away before him. His mother was a truthful woman. They had both to eat their (daily) food. See how God makes His Signs clear to them; yet see in what ways they are deluded away from the truth!' (5: 75)

[12] 'Behold!' the Angel said, 'God has chosen you, and purified you, and chosen you above the women of all nations'. (3: 42)

[13] *Ibid.*

[14] *Ibid.*

[15] 'Every time that he entered (her) chamber to see her he found her supplied with sustenance. He said: 'O Mary! whence (comes) this to you?' She said: 'From God: for God provides sustenance to whom He pleases without measure.' (cf. 3: 37)

[16] We have already mentioned some of the verses of the Qur'an about the renunciation of Jesus. Here I would like to refer to a more detailed account of his birth from the Chapter of Mary:

And make mention of Mary in the Scripture, when she had withdrawn from her people to a chamber looking East,

And had chosen seclusion from them. Then We sent unto her Our spirit and it assumed for her the likeness of a perfect man.

She said: Lo! I seek refuge in the Beneficent One from you, if you are God fearing.

He said: I am only a messenger of your Lord, that I may bestow on you a pure son.

She said: How can I have a son when no mortal has touched me, neither have I been unchaste!

Among the above merits, I think two are most important and involve the rest, that is, to be most truthful and to be purified. Indeed, these are two signs of the perfect people.

According to the Qur'an, there are four groups of people that stand above all others. Those are the people upon whom God has bestowed His blessings and every Muslim at least ten times a day in his prayers asks God to guide him towards their path, the Right Path (1: 6 and 7). The Qur'an says:

> And whosoever obeys God and His Apostle will be in the
> company of those upon whom God has bestowed blessings,
> of the Prophets, the most truthful, the witnesses, and the
> righteous: ah! what a beautiful fellowship! (4: 69)

Thus, the most truthful *(al-ṣiddīqīn)* come in rank immediately after the prophets.[17] In fact, to be most truthful is so important that sometimes prophets are praised as being most truthful.[18] Truthfulness here

---

He said: So (it will be). Your Lord says: It is easy for Me. And (it will be) that We may make of him a sign for mankind and a mercy from Us, and it is a thing ordained.
And she conceived him, and she withdrew with him to a place.
And the pangs of childbirth drove her unto the trunk of the palm tree. She said: Oh, would that I had died before this and had become a thing of naught, forgotten!
Then (one) cried unto her from below her, saying: Grieve not! Your Lord has placed a rivulet beneath you,
And shake the trunk of the palm tree toward you, you will cause ripe dates to fall upon you.
So eat and drink and be consoled. And if you meet any mortal, say: Lo! I have vowed a fast unto the Beneficent, and may not speak this day to any mortal.
Then she brought him to her own folk, carrying him. They said: O Mary! You have come with an amazing thing.
Oh sister of Aaron! Your father was not a wicked man nor was your mother a harlot.
Then she pointed to him. They said: How can we talk to one who is in the cradle, a young boy?
He spoke: Lo! I am the servant of God. He has given me the Scripture and has appointed me a Prophet,
And has made me blessed wheresoever I may be, and has enjoined upon me prayer and almsgiving so long as I remain alive,
And (has made me) dutiful toward my mother, and has not made me arrogant, miserable.
Peace on me the day I was born, and the day I die, and the day I shall be raised alive!
Such was Jesus, son of Mary: (this is) a statement of the truth concerning which they doubt. (19: 16-34)
17 Members of each category enjoy all the merits of the lower categories.
18 For example, the Qur'an says: 'Also mention in the Book (the story of) Abraham: he was a truthful man a prophet.' (19: 41)

is much more than truthfulness in one's speech. The truthfulness here requires truthfulness in speech, in intentions and beliefs, and in acts. In other words, it involves correspondence and harmony between one's heart, mind, tongue and deeds.[19] Mary is the only woman who is mentioned in the Qur'an as being the most truthful (*ṣiddīqa*). Of course, Islamic *hadiths* mention other women, especially Fatima the daughter of the Prophet Muhammad, as being one of the most truthful.

With respect to purification, one must note that the whole point in the spiritual journey is to purify oneself. All the prophets have come to teach and purify human beings.[20] Since God is the purest of the pure, whoever aspires to approximate Him must purify himself. The purification must start with one's own determination to follow the right path. Having done one's best and proving one's real determination to purify one's soul, God will guide and send His favours to this servant in a special way and purify him. Thus, there are two stages: one is the stage of purifying oneself (this is for *mutaṭahhirūn* or *muṭṭahharūn*) and the other is the stage of being purified by God (this is for *muṭahharūn*). One of the merits of the purified (*muṭahharūn*) is that they have access to the secrets of divine revelation. For example, we read in the Qur'an:

> That this is indeed a Qur'an most honourable
> In a Book well-guarded
> Which none shall touch but those who are purified:
> A Revelation from the Lord of the Worlds. [21] (56: 77-80)

It is in this sense that the Qur'an tells us about the purification of Mary (3: 41) and the purification of the Household of the Prophet (*Ahl al-Bayt*) by God.[22]

---

[19] For example, see verse 2: 177.

[20] For example, see verse 62: 2.

[21] Commenting on the above verse, A Yusuf Ali writes: It is a Revelation described by four characteristics. (1) It is most honourable, karim, which implies, besides the fact that it is worthy of receiving honour, that it confers great favours on those who receive it. (2) It is well-guarded, maknun; precious in itself, and well-preserved in its purity ... (3) None but the clean shall touch it,–dean in body, mind, thought, intention, and soul; only such can achieve real contact with its full meaning. (4) It is a Revelation from the Lord of the Worlds, and therefore universal for all.

[22] 'God's wish is but to keep away the uncleanness from you, O people of the House! And to purify you a (thorough) purification' (33: 33)

Now let us refer briefly to some aspects of the Islamic view of Jesus. Jesus is mentioned in the Qur'an more than ninety times and there is a rich literature in Islamic *hadith* on Jesus, including his sayings and his conduct.[23, 24] We have already discussed his virgin birth and the fact that he was one of the five greatest prophets who are known as *Ulū al-'Azm* meaning those of great determination. According to Islamic tradition, all of these five had a universal mission.[25] To be a prophet and, indeed, to be one of the five greatest prophets implies very high qualities, such as sinlessness, purity, and even infallibility.[26] Not only was his birth miraculous as a sign of the omnipotence of God, but also his childhood. As a newborn, he was able to speak: [27]

> He shall speak to the people from his cradle and in maturity, and shall be of the righteous. (3: 46)

During his mission, Jesus was able to work miracles as a sign of the truth of his mission and that he was supported by God. The Qur'an refers to this fact in several verses, such as:

> Behold! the disciples said: 'O Jesus the son of Mary! can your Lord send down to us a table spread with food from heaven?' Said Jesus: 'Fear God if you have faith.'
> They said: 'We only wish to eat thereof and satisfy our hearts and to know that you have indeed told us the truth; and that we ourselves may be witnesses to the miracle.
> Said Jesus the son of Mary: 'O God our Lord! send us from heaven a table set (with viands) that there may be for us for the first and the last of us a solemn festival and a sign from

---

[23] Jesus is mentioned in the Qur'an in different ways, sometimes by his proper name, sometimes by his titles or attributes. For example, the term 'Īsā (Jesus) is mentioned 25 times, al-Masīḥ 11 times, son of Mary 33 times, al-Nabī (the Prophet) once, Rasūl (the Apostle) 3 times.

[24] For example about Jesus' simple life see *Nahj al-Balaghah*, Sermon 159, 324.

[25] For example, Sayyid M H Tabataba'i writes: ' Verily, Jesus was one of 'Ulu al-'Azm like Moses and they were sent for all people of the world.' (Tabataba'i, Vol. 3, 216)

[26] According to Shi'i theology, the infallibility of the prophets includes both their mission activities and their personal life.

[27] We have referred in footnote 16 to the verses of the Chapter 19 indicating his actual words as a newborn baby.

You; and provide for our sustenance for You are the best
Sustainer (of our needs).
God said: 'I will send it down unto you: but if any of you
after that resists faith I will punish him with a penalty such
as I have not inflicted on anyone among all the peoples. (5:
112–115)

Elsewhere the Qur'an refers to some other miracles of Jesus:

I have come to you with a sign from your Lord: I make
for you out of clay, as it were, the figure of a bird, and
breathe into it and it becomes a bird by God's leave. And
I heal the blind, and the lepers, and I raise the dead by
God's leave. (3.49)
Then will God say: 'O Jesus the son of Mary! recount my
favour to you and to your mother. Behold! I strengthened
you with the Holy Spirit so that you did speak to the people
in childhood and in maturity. Behold! I taught you the Book
and Wisdom the Law and the Gospel. And behold! You make
out of clay as it were the figure of a bird by My leave and
you breath into it and it becomes a bird by My leave and you
heal those born blind and the lepers by My leave. And behold!
You bring forth the dead by My leave. And behold! I did
restrain the Children of Israel from (violence to) you when
you did show them the Clear Signs and the unbelievers among
them said: 'This is nothing but evident magic'. (5: 110)

Furthermore, Jesus was the promised Messiah:

Behold! the angels said 'O Mary! God gives you good news
of a word from Him, whose name shall be the Messiah,
Jesus son of Mary, honoured this world and in the Hereafter,
and one of those brought near to God. (3: 45)

The above verse also indicates that Jesus was 'a Word of God',
honourable in this world and in the Hereafter, and of those who are
nearest to God (*muqarrabīn*). Since the only way to get near to God is to
worship and serve Him purely, Jesus was a true 'servant of God' (*'abdullāh*)

(19: 30), 'blessed' or 'a source of blessing' (*mubārak*) (19: 31), and 'a statement of truth' (*qawl al-ḥaqq*) (19: 34). In verse (4: 171), Jesus is described as 'an Apostle of God', 'His Word' which He bestowed on Mary and 'a Spirit (proceeding) from Him' (*rūh-an minhu*). Jesus was also given clear signs and 'aided with the Holy Spirit':

> Those apostles, We have exalted some of them above others:
> of them are some unto whom God has spoken and some he
> has raised in degrees (of honour); And we gave Jesus the son
> of Mary clear Signs and aided him with the Holy Spirit ...
> (2: 253)

Having referred to some aspects of the personalities of Mary and Jesus, now is the time to address Christian- Muslim relations. There are different ways to deal with this increasingly important issue. In what follows, I would like to address the issue in an indirect way, that is, by explaining what I have been frequently telling my Christian friends, that as a Muslim I am very comfortable and pleased with dialogue and solidarity between Muslims and Christians. The reason for such a statement lies in the following facts:

—We both believe in and worship the same God who is the One, the Merciful, the Benevolent, the Omnipotent, the Omniscient and the Omnipresent. Muslims and Christians love God immensely and try to devote themselves to Him and become close to Him. We read in the Psalms (42: 2), 'My soul thirsts for God, the God of life; when shall I go to seek the face of God?' and in the Qur'an (2: 115), 'To God belong the East and the West; whithersoever you turn, there is the Face of God.' There is a very rich and significantly similar spirituality in both religions.

—We both believe in human free will, responsibility and accountability before God and share the same understanding of basic major moral values.[28]

---

[28] 'We think that all people, but especially Muslims, can share with us the values that we have received from Jesus: total obedience to the will of God, witness given to the truth, humility in behaviour, control of one's speech, justice in one's actions, mercy shown in deeds, love towards all, pardon granted for wrong done, maintaining peace with all brothers and sisters.' Cardinal Francis Arinze, Message to Muslims for the End of Ramadan 2000.

—We both believe in the Resurrection and in God's treatment of human beings with justice and mercy on the Day of Judgement.

—We both have a high esteem of the gifts of reason and conscience and at the same time recognize our need for divine revelation in our path towards happiness in this world and hereafter.

—We both believe that all humans come from the same father and mother, that is, Adam and Eve. We have a great sense of fellowship and deny any sort of racism.[29] We believe in the dignity of man and reject any unjust treatment of mankind.[30] We appreciate the value of human life as a great divine gift.

—We both believe in the Prophets and share a long history of the Prophecy, right from the very beginning of the history of mankind.

—We both have great respect for the Prophet Abraham and we take him as a role model and, indeed, as 'the father of all who believe'.

—We both have a great reverence and love for Mary and her son, Jesus, upon them be peace. We believe in his virgin birth and await his second coming.

—We both share great concerns about the challenges of living a life of faith today, caused by the contemporary culture of materialism and secularism.[31]

---

[29] 'This means that religion is the enemy of exclusion and discrimination, of hatred and rivalry, of violence and conflict.' (Pope John Paul II, To Christian, Jewish and Muslim leaders, Jerusalem, 23 March 2000) See also *Catechism of the Catholic Church*, No. 842.

[30] Dr George Carey, Archbishop of Canterbury: 'In neither of our faiths is God a subject of idle intellectual curiosity. We are concerned with the living, loving God who brought all things into being and who seeks to bring his creation to its proper fulfilment, with the human family living together in justice and peace. It is this God whose guidance we seek and whose glory we serve.' (*The Road Ahead: A Christian Muslim Dialogue*, X)

[31] 'They [Christians] must look at the profound transformation which is taking place among nations and work hard so that modern man is not turned away from the things of God by an excessive preoccupation with modern science and technology...' (Second Vatican Council, Decree on the Church's missionary activity, *Ad Gentes*, 7 December 1965, nn. 11, 13.)
'As believers, we do not deny or reject any of the real benefits which modern developments have brought, but we are convinced nevertheless that without reference to God modern society is unable to lead men and women to the goal for which they have been created.

—I believe in a complete harmony between all divine revelations and prophecies. There has never been any rivalry or enmity between the Prophets or between their *true* followers. Indeed, Islam, which is in essence an entire submission to God, is the religion of all Prophets. The Prophet Muhammad confirmed all previous Prophets including Jesus and he himself was prophesied by them.

—As a Muslim I have no need to deny Jesus or his mission. Indeed, to be faithful to my very religion, I *must* believe in all Prophets and revelations. The Qur'an asks Muslims to declare their faith in the previous prophets and revelations:

> Say: 'We believe in God and in what has been revealed to us and what was revealed to Abraham, Ishmael, Isaac, Jacob and the Tribes and in (Books) given to Moses, Jesus and the Prophets from their Lord; we make no distinction between one and another among them and to Allah do we bow our will (in Islam).' (3: 83)

—For me, there is no need to deny or cover up the gifts of Jesus or the valuable qualities of Christianity. These are all signs of greatness of the same God. These are all divine blessings that increase my richness, for which I must be very thankful.

—I have no need to compromise my faith in order to enter into a genuine, sustainable and fertile dialogue with the Christians. Indeed, it is the Qur'an itself that calls for such dialogue with all adherents of the Abrahamic faiths. Thus, for me entering into such dialogue and building upon commonalities is rooted in the Qur'an, and is not just a fashion or formality.

—The Qur'an shows great affection for the Christians because of their humility, their search for truth and their sympathy with the Muslims.

It is here too that Christians and Muslims can work together, bearing witness before modern civilisation to the divine presence and loving Providence which guide our steps. Together we can proclaim that he who has made us has called us to live in harmony and justice. May the blessing of the Most High accompany you in your endeavours on behalf of dialogue and peace.' (Pope John Paul II, To the delegation of the World Islamic Call Society, Rome, 15 January 1990)

For example, we read in the Qur'an:

> ... and you will find the nearest among men in love to the believers (to be) those who say:'We are Christians:' because there are among them priests and monks, and because they are not arrogant. When they listen to that which has been revealed unto the Messenger, you see their eyes overflow with tears because of their recognition of the Truth. (5: 82 and 83)

—Through my close and intimate relations with many Christians I have come to the conclusion that the Qur'anic description and praise of the Christians of the time of the Prophet Muhammad can be witnessed among Christians today. There are sincere, truth-seeking, humble and sympathetic Christians who have devoted their lives to God, and I see no reason why I should not take these people to be the real representatives of Christianity, instead of those who call for separation, enmity and fight among believers and are far from practising the commandment of love. Unfortunately today it is very easy to be deceived. There are people who are called 'Muslims' or 'Christians' or 'Jews' but one can by no means judge their faiths by looking at their behaviour. And this gets worse if there is a deliberate attempt to misrepresent the life of faith in general and Islamic way of life in particular.

—It helps me very much to see that my partners in dialogue reciprocate the love and respect that I have for them and their faith. Here I would like to refer briefly to a Christian understanding of Islam and illustrate the fact that these relations of respect and love are already established.[32] Since this volume is specifically concerned with the dialogue between

---

[32] It is true that there have been sad moments in the history of the encounter between Christians and Muslims. However, there have been many cases of happy life together as well. Unfortunately this side of the coin is rarely noticed. For example, right at the beginning of Islam Muslims who had emigrated to Ethiopia were supported by Najjashi, a Christian king. The Canadian Jesuit Ovey N Mohammed writes:'In keeping with the example of Muhammad in dealing with the Christians of Najran and the teaching of the Qur'an that "there is no compulsion in religion" ' (Q 2: 256), Christians were permitted to remain in the territory of Islam through the making of treaties with the Muslim authorities. Many chose to do so rather than migrate to Christian lands where persecution in the name of orthodoxy was widespread.' (p. 32) He also adds later: 'It should be noted that

Shi'i Islam and Roman Catholicism, I will refer below to Catholic sources.[33]

In my view the attitudes of the Roman Catholic Church towards Islam and Muslims can be summed up as follows:

Willingness for dialogue and cooperation with Muslims: There has been an openness among Christians in general and especially in the Roman Catholic Church after Vatican Council II, towards non-Christian faiths, especially the Abrahamic religions.[34] Many attempts have been made especially in the last few decades to establish fertile dialogue between

---

before the rise of colonialism Christians living in Muslim countries enjoyed, on the whole, a measure of toleration the like of which cannot be found in Europe until quite modern times.' (p. 41)

[33] It has been noted by many writers that in addition to general similarities between Islam and Christianity there are more similarities between Shi'i Islam and Roman Catholicism. For example, see James A Bill and John Alden Williams, 'Shi'i Islam and Roman Catholicism: An Ecclesial and Political Analysis', in *The Vatican, Islam, and the Middle East*, ed. Kail C Ellis, Syracuse, Syracuse University Press, NY, 1987; and Ovey N Mohammed, SJ, *Muslim-Christian Relations: Past, Present, Future*, Orbis Books, New York, 1999. Among the similarities, the following can be listed:

a. The religious hierarchy of the Shi'a has its parallel in Roman Catholicism;

b. The emphasis on the concept of 'martyrdom' and the similarity between the death of Imam Husayn and Jesus. Bill and Williams point out: 'In both cases, the drama of suffering and the legend of martyrdom have been institutionalized and remain living, integral parts of the system of faith.'

c. The similarity between the personalities of Mary and Fatima, the daughter of the Prophet Muhammad as a sorrowful mother figure at the heart of a holy family;

d. 'The importance of mystical movements';

e. 'The recognition of legal systems based on the premise that all power derives from God';

f. 'The drive for the establishment of social and political systems that will provide justice, liberty, and security.'

In a recent work, Bill and Williams write: 'Few in the Western world understand the many fascinating linkages between Catholicism and Shi'ism. For example, in the Qur'an, Jesus is mentioned in over ninety verses. There are more references to Mary in the Qur'an than in the Bible; in fact, Mary is mentioned far more than any other woman. There are twelve Imams (charismatic leaders) according to Shi'i beliefs and twelve disciples in Christianity. The first eleven Imams are believed to have died as martyrs; with the exception of Judas Iscariot and St John, the apostles were also reportedly martyred. Interestingly, the number 72 appears repeatedly in both traditions ...' (*Roman Catholics and Shi'i Muslims: Prayer, Passion, and Politics*, University of North Carolina, Chapel Hill, 2002, 3)

[34] For example, Pope John Paul II on the place of Islam in this dialogue says: 'In this dialogue, the Jews and the Muslims ought to have a pre-eminent place.' (Pope John Paul II, Apostolic letter on preparation for the jubilee year 2000, *Tertio Millennio Adveniente*, 10 November 1994, n. 52)

Muslims and Christians in order to reach mutual understanding and in order to build bridges between the two parties so they might work together to meet the challenges that threaten the whole faith community. On the significance of this dialogue, Pope John Paul II says:

> The Catholic Church wishes to pursue a sincere and fruitful interreligious dialogue with the members of the Jewish faith and the followers of Islam. Such a dialogue is not an attempt to impose our views upon others. What it demands of all of us is that, holding to what we believe, we listen respectfully to one another, seek to discern all that is good and *holy* in each other's teachings, and cooperate in supporting everything that favours mutual understanding and peace. (Pope John Paul II, To Christian, Jewish and Muslim leaders, Jerusalem, 23 March 2000)

High regard for Muslims: On the high regard and respect of the Church for Muslims, one may refer to the following documents:

> The Church regards with esteem also the Moslems. They adore the one God, living and subsisting in Himself; merciful and all-powerful, the Creator of heaven and earth, who has spoken to men; they take pains to submit wholeheartedly to even His inscrutable decrees, just as Abraham, with whom the faith of Islam takes pleasure in linking itself, submitted to God. Though they do not acknowledge Jesus as God, they revere Him as a prophet. They also honor Mary, His virgin Mother; at times they even call on her with devotion. In addition, they await the day of judgment when God will render their deserts to all those who have been raised up from the dead. Finally, they value the moral life and worship God especially through prayer, almsgiving and fasting. (*Nostra Aetate* 3)

Recognizing the salvation of Muslims: The Church believes that there is no monopoly over salvation:

> The plan of salvation also includes those who acknowledge

the Creator, in the first place amongst whom are the Muslims; these profess to hold the faith of Abraham, and together with us they adore the one, merciful God, mankind's judge on the last day. (*Catechism of the Catholic Church*, No. 841 from *Lumen Gentium*, No. 16)

Recognizing Islam as a sister faith and Muslims as sisters and brothers in faith: The Church not only allows for the salvation of Muslims, but also understands Islam as a genuine expression of the faith of Abraham:

They have, like you, the faith of Abraham in the one, almighty, and *merciful* God. (Pope John Paul II, To the Catholic community in Ankara, 3 December 1979)

Your God and ours is the same, and we are brothers and sisters in the faith of *Abraham*. (Pope John Paul II, To young Muslims of Morocco, Casablanca, 19 August 1985)

Respect for the Prophet Muhammad: Naturally the respect of the Church for Islam is not limited to its followers, i.e. Muslims. It also extends to the Prophet Muhammad and the values that he preached. As Cardinal Tarancon, president of the Spanish Bishop's Conference at the 1977 International Muslim–Christian Conference at Cordoba has put it:

How is it possible to appreciate Islam and Muslims without showing appreciation for the Prophet of Islam and the values he promoted? Not to do this would not only be a lack of respect to which the [Vatican] Council exhorts Christians, but also neglect of a religious factor of which account must be taken in theological reflection and religious awareness.[35]

---

[35] In that speech, Cardinal Tarancon called on Christians, as did the Patriarch Timothy of Baghdad (d. 823), that 'Muhammad walked in the path of the prophets.' (Cited in Muhammed, 64) It is interesting to know that there are many faithful Christians who along with the teaching of Paul that there will be authentic prophets after Jesus (1 Cor 14: 29, 39; 12: 10, 28; Rom 12: 6) recognize Muhammad as a genuine prophet. For a sample list of Catholic and Protestant thinkers who have written in support of this idea , see Muhammed, 119, notes 65 and 66. J M Gaskell in his *Explaining Islam: Islam from a Catholic Perspective* (p. 29) writes: 'Many Christians tend to think of prophets as essentially Old Testament figures alternately uttering dire warnings and promising a Messianic age of peace, overlooking the fact that the gift of prophecy is one of the Gifts of the Spirit listed by St Paul …'

I think it is now clear that Christians and Muslims are very close to each other; they share a lot and there is no reason why there cannot be a strong sense of unity between them. Indeed, as we saw above, there are many reasons that call on them to come together and to work together for the betterment of mankind.

MARY AND FĀṬIMA IN THE CATHOLIC
AND SHI'A TRADITIONS

Chris Clohessy

When it was the Day of Resurrection, a caller cried from
the middle of the throne: 'O people of the resurrection,
lower your gaze, for Fāṭima the daughter of Muḥammad is
passing by with a shirt stained by the blood of al-Ḥusayn.'
She embraced the leg of the throne and said: 'O God, settle
accounts between me and those who killed my son, and
God decide for my community.' Then she said: 'O God, let
me intercede for whoever weeps over his misfortune,' and
God let her intercede on their behalf.

This tradition, found in this and analogous forms in almost all the major
Shī'a *aḥādīth* collections, together with those traditions that describe at
some length the glorious entry of Fāṭima into Paradise (arrayed in
vestments of light, mounted on a thoroughbred of light adorned with
pearls and gold, and accompanied by thousands of angels, maidens of
Paradise and important Qur'anic figures) offers us some significant clues
as to how the Shī'a envisage her, and provides us with a context in which
to read the more mundane aspects of her life. On earth she was poor and
weak, but her reward in heaven will comprise incalculable riches, including
habitations for her and her party *(shī'a)* made of pearls. On earth she was
neglected, marginalized, mistreated and deprived of justice, but in heaven
all the populace of that place will lower their gaze before her, and her
company will be the angels and those richly blessed by God. On earth
she wept and grieved after the death of her father Muḥammad: even
after her own death, her grieving continues unceasingly over the murder
of her son al-Ḥusayn and the ill-treatment afforded the people of the
house *(ahl al-bayt)*: but in heaven she will be vindicated, with a dreadful
punishment meted out to her son's murderers, and all her tears will be
wiped away. There in that place, this poor and frail woman, who suffered
under such a burden of weakness during her life, will be endowed with

untold power, making intercession before God for the sinners of her father's community.

It is not hard to distinguish, both in her life and in the traditions built up around her, elements strongly identifiable with the Mariology of the Catholic Church, leading us to the engaging temptation of drawing parallels between Fāṭima and Mary. Such parallels may be regarded as valid without necessarily being unequivocal, as sound without automatically being incontestable. There remains a considerable difference between the claims made by Catholicism about Mary and her Son, and the claims of Shī'a Islam concerning Fāṭima and hers: consequently, we do not suggest absolute equality in the lives compared, but simply attempt to underscore certain virtues.

Within Catholic theology, the life and doctrine of the Virgin Mary might be classified under a number of headings: her Immaculate Conception (that she was conceived without sin in the womb of her mother), the miracle stories surrounding the virginal conception and birth of Jesus, her grief and suffering, chiefly beneath the cross of her Son and her intercessory prerogatives in heaven on behalf of the people of God. It is within these theological categories that this paper attempts to examine the life of Fāṭima according to the traditional texts of Islam.

1

The most Blessed Virgin Mary was, from the first moment of her conception, by a singular grace and privilege of almighty God and by virtue of the merits of Jesus Christ, Saviour of the human race, preserved immune from all stain of original sin.[1]

So it is that the Catholic Catechism speaks of *'the splendour of an entirely unique holiness'*[2] which derives from Christ and His merits and by which Mary is enriched in the very instant of her conception in the womb

---

[1] Pope Pius 1X, 'Ineffabilis Deus', in eds. J Neuner and J Dupuis, *Christian Faith: Doctrinal Documents of the Catholic Church*, New York, 1996, 260.

[2] The Catechism of the Catholic Church, 492, London, 1994.

of her mother. This freedom from original sin extends not to original sin alone, for Mary is entirely without sin, both original and actual.

In terms of the conception of Fāṭima in the womb of her mother, Muhammad's wife Khadīja, there is no hint of an 'immaculate conception' found within the strands of Islamic tradition. But there are transmitters of traditions who invoke a scenario suggestive of a heavenly origin for Fāṭima. Majlisī,[3] for example, records a number of *aḥādīth* in the following vein: that Muhammad is reported to have said that on the night of the *mi'rāj*, when he reached the sixth heaven, Gabriel took his hand and led him into Paradise. There he saw a tree of light, in front of which stood two angels. On the tree he beheld some fragrant dates, one of which he ate, and it became sperm in his loins. When he returned to earth he had intercourse with Khadīja, and she became pregnant with Fāṭima. Fāṭima is thus a human 'houri', because she has the characteristics and moral attributes of a virgin of Paradise and the appearance of a human female form. Muhammad adds that whenever he is near Fāṭima, he smells the odour of Paradise.[4] This divine intervention in the conception of Fāṭima is further accentuated by more than one *ḥadīth* which speaks of her creation from divine light. In fact, a number of traditions assert that God created Muhammad, 'Alī and their descendants before heaven and earth. An example of these comes from the sixth Imām, Ja'far al-Ṣādiq, instructing one of his disciples (al-Mufaḍḍal) about verse 72 of the thirty-eighth chapter of the Qur'ān:

> God (blessed and exalted be He) created the spirits (of men) two thousand years before their bodies. He made the spirits of Muhammad, 'Alī, Fāṭima, Ḥasan and Ḥusayn and of the other imāms the highest and noblest of all. God manifested them to the heavens, earth and mountains and their light dazzled them. He then said to the heavens, earth and mountains: 'These are my beloved ones, my friends and my proofs over my creation and the imams of my human creatures ... For those who love them I created my Paradise,

---

[3] Muḥammad Bāqir al-Majlisī al-Iṣfahānī (d. 1110/1700), the author, amongst other works, of *Biḥār al-anwār*.

[4] For this *ḥadīth*, see for example Muḥammad al-Majlisī, *Biḥār al-anwār*, volume 4, chapter 3, 236.

and for them that oppose them and show enmity towards them, I created my fire.'[5]

More essential in terms of a contrast with Mary is the theology of Fāṭima's impeccability. Like Mary, she is deemed to be sinless, although this is a later development in the theology surrounding her person. She is pure (*ṭāhir* or *muṭahhar*), purified by God with the same purification given to Maryam in the Qur'ān (cf. Q. 3: 42) by virtue of her membership of the 'people of the cloak'[6] and thus the 'people of the house' (the family of the Prophet). This divine favour covered her with purity and holiness whilst still in the womb of her mother Khadīja.

2

The Church has ever taught that Jesus was conceived in the womb of Mary solely by the power of the Holy Spirit, without even a hint of human involvement or intervention. This teaching is precisely articulated by the angel's words to Joseph: '*That which is conceived in her is of the Holy Spirit*'[7] and a fulfilment of the prophecy of Isaiah: '*Behold, a virgin shall conceive and bear a son.*'[8] The doctrine of the virgin birth is extended to embrace Mary's perpetual virginity: that is, she remained a virgin before, during and after the birth of Jesus. To Mary the Church gives the title *Aeiparthenos*, ('Ever-Virgin'), insisting that the New Testament references to the 'brethren of Jesus'[9] refer to close relatives, in accordance with Old Testament custom and usage.

While there is no hint of a virgin birth (at least in the conventional manner of understanding such a term) in the case of Fāṭima's conception of al-Ḥusayn, two factors are noteworthy: the first concerns the miracles surrounding his conception and birth, and the second is her title 'virgin' *(batūl)*. The birth (and martyrdom) of al-Ḥusayn are announced to Muḥammad by Gabriel, in a tradition recorded by, among others, al-Qummī:

---

[5] Shaykh al-Ṣadīq ibn Bābawayh al-Qummī, *Kitāb Ma'ānī al-Akhbār*, Tehran, 1959, 108-9.
[6] *Ahl al-kisā'*, comprising Muḥammad, 'Alī, Fāṭima, al-Ḥasan and al-Ḥusayn. Cf. Q. 33: 33.
[7] Matthew 1: 20.
[8] Isaiah 4: 14 quoted in Matthew 1: 23.
[9] For example, Mark 3: 31-35, 1 Corinthians 9: 5 and Galatians 1: 19.

Gabriel said: 'O Muḥammad, thy Lord sends thee greetings
and informs thee that a child shall be born to thee from
Fāṭima who shall be slain by thy community after thee.'[10]

In Shīʿa piety, Fāṭima remains the sorrowful mother whose
short life is made immeasurably more bitter by the foreknowledge of
the murder of her son al-Ḥusayn, the prediction of which is evocative
of the dire predictions made by Simeon to Mary in the temple—*You
see this child: he is destined for the fall and for the rising of many in Israel,
destined to be a sign that is rejected—and a sword will pierce your own soul
too* ...[11] The nativity of al-Ḥusayn, as it is depicted even by the earliest
writers, sets forth his supernatural character. Shīʿa tradition holds that,
like Jesus, he was only in the womb for sixth months.[12] Fāṭima retreats
from all human contact during her confinement: while she is fed with
heavenly sustenance, requires no lamp even on the darkest night and is
visited by angels, her infant son audibly praises God in her womb.
When he is born, God sends a houri to be her midwife: and an angel
visiting the Prophet declares Fāṭima *the pure one, who is like the Virgin
Mary, the daughter of ʿImrān.*[13] More than one author, desiring to
accentuate these miracles, states that when al-Ḥusayn was born, his
mother was clean and pure, untouched by the impurities of childbirth.[14]
It is partly in this concept that we begin to understand her title 'virgin',
given to her despite clear evidence of sexual intercourse and childbirth.
Quite clearly, the stress laid upon physical virginity in Christianity
does not concur with the Islamic understanding. Fāṭima's virginity lies
in her lack of menstruation. While some traditions hold that this is the
very meaning of her name—that she has been 'weaned' or 'separated'
(the root meaning of her name) from menses—others clarify the
meaning of her virginity. A number of Shīʿa authors record traditions
insisting that Fāṭima was freed from menstruation by God (for such a

---

[10] Cf. Jaʿfar b. Muḥammad b. Qawlawayh al-Qummī, *Kāmil al-Ziyārāt,* Najaf, 1937, 56-7.

[11] Luke 2: 34-35.

[12] Cf. al-Majlisī, *Biḥār al-anwār*, volume 14, 207.

[13] Aḥmad al-Makkī al-Khawārizmī, *Maqtal al-Ḥusayn*, Najaf, 1948, 161.

[14] Cf. Abū al-Ḥasan al-Masʿūdī al-Dihlī, *Ithbāt al-walīyah li-l-Imām ʿAlī bin Abī Ṭālib*, Najaf,
1954, 159-60. Some contemporary scholars doubt the authenticity of this historical work.

phenomenon did not befit the daughter of the Prophet) and that she shed no blood in childbirth.[15]

3

> Worn out with grief, Mary, the ewe, seeing her own lamb taken to the slaughter, followed with the other women and cried: 'Where are you going, my child? For whose sake are you finishing this swift race?' Mary cried thus, from her heavy grief; and as she wailed and wept in her very deep sorrow, her son turned to her and said: 'Why, mother, do you weep?[16]

There is perhaps no area where Mary and Fāṭima are more closely united than in that of grief. Although the image of Mary as the 'Lady of Sorrows' with her inconsolable weeping was eagerly seized upon by medieval mystics such as John Tauler (d. 1360) and Henry Suso (d. 1366), it is in fact a devotion that predates them and finds its roots in Scripture. A sufficient number of Gospel passages suggest the hardship, grief and suffering of Mary's life: the dire prophecy of Simeon (Luke 2: 34-5), the flight into Egypt (Matthew 2: 13-21) and the whole Calvary event where she shares intensely in the sufferings of Christ (John 19: 17-42). It is here that Mary's sorrows, spread throughout her life, reached their climax as, standing beneath the cross of her Son, she offered her suffering as a participation in the redemptive act. Other events from which her sorrows may be inferred are the physical difficulties surrounding Jesus' birth, the massacre of the innocents, Jesus' loss for a period of three days and the threats against his life. Long before the medieval mystics, with their stress on suffering and asceticism, other theologians were already pondering the grief and suffering of Mary. These include the 5th-century Abbot Poeman in his 'Apothegms'

---

[15] These authors include al-Majlisī in *Biḥār al-anwār*, Shaykh al-Ṣadīq b. Bābawayh al-Qummī in *Man lā yaḥḍuruhu al-faqīh* and *Kitāb al-amālī*, Muḥammad b. ʿAlī al-Ḥusayn al-Ḥurr al-ʿĀmilī in *Wasāʾil al-shīʿa* and finally in the *Ṣaḥīfat al-Riḍā* attributed to the Eighth Imām. Suffice to say that it is a well-documented tradition.

[16] Romanos the Melodist, 'Mary at the Cross', in Constantine Trypanis, trans., *The Penguin Book of Greek Verse*, Harmondsworth, Middlesex, 1971.

('Would that I could weep with her always'), the 4th century Ephrem the Syrian and the 6th century Romanos the Melodist, quoted above. Later writers and theologians who took up this image and devotion were St Bonaventure (d. 1274), St Albert the Great (d. 1280), Jacopone da Todi (d. 1306) and St Alphonsus di Liguori (d. 1787). Nor is this theme absent in the contemporary Church: in recent Marian apparitions such as La Salette (1846), Fatima (1914), Sicily (1953) and Japan (1973), Mary was reported to have been weeping. Pope John Paul, speaking in 1984, insisted that:

> Our Lady's tears belong to the order of signs: they testify to the presence of the Mother in the Church and in the world. A mother weeps when she sees her children threatened by evil, be it spiritual or physical. Mary weeps when sharing in Christ's tears over Jerusalem, or at the tomb of Lazarus or finally on the way of the Cross.[17]

A recent authoress has given a fresh interpretation to Mary's sorrows, elements of which are already to be found in the writings of Pope Paul VI:[18]

> Mary is the woman butchered in Rwanda, the Muslim woman raped and brutalized and left pregnant by soldiers, the single mother on welfare, working at subsistence wages, raising her children without help from the church or community or her ex-husband. She is all the women, one third of the world's population always on the move, fleeing from starvation, war, and disasters of flood, earthquake, and draught. She is the woman who mourns the slaughter of the children, the executions of the state, the torture and disappearances of men and women. She is the shadow of the old ones battered or shunted aside, institutionalized or left on the streets to wander and scavenge for a living ... She is the one who belongs to those who have no one else.

---

[17] Pope John Paul 11, homily in Syracuse, Sicily, 6 November 1994.
[18] Pope Paul V1, Apostolic Exhortation for the Right Ordering and Development of Devotion to the Blessed Virgin Mary (Marialis Cultus), 2 February 1974.

She is the one who mourns injustice, violence, insensitivity, and selfishness. She is both victim and advocate. She is singer and crier for an end to evils and unnecessary hurt.[19]

Of fundamental importance to Shī'a piety is the grief and lament of Fāṭima al-Zahrā' (the Radiant), who in her weakness, suffering and sorrow has become an archetypal figure for Shī'a Islām in all its history of anticipation and frustration. Both in this world and in the world to come, and until the Day of Resurrection, she is considered as the Mistress of the House of Sorrows *(bayt al-aḥzān)*, where even now she grieves over her slain son. Not the angels alone, but all of creation shares her incessant weeping, as recorded in a tradition attributed to the sixth Imām, Ja'far al-Ṣādiq:

For truly Fāṭima continues to weep for him, sobbing so loudly that hell would utter such a loud cry which, had its keepers not been ready for it ... its smoke and fire would have escaped and burned all that is on the face of the earth. Thus they contain hell as long as Fāṭima continues to weep ... for hell would not calm down until her loud weeping had quieted ... the angels too weep for the weeping of Fāṭima, praising God and invoking his mercy.[20]

Most Shī'a sources depict Fāṭima in the last days of her short and difficult life weeping inconsolably, not only over the death of her father the Prophet but also over the injustices and rough treatment meted out to her (and to the household of the Prophet) after Muḥammad's death. So much did she sob and cry that, it is said, the citizens of Medina protested to 'Alī that her wailing disturbed them. Fāṭima then took to going to the graveyard to weep at night and, some traditions report, was consoled by an angel. Now, in Paradise, her lament continues: there, she weeps incessantly over her martyred son and over the ongoing sufferings of her community. It is precisely her tears that will enkindle the wrath of God against the murderers of al-Ḥusayn, and win His mercy and forgiveness for her Shī'a. Here, she represents a sorrowing correlation

[19] Megan McKenna, *Mary, Shadow of Grace*, Maryknoll, 1995, 4.
[20] Al-Qummī, *Kāmil al-Ziyārāt*, 82–3.

between the people of the house *(ahl al-bayt)* and their devotees. As one author notes,

> All things weep in emulation of her tears, and the tears of the faithful here on earth are but a way of sharing in her sorrows and a means of bringing consolation to her broken heart.[21]

Her heart is principally broken by the murder of her son at Karbalā'. This definitive event at such a critical hour of Islamic history is purported by the Shī'a to be *'the greatest suffering and redemptive act in history'*.[22] This redemptive act is sustained or extended and shared in by the grief and mourning of his devotees, the faithful community. Not only humanity, but also the whole of creation shares in this sorrowing and, consequently, in the power of intercession on the Day of Judgment *(yawm al-dīn)*. The intercessory prerogatives of Fāṭima are assured for those who wept with her and for her over the killing of Imām al-Ḥusayn. But as McKenna, quoted above, gives a fresh interpretation to the sufferings of Mary, so too Fāṭima, the weak and sorrowing daughter of the Prophet, has been 'reinterpreted' for contemporary times:

> Fatima acts as a halo for the visages of all the oppressed who later became the multitudes of Islam. All of the usurped, extorted, oppressed sufferers, all of those whose rights have been destroyed and sacrificed by pressure and force, and have been deceived had the name Fatima for a slogan. The memory of Fatima grew with the love, emotions and wonderful faith of men and women who throughout the history of Islam fought for freedom and justice ... she inspires the seekers of justice, the resisters of oppression, cruelty, crime and discrimination. Fatima is the woman that Islam wants a woman to be.[23]

---

[21] Mahmoud Ayoub, *Redemptive Suffering in Islam*, The Hague, 1978, 144.

[22] Peter Chelkowski, 'Ashura' in *The Oxford Encyclopedia of the Modern Islamic World*, Volume 1, Oxford, 1995, 141.

[23] 'Alī Shariatī, *Red Shi'ism*, Tehran, 1979, 4.

But for the Shī'a, the gloom and sorrow that comprised Fāṭima's brief and difficult life are amply rewarded in Paradise where, in addition to the honour and status accorded her, she is given powerful intercessory prerogatives by God as a reward for the sufferings inflicted upon her. The first, together with her husband, to enter Paradise and the head, according to traditions found in both Sunnī and Shī'a sources, of all the women there, her great personality will be made manifest on the Day of Resurrection, as by her prayers she saves her Shī'a from the Fire.

4

Taken up into heaven, she ... by her manifold intercession continues to procure for us the gifts of eternal salvation. Therefore the blessedVirgin is invoked in the Church under the titles of advocate, helper, benefactress and mediatrix. This, however, is understood in such a way that it neither takes away anything from nor adds anything to the dignity and efficacy of Christ the one Mediator.[24]

The intercessory role of Mary is quite clearly evident in the New Testament, in the account of the wedding at the Cana,[25] where by her intercession she initiated the first of Christ's miracles recorded by St John, and in her prayerful presence in the early Church, especially with the Apostles before the day of Pentecost. Having been assumed into heaven and clothed in unsurpassed glory as Queen, far from putting aside this mediatory role, she continues to exercise a mission of intercession for the salvation of all her children. While there remains only one Mediator between God and humankind—Jesus Christ[26]—the Church insists that

Mary's function as mother of humankind in no way obscures or diminishes this unique mediation of Christ ... it flows forth from the superabundance of the merits of Christ, rests

---

[24] Dogmatic Constitution on the Church (Lumen Gentium), number 62. Cf. ed. A Flannery, *Vatican Council 11. Constitutions and Decrees*, New York, 1996, 62.

[25] John 2: 1-10.

[26] Cf. 1 Timothy 2: 5-6.

on his mediation, depends entirely upon it and draws all its power from it.[27]

Faith in her intercessory power is expressed from earliest Christian times and is found articulated, for example, in the first extant prayer to Mary, the Greek text of the 3rd-century prayer *Sub tuum praesidium.*

> It was reported that when she heard that her father was giving her in marriage, and had fixed dirhams as a dowry for her, she said: O Messenger of God, the girls of the people are given in marriage with dirhams, and what is the difference between me and them? I ask you to return them, and to ask God the Most High to make my dowry intercession for the sinful of your community. Gabriel came down, and he had a slip of silk upon which was written: God has fixed the dowry of Fāṭima the Radiant as intercession for the sinners of her father's community. When she dies, I order that you place this slip upon her breast under the shroud. She took it and said: When I am gathered on the Day of Resurrection, I will hold this slip in my hand and intercede for the sinners of my father's community.[28]

This tradition, appearing in numerous forms, is not found in the major Shī'a collections. Nevertheless, it expresses the faith of the community in the intercessory prerogatives given to the daughter of Muḥammad, the Mistress of the Day of Judgment, as a reward for her manifold sufferings and as a sign of her status. In sharp contrast to the weak and ill-treated woman on earth, we are presented with a woman whose only weapon is still her tears: on earth, these were a source of embarrassment to the people of Medina, but in heaven they are intercessory, kindling the grief and anger of the angels and the wrath of God against those who have mistreated her and her community. There is a fairly substantial corpus of *aḥādīth* describing the features of Fāṭima's intercessory powers in which, at times, she seems to be given the authority

[27] Dogmatic Constitution on the Church (Lumen Gentium), 60. Cf. A Flannery, ed., *Vatican Council 11. Constitutions and Decrees*, 85.
[28] Transmitted by Aḥmad b. Yūsuf al-Dimashqī. Cf. Muḥammad al-Qazwīnī, *Fāṭima al-Zahrā' min al-mahd ilā al-laḥd*, Beirut, 2002, 113.

131

to offset the Divine command: her intercession is not that punishment should be lightened, but that the sinner be saved from Hell altogether. Sharing with the Imāms not only their suffering (indeed, their martyrdom) but also their high status with God, the poverty and privation of her life is matched with inexpressible glory. Her intercession appears to be twofold: positive, on behalf of all who loved the 'people of the house', and negative, as she asks Divine retribution for the injustices she and her martyred son suffered. Standing before the gates of Hell with al-Ḥusayn's bloodstained shirt in her hands, she will read the foreheads of all who pass, upon which will be written 'believer' *(mu'min)* or 'unbeliever' *(kāfir)*, interceding especially for those who have led good lives, but whose balance of good and evil deeds inclines more to the latter. Those saved comprise also those who, in their hearts, had love for her and her progeny, and those who loved those who loved her, as well as those who fed, clothed, gave drink to others and prevented backbiting, all for the love of Fāṭima. But those who killed al-Ḥusayn, as well as their sons and their grandchildren, will be flung into the worst part of Hell by a God grown angry at the tears and suffering of the Prophet's daughter, a God who grows angry when Fāṭima is angry, and is satisfied by her satisfaction.[29]

The parallelism between these holy women, coming as they do from two patently distinct religious cultures, remains captivating, and must surely go beyond a simplistic argument of 'theological borrowings', which would be to disallow each system an independent religious vision. Both were poor and weak in worldly terms, both chaste and pure virgins (within the framework of different understandings of such a concept: for whilst virginity has a particular place in Catholic piety, it is marriage that is strongly emphasized in Islam), both apparently marginalized (in Mary's case, this marginalization is only ostensible: Jesus appears to make her subsidiary to those who hear and keep God's word, but he is in fact highlighting her virtue as the model of such behaviour).[30] Both experience divine intervention not only in their own conception and birth but also in the conception and birth of their sons. Both are women of intense and enduring sorrow and grief, and receive prophetic warnings of future suffering; and while Mary witnesses the killing of her son, Fāṭima knows it to be a thing foreordained, and laments over it. Both, after a life of

---

[29] Cf. al-Majlisī, *Biḥār al-anwār*, volume 43, 8.
[30] Cf. Matthew 12: 46, Mark 3: 31 and Luke 8: 19, 11: 27.

hardship, poverty and sorrow are given immense status in Paradise, incomparable glory and crucial intercessory prerogatives. Together, these two women present an interesting case: each belongs to a religious system which has been severely censured for its policy towards and theology concerning women. As authors like Frithjof Schuon point out, Mary and Fāṭima exemplify absolute sanctity, and yet during their earthly lives both are marginalized, thwarted, neglected and even at times treated harshly. In the case of Fāṭima we see this in her treatment by the first caliph, who refused her certain prerogatives, such as the Fadak property left her by her father. As for Mary, she is almost completely overlooked by the New Testament, and apparently cast to one side in the Gospel. Yet both women would emerge at a later time, endowed by their own traditions with extraordinary glory. Without blurring the arrant inimitability of each, the words of Pope Paul V1 about Mary might no less be applied, at least in some of its aspects, to Fāṭima:

> The modern woman will note with pleasant surprise that Mary of Nazareth, while completely devoted to the will of God, was far from being a timidly submissive woman or one whose piety was repellent to others; on the contrary, she was a woman who did not hesitate to proclaim that God vindicates the humble and the oppressed, and removes the powerful people of this world from their privileged positions. The modern woman will recognize in Mary, who 'stands out among the poor and humble of the Lord,' a woman of strength, who experienced poverty and suffering, flight and exile ... the figure of the Blessed Virgin does not disillusion any of the profound expectations of the men and women of our time but offers them the perfect model of the disciple of the Lord: the disciple who builds up the earthly and temporal city while being a diligent pilgrim towards the heavenly and eternal city; the disciple who works for that justice which sets free the oppressed and for that charity which assists the needy ...[31]

---

[31] Pope Paul V1, *Marialis Cultus*, 1974, 37.

MYSTICISM, POLITICS, DIALOGUE: CATHOLIC ENCOUNTERS WITH SHI'A ISLAM IN THE LIFE AND WORK OF LOUIS MASSIGNON

Anthony O'Mahony

This paper seeks to introduce the life and thought of Louis Massignon and his encounter with Shi'a Islam, with Iran and with the modern Iranian Shi'a religious thinker, 'Ali Shari'ati. Massignon's relations with Shi'a Muslim tradition is one of the most interesting episodes in the modern Christian-Muslim encounter, for it encompasses a wide range of endeavour—a mysticism which lead to a political spirituality, which in turn opened up an interreligious engagement and dialogue between Catholicism and Shi'a Islam.[1]

Abbé Harpigny in his important study *Islam et Christianisme selon Louis Massignon,*[2] divides Louis Massignon's *itinéraire* into three episodes: *le cycle hallagien*—which ended with the submission of his doctoral thesis: *La Passion d'al-Hosayn-ibn Mansour al-Hallâj, martyre mystique de l'Islam* in 1922; *le cycle abrahamique*—up until his ordination as a priest in the Greek Catholic Melkite Church in Cairo in 1950; and *un cycle gandhien*—a period of political activism which ended with his death in 1962. Massignon's colloquy with Shi'a Islam started with his conversion to Christianity in Iraq in 1908,[3] and developed into a deep appreciation of the mystical dimension of politics or desire for

---

[1] See also my other studies which attempt to chronicle the encounter between Christianity, Iran and the Shi'a tradition: 'Cyprian Rice, OP, L'Islam chiite et la mission dominicaine en Perse-Iran, 1933-1934', *Mémoire dominicaine: Les Dominicains et les mondes musulmans*, No. 15, 2001, 217-225; 'Mysticism and Politics: Louis Massignon, Shi'a Islam, Iran and 'Ali Shari'ati— A Muslim-Christian Encounter', *University Lectures in Islamic Studies*, Vol. 2, 1998, 113-134; 'The Image of Jesus and Christianity in Shi'a Islam and Modern Iranian Thought', *A Faithful Presence: Essays for Kenneth Cragg*, ed. David Thomas with Clare Amos, Melisende, London 2003, 256-273.

[2] Guy Harpigny, *Islam et Christianisme selon Louis Massignon*, Université Catholique de Louvain, Louvain, 1981, 27-28.

[3] Daniel Massignon, 'Le Voyage en Mésopotamie et la Conversion de Louis Massignon en 1908', *Islamochristiana* (Rome), Vol. 14, 1988, 127-199.

justice in this world. Louis Massignon's encounter with Ali Shari'ati[4] occurred during *le cycle gandhien*; however, the themes, which acted as axis points for the relationship between these two important thinkers, had been of concern to both of them prior to their meeting.[5]

Louis Massignon: a Christian encounter with Islam

Louis Massignon (1883-1962) was arguably one of the most important orientalist scholars in the European tradition of the 20th century,[6] a dominant presence in the field of Islamic studies, whose career which began in 1900 and spanned more than sixty years.[7] However, distinguished as his career was, today his name would probably be known only within the scholarly world as related to Islamic studies, were it not for a life whose range defies easy categories.[8] He made a special contribution to our knowledge of Islamic mysticism, Sufism, and sociology,[9] and had a deep and lasting influence upon Islamic studies in general, particularly in

---

[4] N Yavari-d'Hellencourt, 'Le radicalisme shi'ite de 'Ali Shari'ati', *Radicalismes Islamiques I: Iran, Liban, Turquie*, ed. Oliver Carré and Paul Dumont, L'Harmattan, Paris, 1985, 83-118 and *Ali Shari'ati: Histoire et destinée*, textes choisis et traduits du persan par F Hamed et N Yavari-d'Hellencourt, Sindbad, Paris, 1982; Ali Rahnema, *An Islamic Utopian: A Political Biography of Ali Shari'ati*, I B Tauris, London, 1998.

[5] See Michel Cuypers, 'Une rencontre mystique: 'Ali Shari'ati—Louis Massignon', *Mélanges de l'Institut Dominicain d'Etudes Orientales*, (Cairo) 21, 1993, 291-330 and *idem*, 'Une rencontre mystique: 'Ali Shari'ati—Louis Massignon', *Louis Massignon et ses contemporains*, in ed. Jacques Keryell, Editions Karthala, Paris, 1997, 309-328.

[6]   Albert H Hourani, *Islam in European Thought*, Cambridge University Press, Cambridge, 1990, 43-49.

[7] On Louis Massignon, see the following: *Présence de Louis Massignon: Hommages et témoignages*, textes réunis par Daniel Massignon à l'occasion du Centenaire de Louis Massignon, Editions Maisonneuve et Larose, Paris, 1987; Mansour Monteil, *Le Linceul de Feu, Louis Massignon (1883-1962)*, Vega Press, Paris, 1987; J Moncelon, 'Louis Massignon', *La Vie Spirituelle*, 680, 1988, 363-379; J Moncelon, *Massignon: l'Ami de Dieu*. Thèse de doctorat, Nanterre, 1990; C Destremau and J Moncelon, *Massignon*, Plon, Paris, 1994; G Zananiri, 'Massignon' , *La Vie Spirituelle*, 138, No. 659, 1984, 226-231; *Louis Massignon: mystique en dialogue* (Collection 'Question de', No 90), Albin Michel, Paris, 1992.

[8] See Mary Louise Gude's important study: *Louis Massignon: The Crucible of Compassion*, Notre Dame University Press, Notre Dame, Indiana, 1996.

[9] Pierre Rocalve, *Place et rôle de l'Islam et de l'Islamologie dans la vie et l'œuvre de Louis Massignon*, Thèse de doctorat, Sorbonne, 1990, which has now been published as P Rocalve, *Place et rôle de l'Islam et de l'Islamologie dans la vie et l'œuvre de Louis Massignon*, Institut Français de Damas, Collection Témoignages et Documents, No 2, 1993.

France,[10] and upon the understanding of Islam within the Catholic milieu.[11] By the force of his personality and the originality of his ideas Louis Massignon was perhaps the only Islamicist scholar who was a central figure in the intellectual life of his time.

However we understand or measure the work and personality of Louis Massignon, there was a deep symmetry between his writings, his acts, and his beliefs.[12] At the centre of Massignon's scholarly endeavour was the search for what was, or is, original in a person, a society or a work. Authenticity, where present, was one of the qualities he sought: there took place what was worthwhile and essential. Such authenticity could lie in the subject matter that was expressed or in the way in which such subject matter was expressed. His interest was aroused by the particular traits pointing to a certain authenticity. Behind such originality or authenticity Massignon could detect, in some cases, a testimony and sensitivity to such *témoignage*. This sensitivity was at the basis of his never ending attention to expressions of the human soul, especially those of a religious connotation. Massignon's research constantly faced the methodological difficulty of proving that something was or was not a borrowing from something else.[13] This was particularly true of his debates with the Spanish Catholic priest-scholar Miguel Asin de Palacios over the connection between Christian antecedents of Islamic mysticism.[14] However, if Massignon could not present strict evidence, he always attempted to discover hypotheses other than those of direct literary or historical derivation, in order to explain similarities between different

---

[10] E Said, 'Islam, the Philological Vocation and French Culture: Renan and Massignon', in ed. Malcolm H Kerr, *Islamic Studies: A Tradition and its Problems*, Undena Publications, Malibu, California, 1980, 53–72; and *idem, Orientalism: Western Conceptions of the Orient*, Routledge & Kegan Paul, London, 1978, 263–274.

[11] Neal Robinson, 'Massignon, Vatican II and Islam as an Abrahamic Religion', *Islam and Christian-Muslim Relations*, 2, 1991, 182–205, and Robert Caspar, 'La vision de l'Islam chez Louis Massignon et son influence sur l'Eglise', in ed. J-F Six *L'Herne Massignon*, Paris, 1970, 126–147.

[12] For an attempt to assess Massignon's mysticism, see J Keryell, *Jardin Donné, Louis Massignon à la recherche de l'Absolu*, Éditions Saint-Paul, Paris-Fribourg, 1993.

[13] See the following works by Jacobus Waardenburg: 'L Massignon's study of religion and Islam; an essay *á propos* of his Opera Minora', *Oriens*, 21-22, 1968-69, 136–158; 'Massignon: notes for further research', *The Muslim World*, 56 (1966), 157–172; *L'Islam dans le miroir de l'occident*, Mouton, Paris, 1963; 'Regard de phénoménologie religieuse', in ed. J-F Six, *L'Herne Massignon*, 148–156.

[14] Mikel de Epalza, 'Massignon et Asin Palacios: une longue amitié et deux approches différentes de l'Islam', in ed. J-F Six, *L'Herne Massignon*, 157–169.

phenomena without any apparent relationship. For example, he showed considerable interest in such coincidences as existed both in Islam and in Christianity and sought to link them with each other or find some connection between them at a deeper level.[15]

A clear record of how Massignon reconciled his scholarly work on Islam with his orthodox Catholic beliefs is found in *Les trois prières*

---

[15] Louis Massignon's bibliography as a scholar is impressive. For the complete bibliographic survey, see Youakim Moubarac, *L'Oeuvre de Louis Massignon; Pentalogie Islamo-Chrétienne I*, Éditions du Cénacle Libanais, Beirut: 1972-73. Amongst his studies, the first place must go to his two doctoral theses of 1922: (i) *La Passion d'al-Hosayn-ibn Mansour al-Hallâj, martyre mystique de l'Islam* Geuthner, Paris, 1922, first edition, 2 Vols. Massignon continued to work on a new edition of this work until his death in 1962. After his death, the new edition was assembled by a group of scholars working together with the Massignon family and friends, which was published as *La Passion de Husayn ibn Mansur Hallâj, martyre mystique de l'Islam*, Gallimard, Paris, 1975, second edition, 4 Vols. The second edition was translated into English by Herbert Mason as *The Passion of al-Hallâj: Mystic and Martyr of Islam*, Bollingen Series XCVIII. Princeton University Press 1982, 4 Vols. An abridged version appeared as *Hallâj: Mystic and Martyr* edited and translated by Herbert Mason, Princeton University Press, 1994. And (ii) *Essai sur les origines du lexique technique de la mystique musulmane*. first edition, Geuthner, Paris, 1922; second edition, Vrin, Paris, 1954; third edition, Vrin, Paris, 1968. Now being translated into English by Benjamin Clark as *Essays on the origins of the technical language of Islamic mysticism*. University of Notre Dame Press, 1997. Secondly, there are the editions of religious texts, most of which are related to al-Hallaj: *Kitab al-Tawâsîn d'al Hallâj*, Geuthner, Paris, 1913; *Quatre textes inédits, relatifs à la biographie d'al-Hallâj*, Geuthner, Paris, 1913—including *Akhbar al-Hallâj*, which was re-edited with new materials in several editions: Paris, 1936 and Vrin, Paris, 1957; *Diwân d'al-Hallâj*, first edition, *Journal Asiatique*, Paris, 1931; second edition, Geuthner, Paris, 1955; third edition, Documents spirituels des Cahiers du Sud, Paris, 1955; fourth edition, Éditions du Seuil, Paris, 1981; and *Recueil des textes inédits concernant l'histoire de la mystique en pays d'Islam*, Geuthner, Paris, 1929. Thirdly, there are archaeological and sociological studies: *Tableau géographique du Maroc dans les quinze premières années du XVIe siècle d'après Léon l'Africain*; and the two volumes of *Mission en Mésopotamie (1907-1908)* as well as *Enquête sur les corporations d'artisans et de commerçants au Maroc*. L Massignon: *Tableau géographique du Maroc dans les quinze premières années du XVIe siècle d'après Léon l'Africain*, Jourdan, Algiers, 1906. L Massignon, *Mission en Mésopotamie (1907-1908)*, Volume I: *Château d'al-Okheïdir, Relevés archéologiques*, Mém. 28, Institut Français d'Archéologie Orientale, Cairo, 1910; Volume II: *Topographie historique de Bagdad. Epigraphie (Mosquée Mirjân)*, Mém. 31, Institut Français d'Archéologie Orientale, Cairo, 1912). L Massignon, 'Enquête sur les corporations d'artisans et de commerçants au Maroc', *Revue du Monde Musulman*, Leroux, Paris, 1924, and 'Compléments' *Revue d'Études Islamiques*, Vol. 2, 1927, 273-293. Under this category fall also the four editions of *Annuaire du Monde Musulman*, first edition, *Revue du Monde Musulman*, Paris, 1922-23; second edition: Paris, 1926; third edition: Leroux, Paris, 1929; fourth edition (with V Monteil), Presses Universitaires de France, Paris, 1955. Fourthly, there are the numerous articles in *Encyclopaedia of Islam* and the privately published and circulated *Les trois prières d'Abraham* (first and third parts in 1935, second part in 1929, republished in 1949; the fourth part never appeared); and a vast number of book reviews published in the *Revue du Monde Musulman* and *Revue des Etudes*

d'Abraham: Seconde prière, which is a meditation on Abraham's prayer for Ishmael, as reported in Genesis. Massignon stresses that Ishmael's exile took place after he had been circumcised and had received God's blessing in response to Abraham's prayer (Genesis 17:18-20). He sees in Muhammad's own forced emigration, or *hijrah*, from Mecca, a repetition of Ishmael's banishment at the instigation of Sarah. He suggests that, when Muhammad encountered the Jews in Medina, he therefore declared before God that he drew his inspiration from Abraham and claimed Abraham's entire spiritual and temporal heritage for the Arabs alone.[16] In later years, he became particularly interested in those phenomena which show a convergence or dialogue between Islam and Christianity: the meeting of Muhammad and the Christians of Najran, the cult of Fatima as a parallel to the veneration of the Virgin Mary, the veneration of the Seven Sleepers of Ephesus by Christians and Muslims alike, vocations within Islam of mystical compassion and substitution like that of al-Hallaj. Massignon, who was very interested in biography, liked to plot on the graph what he called 'the curve of life', the life stories which attracted his attention and where he also thought that there were Christic figures within Islam who could ultimately play a role in bringing Muslims to confess the divine sonship of Jesus, the Christ, if only at the last judgement; such figures included Salman Pak,[17] al-Hallaj,[18] al-Ghazali and others.

The renewal of Massignon's Christian religious consciousness was directly linked in his own mind to Islam. Hallaj, particularly, had

Islamiques. We also have three volumes of *Opera Minora* (1963), containing some 207 of Massignon's articles together with an anthology, *Parole donnée* (1962) with 31 articles, some of which are not found in *Opera Minora*. Louis Massignon: *Opera Minora*, ed. Y Moubarac, Dar al-Maaref, Beirut, 1963 and Presses Universitaires de France, Paris, 1969. Louis Massignon, *Parole donnée*, Julliard, Paris, 1962. This collection has appeared in two subsequent publications: Collection de Poche 10/18, Paris, 1970, and Le Seuil, Paris, 1983. One important edition to this bibliography is *Testimonies and Reflections: Eassys of Louis Massignon*, selected and translated by Herbert Mason, University of Notre Dame Press, 1989.

[16] Sidney H Griffith, 'Sharing the Faith of Abraham: the "Credo" of Louis Massignon', *Islam and Muslim-Christian Relations*, 8, no. 2, 1997, 193-210; Roger Arnaldez, 'Abrahamisme, Islam et christianisme chez Louis Massignon', *L'Herne Massignon*, 123-125, and *idem* 'Figures patriarcals et prophéiques', *Lumiere et Vie*, No. 188, 1988, 81-96.

[17] Jean Moncelon, 'Salmân Pâk dans la spiritualité de Louis Massignon', *Luqmân*, (Tehran), automne-hiver 1991-1992, 53-64.

[18] R Arnaldez, *Hallaj ou la religion de la croix*, Plon, Paris, 1964; Herbert Mason, *Al-Hallaj*, Curzon Press, Richmond, 1995; and Herbert Mason, *The Death of al-Hallaj: a dramatic narrative*, University of Notre Dame Press, Notre Dame, Indiana, 1979.

moved forever beyond the realm of mere academic interest to become an actual guiding fraternal force. Their extraordinary friendship 'filled the heart of Massignon and shaped his mind so thoroughly that he can be seen as the greatest Muslim among Christians and the greatest Christian among Muslims.'[19] Massignon, with his involvement in the political issues of his time, Jerusalem, Palestine, Morocco, Algeria, was not just a radical activist, but a radical exemplar of a Hallajian synthesis, old but little known in our world, of the heart and mind, *qalb* and *'aql*, unalienated from one another. This was his full achievement as a human being and the simplest, profoundest fruit of his friendship with Hallaj. In a letter to the American mystic and Trappist monk Thomas Merton, he wrote:

> My case is not to be imitated; I made a duel with our Lord,
> and having been an outlaw (against nature in love), against
> law (substituted to Moslems), and Hierarchy ... (leaving my
> native proud Latin community for a despised, brided and
> insignificant Greek Catholic Melkite church), I die lonely
> in my family, for whom I am a bore ... I am a gloomy
> scoundrel.[20]

He died during the night of 31 October-1 November 1962.

Louis Massignon and Iran[21]

Like all Orientalists, Louis Massignon is principally known as an Arabist because of his very close links to the Arab countries, although he had a good knowledge of Turkish and Persian. But whereas Turkey for him was mainly a source of documentation and research on al-Hallaj, he had very close links with Iran, mainly after 1945, which I will attempt to outline below. We can distinguish three stages in this encounter: the time

---

[19] Ibrahim Madkour, 'Louis Massignon', *L'Herne Massignon*, 68.

[20] Louis Massignon to Thomas Merton, 31 December 1960, Thomas Merton Study Centre, Bellarmine College, Louisville, Kentucky quoted in Sidney H Griffith, 'Thomas Merton, Louis Massignon and the Challenge of Islam', *The Merton Annual*, Vol. 3, 1990, 151-172.

[21] For this section I am indebted to the study by Pierre Rocalve, 'Louis Massignon et l'Iran', *Louis Massignon et le dialogue des cultures*, textes réunis par Daniel Massignon, Les Éditions du Cerf, Paris, 1996, 307-339.

when he worked on al-Hallaj; the time after 1930 when Iran became for him an area of exploration and of dialogue; and finally, during the last years of his life, the time when he was concerned with broad topics of Shi'a resonance; this will eventually enable us to assess the influence of Louis Massignon in Iran.

In Islam there was no clear demarcation line between the Arab and Persian culture, particularly during the lifetime of al-Hallaj, an 'arabicized Persian'. In order to embark on his great quest, Massignon had to place himself between two cultures, the junction of which was Ctesiphon, capital of the Sasanid empire, now al-Mada'in, i.e. practically the place where he returned to his Catholic faith and also the place where the tomb of Salman Pak, the Persian companion of the Prophet (Salman Farsi), can be found. For Massignon it is the Iranian world which realized the supranational nature of Islam to which he was very attached, emphasizing repeatedly the role, in Islam, of the *mawali* or 'adopted ones', considering himself to be one of them.[22] It is well known that Islam spread from Persia and in Persian cultural form to Turkestan and India. It is for this reason that the Arab and Persian civilisations mutually penetrate each other in the work of Massignon.

The importance of Iran as source of documentation on al-Hallaj becomes clear when one runs through the list of Persian authors in the bibliography of *La Passion d'al-Hosayn-ibn Mansour al-Hallâj, martyre mystique de l'Islam*—and also authors situated 'at the crossroads' with Arab culture: 145 of those authors are listed as Persians, plus 3 Persian and Afghan Apocrypha, and 14 additions were added in the second edition. One can also record, like him, the name of the authors mentioned in the Shi'a and Persian bibliographical sources on al-Hallaj, for example Nur Shustari (d. 1019), Bihbihani (d. 1216) and 'Abbas Qummi (17th century).[23]

Massignon undertook his research initially in the oriental collections of the libraries in Paris, London, Berlin, Vienna, Rome, St Petersburg and those of the mosques in the great Arab cities (Damascus, Cairo, Baghdad) and also Constantinople. He also made wide use of the al-Hallaj collection in Persian manuscripts in Calcutta, Bombay, and

---

[22] *Annuaire du monde Musulamn*, Presses Universitaires de France, Paris, 1955, 4e edition, 12, quoted in P Rocalve, 'Louis Massignon et l'Iran', 308.

[23] *La Passion d'al-Hosayn-ibn Mansour al-Hallâj, martyre mystique de l'Islam*, Vol. II, 510.

Lahore. After 1930, he worked directly in the libraries of cities in Iran, mainly Tehran (Sipahsalar mosque) and Mashhad (Imam Reza mosque).

He himself gave the following summary: 'Hallaj is even more than Salman Pak at the origin of the Muslim vocation which Iran fulfilled in the world for the God of Abraham, for the second time after Cyrus and the restoration of the temple.'[24] Volume II of *La Passion d'al-Hosayn-ibn Mansour al-Hallâj, martyre mystique de l'Islam,* is entitled *La Survie de Hallaj* ('The survival of Hallaj') and his 1946 study on the *isnad* or 'chains of fundamental witnesses in the Muslim tradition of Hallaj'[25] is largely devoted to locating where in Iran they survived. Important lines of Hallaj transmission can be found in Iran in two main areas, the provinces of Fars and Khurasan.

In Fars province,[26] outside of Baghdad, the main transmission line is to be found in Shiraz, namely through a disciple of al-Hallaj, ibn Khafif, who visited him in his last prison and returned to his native Shiraz where he drafted a treatise setting out the arguments for and against al-Hallaj. His Sufi disciples, the *murshidun,* secretly venerated al-Hallaj in Baiza, the native town of al-Hallaj. One of them, a descendant of al-Hallaj, a Baydawi, is said to have transmitted the initiation into al-Hallaj to Shiraz in around 710/1310.

From then onwards, the *ribat* or mystics' 'monasteries' transmitted al-Hallaj's *isnads* to each other. Thus Ruzbihan Baqli (d. 1209), the greatest Muslim commentator on al-Hallaj, found his documentation on al-Hallaj in the Kazaruniya monasteries of Shiraz to which he was initiated. This could constitute another chapter heading: the brotherhoods, their creation and implantation in Persia which Massignon mainly studied in his *Essai sur les origines du lexique technique de la mystique musulmane.* He also examines their pro-al-Hallaj (the Kubrawiya) and anti-al-Hallaj (the Karramiya) viewpoints in *La Passion d'al-Hosayn-ibn Mansour al-Hallâj.*

Khurasan province[27] was also an important place of prediction for al-Hallaj, and documentation on al-Hallaj survived in its theological

---

[24] *La Passion d'al-Hosayn-ibn Mansour al-Hallâj, martyre mystique de l'Islam,* Vol. II, 97.

[25] L Massignon, 'Etude sur les 'Isnad' ou Chaînes de témoignages fondamantales dans la tradition musulmane hallagienne', *Opera Minora* (OM), ed. Y Moubarac, Dar al-Maaref, Beirut, 1970, Vol. II, 61-92.

[26] *La Passion d'al-Hosayn-ibn Mansour al-Hallâj, martyre mystique de l'Islam,* Vol. II, 192-206.

[27] *Ibid.,* 206-240.

libraries, particularly in Nishapur: it is here the collection by one of the most famous commentators on the Qur'an, Sulami, was found, who left his library to the person who in the 5th century of the Hegira wrote the first al-Hallaj biography, Ibn Bakuya. Known as a mystic under the name of Baba Kuhi, Ibn Bakuya following a request, succeeded in having Ibn Hafif's treatise published and distributed, despite the fact that everything concerning al-Hallaj was forbidden. Soon after, the famous mystical master of Nishapur in the 5th century, Abu Sa'id Abi'l-Khayr (d. 440/ 1049) venerated al-Hallaj; but it is well-known that he was in contact with the great philosopher Ibn Sina, Avicenna. Thus one passes from the mystics to the philosophers. Among the Persian mystical disciples of al-Hallaj one should also point out—this time in Hamadan—'Ayn al-Qudat Hamadhani (killed in 525 1131) who took up again al-Hallaj's themes on Iblis/Satan and who wanted to die a martyr, like al-Hallaj.[28]

Despite the fact that the religious establishment were generally prejudiced against al-Hallaj, Massignon notes some exceptions including the Avicennan Nasir al-Din Tusi (672/1273)) who was influential at the Mongol court of Tabriz and, as inspector of the *waqfs*, had the tomb of al-Hallaj in Baghdad restored when he was a councillor of Hulagu. Tusi, the author of a prayer to Fatima, that Massignon compared to the *Stabat Mater*, considered al-Hallaj to be a saint. This view was shared much later, in the 17th century, by most masters of the school at Isfahan, particularly Mulla Sadra Shirazi (d. 1050/1640) to whom Henry Corbin, Massignon's successor, was to devote important studies.

Generally speaking, Massignon has shown that there was a very lively cult of al-Hallaj in Shi'a circles among the most fervent partisans of innovation, the *usuliyun*, unlike the traditionalists, the *akhbariyun,* who rejected him. As we know, Iran was a special place of Muslim mysticism and therefore was a key place of study for an expert on Muslim mysticism such as Massignon.

In his *Essai sur les origines du lexique technique de la mystique musulmane,*[29] Massignon rejected above all the theory put forward chiefly by Renan, that mysticism was Aryan; instead, he set out to prove that its main source was qur'anic. Massignon put forward the following arguments

[28] *Ibid.*, 176–179, and P Rocalve, 'Louis Massignon et l'Iran', 311.
[29] *Essai sur les origines du lexique technique de la mystique musulmane*, 45–50.

against Iranian influence: Iran is not purely Aryan—Shi'ism was spread in Persia through Arab settlers from Kufa; the notion of great thinkers 'of Persian origin' (due to a *nisbah* attached to a town in Persia) is false according to him because either they often only wrote in Arabic, or they were *mawali*; Persian thinkers and writers sacrificed their personal tendencies in order to safeguard the universal nature of their belief— Persians were great Arabic grammarians. However, Massignon admits that there were some Iranian influences on Muslim mysticism, through the day-to-day contact of Arab milieu with the Mazdeans and particularly the Manicheans; there also existed an oriental syncretistic milieu where the Persian influence played its role: the Manicheans notably introduced gnostic and astrological elements.

Later on, Massignon did more justice to the 'Iranian genius'[30] when he studied, in *L'Âme de l'Iran* (a collective study compiled in collaboration with H Massé and R Grousset) 'the co-operation of the Iran thinkers of the Middle Ages in the blossoming of Arab civilisation' and pointed out the decisive influence of an Iranian mystic, Bayazid Bistami who, being Persian, was able to 'engage in dialogue with God' by means of *shatahats*, extreme theopathic phrases, in Persian—although he wrote in Arabic, with a violence which, he wrote, 'no Semite, in his reverential fear of Transcendence, would have dared.' He added, 'the whole vocabulary of Arab mysticism depends on this first start, this attempt by Persians to seize the divine language through the Qur'an.' The mystical momentum of Bistami was to be taken up by other mystics born in Iran, such as al-Hallaj.

Massignon also widely studied the influence of al-Hallaj on the great Persian mystical poets, seeing in him 'a great Semite spiritual person', certainly, but one who nevertheless remained for Iran 'the heroic source of a great river of poetry as far as 'Attar and Rumi'.[31] It was through 'Attar (d. 607/1220), the author of the *Mémorial des saints*, that Massignon got to know about al-Hallaj, when he was in Cairo and wanted to read some Persian.

---

[30] 'Valeur culturelle internationale de la co-opération des penseurs Iraniens du Moyen Age à l'essor de la civilisation arabe', *Opera Minora*, Vol. I, 534-549.

[31] P Rocalve, 'Louis Massignon et l'Iran', 313.

It is 'Attar[32] who—having been a disciple of Yusuf Hamadhani, his mystical master—spread the Hallajian theme in Persian mystical poetry, whence it spread to everywhere in Islam, with the love of Persian poetry. 'Attar took al-Hallaj as model and herald of annihilation for love, the symbol of death by love which through its derivative deifies the theme of decapitation (*Bisarnama,* 'book of the decapitated'); in *Asrarnama,* Hallaj appears decapitated in a dream: 'when the body disappears, love is purified.'[33] The subject is dealt with by Rumi, Jami, 'Iraqi (the *Lama'at*), Kubra, Nasafi and Hafiz. Hafiz admired in al-Hallaj 'the lover whom the cross has attached to his desire so much, to whom it has become such a consolation, that he does not detach himself from it any more.'[34] Massignon also brought Shabistani, a Sufi and 16th century poet, closer to al-Hallaj because of his themes and images in the rosary of the mysteries.

Finally, Iran was for Massignon—still in the context of his work on al-Hallaj—a privileged place of Muslim thought. He showed that after the controversies of a theological nature on the condemnation or damnation of al-Hallaj, it was the Iranian philosophers—with 'Ibn Sab'in de Murcie'—who first saw al-Hallaj as a supra-Muslim intercessory saint who did 'not contradict primitive and universal monotheism'.[35] This is the case of Suhrawardi Maqtul of Aleppo, a master of Persian prose, and 'a passionate rather than mystical metaphysician' whom Massignon in a way entrusted to Henry Corbin. As he tells us, 'he has clearly uncovered the proper philosophical, metaphysical and ontological value of the case of conscience which was Hallaj,' working from 'direct quotations taken from the *Tawasin* and the *Akhbar*'.[36]

This also applies to Ruzbihan Baqli, an Iranian theosophist born in Fars and who died in Shiraz (1209); he wrote in Arabic and Persian and composed a corpus of *shatahat*, a true 'summa of Sufism', more than

---

[32] *La Passion d'al-Hosayn-ibn Mansour al-Hallâj, martyre mystique de l'Islam,* Vol. II, 380-406; and Jacques Keryell, 'La place du poète persan 'Attâr dans l'oeuvre de Louis Massignon', in ed. Eve Pierunek and Yann Richard, *Louis Massignon et l'Iran,* Travaux et mémoires de l'Institut d'études iraniennes, 5, Paris–Teheran, 2000, 89-96.

[33] Louis Massignon, 'L'Œuvre hallagienne d'Attar' [published in *Revue des études islamique* 1947], *Opera Minora,* Vol. II, 140-66.

[34] L Massignon, 'Le Cas de Hallaj martyr mystique de l'Islam' [1945], *Opera Minora,* Vol. II, 188.

[35] *Opera Minora,* Vol. II, 187; P Rocalve, 'Louis Massignon et l'Iran', 312-13.

[36] *La Passion d'al-Hosayn-ibn Mansour al-Hallâj, martyre mystique de l'Islam,* Vol. II, 434.

half of which—including the *Tawasin* in Persian—are by al-Hallaj.[37] Massignon considers in a 1953 study for *Studia orientalia* that the *Mantiq* of Baqli with the collection of *shatahat* is 'the most important work on Hallaj, the whole of his oeuvre and the formation of his thought.' Baqli— whose Kazaruniya relation through an ancestor of al-Hallaj from Baiza has been discussed—was profoundly Hallajian; he is the only one who commented on the *Riwayat* by al-Hallaj.[38]

Louis Massignon did not go to Iran before the age of 47 in 1930.[39] In 1930, between 20 November and 14 December he visited the Fars region, this time for a longer period, passing through Isfahan and notably (on 28 November) through Baiza, the native village of al-Hallaj near Shiraz. Coming from Soviet Russia he entered Iran via Rasht on the Caspian Sea, then went on to Nishapur to the tomb of Ibn Bakuya. In December, he went to Tehran and was received by the French ambassador Gaston Maugras whom he had met during the First World War; from there he went to Kirmanshah and then to Iraq. He gave four talks in Tehran, two at the legation, one on the Latin alphabet (on 6 December) and one on the Isma'ilis and scientific propaganda (on 9 December). Also on 9 December he talked to the Minister for Public Education on Iran's originality concerning mystical love, and on 12 December he gave a talk at the Irané Djavan Club, again on the latinization of the alphabet. He had already talked about this subject in Paris and Beirut in 1928. At the time, the Turkish example had impressed him and he was favourable to the Arabic alphabet being latinised. It is thought that he studied the subject in Iran. We know that he subsequently—albeit much later—strongly advocated that the Arabic alphabet should not be latinized, and defended this view at the Arabic language Academy in Cairo in 1953. In his report to the Ministry of Foreign Affairs he declared that 'an elite was working on [the latinization] and that several ministries had been rallied to it so that a sudden reform might suddenly take place in two years' time.' However, he noted the objections made by Persian scholars who feared for the masterworks of literature.[40]

---

[37] *Ibid.*

[38] *Ibid.*, Vol. II, 406-414 and 498-501.

[39] P Rocalve, 'Voyages et missions de Louis Massignon en Iran', *Louis Massignon et l'Iran*, 17-22.

[40] See also the example of Turkey relating to the latinization of the alphabet: Jean-Louis Bacque-Grammont, 'L'ambassade de France en Turquie et l'adoption du nouvel alphabet en 1928', *La Turquie et la France a l'Epoque d'Atturk*, réunis et présentés par Paul Dumont et Jean-Louis Bacque-Grammont, Paris, 1981, 229-256.

On 30 May 1933, he was invited by the Society of Iranian Studies to give a talk at Musée Guimet, which he did on Salman Pak, a relatively new subject for him (as he had not really 'discovered' him until 1927).The study of Salman Pak put him on track for a spirituality which he encountered, in a particularly lived way, first of all among the Nusayris (in Syria, then under Frnch mandate), but also in the whole of Iran. In his magisterial study on Salman Pak and the spiritual premises of Iranian Islam, which was published in 1934, he was to discern, according to the words of Henry Corbin, 'the presence of a more ancient gnosis, a presence which guarantees and witnesses very rightly the continuity of the Iranian religious conscience.'[41] As Massignon explained, the birth of Iranian Islam resulted 'from the ardent acceptance of a new and *surnatural* faith by a milieu of ancient culture which, in the light of its new faith, contemplates the visible universe through the illuminated prism of its ancient myths.' We know that he was to pursue this topic during the 1950s and that after looking at Iran from an al-Hallaj angle, he was to see Iran as a part of Islam where Salman Pak and Fatima are particularly venerated and hence closely associated with themes in his own spirituality.

It was especially in 1952 in his study titled 'La Futuwwa ou pacte d'honneur artisanal entre les travailleurs musulmans du Moyen Age' ('The *Futuwwa* or craftman's pact of honour between Muslim workers in the Middle Ages'),[42] that he drew attention to the legendary role of Salman Pak in the origin of the corporations and how the 'Muslim corporations were established on models borrowed from Mada'in, i.e. Persia, and not from Damascus or Cairo' and that 'if all of Muslim art is impregnated by Persian procedures it is because Mada'in, the metropolis of the Sasanid empire, supplied the nouveaux riches among the Muslim conquerors with masterpieces and specialized craftsmen in all branches.'

In 1934, he had accepted an invitation to the inauguration of the Iranian Academy in Tehran, but as it was delayed he was unable to attend because of prior engagements. In April 1939, he was designated to accompany General Weygand, who represented France at the first marriage of the future shah, Reza Pahlavi (with the sister of King Farouk).

---

[41] *Cahier de l'Herne*—Louis Massignon, Éditions de l'Herne, Paris, 1970, 60, quoted by P Rocalve, 'Louis Massignon et l'Iran', 316.

[42] 'La Futuwwa ou pacte d'honneur artisanal entre les travailleurs musulmans du Moyen Age', *La Nouvelle Clio,* Opera Minora, Vol. I, Brussels, 396–422.

In May 1940, he was appointed to the Iranian Academy but because of the war he was not received until 1945 (aged 69). He gave his reception speech on 15 May in the presence of the Minister of the Court, M Samii, on the role of the Iranian genius in the presentation of the ideas and the development of the technical vocabulary of Arab civilisation.

Here are outlined the main conclusions of Massignon's work which are relevant to our subject: 'During the entire Muslim period, the Iranian genius was far from deforming the possibilities of expression of Arab vocabulary; rather it enabled the Arabic language to unfold the definitive meaning in technical terms in order to allow them to have an international role.' Massignon also attempted to show that thanks to a cultural sophistication Iran played the same role for Islam as Greece did for Christianity. He wrote that 'Iran has been able to teach the Muslim missionaries the catechetical technique of language, as Greece was able to teach the Christian missionaries.' 'In fact, Persian compelled Arabic thought and made it more explicit,' Persian being an Aryan and circumlocutory language which does not allow the ambiguity in which the Semitic Arabic language demonstates. Thus Iranian thought was able to 'perfect the work of translation of Greek philosophy which was started in Syriac' and to 'construct Arabic's technical, philosophical and theological vocabulary starting with Ghazali and Suhrawardi Maqtul.' 'The symbolic work of Iranian thought on the concrete vocabulary of the Arabs has thus meant a gain for humanity, a recovery of its pre-eternal beauty'—that of the symbol.

Overall, despite his prejudices, Louis Massignon managed to show, as outlined by Henry Corbin that 'Iranian Islam is, par excellence, a witness of the supranational character of Islam.'[43] In the same text, Massignon follows on from a study undertaken in 1939 on the gardens and mosques in Islam and makes his now famous comments (which were taken up in *L'Âme de l'Iran*) on Persian, Chinese and Latin gardens. He also studied the role of the Iranian genius in Muslim art whose 'methods of artistic realization' (the theme of a lesson at the Collège de France on 25 February 1920 and an article in *Syria* I and II in 1921), as is known, Massignon had spent a long time analysing. He showed how the dramatic Manichaean notion of light was used in the art of Persian liturgical

---

[43] *Cahier de l'Herne—Louis Massignon*, 59, quoted by P Rocalve, 'Louis Massignon et l'Iran', 317.

illuminations ('Mani—creator and great master of pictorial art—assigned an apologetic goal to painting') and was then utilised in Muslim art in a more relaxed manner and put to the service of an inspiration.

In Henri Massé's article in the *Cahier de l'Herne* dedicated to Louis Massignon's relations with Iran, Massé pointed out the originality of Massignon's views on art and miniature were. Massignon had developed these ideas in 1939 in *A Survey of Persian Art: the Origins of the Transformation of the Persian Iconography by Islamic Theology*, which were summarised beforehand in a very short article published in the *Nouvelle Revue Française* in March 1936, entitled 'Sur l'origine de la miniature persane'.[44]

The study contained in the *Survey* which was subtitled, *The Shi'ite School of Kufa and its Manichean Connexions*, contained apart from its conclusions on the art of miniature, very original views on the origins of Shi'ism and its penetration of Iran. Massignon in fact showed how Mesopotamia, 'an Aramaic zone with a social texture subjected to strong Iranian influences', particularly Kufa—whose population consisted of a mixture of Aramaeans, Nestorian Christians, Arabs (Qahtanids from Yemen), Christianised or 'Sabaeanised' perhaps, and of Persian settlers who adopted 'Alid legitism'—was prone to infiltration by Manicheanism, or rather Mazdakism. As Massignon shows, the Muslim settlement of Persia took place from Kufa and Basra, but whereas Basra was a cradle for Sunni Islam and its settlers spread mainly in Khurasan and the towns Balkh, Merv, Nishapur,[45] the settlers coming from Kufa where Isma'ili or Zaidi Shi'ites—whose 'legitism' was complicated by extremist sects' which reflected the gnostic conflicts of the Manichaean schools—rooted themselves in centres such as Kashan, Ava near Rayy, and especially Qum during the 8th century. He added that, 'Islamic astrology and alchemy are rooted in Kufa among Shiite extremists, and their themes have played such an important role in Persian poetry and miniature ...' In poetry, Kufa moreover suggested an 'ideal of pure love which exerted a decisive influence on Persian poetry and painting.'

At the same time, in May 1945 during his stay in Tehran, he was received at the University of Tehran as professor *honoris causa* under the presidency of Vice-Principal Rahnema, in the absence of the Rector, Dr Siassi. He devoted his inaugural speech to the beginnings of Arab

---

[44] *Cahier de l'Herne—Louis Massignon*, 100, quoted by P Rocalve, 'Louis Massignon et l'Iran', 319.
[45] Louis Massignon, 'Explication du plan de Basra', *Opera Minora*, Vol. III, 75.

politics in Iran andYemen and the importance of the Prophet's *mubahala*—among the Shi'ites the episode of the *mubahala* is considered to be the 'spiritual enthronement' by Muhammad of his family.

His lectures were given in French but also in Persian. He gave two talks in Persian about mysticism, which were attended by the shah, as well as the summary (in which he was helped by an interpreter) of his inaugural speech to the Academy. In fact, he had begun to study Persian very seriously again, of course for intellectual reasons but also because the intrigues of his colleagues had led to him losing the presidency of the Institute of Islamic Studies founded by him in 1929 together with W Marçais and Godefroy Demombynes. As an act of defiance, he therefore decided—he, the Arabic scholar—to make himself a new name, this time in Iranian studies. This he was to achieve very rapidly, as already in 1947 he became director of the Institute of Iranian Studies and was to keep this post until his death (he outlined the activities of the Institute in the *Annales de l'université de Paris,* 30th year, No 3, July-September 1960).[46]

This visit to Tehran in 1945 was part of a mission in the Near and Middle East which had been commissioned by the French Ministry of Foreign Affairs with a view to renewing the cultural relationship after the war. In Iran, his mission—which he had to define himself—was to examine 'the persistence of an Arabic vocabulary of civilization and its connexion with the Islamic solidarity of the new nations being formed in the Middle East.' In his report dated 25 November, he noted that in Iran 'the archaistic reform of the lexicon is stuck' but discovered an interest for the classics (recently published critical studies dealing with Rumi and Hafiz). His visit to Iran lasted from 30 April and 25 May. He revisited the Fars region (Khurramshahr, Ahvaz), Mashhad (twice, on 6 and 23-24 May), and the American excavations of Nishapur.

In 1954, during his last visit to Iran—he was aged 71—he participated in several exhibitions for the millennium of Avicenna, first in Iran itself where he took part, in April, in the ceremonies organized in Tehran and Hamadan. In Tehran, he had an audience with the shah who declared his willingness—as pointed out by Daniel Massignon—to

---

[46] On Louis Massignon and the Institute for Iranian Studies, see Gilbert Lazard, 'Histoire de l'Institut d'études iraniennes', *Louis Massignon et l'Iran,* 7-12. The actual report can be found Pierre Rocalve, 'Louis Massignon et l'Iran', *Louis Massignon et le dialogue des cultures,* 331-339.

grant Massignon a favour. Massignon asked for permission to visit a political prisoner, Dr Sadighi, former Secretary General of the University of Tehran, a francophone, which was granted by the shah. After this second talk, the shah granted him another favour. This time Massignon asked for the prisoner to be liberated whereupon the shah replied that Massignon was asking for the impossible. The prisoner was, however, subsequently liberated, of which the shah informed Massignon. He was not to return to Iran. However, in December 1962, he was given a homage at the Faculty of Humanities of the University of Tehran by Henry Corbin, M Siassi, Fr Naficy and Dr Moin.

In recent times Louis Massignon is less known in Iran than in the Arab countries, although in university and in religious circles his memory is held in respect and esteem.[47] However, his name is nowadays associated with that of Henry Corbin,[48] who is known to have been Massignon's pupil, but whose exceptional place in Iranian studies has in some way eclipsed the memory of his teacher. Together, both of them escape the reprobation to which orientalists in general are subject. In Iran as has been pointed out by Pierre Rocalve, Louis Massignon and Henry Corbin are generally considered to be exceptions because of their work, but also because their sincerity is not doubted and their attachment to the Muslim world is known.

The memory of Louis Massignon is nowadays also linked to that of Ali Shari'ati, an eminent figure of the Iranian intelligentsia who was one of the masters of thought for the Iranian intelligentsia and youth. He indisputably influenced the Islamic revolution and inspired the current 'progressive' religious leaders. He died in London in 1977. Together

---

[47] Ehsan Naraghi, 'Massignon et les Iraniens, rencontres' and Nasrollah Pourjavady, 'Importance de la connaissance de Massignon', *Louis Massignon et l'Iran*, 23-29, 105-110.

[48] Henry Corbin (b. Paris, 14 April 1903, d. Paris, 7 October 1978), French philosopher and orientalist best known as a major interpreter of the Persian role in the development of Islamic thought. The most important moment in his life was his introduction to Shihab-al-Din Yahya Suhrawardi (d. 578/1191). Louis Massignon gave him a lithographed edition of Suhrawardi's principal work, *Hekmat al-esraq*. 'The young platonist that I was then could only take fire from contact with 'the imam of the platonists of Persia' ('Post-Scriptum à un entretien philosophique', Christian Jambet, *La Logique des Orientaux: Henry Corbin et la science des formes*, Éditions du Seuil, Paris, 1983, 41). For the relationship between Massignon and Corbin, see Jean Moncelon, 'Louis Massignon et Henry Corbin', *Louis Massignon et ses contemporains*, 201-219; Pierre Rocalve, 'Louis Massignon et Henry Corbin', *Luqman* (Tehran-Paris), Vol. X, no. 2 (1994), 73-86; Christian Jambet, 'Le Soufisme entre Louis Massignon et Henry Corbin', *Louis Massignon et l'Iran*, 31-42.

with Bazargan, Shari'ati had set up a meeting place in Tehran, *Hoseyniyye Ershad*, where he taught Islamic studies. Between 1960 and 1962, Shari'ati had worked together with Louis Massignon, helping him with the compilation and translation of documents concerning Fatima, daughter of the Prophet. Shari'ati himself translated two studies by Massignon, '*Une courbe personnelle de vie, le cas de Hallaj, martyr mystique de l'Islam*', into Persian, as well as *Salman Pak et les premises spirituelles de l'Islam iranien*'.[49] However, he only published the article on Salman; as he explained in his autobiography, *Kavir* ('The Desert') with al-Hallaj he did not want to 'accentuate the spirit of mysticism which is already profoundly anchored in the Iranians.' His published study on Salman is well-known in Iran, especially in religious circles. By contrast, although he intended it, Shari'ati did not translate Massignon's studies on Fatima, to which he had contributed.

Shari'ati, a thinker and tribune at the same time, was however an extraordinary and excessive personality. These excesses to which he gave himself when writing about Louis Massignon in *Kavir*—especially in a section entitled 'My idols' (*Massignon but-ha-yi man*)—were, as has been observed by Rocalve, judged badly in Iran. They have resulted in a certain discredit on the memory of Massignon among some of them, especially in conservative religious circles which only know Massignon by Shari'ati's narratives.

Narrating a scene where Shari'ati gives himself the role of having pronounced 'profound' words in respect of Massignon's famous comparison between Persian and European gardens, Shari'ati writes: 'It will have taken for fortunate destiny to take you [i.e. himself, Shari'ati] by the hand, one fine day, to make you sit down in front of a man of his calibre ... It will have taken for you to sit next to him, for you to pour out your heart to him, to open all windows of your soul, for you to understand finally in all its depth the gushing forth of a source of limpid and abundant water which flows and flows ... In short: I regarded Massignon as sacred [...] [He] quenched my soul and inundated my heart. More than his knowledge and his ideas, I appreciated in him his goodness which was sublime ...'[50]

---

[49] Jean Moncelon, 'Salmân Pâk dans la spiritualité de Louis Massignon', *Luqmân* (Teheran-Paris), Vol. VIII, no. 1, 1992, 53-64.

[50] Quoted in Pierre Rocalve, 'Louis Massignon et l'Iran', *Louis Massignon et le dialogue des cultures*, 324.

However, it is probably mainly through Henry Corbin[51] that the memory and influence of Massignon in Iran was perpetuated. This did not, however, occur without a certain degree of ambiguity. We know—Corbin himself told the story in the *Cahier de l'Herne* dedicated to him—that 'around 1927-28' when studying at the Collège de France, Massignon definitely reoriented his career by giving him a copy of Suhrawardi's 'Theosophy of the Orient of the Enlightenment' (*Hikmat al-Ishraq*). Their intellectual and increasingly friendly relationship—judging by the extracts of their correspondence published in the *Cahier de l'Herne* dedicated to Corbin—deepened as time went on. Of course, Massignon followed the work of Corbin very closely, right until his death. As observed by Pierre Rocalve, in the Collège de France, where part of Massignon's library is located, signed copies of Corbin's work can be found, particularly the translations by the Hallajian Ruzbihan Baqli and his works which make up the 'Isma'ili trilogy'. Corbin was to succeed Massignon as director of Islamic Studies at the École Pratique des Hautes Études, Section des Sciences Religieuses. It is well known that Massignon was interested in Isma'ilism and in the Nizaris. It is in the Nizari texts that he first of all discovered the role of Salman Pak and Fatima in Shi'ite spirituality. His study on the 'gnostic cult of Fatima in Shi'ite Islam' (in German) was dated 1938 and is based mainly on Nizari texts (*qasida* by Ibrahim Tusi (d. around 750/1350). At that time, he thought that for the Shi'ites Fatima was above all 'the incarnation of divine vengeance' whereas in his subsequent work he mainly emphasised the role of Fatima as compatient, likening her cult to that of Our Lady.

In the scholarly study of 'extremist' Shi'ism, the exchange between Massignon and Corbin covered the whole range of the Shi'a tradition. Corbin, Massignon's pupil, then worked in the areas which the master had opened up to him. It was probably at the time of the encounters at the Éranos Circle in Ascona which Corbin—who later on was to play an important role—joined in 1949 (whereas Massignon took part in 1937 until 1956), that the exchanges between the two scholars were at the height of their intensity.[52] Massignon also orientated his work to the devotion to

---

[51] Daryush Shayegan, *La topographie spirituelle de l'Islam iranien*, Éditions de la Différence, Paris, 1990; and Seyyed Hossein Nasr, 'Henry Corbin: The Life and Work of the Occidental Exile in Quest of the Orient Light', *Sophia Perennis*, Vol. III, 1, 1977, 88-106.

[52] On Henry Corbin and Eranos, see the study by Steven M Wasserstrom, *Religion After Religion: Gershom Scholem, Mircea Eliade and Henry Corbin at Eranos*, Princeton University Press, Princeton, New Jersey, 1999.

Fatima in Shiʻite circles, and the 'private liturgies' of Shiʻite women in Persia which he undertook with Dr Moin and Corbin in Tehran in 1954[53]

Their intellectual paths were, however, soon to diverge. Massignon respected the personality of his student even though he noted that within the context of 'existential monism' Corbin was developing a true 'doctrine' of gnosis, of Iranian theosophy which drifted increasingly apart from the only monism acceptable to Massignon, i.e. the testimonial monism of al-Hallaj. However, he refrained from stating their differences publicly. Nevertheless, he would occasionally tease Corbin regarding Ibn ʻArabi, the 'Prometheus without culture', these teases being accompanied by invitations to a certain humility of spirit. Corbin narrated in his 'Post-scriptum biographique à un entretien philosophique' ('Biographical postscript to a philosophical conversation') how much Louis Massignon warned him against his 'ultra-Shiʻism'; he also issued the recommendation 'not to Mazdeanise too much'.[54]

By contrast Corbin, in his homage to Massignon in the *Annuaire 1963-64 de l'École Pratique des Hautes études* which was reprinted in the *Cahier de l'Herne,* did not hesitate to outline the 'areas of darkness', expressing regret at the fact that 'clauses of intimate safeguard', 'pre-existential options which escape scientific justification' had prevented Louis Massignon from applying the golden rules of 'understanding' to Shiʻism, Avicenna and especially to Ibn ʻArabi and his school, rules which he had defined for his own approach to religious sciences and in his reserach on al-Hallaj.[55]

Moreover, Corbin noted not without spite that Louis Massignon in his work on Salman Pak and Fatima conducted in the 1950s had been 'preceded by all the exegesis of Shiʻite gnosis' which by the way he had rejected. Indeed, Louis Massignon knew that his work on Fatima to which he was so attached could be carried out on Iranian Islam and wished Corbin to realise the corpus on Fatima which he would have liked to put together (letter to Corbin dated 17 September 1959). He was hoping to leave this corpus with the library of the Institute of Iranian Studies, as stipulated in the *Annales de l'université de Paris* in 1960 (as well as a collection on al-Hallaj).

---

[53] L Massignon, 'La Notion de vœu et la Dévotion musulmane à Fatima' [1956], *Opera Minora,* Vol. I, 576, note 1.

[54] Rocalve, 'Louis Massignon et l'Iran', *Louis Massignon et le dialogue des cultures,* 326-327.

[55] *Ibid.,* 327.

Having thus—by virtue of his work on Salman Pak and Fatima—come increasingly close to Shi'ite spirituality and sensibility at the end of his life, Massignon recognised in Corbin the person who was 'in fact, closest to [his] thought, whose vocation [was] closest to [his], *sub specie aeternitatis*' 'when I go I count on you first of all to defend the sacred friendship which God inspired me with for al-Hallaj and Fatima Zahra and through them with Salman Pak and Muhammad.' He added: 'With that nuance of mine which besides you have already mentioned in your work: that I am for the *wahdat al-shuhud* and that I for the superiority of the *Fiat* of Our Lady, i.e. of redeemed humanity over the angels' act of adoration' (alluding to the fact that Corbin was a theosophical and Protestant). In other words, for the Immaculate Conception and Christ the Redeemer and not for gnostic theosophy.[56]

Massignon was fair minded and nevertheless gave homage to Corbin in his account of the activities of the Institute of Iranian Studies, writing that it was with his 'most warm encouragement and the most comprehensive welcome of the Iranian thinkers who were most taken by the Iranian "genius"' that Corbin published a series of precious unpublished texts. They were Isma'ili gnostic texts and extremist mystical texts, 'an unexplored territory of religious psychology to be investigated'. In what is a significant acknowledgement, Massignon even went as far as considering that 'it was for [him] the expansion of this 'participation of liking' which had linked [him] with the meditations of the Persian pilgrims in Iraq, before their *atabat 'aliya*, their supreme monuments, Salman Pak, and al-Hallaj, and the martyrs of Kerbela.' Thus in 1960 the master gave his blessing to his student's work on extremist Shi'ism and even went so far as to recognise them as being an extension of his own work.

To finish I will entrench myself behind Louis Massignon, a Massignon whose whole work—as has just been seen—is marked by the mutual penetration of his work on the Arab and Iranian civilisation.

As he wrote in 1960, 'It is as director of the Institute of Iranian Studies, by the diffraction of *Iranian* cultural themes and motifs [emphasis added by him] that the whole of the Muslim world has elaborated an aesthetic which is common to the various Islamic nations and even an

---

[56] *Ibid.*, 327–328.

'Oriental' philosophy [term borrowed from Suhrawardi] which is distinct from classical Greek–Arab philosophy.'[57]

Louis Massignon and Shi'a Islam—a spiritual encounter[58]

Two contradictory accusations have been levelled against Massignon concerning Shi'ism.[59] On the one hand, some of his former pupils such as Corbin have criticized him for neglecting Shi'ism, for not emphasising the thoughts of Avicenna and Ibn 'Arabi sufficiently and for thus having been too respectful of Sunni orthodoxy. On the other hand, numerous orientalists have accused him of showing an intent and almost unhealthy interest in secondary or accessory aspects of Islam, in the extremist and hermetic sects, such as the Yazidis, Qarmatis, Nusayris, Isma'ilis and Druze which do not strictly speaking stem from Shi'ism but are rather part of the larger Shi'ite family. [60] It is his concept of history which is questioned: his detractors consider that an understanding of history as a witness and not as science, an attempt to make it 'speak' is metahistory, even metapsychology.[61]

---

[57] *Ibid.*, 328–329.

[58] Again I am indebted to the work of Pierre Rocalve, 'Louis Massignon, Le Shi'isme et les sectes', *Place et rôle de l'Islam et de l'Islamologie dans la vie et l'œuvre de Louis Massignon*, Institut Français de Damas, Collection Témoignages et Documents, No 2, 1993, 67-84.

[59] Michel Boivin, 'Ghulât et chi'ite salmanien chez Louis Massignon' and Pierre Lory, 'L'islam chi'ite dans l'oeuvre de Louis Massignon' *Louis Massignon et l'Iran*, 77-88.

[60] See the very interesting study on a contemporary 'Alawite thinker by the Chaldean Christian and Jesuit scholar Antoine Audo, SJ, *Zaki al-Arsouzi, une arabe face a la modernite*, Dar el-Machreq, Beirut, 1988 with regard to his remarks on Louis Massignon and his understanding of the 'Alawite tradition.

[61] Massignon held a view of history, which sees the handing on of knowledge of God from one individual to another as the only significant process and therefore most deserving of study. Louis Massignon developed a theme of history in which the meaning of history is to be found not in the impersonality of social evolution, but in the divine word in the individual seed. Such encounters can take place within the ordered framework of an established tradition: but they can also be sudden confrontations: the unexpected 'Other' breaks in on ordinary life, shattering and transforming it. In a moment of illumination a man can transcend his worldly images and see beyond them another beauty. History is a chain of witnesses entering each others' lives as carriers of a truth beyond themselves, and a chain which can run across the habitual frontiers of different religions. Massignon believed that he himself had been drawn into this chain, in an event of which it is difficult to accept all the details as he has described them, but which certainly decided the direction of his life. The event was his initiation as a witness, a participant in the mystery of substitution, by which a man can provide for others what they cannot obtain for themselves. Having acquired through Muslims the knowledge of transcendence, how could he himself serve as a channel through which they could come to knowledge of incarnation?

In fact, Massignon sensed that Shi'ism would have a major place in the contemporary world, and he was right. Since his death Shi'ism has asserted itself more explicitly religiously and politically in the world. It is obvious that Massignon would have judged the current trends and currents of Shi'ism in Iran, Lebanon, even in Saudi Arabia, in Bahrain and in Pakistan in a way which it is not our place to imagine, but it surely would have been very different from what can currently be read on this matter.[62]

We have Massignon's lectures and his *oeuvre* to examine his position regarding Shi'ism; but we can also, through his life and his writings, try to understand the reasons for what some considered to be reservations and some, an excessive complacency but which was definitely a unity of spiritual affinities.

The Islamic specialist Massignon placed himself in the great tradition of studies of 'orthodox' Sunni Islam and his chief concern was to demonstrate a mystical dimension in the tradition and that it was essentially Sunni in character. But, be it through his principal research topic, al-Hallaj, or in the remainder of his work—his lectures at the Collège de France and at the École des Hautes Études, his continual visits to Iran, Syria and Lebanon—he was confronted with Shi'ism at all crossroads of his life, scholarly, spiritual and political.

First of all, he studied Shi'ism in relation to al-Hallaj, either in order to situate the latter within Shi'ism, or as a historian in order to outline the historical context at the time of the 'Abbasids. Massignon showed that al-Hallaj was Sunni. However, the question of his relationship with Shi'ism and especially with the extremist Shi'a sects came up both at the beginning and at the end of his life. Al-Hallaj was born in Persia, in Baiza near Ahvaz, a Shi'a area, and may therefore have been Shi'a initially. Although he was ostensibly Sunni, al-Hallaj preached before the Imamites—let us not forget the place of the Shi'ites at the 'Abbasid court which was the object of several works by Massignon;[63] and his numerous trips to Persia and Afghanistan meant that al-Hallaj passed off as Shi'a. When al-Hallaj was first arrested near

---

[62] However see the interesting studies by Nikki R Keddie, 'Shi'ism and Revolution', in *Religion, Rebellion, Revolution*, ed. Bruce Lincoln, Macmillan, London, 1995, 157-182; Na E Kohlberg, 'The Evolution of the Shi'a', *The Jerusalem Quarterly*, no. 27, 1983, 109-126.

[63] Louis Massignon, 'Les origines shi'ites de la familie vizirale des Banu l'Furât'; *Opera Minora*, Vol. I, pp. 484-487; 'Cadis et naqibs bagdadiens' *Opera Minora*, Vol. I, 258-265.

Wasit at the beginning of his career as preacher (272-273) he was taken for a Zaydi or Qarmati spy.

Massignon considers that al-Hallaj was initially sensitive to Fatimid Isma'ilism and notes that he 'used without hesitation the terminology of his Salmanian Shi'a adversaries to set it right and sublimate it.'[64] He drafted a long list of Hallajian terms of Qarmati origin, noting that al-Hallaj 'warped' them (cf *Riwaya* XXV by al-Hallaj).[65] And 'certain apocalyptic words attributed to Ali deified by extremist Shiites seem to have been used by Hallaj in his own name.'[66] His vocabulary, he explained, 'like the Isma'ili vocabulary often borrows technical terms from Siniya.'[67] Al-Hallaj's teaching on the imminence of the judgement was, in any case, very close to the *raja'*—the Shi'a theory of return.

The sentencing of al-Hallaj—his trial—brought highly complex motifs into play. However, one of the key features of his sentencing is within the context of one of the great theological debates of the time which itself relates to Qarmati effervescence: the *qibla* in Mecca. For al-Hallaj, the pilgrimage was an internal prayer and not a great ostentatious gathering. Yet did not the carrying-off of the black stone by the Qarmatis take place in 317/930, that is eight years after al-Hallaj's death? Massignon studied the role of the Qarmatis in the weakening of the 'Abbasid empire.[68]

Once al-Hallaj had been condemned and executed both the Shi'ites and the Sunnis questioned themselves—and separated over the question—on the validity of his sentencing. For the 'duodeciman Imamites' the sentence of the Sunni judges in 922 is a simple political measure which was pronounced by a usurper without mandate. However, the Imamites pronounced an excommunication order on al-Hallaj whose theory of sainthood undermined the bases of Shi'ism, the privilege of the imams and the political and theological Mahdism of the 'Alids. The *ahbariyya* Imamite theologians even classed the *hallajiyya* in the category

---

[64] *Diwân d'al-Hallâj, Journal Asiatique*, first edition, Paris: 1931; second edition, Geuthner, Paris, 1955; third edition, Documents spirituels des Cahiers du Sud, Paris, 1955; fourth edition, Éditions du Seuil, Paris, 1981, 15.

[65] *La Passion d'al-Hosayn-ibn Mansour al-Hallâj, martyre mystique de l'Islam*, Vol. 1, 246, quoted in P Rocalve, 'Louis Massignon, Le Shi'isme et les sectes', 68.

[66] *La Passion d'al-Hosayn-ibn Mansour al-Hallâj, martyre mystique de l'Islam*, Vol. 1, 156, quoted in P Rocalve, 'Louis Massignon, Le Shi'isme et les sectes', 68.

[67] Rocalve, 'Louis Massignon, Le Shi'isme et les sectes', 67.

[68] *Ibid.*, 69.

of fanatics. On the other hand, Massignon noted that two important Shi'ite theologians, Nasir al-Tusi in the 13th century and Mulla Sadra Shirazi in the 17th century, made al-Hallaj into a 'saint' and that his cult was revived in Persia among the *usuliyyun* so much so that there is an al-Hallaj tradition in some Shi'ite religious orders. The same applies to the Babis, the Bahai, who see al-Hallaj as a precursor, not counting the Yazidis who consider him the last divine envoy. The Nusayris, however, excommunicated al-Hallaj.[69]

Numerous courses at the Collège de France and the École Pratique des Hautes Études dealt with Shi'ism.[70] Massignon, who was mainly known as an Arabic specialist and was attached to the Arabic

---

[69] *Ibid.*, 69.

[70] Pierre Rocalve, 'Louis Massignon, Le Shi'isme et les sectes', 83–84, helpfully lists all of the lectures and seminars delivered by Massignon on Shi'a themes. The Saturday lectures of 1930-31 at the Collège de France which paint a picture of Shi'ism throughout the centuries (Massignon had returned from a mission in Iran, Iraq and Syria): doctrinal and social role, geographical spread, documentation, breakdown by sect. This obviously came within his *Annuaire du monde musulman,* an inventory undertaken during his supply post to Le Châtelier. In his lectures, Massignon defined Shiism as 'proceeding from a collective psychological origin, meditation, in the conscience of some first believers, on the rules of conduct adopted by 'Ali before his election to the caliphate, on the drama of Karbala', on the final triumph of justice in this world and the moral significance of the sequence of historical events' (it should be noted that for Massignon Shi'ism is defined notably by its philosophy of history). In 1931-32 he pursued the same theme which he titled, 'Collective meditation of the Shiites on the basis of unpublished Nuseyri texts'. During his trip to Syria he met up with Nusayri friends and discovered manuscripts. He dealt with the gnostic vocabulary of the first Shi'ite cosmogonies (with their Mazdean, Madakite origins which can be explained by the Islamicisation *in situ* in Kufa of a Persian colony which was Arabicised in the 7th century). According to Massignon, Yemenite emigrants from Kufa have implanted Shi'ism in Persia from the first century of Islam onwards; it should thus be noted that Massignon was interested in the origins of Shi'ism through his interest in Kufa and Ctesiphon (destination of his first mission and of the 'visitation of the stranger'). In 1932-33 and 1933-34, he studied the formation of the scientific vocabulary among Qarmati encyclopedians of the 10th century (*Ihwan al-Safa'*) and entitled his 1933-34 lectures, 'The Islamic renaissance in the 10th century'. At the same time, he gave talks at the École Pratique des Hautes Études, department of religious sciences, in 1932-33 on 'The critique of the sources on the armistice of Ciffin *[waq'at Siffin]* of Naçr ben Mozahem', and in 1933-34 on 'The first religious struggles of Islam' according to Dinawari (d. 282/895). In 1934-35, his second series of lectures at the Collège de France dealt with the religious thought of extremist Shi'ites on the basis of Druze, Nusayri and Isma'ili texts, Druze and Nusayri catechisms which had appeared in Syria during the 18th century in reaction to Christian proselytism. In 1935-36, he studied the distribution crisis among the Nuseyris in Syria and the role of 'Ali in Islam: he provided the alternatives of a colourless personality ('a factitious effigy which through the events has been pounded onto a colourless personality') or 'a personality presenting an

---

language, acquired a wide knowledge of Iranian religion and history as a result of his work on al-Hallaj. He was adopted by the Institute of Iranian Studies especially after his departure from the Institute of Islamic Studies and became president of the Institute in 1947. He perfected his knowledge of Persian and gave lectures in Persian when in Iran.[71]

Already in 1939 he had published a study on Persian miniatures, written in English. In 1945, he was invited by the Iranian Academy and gave a speech on the role of Iranian engineering in maintaining the idea and formation of Arabic technical vocabulary. In 1951, he produced a study together with Grousset and Massé on 'The international cultural value of co-operation between Iranian thinkers from the Middle Ages to the rise of Arab civilisation'.[72] His contribution to Iranian studies thus mainly concerned the mutual penetration of the Arab and Iranian cultures. He made much use of Iranian sources—philosophers, theologians, theosophers such as Ruzbihan Baqli and Shirazi, especially for his work on Fatima. His courses at the Collège de France in fact orientated his lectures and publications towards Shi'a themes, be it on the fringe of his teaching activities or as reflections towards the end of his life.

In 1933, he gave a conference at the Society of Iranian Studies with the significant title, 'Salman Pak and the spiritual premises of Iranian Islam'.[73] One might ask whether he moved from the Druze and the Nusayris on to Salman Pak or *vice versa*, as his missions in Syria in 1927

---

authentic series of original reactions, truly matured?' He tended towards 'a very slow and restricted, albeit real realisation of his responsibilities as religious leader, more perceptible than among his predecessors.' He then studied the genealogy of the family of 'Ali, his brothers, sons, daughters, sister and their clients in Kufa (still his personal interest in Kufa) before 686, dissent between 'A'isha and Fatima to measure the part of female pressures in the family on the formation of 'Ali's mentality. He compares the *hadiths* of the partisans of 'Ali with the later critics claiming to have their roots in these partisans. In 1936-37, he held five series of lessons on the idea of the Mahdi, the case of the 12th imam and the Shi'ite eschatological accounts, with a parallel study of the Jewish, Christian and Mazdean apocalypse. 1937-38, he gave a conference at the École Pratique des Hautes Études on the Harigite sect. 1941-42, he examined unpublished Shi'ite texts: *khutbas* attributed to 'Ali on the divinisation of Fatima, on the *mubahala,* texts mentioned in 1939 in 'Outline of a Nuseyri bibliography' given to *Mélanges Dussaud.* 1944, his lectures dealt with the role of Iran in the expansion of Islam.

[71] Yvon Le Bastard, 'La question des langues chez Massignon: aryanisme et sémitisme, profane et sacré', *Louis Massignon et l'Iran*, 43-50.

[72] 'La valeur culturelle internationale de la co-operation des penseurs iraniens, du Moyen Âge à l'essor de la civilisation arabe', *Opera Minora,* Vol. 1, 534-549.

[73] 'Salman Pâk et les prémices spirituelles de l'Islam iranien', *Opera Minora,* Vol. 1, 443-483.

had—as he pointed out in his 1959 conference on the Nusayris during a colloquium held at Strasbourg University—led him to become bound 'by friendship with qualified Nusayris [...] who lived from their faith in transhistorical intercessors such as Salman and Fatima and who like me put faith in apotrope witnesses who suffered for justice.'[74]

It was also in 1927 that he discovered, as mentioned earlier, the tomb of Salman Pak at Ctesiphon and was led to assign to the 'barber of Mohammad' the role of intercessor in his conversion, similar to that of al-Hallaj: 'A personal experience (that of the intercessors) which was aborted, secret, and did not consciously emerge from the terrain of my scientific research until 20 years later'—20 years after first taking part in the pilgrimages to Shi'a sites in Iraq.[75] He was to continue his meditation on Salman Pak throughout his life, from 'La "futuwwa" or "craftsmen's pact of honour" between the Muslim workers in the Middle Ages' to 'New research on Salman Pak' in 1962 towards the end of his life.[76]

At the same time, his work on the Shi'a sects—which, as we have seen, came out of his studies on al-Hallaj—remained important. In 1937 and 1938, for the Eranos Colloquia at Ascona dealing with esoteric subjects, Massignon studied the origins and the reach of gnosticism in Islam—Shi'a initiations and Salmanian texts, gnostic aspects of Sufism. He started to deal with the subject of Fatima which he was to enrich constantly from then onwards, starting in 1938 with 'The gnostic cult of Fatima in Shia Islam', followed by 'The Mubahala of Medina, study of the propositions of ordeal made by the prophet Mohammad to the Christians B el-Harith of Najran in Medina in 631' in 1943, 'The Mubahala of Medina and the hyperdulia of Fatima' in 1952, 'The Muslim experience of compassion ordained universally concerning Fatima and Hallaj' in 1955; and in 1956, both 'The oratory of Mary at Aqsa seen under the veil of pain of Fatima' and 'The notion of wish and the Muslim devotion to Fatima'.

Massignon found in Shi'ism a spirituality and spiritual themes which were dear to him and which—in certain respects—corresponded to his own religious sensibilities. Some affinities existed, and this was both an advantage and a drawback in terms of scientific objectivity. The main

---

[74] Quoted in P Rocalve, 'Louis Massignon, Le Shi'isme et les sectes', 70.

[75] For Massignon and Salman Pak, see Moncelon, 'Salmân Pâk dans la spiritualité de Louis Massignon', *Luqmân*, Teheran-Paris, Vol. VIII, no.1, 1992, 53-64.

[76] P Rocalve, 'Louis Massignon, Le Shi'isme et les sectes', 70.

theme, and also the most specifically Shi'a one, is suffering, as well as—typically Massignonian or of his time—the reparative value of suffering. As mentioned earlier, Massignon significantly brought al-Hallaj and Fatima closer together concerning the subject of suffering, during the conference which he gave at the Eranos circle in 1955. He showed how they were both objects of meditations on suffering, both mystics—Sunni in the case of al-Hallaj, Shi'a in the case of Fatima. As Massignon pointed out, both prayed for the oppressed and for a mutation of the will of God. This compassion for the victims of evil—including the evil to come—only became partly effective in both cases al-Hallaj and Fatima, by means of a sacrificial offering. This was a vital theme for Massignon and stood at the basis of his own vocation. It is in the footsteps of al-Hallaj who partakes in the suffering of the sinners, and of Fatima weeping for the 'Alids, that Massignon himself with age increasingly placed himself in the lineage of those compatient with Islam, with the aim that one day all human beings would recognize the transcendence and mystery of God. Massignon sees in Fatima the Islamic counterpart to Mary and strongly pushed the similarities, especially the suffering and *compassion*, the oratory of Zachary where Mary vowed herself to virginity, linked with the birth of Fatima, the tears of Fatima and those of Mary at La Salette.[77]

In 1952, following a visit of the Church of the Blachernes in Constantinople, he responded to the tears of Fatima by placing the Badaliyya under the patronage of Our Lady of the Veil (Our Lady of Pokrov, patron of Moscow), the one who 'wept tears of light, this great veil on the City of Christian Triumph, Constantinople, in order to protect it from pagan Russians.'[78] 'Tears on the Greek Church, such as at La Salette on the Latin Church'. He thought that she 'would link up again the return of communist Russia to Christ and the return of Islam to Mary, "Queen of the World" (Our Lady of Fatima)' (Letter no. X from Massignon to Badaliyya, Christmas 1956). In this letter, he requested a union of prayers with the Persian Shi'ites celebrating the 700th anniversary of Nasir al-Din Tusi, a 13th century Shi'a theologian, around a prayer to Fatima, 'Lady of Sorrows', equivalent to the *Stabat Mater*.[79]

---

[77] See the interesting study by Tim Winter, '*Pulchra ut Luna*: Some Reflections on the Marian Theme in Muslim-Catholic Dialogue', *Journal of Ecumenical Studies*, 36, no. 3-4, 1999, 439-469.

[78] Jacques Keryell, *Louis Massignon, L'Hospitalité sacrée*, Nouvelle Cité, Paris, 1987, 302.

[79] P Rocalve, 'Louis Massignon, Le Shi'isme et les sectes', 72.

Fatima was for Massignon also a symbol of the link between Arab and non-Arab believers, as she is present at the *mubahala* of Medina and is the patron of the *mawali*; the Shi'ites have made the *mubahala* into the feast of spiritual adoption of non-Arabs converted to Islam.[80] Besides, Massignon is part of the gnosis in the analysis of the role of Fatima, as his first study on her is devoted to 'Fatimid' sources of Nusayri and Druze gnosis, by taking up the Nusayri work on numeric symbolism based on the numeric value of the names of Mary (Maryam) and Fatima according to the philosophical alphabet of Arab numerology (Fatima is equivalvent to 290 of the Hegira—902, the year of the Isma'ili Hegira, the Fatimid revolt).[81]

The importance attached by Massignon towards the end of his life to this Christian-Muslim spirituality cannot be overestimated. It is evidenced notably by a letter by Massignon to Henry Corbin dated September 1959 and reprinted in the *Cahier de l'Herne* dedicated to Corbin: 'I count on you first of all to defend the sacred friendship with which God has inspired me for Hallaj and for Fatima Zahra' and, *through them,* for Salman and Mohammad.' He wanted to have a corpus of Fatima drawn up by French-speaking Iranian scholars. As he wrote to Corbin, 'this corpus can be a powerful means of unifying Shi'ism and Sunnism, Islam and Christianity.' [82]

Massignon very naturally links suffering and compassion with his favourite subject i.e. *substitution,* as it is said in the Qur'an (164): 'Every man commits evil only to his own detriment. No one will carry the burden of another' (the only exception being pilgrimages where one can receive pardon for one's sins through someone else if one cannot attend oneself). Massignon incessantly researched all traces of a devotion to reparation in Islam. He did not turn it into a specifically Shi'a theme, as he found the model of the 'substitute' in al-Hallaj who offered himself in solidarity with the suffering of sinners for whom he implored divine forgiveness, and as it is in Sunni Sufism that the theory of *abdal,* or apotrophe substitutes, developed. The cosmic order is maintained by a fixed number of saints who succeed each other by permutation, a kind of spiritual pillar without whom the world would crumble under the

---

[80] L Massignon, 'L'expérience musulmane de la compassion ordonnée à l'universal à propos de Fâtima et de Hallaj', *Opera Minora,* Vol. III, 642-653.

[81] P Rocalve, 'Louis Massignon, Le Shi'isme et les sectes', 73.

[82] *Cahier de l'Herne—Henry Corbin,* Paris, 1981, 338.

wrath of God. However, the premises of *La Passion d'al-Hosayn-ibn Mansour al-Hallâj, martyre mystique de l'Islam* 'Islamic substitution', to use his expression, can be found among the Shi'ites: 'Ali was the first substitute, Fatima is the female role model in Islam, and Salman Pak, whose role among Shi'ites is known, particularly among extremist Shi'ites, was the first (or second) of the *abdal*, or apotrophe substitutes, in this continuous spiritual chain which follows the work of redemption of humanity.[83] This theme of substitution was one of the foundations of the historical method employed by Massignon whose work—as we will see—is based on a spiritual and messianic philosophy of history. In the preface to the second edition of his study on al-Hallaj, he explained that one of his basic hypotheses was a concept of history as 'real and efficient solidarity of the misery of the masses with the holy saving and repairing sorrow of some heroic souls called apotrophe substitutes.'[84]

Catholic theologians stressing that Massignon's theology of redemption is old-fashioned or at least typical of the religiosity of his age, or Muslim theologians pointing out that Islam refuses the cross, suffering and the death of Christ, undoubtedly have arguments to challenge Massignon's hypothesis. But Massignon based himself on his experiences, especially towards the end of his life where he saw the persecutions to which he was subjected because of his political activism in favour of, first Muslims and political refugees, and then of all those disinherited, as forming part of the apotrophe chain of 'hostages of Justice': 'Let us turn our eyes to heaven, towards life eternal, towards the "cloud of witnesses who have come before us"; they, *too,* have been marked, abandoned, hostages and ransoms of Justice; before time, they await us in the participation of the Chalice of Passion, in the Solitude with only the Lord, in the forsakenness of the essential Desire.'[85]

Salman Pak, the first of the *abdal* at the time of the Prophet, was at the edge of Shi'ism, one of the recurrent themes in the work of Massignon from 1927 and the discovery of his tomb onwards, as seen earlier.

Massignon was aware of the numerous works undertaken by orientalists on the subject of Salman Pak, notably Horovitz' thesis which

[83] P Rocalve, 'Louis Massignon, Le Shi'isme et les sectes', 73.

[84] *Ibid.*, 74.

[85] Louis Massignon, ' À la limite', *Parole de l'Donnée* quoted in P Rocalve, 'Louis Massignon, Le Shi'isme et les sectes', 74.

in 1922 denied the existence of Salman Pak. He entered into the controversy with great passion; basing himself on the studies by Caetani, Levi della Vida and, especially, Ivanow, whom he had met in Basra in 1907 and who between 1922 and 1932 edited a book, *Umm al-kitab*, in which the gnostic legend of Salman Pak occupied an important place. Massignon expressed his conviction that Salman Pak was an authentic person and even that he persisted in his fidelity to Christ.[86] Massignon considered Salman Pak to be the spiritual ancestor of Shi'ism, the symbol of the precursor, the initiator, the intercessor, the *'ajami* mentioned in Sura XVI (The Bees). From a Shi'a point of view, Salman Pak was the special adviser to the Prophet, his confidant, the one through whom he checked the scriptural antecedents of his revelations; for the Nusayris, Salman Pak is even the one who helped Muhammad memorise the Qur'an. He was passed on by the Prophet to 'Ali. In the Shi'a tradition, it is also Salman Pak who had 'Ali recognized as legitimate chief, the imam. It was therefore Salman Pak who gave rise to the problem of the legitimate imamate, as proved by the sentence attributed to him during the election of Abu Bakr, *Kardid o nakardid*, a kind of courteous rejection of an opinion or act. Salman Pak is also the symbol of the loyalty of a friend (cf. the prayer by a Shi'ia pilgrim on his tomb: 'May I live and die as loyal as you who have not betrayed'). He was one of the seven through whom 'Ali had Fatima secretly entombed. After the death of the Prophet he counselled the 'Alids and defended their rights.[87]

The vital importance of Ctesiphon and Kufa for Massignon has already been mentioned; they were places of his conversion but also places where the encounter of Manichaeism and of the beginning of Islam led to a bubbling up of thought and gnosis, to which he dedicated a study at Eranos in 1937. Ctesiphon, Mada'in, is also the point of departure of esoteric corporatism which went from Mada'in, the capital rich in Christian and Manichean artisans, to the Baghdad of the 'Abbasids. Popular catechisms make Salman Pak the founder of the corporations, as he is said to be the fourth initiated. He was a barber, and it was he who shaved the heads of the companions of the Prophet. All the initial structures of artisans are said to go back to Salman Pak. Today, his tomb is visited by the corporations on 15 Sha'ban. He is said to have initiated the 17 or 33 or 57 companions

---

[86] P Rocalve, 'Louis Massignon, Le Shi'isme et les sectes', 75.
[87] *Ibid*.

who founded Muslim corporatism. The Shi'a devotion to Salman Pak must have begun around 113-121 of the *Hijrah* but it is particularly important for the Isma'ilis. Massignon, who as we know was very interested in the corporations, considered Salman Pak, with his usual extrapolations, to be 'the precursor of this reconciliation of all out, and in a discipline of work in a fraternal community'.[88] This hypothesis is completed, if not contradicted, by the fact that he saw Sodom as the city of trade corporations, societies of thought whose recruitment is not done by family genealogy but rather by technical, even 'Socratic' initiation.[89]

In his outline of a Nusayri bibliography dated 1939, Massignon showed that the popular themes taken up in Nusayri manuscripts transpose 'a very ancient Shi'a tradition from Kufa and Madain, that of the *mukhammisa* [pentainds] whose legendary founder was Salman' (he also showed the role of the great Iraqi financiers' *mukhammisa* who made their fortune in the Baghdad of the 'Abbasids, at the same time being in the service of Shi'a conspiracy[90]). The Nusayris assimilate Salman Pak to the divine prototype, *ruh al-amr,* who is named by his initial *sin*. He thus becomes the *missing link* between Mohammad and 'Ali, the *sin* between the *mim* and the *'ayn*. 'It is to none better than this stranger that the word of imam Jaafar ("Islam began expatriated and it will become expatriated again; happy are those among the members of the Community who expatriate themselves to find again the Qayim"): Shi'a call to temporal heroism.' 'Because Salman is the prototype of the expatriates, of these strangers, of these *mawali* (= 'adopted ones') welcomed by Islam which have helped it advance.'[91] Massignon who, like Salman, has been adopted (*min ahl al-bayt,* 'of the family') by Islam and is a modern witness of the sincerity of Muhammad, does not hesitate to consider himself one of the *mawali* (cf. the conclusion of *Signe marial*).

In his work on Salman Pak, Massignon showed how the desire for temporal justice which characterizes Shi'ism and the devotion to the 'Alid cause and to the expected Mahdi meet in Salman Pak. The theme of Mahdi, with strong Shi'a resonance, occupies an important place in

---

[88] L Massignon,' "La 'Futuwwa" ou "pacte d'honneur artisanal" entre les travailleurs musulamns au Moyen Âge', *Opera Minora*, Vol. I, 396-421.

[89] P Rocalve, 'Louis Massignon, Le Shi'isme et les sectes', 75.

[90] L Massignon, 'Recherches sur les shi'ites extremistes à Bagdad à la fin du IIIe siècle de l'hégire', [1938], *Opera Minora*, Vol. 1, 522-526.

[91] *La Passion d'al-Hosayn-ibn Mansour al-Hallâj, martyre mystique de l'Islam,* Vol.I, 62.

the work of Massignon. Massignon himself had a cast of mind and style which were readily apocalyptic, especially after the Second World War, at the time when he contributed to the French Christian review *Dieu Vivant* as well as to the Eranos circle and rose up against nuclear power and technology. He wrote that 'The Mahdi would certainly not be a "polytechnicien" but would appear instead among the oppressed.' This is also the tone of his letters to the Badaliyya from 1947 onwards. His personal meditation was then strongly directed towards the last ends, and his philosophy of the history and philosophy of man confirm each other: the death of the individual or the end of time are recapitulations which enlighten the sense, the purpose of a life and of history. In this respect, he was himself probably closer to Shi'a eschatology and its emphasis on the justice of the final resurrection than to Sunni orthodoxy for which the end is a reminder of the new beginning, a return to the origins, towards God. The Qur'an certainly contains numerous verses on the 'Last Judgement' as Massignon showed in *La Passion d'al-Hosayn-ibn Mansour al-Hallâj, martyre mystique de l'Islam*, but this judgement is not a purpose of history.[92]

Massignon must have felt profoundly torn between his attachment to Sunni orthodoxy and his passion for justice, which was so close to Shi'ism, especially towards the end of his life. But when he deepens the apocalyptic aspects of Islam, he does so as a historian who is concerned with discerning all aspects of a subject matter which leads to a certain level of confusion. His study on 'the perfect man in Islam and his eschatological originality', dated 1948, is characteristic in this respect. He draws up an extraordinarily erudite inventory of the historical traditions surrounding the Mahdi and the Last Judgement; but he does not establish a hierarchy between the Shi'a and Sunni traditions. However, he recognizes that, although the Mahdi could be Jesus in the first centuries of Islam, nine centuries after Muhammad the majority of Muslims think that he belonged to the family of the Prophet, was an 'Alid and, even more restrictively, that he was a Fatimid. Yet Massignon was too strongly attached to the Semitic conception of Islam rather than the Mazdean-Iranian instinct which is linked with Shi'ism.

In *La Passion d'al-Hosayn-ibn Mansour al-Hallâj, martyre mystique de l'Islam*, however, he showed that the predication of the Mahdi by al-

---

[92] *Ibid.*, Vol. I, 344.

Hallaj in Khurasan makes him appear a Shi'ite, and although the subject of the Mahdi 'finds its beginnings in the *Koran*,' it was 'worrying not just for the established power but also for strict orthodoxy: it is a revolutionary and levelling spirit which was able to unleash itself against all profane privileges, especially against the hegemony of the Arab race [...].' Massignon showed that the classes of the oppressed converts (*mustad'afun*) meditated on this theme of the Mahdi first. [93]

In any case, what becomes clear for him is the aspect of social claims of the 'Last Judgement'. For both him and for the Shi'ites the resurrection was more and more a justification, reparation of the oppressions, and a condemnation of the persecutors and a rehabilitation of the persecuted. It therefore signifies the intimate union of the excluded in this world, of the deprived, with the Saviour, the Mahdi. In this respect, Letter no. X to the Badaliyya dated Christmas 1956 is significant, as it highlights the convergence of the Muslims' desire for social justice with that of the 'badaliyyots', to whom he wrote 'Let us substitute ourselves for this desire by a Mahdi which will fill the world with justice just as it has been filled with iniquity.' It is not about 'converting' the Muslims but to 'live eschatologically from the convergence of their desire for social justice with ours' (p. 20). And (on p. 16): 'We want to share the humble experience of the poor Muslim workers themselves, the experience in one day of justice, threshold of eternal life.'[94]

Although Islam from the very beginning protested against the privileges enjoyed by the Christians, for Massignon it has nevertheless never ceased to enjoin Christians to take their responsibility towards all those who are deprived, who will constitute the 'cortège of the Last Judgement'. From this theme he also draws a proof of Islamic-Christian convergence: the same desire for justice, but also the same expectation of the return of Jesus: 'Our prayer, going back generations of Muslims until the first, recapitulates through the generations the desire conceived in the masses of a Fatimid Mahdi who will bring the Son of Mary to Jerusalem for the Judgement' (Letter to Badaliyya no. X, p. 19). Massignon detects an assimilation of Jesus and the Mahdi in strains of Muslim thought throughout the centuries. These can be found in the legend of the Seven Sleepers, a cult that can be found among both Christianity and Islam—

---

[93] . *Ibid.*, 344-345.
[94] P Rocalve, 'Louis Massignon, Le Shi'isme et les sectes', 77.

Sura XVIII, called 'sura of the cave'. The provisional resurrection of the Seven Sleepers symbolises, as Massignon puts it, 'The apocalyptic impatience of the expatriates, the poor, the persecuted who hunger and thirst for justice'. 'At the end of time, he [Jesus] will return personally with the Seven privileged witnesses which Sura XVIII associates with him.'[95] There is only one congregation of apotropean saints, that of Elijah and the Seven Sleepers.'The 'sura of the cave' which is based on apocryphal texts, in fact concentrates the three apocalyptic themes, the Seven Sleepers, Elijah and Moses and Alexander *dhu al-qarnayn*.[96]

Together with the Seven Sleepers (Christian martyrs), the themes of Elijah (a Jewish prophet who is, however, common to the three 'Abrahamic' monotheistic religions), Ilyas, al-Khidr—a theme which he himself describes as 'decorative'—also has echoes in Shi'ism and—this is important in the spirituality of Massignon—is also found among the Carmelites.

The faith in the invisible and consoling intercession of Khidr-Ilyas—he assures us that he has no doubt that the two are in fact the same[97]—is deeply ingrained in the devotion of pious Shi'ites and Sunni mystics. Massignon in his 1955 study enumerates the Shi'ites' devotion to Elijah, notably in Baghdad. He even notes a 'liturgical conjunction between Mary and Elijah, symmetry of the geographical connection between the cavern of the Seven Sleepers and the "house" of Mary in Ephesus and especially of the "copatronage" of Elijah and Mary on the order of the Carmel.'[98] For the Shi'ites, Khidr will return with the Seven Sleepers at the end of time, 'at the head of the vanguard of the Mahdi's army to guide it until Jerusalem and to bring Jesus, the Son of Mary.' He announces the arrival of the Shi'ite Mahdi. Massignon quotes a long list of apparitions by Khidr in the Shi'ite traditions, to the Prophet, to Fatima and to the 'Alids, including Husayn in Karbala.[99]

In all his historical apparitions Elijah is the symbol of the spiritual director who 'entails the foundation of religious orders and the adoption of special frocks and scapulars:' the Carmel among the Latins, the order

---

[95] L Massignon, 'Les saints dormants d'Éphèse, apocalypse de l'Islam' [1950], *Opera Minora*, Vol. III, 104.

[96] P Rocalve, 'Louis Massignon, Le Shi'isme et les sectes', 78.

[97] L Massignon, 'Élie et son rôle transhistorique, Khadiriya, en Islam', [Études carmélitaines, 1955], *Opera Minora*, Vol. 1, 142-161.

[98] L Massignon, 'Élie et son rôle transhistorique, Khadiriya, en Islam'*Opera Minora*, Vol. 1, 147.

[99] P Rocalve, 'Louis Massignon, Le Shi'isme et les sectes', 79.

of the Hadiriyya among Muslim spirituals from which the Idrisiyya and the Senussi have sprung. In the Sura of the Cave, the three scandalous acts by which he makes Moses lose his patience show that Elijah is a saint who surpasses the prophet: in this account, grace surpasses Law. Elijah is the master of mystical fraternities. He 'transfigures Law'. He is 'the sign of hope in the beyond, by vows of virginity and silence, by the discipline of fasting.'[100]

Thus the theme of sanctity also brings Massignon closer to Shi'ite sympathies. Faced with the majority Sunni faith, the Shi'a faith is more eschatological, but also more devotional and more accessible to the cult of the saints which is challenged by orthodox Islam. The place of the cult of the saints in the life of Massignon is well known, as just like the *abdal,* the saints are witnesses and for Massignon history is a recapitulation of witnesses. However, we are now in a very delicate area as far as the interpretation of Massignon's thought is concerned, where his reservations concerning Shi'ism were inextricably mixed with its attractions which converged with his own thought. Massignon, an exalter of Sunni Sufism, could not follow Shi'ism in the area of the *walaya* or imamology. Sufism eliminates the imamate.[101]

However many affinities there might have been between Massignon and certain points of Shi'ite religiosity, there was also a fundamental difference, which for him was unbridgeable due to a different interpretation of the quality of the mystical. Henry Corbin, who suffered from this 'misunderstanding' (according to Massignon), regarding Iranian Islam. Corbin himself would have wanted to build bridges allowing a coming closer of his master and Shi'ism. But the whole career of Massignon was built on the idea and conviction that 'orthodox' Islam is authentically spiritual and carries the mystical. In his thesis on al-Hallaj in *Essai sur les origines du lexique technique de la mystique musulmane* he showed—as outlined earlier—that it is the interpretation, the reading of the revealed book—the Qur'an—which leads to the mystical. He explained that Sufism is the bearing fruit of the spiritual experience of the Prophet, the *mi'raj*, a prototype of mystical experience, 'ecstatic assumption'. In all his work he protested against those orientalists or Christians who see Islam as a legalistic and literalist religion. For him,

---

[100] Massignon, 'Élie et son rôle transhistorique, Khadiriya, en Islam', *Opera Minora,* Vol. 1, 161.
[101] P Rocalve, 'Louis Massignon, Le Shi'isme et les sectes', 79.

Islam is, on the contrary, a religion which is charged with an essentially spiritual message: the *tawhid,* divine uniqueness, the transcendence from which Islam allowed the development of a spiritual asceticism, the degrees of which call for metaphysics: between the law *(shari'ah)* and the mystical path *(tariqah)* there is spiritual truth *(haqiqah).* The spirituality of Islam is therefore essentially orthodox and does not need to seek refuge among 'schisms or sects'. Sufism is Sunni and, moreover, it is Arab, as the Arabic language is a carrier of divine incandescence, of mystical 'calcination'.[102]

This shows clearly what separates Massignon from Shi'ism. Massignon is attached to transcendent Semitic Shi'ism, to what he calls testimonial monism, that of al-Hallaj. He profoundly mistrusts—as could be seen in connection with Sufism—not only all dualism but also the existential monism of the Qarmatis and after them the Shi'ites or thinkers close to the Shi'ites who are filled with the thought of Ibn 'Arabi and have an immanent, pantheistic, aesthetic concept of mystical union—everything emanating from God. Massignon reproached Ibn 'Arabi, who is taken by formal logic, 'to have eliminated all transcendent intervention by the divinity.'[103] In fact, there is no other mysticism but the Semitic-Sunni one; Persian mysticism is not mystical but is a gnosis; a Semite witnesses divine transcendence directly, as Abraham did. Indo-Europeans, Persians who are impregnated with Manicheanism or Mazdeism, are in search of a symbolic interpretation of the universe, whose significance they seek using an initiation that is more or less aesthetic in nature. For Persians, Shi'ites and extremist Shi'ites, the soul reaches God through a series of initiations or even reincarnations under the direction of the imam at the time. They search for the knowledge which they want to penetrate, whereas for Sufis, the soul is reached by God directly. As Henry Corbin showed—this explains *a contrario* the position of Massignon—Sufism is not useful for Shi'ism as Sufism is esoteric in itself; the Shi'ite milieu is virtually initiational. In his *Essai sur les origines du lexique technique de la mystique musulmane* Massignon showed that Shi'ism has from the beginning been distant with regard to Sufism. After a period when Sufism was more or less indistinctly Sunni or Shi'ite, i.e. from the 3rd century onwards, the Eighth Imam used harsh words against Sufism which does not accept 'imamology', and the imamites criticize the dogmatic theses

[102] P Rocalve, 'Louis Massignon, Le Shi'isme et les sectes', 80.
[103] L Massignon, 'Die Ursprünge und die Bedeutung des Gnostizismus in Islam', *Opera Minora,* Vol. 1, 499.

put forward by Hasan al-Basri. This statement, however, has to be qualified as there was a renaissance of Shi'ite Sufism from the 13th century onwards, and most *tariqat* took one of the imams as starting point. There are Shi'ite *tariqat*. Nevertheless Shi'ism does not relate to Sufism, and although Massignon studied the Shi'ite gnostics he had no time for them.[104]

More generally speaking, Massignon only felt reluctant towards the separatist movements and the sects, contrary to what has been claimed by some of his detractors; for Massignon, Islam was above all a community *(umma)* and Sunni. In 1959, he confessed to the audience at the University Colloquium at Strasbourg, that 'It was not with my full own will that I was led to scrutinize [...] the Nuseyri religious fact. Having had my debut in Islamic studies among Salafiya Sunni friends in Baghdad, I learnt to "philosophically" side with the Umayyads against the Alids.'[105]

Massignon had a vision of an ideal Islam, rich in spirituality, in mystical transcendence in which the existential monism and Shi'ite spirituality were deviations. Moreover, he mistrusted all derivations of neo-Platonic philosophies such as can, for example, clearly be seen among the Ikhwan al-Safa', and of all Hellenic influences with which the extremist sects have been impregnated.

If one moves even further into Shi'ite religiosity one notes that it was inevitable that it should converge with Massignon and his vital commitment, especially at the end of his life. He was not at all sensitive to the profound ethos of Shi'ism, to what Henry Corbin called the *desperatio fiducialis*. Shi'ism is nourished by a gnosis that awaits the Mahdi, the Resurrection. It waits. By contrast, with advancing age, Massignon became more and more impatient to see immanent justice. He attached himself to the heritage left by Gandhi. He had a philosophy of history which was profoundly different from that of Islam and, within Islam, from that of Shi'ism. For Islam, history is occasionalist whereas Massignon—as we will see—was attached to a eschatological vision, to the notion of promise. This promise gives history a meaning and orientates it towards a centre of Messianic convergence. For Islam, history is only captured as lightning moments between two events, the creation and the resurrection, although for Shi'a Islam it can be an esoteric spiritual deepening of Truth *(haqq)*.

---

[104] P Rocalve, 'Louis Massignon, Le Shi'isme et les sectes', 80.
[105] Quoted in P Rocalve, 'Louis Massignon, Le Shi'isme et les sectes', 81.

In this area also, Massignon thus does not fall short of contradicting himself, or to be more precise, he has moved beyond contradictions. With advancing age he came closer to Shi'ite spirituality and devotions (through the notions of suffering and compassion, through the Badaliyya, and through the cult of saints), whereas his vision of Abrahamic, Semitic Islam which is always deepened within the meaning of the *tawhid,* made him divert from it. It is in Shi'ism that he found the clearest signs of a rapprochement between Islam and Christianity: Fatima-Mary, Jesus-the Mahdi, the Seven Sleepers and the Last Judgement, the Resurrection and Justice to the deprived, all themes which he exploited to the full. Like Shi'ism, his religion was more and more sorrowful, expiating. But what attracted Massignon most to Islam was the transcendental void, so much so that there is something of a dissociation, a dichotomy between Massignon's devotional obsessions and his philosophy of religion.

The same contradiction and feeling of being torn can be found in his 'cult' of Salman Pak, in whom he perceived one of his intercessors, although it was through Salman, venerated by the Nusayris and legendary founder of the *mukhammisa,* that the Hellenic infiltrations which he detested so much took place. And even in his 'cult' of Fatima, a person at the origin of the 'Fatimid' Isma'ili conspiracy, 'that conspiracy of former bandits turned righters of wrongs' that 'he hardened the legendary physiognomy of Fatima of whom they only understood her external indignation without her interior life of *soledad.*'[106]

Louis Massignon and Ali Shar'ati—a mystical encounter

The memory of Louis Massignon in Iran (as well as that of Henry Corbin noted above) is also nowadays linked to that of Ali Shari'ati. As already observed, Shari'ati, a thinker, was however an extraordinary and excessive personality. This excessive style is the style to which he gave himself when refelecting on Louis Massignon in his *Kavir.* They have resulted in a certain discredit on the memory of Massignon among especially in conservative religious circles which only know of Massignon through Shari'ati's writings. Read for example the following:

---

[106] P Rocalve, 'Louis Massignon, Le Shi'isme et les sectes', 82.

I have never in my life seen anything more sublime that this old Frenchman aged 69; I do not only refer to his moral and intellectual superiority, but also to his physical charm, making all the faces which I observed in Paris appear insipid. His white hair was cut short, with two slight tufts growing behind his ears, casting reflections of light and giving the whole of his physiognomy a divine and extraordinary purity from which I found it very difficult to detach my gaze ...[107]

In another reference to Massignon during a conference on '*Shiah, where the Spirit of Semitism Meets that of Aryanism*', Shari'ati wrote with intensity about of his spiritual and emotional links with his former teacher.

Amongst the faces, voices, views, spirits, in short, amongst the people of kinds whom I have seen file past me in the course of the years there is one to whom I am attached in such a way—I did not know, and still don't know exactly how he seduced and delighted me thus—that henceforth, I can no longer feel alone, independent of him. Just as I cannot imagine myself without my own face I cannot feel or understand myself without him. Twelve years have gone past since our first encounter. Remembering him makes me suffer more and more each day. I love him to the extent of feeling sometimes that my soul can no longer contain my affection for him, that it will overflow and that my heart is about to burst and can no longer bear it. Sometimes remembering him would seem to make all the blood in my body flow towards my heart, it rushes there attempting to engulf it by force, without success, in an impossible struggle which makes me suffer. My heart aches, my breathing stops, there is a lump in my throat and my eyes and my whole body burn. This torments me considerably; I would like to cry a little, to cry hot tears, in order to find relief, but I am ashamed to be told: 'Look at him, this respectable man, crying for his teacher! Are you a little boy in nursery, or a primary school

---

[107] Quoted by Pierre Rocalve, 'Louis Massignon et l'Iran', *Louis Massignon et le dialogue des cultures*, 324.

child? What is there to this Massignon? Is there really need
to make such a fuss about him? ...'

I fear, I am afraid that something like this be told to
me, to him, to us ... That would be terrible. I believe that if
one day my ears were to hear this, I would lose my sight
and my speech, and my legs would be paralysed. It is six
years ago that he left. And here I am, dragging on in this
bitter and painful 'without you', O my dear Massignon,
my incomparable angel. During those six years I have not
ceased to write, to talk about you: my pen has not left my
fingers one instant. It is the only companion capable of
soothing some of the emptiness which your absence has left
within me, of reducing its implacable cruelty ...'[108]

Shari'ati was born in 1933 in Khurasan in the northeast of Iran
and came from a religious Shi'a family. His father was from a long line
of scholarly clerics who in Shari'ati's own words had 'resisted the
temptation' to forsake their village of Mazinan, whose mosque they had
built, for the 'attractions' of either Tehran or Najaf. Shari'ati grew up
partly in Mazinan, partly in Sabzavar; and partly in Mashhad where he
attended secondary school and then the local teachers' college. His father,
Muhammad Taqi Shari'ati, a religious progressive, provided him with
an open and modern education during which he was made aware of the
problems of Islam and nationalism. These early years were spent very
much under the intellectual influence of his father, who was in many
ways a highly unconventional cleric. In the early 1940s, he set up a small
publishing house named the *Centre for the Propagation of Islamic Truth* and
later on in that decade he formed the local branch of a short-lived
organization known as the Movement of Socialist God-Worshippers
(Nehzat-e Khodaparastan-e Sosiyalist). In the early 1950s he enthusiastically
supported Mosaddeq and the National Front. The younger Shari'ati later
described the elder Shari'ati as his 'first real teacher'. Whilst doing an

---

[108] Ali Shari'ati, *Œuvres complètes (Majmu'e-ye athar)*, Elham, Tehran, Vol. 27, 288-289. Quoted in
Michel Cuypers, 'Une rencontre mystique: 'Ali Shari'ati—Louis Massignon', in *Mélanges
de l'Institut Dominicain d'Etudes Orientales*, Vol. 21 (1993), 291-330, 292. The enterprise of
publishing all of Shari'ati's works or *Œuvres complètes* was started by the *Hoseyniye Ershad*
foundation until 1985, however, the project was subject to numerous difficulties and was
published by various presses.

arts degree at the University in Mashhad he first came across the name of Massignon in an article of the *Revue de la Faculté de Lettres* signed by the philosophy professor Abul Hasan Khan Farughi.

Between 1959 and 1964 he continued his studies in France completing them with 'an (average) PhD in Iranian philology'. He was, however, less interested in linguistics than in sociology and Islamic studies. He attended lectures by George Gurvitch, Jacques Berque and Louis Massignon. Massignon very soon discovered his student, probably because they shared a passion for the study of Islam and for anti-colonialist action (the Algerian war was at its height during this time), but very likely also because of a certain kinship of spirit. Between 1960 and 1962, Shari'ati had worked together with Louis Massignon, helping him with the compilation and translation of documents written in various Persian dialects on Fatima, the Prophet's daughter (this project was never completed and remains unpublished).

Shari'ati himself translated into Persian two works of Massignon, *Étude sur une courbe personnelle de vie, le cas de Hallaj, martyr mystique de l'Islam*[109] and *Salmân Pâk et les prémises spirituelles de l'Islam iranien*.[110] The translation, he says took him two years, which he published mainly with the intention of providing the Iranian intelligentsia with a model for scientific research of the highest quality. However, he only published the article on Salman Pak, as he explained in his autobiography, *Kavir*, and not that of Hallaj because he did not want to 'accentuate the spirit of mysticism which is already profoundly anchored in the Iranians.' However, although he intended it, Shari'ati did not translate Massignon's studies on Fatima, to which he had contributed. After his death, the Shari'ati Foundation published the English translation of one of his talks on the role of women in Islam entitled 'Fatima is Fatima' which bears the sign of this collaboration and which, moreover, was dedicated to Louis Massignon.[111]

Does this mean that the relationship between Massignon and Shari'ati was situated at the level of influences of ideas? In order to

---

[109] 'Étude d'une courbe personnelle de vie, le cas de Hallaj, martyr mystique de l'Islam', *Dieu Vivant*, cahier 4, 1945, 11-39.

[110] *Salmân Pâk et les prémises spirituelles de l'Islam iranien*, Société d'Etudes Iraniennes, Paris, Cahier 7, 1934, 52.

[111] Ali Shari'ati, *Fatima is Fatima*, trans. L Bakhtiar, Shari'ati Foundation and Hamdami Publishers, Tehran, 1980. M K Hermancen, 'Fatima as a Role Model in the works of Ali Shari'ati', *Women and Revolution in Iran*, ed. G Nashat, Westview Press, Boulder, Colorado, 1983, 87ff.

answer this question, a more in-depth analysis would be required. To turn to what Shari'ati says on this subject in the texts where he talks of Massignon, there can be no doubt that the importance which persons such as Salman Pak and more even, Fatima, had for Shari'ati's thought was directly due to Massignon. It is also certain that the very 'committed' attitude of Massignon regarding Islam and the Muslims contributed to giving Shari'ati a very practical concept of Islamology, which he did not at all conceive as an academic study, but rather as an *ideology* transforming the mentalities and society. We should note that these 'ideas' already all have a practical scope: Salman and Fatima are examples of committed lives, which should be followed, and Islamology has to carry a revolutionary message. What Shari'ati took on from his master Massignon were not his purely theoretical ideas on Islam but his ideas or attitudes leading to action. We should also add that Massignon to Shari'ati was more than a professor or a teacher of ideas, but a *master of life*. Shari'ati is not so much seduced by Massignon's ideas strictly speaking, but rather by his *intellectual asceticism*, his attitude as that of a scientist with total integrity when facing reality, his concern for the only truth in the presence of facts. Reflecting on his years in Paris, Shari'ati concludes: 'More than anything else, the merit for what I have learnt and above all, *for what has become of me* belongs entirely to Louis Massignon who united within himself the Orient and the Occident.' In a long autobiographical letter to his son in early 1977 (i.e. only a few months before his death), he recounts how he renounced his personal preferences which went more towards philosophy, mysticism and poetry (and which could have made him into a brilliant intellectual academic). Instead, he studied sociology and history, which he considered to be more useful for the Islamic society of his time which needed to abandon its metaphysical idealism and discover concrete social realism. Shari'ati deliberately wanted to be and effectively was a socially committed intellectual. For him, it was a prime moral obligation to put his intellectual work to the service of society, a theme runs through all his works. But this choice was certainly made at a great cost:

> The *highest degree of martyrdom*, the giving of oneself and the generosity, he writes to his son, does not consist in renouncing just one's goods and one's life, but also one's own growth and own total fulfilling in respect of existence, spirituality

and science. It means making yourself available to the others, talking to them, responding to the elementary and ordinary needs of their lives.

Moreover, Ervand Abrahamian, one of the foremost historians of Iran and political scientist of the Islamic revolution and its thinkers, writes about other Catholic influences upon Shari'ati:

> Through Massignon, Shariati was exposed to a radical Catholic journal named *Esprit*. Founded by Emmanuel Mounier, a socially committed Catholic, *Esprit* in the early 1960s supported a number of left-wing causes, particularly national liberation struggles in the Third World. It carried articles on Cuba, Algeria, Arab nationalism, economic underdevelopment, and contemporary communion— especially the different varieties of Marxist thought. Its authors included Massignon, Michel Foucault, Corbin, Fanon, radical Catholics, and Marxists such as Lukacs, Jacques Berque and Henri Lefebvre. Moreover, *Esprit* in these years ran frequent articles on Christian-Marxist dialogue, on Left Catholicism, on Jaure's religious socialism, and on Christ's 'revolutionary, egalitarian teachings'. Despite the influence of Massignon and *Esprit*, Shariati later scrupulously avoided any mention of radical Catholicism. To have done so would have weakened his claim that Shiism was the only world religion that espoused social justice, economic reality and political revolution.[112]

On his return to Iran in 1964, Shari'ati was arrested and imprisoned for six months. After his release he took on a range of minor teaching posts until he was finally accepted as lecturer at the University in Mashhad. Here Shari'ati rapidly became well known. His lectures were not very academic and were designed above all to awaken his listeners to a renewed Islam, which would liberate his country from its dependence on the West. He was chased from the university by the authorities and

---

[112] Ervand Abrahamian, *Radical Islam: The Iranian Mojahedin*, I B Tauris, London, 1989, 108.

became a successful speaker at the *Hosseyniye Ershad,* a progressive Islamic institute in Teheran of which he was the co-founder. His popularity amongst young Muslim students was such that, in 1973, *Hosseyniye Ershad* was closed down and Shari'ati was imprisoned shortly thereafter, being released eighteen months later. The imperial police monitored him closely but he nevertheless managed to leave Iran in the spring of 1977; soon after, on 19 June 1977 he succumbed to a heart attack and died in London aged 44. His premature death under somewhat mysterious circumstances was soon interpreted by Shari'ati's followers as a political assassination conducted by the shah's secret police. For them, the doctor had become a martyr, a *shahid*.[113]

In his memoirs, *Kavir,* Shari'ati reflects on some of Massignon's other moral and spiritual qualities, of which the most shining example is 'his absolute, transcendent goodness'. It is this quality which enables us to penetrate into the secret of the relationship between these two men. Certainly, Shari'ati had been charmed by this goodness when in direct contact with his master; however, it is only much later, after Massignon's death, that Shari'ati experiences it afresh and in a more intimate manner. Speaking indirectly about himself, Shari'ati writes:

> All of a sudden, the flash of lightning came down on him, and in a great blazing turning everything upside down the horizons suddenly seemed different to him, the heavens above were transformed, the earth, the air we breathe, our outlook, our heart, our imagination, everything changed ... The world, man and *God* himself are transfigured—This is a new Birth, a new Life.

And as if to avoid any misunderstanding, further on in the text he explains: 'He [Massignon] was this flash of lightning for me, but a

---

[113] M Bayat-Philipp, 'Shi'ism in contemporary Iranian politics: the case of Ali Shari'ati', in ed. E Kedourie and S G Haim, *Towards a Modern Iran,* Frank Cass, London 1980; Abdulaziz Sachedina, 'Ali Shari'ati: ideologue of the Iranian revolution', in ed. John L Esposito, *Voices of Resurgent Islam,* Oxford, 1983, 191-214; Ervand Abrahamian, 'Ali Shari'ati: ideologue of the Iranian revolution', in ed. Edmund Burke III and Ira M Lapidus, *Islam, Politics and Social movements,* University of California Press, Berkeley, California, 1988, 289-297; and Ali Rahnema, 'Ali Shari'ati: teacher, preacher, rebel', in ed. Ali Rahnema, *Pioneers of Islamic Revival,* Zed Press, London, 1994, 208-250.

flash of lightning which came down on my heart after his death.' Shari'ati does not hesitate to compare this event to the Burning Bush of Moses or the Enlightenment of Buddha. But the first comparison which springs to his mind is that of the encounter of Jalal al-Din Rumi (Mawlavi) with Shams of Tabriz. The story of this fulminating encounter between Rumi and the one who, in an instant, transformed Rumi's life and made him into one of the greatest Iranian mystics. In Shams, Rumi did not only recognize a spiritual master, he saw in him the living presence of the Divine Light which henceforth was to enlighten his whole life like a sun (in Arabic, *shams*).

However, there is a whole essential aspect to the personality and spirituality of Massignon which is inseparable from his mysticism, and of which Shari'ati seems not to have so much as an inkling: what to Massignon meant his approach of Christian benevolently encountering Islam, of which he had made himself the host. And that the love of charity does not only address itself to those who in some way or other are already *one* with me (even through shared solitude in exile), but finds its supreme accomplishment in the love *of the other* as such, in total respect of his/her otherness. It is this which plunged Massignon into the study of Islam for the whole of his life, pushed him to visit the Algerian prisoners of Fresnes, made him explain the Qu'ran to the Maghrib workers of the mosque in Paris. Shari'ati recalls:

> The most remarkable lecture by Professor Massignon I ever attended was not held at the Sorbonne or at the Collège de France ... but at the foot of the columns of the mosque of the Muslims of Paris. He was sitting there, with a few vegetable salesmen and some unhappy Algerian Arabs who had, in colonialist France, forgotten even their religion and their language; and he taught them the Qu'ran.

Shari'ati is certainly conscious of the immense intellectual effort accomplished by his master in order to get to know Islam and its most elevated spiritual aspects, and he is profoundly grateful to him for it, as though justice has finally been rendered. However, it never occurred to him that Massignon's was a prophetic gesture of dialogue between these two great religious traditions. Massignon as a pioneer of Muslim-Christian dialogue escaped him totally. Shari'ati profited from his research on

Hallaj, Salman Pak and Fatima, but he apparently never thought that this gesture on behalf of Massignon could postulate a similar response, a benevolent interest in Christianity. Admittedly, their vocations were different, and Shari'ati felt his call to lie somewhere else. One cannot, however, fail to be surprised, when looking through his work, to see how little he knows about Christianity, despite his five years spent in Paris and his friendship with Massignon. He obviously admired Massignon, 'a convinced Catholic, filled with Christianity', but the study of Christianity as such never seems to have interested him. He was more attracted by Buddhism or the Upanishads than by the Gospels. When talking of Jesus, always respectfully, it is the Jesus as seen by Islam.[114] But how are we to consider Shari'ati's Mariology:

> It is Mary, who made that dry and haughty Yahweh descend from his throne, he who was indifferent in his omnipotence, who was enthroned with his angels and who stamped on creation like a ruined village, and from time to time used to throw a look of pity in its direction, it was she who made him come to earth, made him tender and tame on Earth. He who was accessible to no one was made incarnate in the sinless and good face of his Jesus. Yes! So wasn't Jesus God! It was Mary who made God come to Earth and fashioned him in the image of a man and it is Caesar who put him on the cross and nailed his four limbs to it. But still it was still the work of Mary: it was she who made God descend to Earth and made him go up from the Earth into the heavens of the gibbet and that time God ascended from his gibbet into the heaven of his solitude ... But thanks to this descent and ascent, in his essence some very important transformations happened ... Because Christ is the Holy Spirit and the Word of God, is the pure blood of God that had been nailed to the cross, and he had done all this to save the spirit of man from original sin and he saw that peace and reconciliation and charity and love, on earth, have stretched their wings and that hearts have been raised from

---

[114] On Christ in Islam, see Roger Arnaldez, *Jesus fils de Marie, prophète de l'Islam*, Desclée, Paris, 1980; R Arnaldez, *Jesus dans la pensée musulmane*, Desclée, Paris 1988; Neal Robinson, *Christ in Islam and Christianity*, Macmillan, London, 1991.

their rottenness, their hate, their jealousy, their ugliness and their baseness.[115]

In his writings, the Church and what it has made of the teachings of Jesus always appear with negative connotations, a mixture of the secular polemics of Islam against Christianity and of primary ideas reaped in Marxist, existentialist or positivist circles of the French university milieu of the 1960s. Thus, after the very beautiful pages we have just related, the Christian reader will be quite unpleasantly surprised by certain remarks. For example, talking about Sartre, Shari'ati describes him as a spirit sacrificed by *The Church and the Capital,* disgusted by the world and religion which, over there [in the Occident] are two sides of the same coin. It could be wished that Shari'ati in his praise of the author of *Salman Pak* be more nuanced about the 'sordid calumnies of the priests' (he obviously did not know that Massignon had become a priest himself in 1950). And Massignon probably would not have read the following sentence in his praise without raising his eyebrows: 'His energetic pen ... always defended the truth of Islam and of the defenceless personality of what is Oriental, *when in the face of the accusations by the Church ...*' Very well, Shari'ati talks with the liberty and outspokenness of an outsider. But that is precisely what Massignon never did: he always talked about Islam 'from the inside', as much as about the Church of which he formed part and which he venerated—which left him all the more freedom to violently criticize some of its members, even its high dignitaries, who disfigured its face by their hardly gospel-like attitude, notably during the Algerian war. In this, Shari'ati was not his 'disciple'.

There is another sentence which cannot be silently passed, as it is too much out of place in the text as a whole, and which runs as follows:

And Mohammed, that man in whose breast the heart of Jesus beat, and who held in his hand the bloodstained sword of Caesar: humanity held captive needs both for their salvation: Caesar, on his own, only spreads the blood, and

---

[115] The passages quoted here are taken from an article by Yann Richard, 'Lettre à mes amis d'Iran sur Dibâtch et Shari'ati', *La Croix l'événement*, 3 août 1994, 13, and are taken from the two final volumes (33/1 et 33/2) of Shari'ati's *Œuvres complètes*, Vol. 1, 49–50 and Vol. 2, 718–719. See also Dorothy C Buck, 'Mary and the Virgin Heart: a reflection on the writings of Louis Massignon and Hallaj', *Sufi*, 24 (1994–95), and 28 (1995–96), 6–11.

Jesus, on his own, only loves—each one without the other is
without the power to bring salvation.

Here, the Islamic ideologist asserts himself again, unconscious
of the contradictions of this sentence with its context. The love which
had seduced Shari'ati so much in Massignon, had led the latter to always
look for more routes for human and political salvation, in non-violent
resistance, following Gandhi. On this route, Shari'ati did not follow his
master either, was not his disciple.

As a Muslim, Shari'ati could not help asking himself the
following question with regard to Massignon: was he, in the eyes of God,
an infidel (a *kafir*) or a believer? In other words: was he saved or not? In
1967, the same year as he wrote the chapter in *Kavir* on Massignon, he
composed a long prayer where he talks very freely with God, 'just like a
child with its Father' and gave up to him all his questions and hopes. In
one passage, he asks God as follows:

> O God, who is an infidel (*kafir*)? Who is Muslim? Who is
> Shi'a? Who is Sunni? What is the exact border that separates
> each of them? ... Massignon, that ocean of science, who for
> 27 whole years has plunged into the life of Salman, the first
> historical founder of Shiism in Iran, who throughout his
> life researched the personality and posthumous influence of
> Saint Fatima in the history of the people, gathering all
> information which in the course of history had been
> dispersed in Arabic, Persian, Turkish, Latin and even Mongol
> sources, he whose whole being took fire each time he spoke
> about Fatima, Islamic mysticism or Salman ... is he an infidel?
> ... Oh God, tell me, how you see things? How do you judge?
> Falling in love with 'names' is that Shiism? Is it not rather to
> know those who are called these names? Or, more even, *to
> imitate their manners?'*

Four years later, in 1971, when performing a pilgrimage to
Mecca,[116] Shari'ati gave a lecture to Iranian pilgrims in Medina. He

---

[116] Steven R. Benson, 'Islam and Social change in the writings of 'Ali Shari'ati: his Hajj as a
mystical handbook for revolutionaries', *Muslim World*, 81, 1991, 9-26.

came to speak of 'Professor Massignon, my master, a Christian and European Orientalist' and of his work on Salman. In the published version of this talk, Shari'ati added the following note:

> How lucky it is that I should remember him in this circumstance [in Medina]; assuredly, God, who does not judge by appearances but by the heart, has undoubtedly forgiven him and given him a great recompense.'

Unlike Massignon, Shari'ati did not practise interreligious dialogue. But he nevertheless perceived its essential foundations: the conviction that the salvation of mankind does not in fact spring from pure doctrinal obedience of any religion, but of putting into practice authentic moral values; that it is not the letter which saves, but the *spirit*; that there is no use 'falling in love with "names"', but that what counts is to 'imitate their habits'.

An end and a beginning

In a corner of the cemetery abutting on the great Shi'a sanctuary of Zaynab (Sayyida Zaynab, sister of Imam Husayn, much venerated by Shari'ati), in the suburbs of Damascus, a modest funeral chamber can be found, housing a just as modest tomb: it is that of 'Ali Shari'ati. This is where he was buried, as when he died, the Iranian authorities were afraid that the repatriation of his body to Iran might provoke unrest. Since the Iranian Revolution in 1979, Iranian pilgrims have been unable to visit the Shi'a sanctuaries in Karbala' and Najaf in Iraq and therefore flock to the sanctuary of Sayyida Zaynab, which is gleaming with mirrors and lights. Those who make a detour to go and meditate at the humble tomb of Shari'ati are fewer. But there are some: the numerous 'graffiti' left by them are a sure sign. They include slogans dear to the ideologist, which his pious disciples have remembered. One of them some years ago wrote the following short sentence above the door of the funeral chamber, with large traits of fire red

---

[117] Sabrina Mervin, 'Sayyida Zaynab: banlieue de Damas ou novelle ville sainte chiite?', *CEMOTI*, no. 22, 1996, 149-62; and 'En syrie, le "pèlerinage de pauvres" à la mosquée Sayida-Zaynab', *Le Monde* (Paris), 3 January, 1998.

paint, which was recorded by a follower of Charles de Foucauld, Fr Michel Cuypers who found three words in Persian visible: *Khuda muhabbat ast*, 'God is Love'. With what intention did this anonymous hand want to ornate the tomb of the *Docteur* with this sentence from the First Letter of St John? Did it want to bring a definitive response to the questions of its master? Or did it simply want to summarize in one word the best teaching it had received from Shari'ati-Massignon?[118]

---

[118] Michel Cuypers, 'Une rencontre mystique: 'Ali Shari'ati—Louis Massignon, *Mélanges de l'Institut Dominicain d'Etudes Orientales*, 21, 1993, 330, and *idem*, 'Une rencontre mystique: 'Ali Shari'ati—Louis Massignon', in ed. Jacques Keryell, *Louis Massignon et ses contemporains*, Karthala, Paris, 1997, 309-328. For a political-theological comparison between Catholic Christianity and Shi'a Islam, see James A Bill and John Alden Williams, 'Shi'a Islam and Roman Catholicism: An Ecclesial and Political Analysis', in ed. Kail C Ellis, OSA, *The Vatican, Islam and the Middle East*, Syracuse University Press, NY, 1987, 69-105.

THE REMEMBRANCE OF GOD
Ayatollah Mushin Araki

According to the Glorious Qur'an, man has a particular status in the cosmic order and that is to act as the vicegerent of God. This particular status in the whole universe lends man superiority over other creatures, including angels. Man's vicegerency is not merely a kind of formal superiority over all things other than God; rather it means management and governing, and the ability to take action and to determine one's destiny. In Islam this ability is referred to as *wilāya* (guardianship).

Man's particular status and authority can lead to his happiness, prosperity and delightful life on the one hand, and to the flourishing and progress of the whole world on the other, providing he acts in conformity to the inner order of the universe, governed and dominated by God and His will. In this case, his actions will be in line with the overall orientation of the order of creation and the esoteric orientation of things, and this brings peace, joy and prosperity to the human community and to the world in which man lives, enabling man to attain spiritual development, sublimity and perfection, and eventually leads to the fulfilment or flourishing of his inner potentialities. The Glorious Qur'an describes the situation in the following verse:

> 'And if the people of the towns had believed and guarded (*themselves against evil*) we would have opened up for them blessings from the heavens and the earth but they believed, so we seized them for what they did earn.' (7: 96)

If man deviates from the path of obedience, submission and service of God, takes the way of disobedience towards God, rebels against God, does not perform the duties incumbent upon him and does not act in accordance with the Divine Commandments, which constitute the justice-based order of creation, the result will be nothing but serious and long-lasting conflict between man's illegitimate and unfair desires on the one hand, and the reality of the justice-based order of the creation

185

which governs all things, and the reality of man's needs and the orientations determined by God, on the other. As a result, this conflict not only causes man and the world around him to lose the course of development and flourishing, but it also brings many terrible harms and calamities which, in turn, leads to misery, great loss, helplessness, wickedness, and backwardness for man and for his surrounding world. Such a tragic situation is the effect of man's rebellious illegitimate desires and aspirations.

The service of God, which is taken to mean acting in conformity with the justice-based created (cosmic) order governing all things, originates from the invocation of God, for it is the constant invocation of God that paves the way for man's obedience and submission to God and his service, and it is the forgetfulness of God that obstructs the way to the obedience and service of Him. This is why God's teachings and guidance, which have been sent down through the prophets to mankind, are referred to as a 'reminder' *(dhikr)*, and turning away from divine teachings is referred to as 'forgetfulness' *(ghafla)*.

Concerning the Torah, the set of teachings revealed to Moses and Aaron, the Glorious Qur'an says:

'And indeed We did grant unto Moses and Aaron the (book) of Criterion (*between the right and wrong*), and Light and a Reminder for the pious.' (21: 48)

It also introduces the Gospel and its teachings revealed to Jesus as a means of remembrance of God and criticizes those who have forgotten his teachings and do not act according to them:

'And of those (also) who say "Verily, We are Nazerenes," We did take their covenant, but they have forgotten a portion of what they were admonished with, therefore we stirred up among them enmity and hatred (to last) till the day of resurrection; and soon will God inform them of what they have been doing.' (5: 14)

Furthermore, the Glorious Qur'an introduces itself as the Book containing a collection of 'invocations', including the reminder sent down through the prophets to the past generations and also a reminder for the followers and companions of the Holy Prophet Muhammad (may peace be upon him and his household):

> 'This (Qur'an) is the Reminder unto those before me: Nay! Most of them know not the truth, so they turn aside.' (21:24)

Dhikr, or 'reminder', is referred to in many Qur'anic verses and in a set of teachings revealed to the Prophet Muhammad. Here are a few examples:

> 'It (the Qur'an) is nought but a Reminder unto (all) the worlds, ... ' (81: 27)

> 'Verily this is a Reminder, so whosoever pleases, takes unto his Lord the (Right) way.' (76: 29)

> 'Verily We have sent down the Reminder (the Qur'an), and verily We (ourself) unto it will certainly be the guardian.' (15: 9)

> 'And this (Qur'an) is a Reminder full of blessings which We have sent down (unto Our Apostle Muhammad) Do you then deny it?' (21: 50)

> 'It is nought but a Reminder and manifesting Qur'an.' (36: 69)

Elsewhere in the Glorious Qur'an, the very Qur'an, which is defined as a reminder, is introduced as light and as a means of guidance to the paths of peace, tranquillity and to the path which takes one from darkness to the world of light and illumination, a guide to the right path:

> 'Indeed has come unto you from God, Light and a Manifesting Book (Qur'an). Whereby God guides him who follows His pleasures, into the ways of peace and takes them out from darkness towards the Light but His will and guides them to the path (that is) straight.' (5: 16)

To sum up, according to the Qur'anic point of view:

a) The teachings of prophets direct mankind to peace.
b) It is through the invocation of God that human beings overtake the path which leads them from darkness to Light and accomplish peace, happiness, honesty and righteousness.
c) The essence of all the teachings communicated to mankind through the prophets is the invocation of God.

In giving a brief account we will not go through the philosophical and scientific arguments for the facts mentioned above or through the results obtained from scientific observations. However, we will point in brief to the fact that the invocation of God nurtures some characteristics or qualities in man which bring about peace, tranquillity, happiness and joy in this life, and lead men to the divine eternal paradise and the infinite joyful pleasures of God in the other world, i.e., the Hereafter.

In brief, the invocation of God develops in mankind such kinds of insight, worthiness, character and life-style that his relationship with others grows together with love, self-sacrifice, benevolence, forgiveness, kindness, and selflessness, and thus enmity is replaced by love and friendship, selfishness by compassion and self-sacrifice, violence by benevolence, and wrath and retaliation by forgiveness and mercy.

Concerning a person's world view, it can be said that one who performs the practice of invocation thinks that life is infinite, and that this world is only the first stage, a period in which man prepares himself to forsake this world for the eternal life in the Hereafter. Man in this world is capable of achieving utmost happiness and fulfilling his desires and needs when he depends on the absolute power, i.e., God, the Omnipotent, who has control over the whole universe, who created mankind to achieve happiness and prosperity, and paved the way for him, so that all existence is destined to be at man's disposal so that he might access to his desires and aspirations and finally attain utmost felicity and all-embracing prosperity:

'God is the One Who created Heaven and Earth and sends down water from the sky. He brings forth produce by means of it as sustenance for you. He has subjected ships to you so they may sail at sea by His command; and subjected rivers to you. He regulates the sun and moon for you, both journeying on and on, and regulates night and day for you. He gives you everything you ever ask Him for. If you counted up God's favour(s), you would never [be able to] number them; yet man is so unfair, ungrateful.' (14: 32-34)

This fact is also mentioned in other verses of the Glorious Qur'an:

'God is He Who made subservient unto you the sea that may traverse the ships therein by His command and that you seek of His grace and that you may seek of His grace and that you may be thankful.
'And made subservient unto you whatsoever is in the heavens and whatsoever in the earth, all, on His behalf.Verily in this are signs for people who reflect.' (45: 12 and 13)

Concerning values, it can be said that according to this mode of thought, all human beings are equal before God and no human being has any superiority or preference over another save in piety and obedience to God.Thus, those who have taken precedence in piety and obedience to God are more honoured than the others. In other words, the more honoured person is the one who is nearer to God and who has precedence over the others in justice and virtue and who guards (himself) against evil.

If piety and virtue are to be taken as the criteria for social eminence, people will surely compete to gain supreme values, and will not act according to their own personal or group interests. If individuals in a society compete with one another to attain more piety and supreme virtue, then love, humility, compassion, self sacrifice and the like will prevail in that society and people will work hard to attain supreme values instead of pursuing inferior interests which bring about nothing but oppositions and disputes. Evidently, those who have precedence over the others in humility, compassion and self-sacrifice and try to serve others will always be happy and fulfilled.

When we speak of human characters we mean the individual and social aspects of human entity. According to this conception, the 'service of God' represents the real nature of human beings. The service of God implies negation or refutation of the domination over human personality of any power other than God's power on the one hand, and utter obedience to God, the Almighty, who is All-Just and All-Powerful, on the other.

Anyone who has this quality, i.e., service of God, seeks nothing but God's pleasure and stands against the temptation of any transient pleasures, ephemeral pursuits, material interests, lower desires and aspirations that drive man to be in opposition to justice, piety and virtue.

It is quite evident that all oppression, discrimination, inequality, disastrous wars, bloody massacres, transgressions, gross violations of human rights, robberies and all sorts of major or minor crimes originate from the selfishness and arrogance of those people who seek only to satisfy their own ephemeral material interests, pleasures and lower desires. The Glorious Qur'an reminds those who have forgotten to invoke God and turned away from the Qur'an and other divine reminders as those who have lost their genuine nature and their real self, which is indeed the only capital or resource in the battlefield of this worldly life:

'Do they wait for anything but the final fulfilment (the resurrection)? On the day the final fulfilment comes, those who have neglected it before will say: "Indeed came the apostles of our world with the truth; Are there for us (now) any intercessors that they may intercede for us? Or could we be sent back so that he might act other than what we did act?" Indeed they have lost their souls, and what they forged has gone away from them.' (7: 53)

As regards 'life-style', when one's personality is formed on the basis of the divine worldview, value and character mentioned above, a person's life-style, whether in connection with himself or with others, will originate from virtue and piety and will be based on justice and righteousness.

In a sermon addressed to someone known as Hammām, Imam 'Alī (may peace be upon him) gives a sketchy but comprehensive and full picture of the pious people who live by the invocation of God and describes their characteristics on the basis of their worldview, values, character and life-style:

The pious in this world are the people of distinction. Their speech is to the point, their dress is moderate and their gait is humble. They submit to Allah with obedience. They keep their eyes closed before what Allah has made unlawful for them, and they put their ears to knowledge. They remain in the time of trials as though they remain in comfort due to their satisfaction with the act of Allah. If there had not been fixed periods of life ordained for each, their spirits would not have remained in their bodies even for the twinkling of an eye because of the eagerness for the reward and fear of chastisement. The greatness of the Creator is seated in their heart, and so, everything else appears small in their eyes. Thus, to them, Paradise is as though they are seated there and are enjoying its favours. To them, Hell is also as if they see it and are suffering punishment in it.

... The peculiarity of any one of them is that you will see that he has strength in religion, determination along with leniency, faith with conviction, eagerness in seeking knowledge, courtesy in lenience, clemency in alms–giving, understanding in awareness, knowledge in forbearance, moderation in riches, devotion in worship, gracefulness in starvation, endurance in hardship, mercy for the exhausted, fulfilment of the right, leniency in earning, desire for the lawful, pleasure in guidance, hatred of greed, piety in straightforwardness, and abstinence in appetites. The approval of him who ignores him does not deceive him. He does not stop judging his deeds. He performs virtuous deeds but still feels afraid. In the evening he is anxious to offer thanks to Allah. In the morning his anxiety is to remember Allah. He passes the night in fear and rises in the morning in joy-fear lest night is passed in forgetfulness and joy over the favour and mercy received by him. If his self refuses to endure a thing, which it does not like, he does not grant its request towards what it likes. The coolness of his eye lies in what is to last forever, while from the things of this world that will not last he keeps aloof. He transfuses knowledge with forbearance, and speech with action.

You will see his laziness aloof, his activity uninterrupted, his hopes simple, his shortcomings few, his heart fearing, his spirit contented, his ignorance absent, his affairs simple, his religion safe, his desires dead, his anger suppressed, his mannerism pure. He does not brief about what is kept secret with him. He does not conceal the testimony against his enemies. He does not do any practice ostentatiously. He does not leave anything shyly. Good alone is expected from him. Evil from him is not to be feared. Even if he is found among those who forget Allah he is counted among those who remember him. He forgives him who is unjust to him, and he gives to him who deprives him. He behaves well with him who behaves ill with him.

His forbearance is not absent; he does not neglect what adorns him. Indecent speech is far from him, his utterance is lenient. His evils are non-existent. His virtues are ever present, his good is ahead, and mischief has turned its face from him. He is dignified during calamities, patient in distress, and thankful during ease. He does not commit excess over him whom he hates, and does not commit sin for the sake of him whom he loves. He does not claim the possession of things that are not his. He does not deny others' rights that are obligatory upon him. He admits truth before evidence is brought against him. He does not misappropriate what is placed in custody. He does not call others bad names. He does not oppress or threaten others. He does not cause harm to his neighbour, he does not feel happy at others' misfortunes. He hurries to the right. He fulfils the trusts. He is slow in ill deeds. He enjoins good and forbids evil. He does not enter into the wrong and does not leave behind right.

If he is silent his silence does not grieve him, if he laughs he does not raise his voice. He is satisfied with what is his. Malice does not agitate him. Whims do not overcome him. Stinginess does not prevail over him. He does not desire for what is not his. He associates with people so as to learn. He keeps silent so as to be safe. He asks so as to understand. He does not listen to the good word so that others will not find themselves neglectful in comparison with him. He does not speak of his good actions so as to avoid taking pride in it before others. If he is wronged he endures till Allah takes revenge of his behalf. His own self is in distress because of him while the people are in ease from him. He puts himself in hardship for the sake of his next life and makes people feel safe from himself. His keeping away from others is by way of asceticism and purification, and his nearness to those to whom he is near is by way of leniency and mercifulness. His keeping away is not by way of vanity or feeling of greatness, nor his nearness by way of deceit and cheating. He follows the examples of the past men of virtue and he is the example of the coming people of virtue. (*Nahj al-Balāgha*, Sermon: 191)

The society in which such people are brought up and which models itself on the characters and life-style of such pious people will never suffer from dangerous social calamities, moral deviations and bloody struggles over private, group or class interests; rather it can take the seat of God's vicegerency and will become the real king of the universe, and all the creatures in the world are made subservient and obedient to Him and His commands.

The definition of the invocation of God

The definition of the invocation of God can be summarized as follows: 'Man's awareness of God's Lordship and his service of Him.'

Man's service of God is a reality to which he submits, whether he likes it or not. It is a reality in which he believes, even though he may make a great show of reluctance in his words and actions. The Glorious Qur'an puts emphasis on the fact that all human beings, including the most stubborn disbelievers, acknowledge God's divinity and express their inner submission and service of God, even if they rise up in open rebellion and show their opposition in words and actions. This acknowledgement of God's divinity is clearly expressed by the Glorious Qur'an:

'And if you ask them who created them, they would certainly say: "God". Whence are they then deluded away (from the truth)?' (43: 87)

The Glorious Qur'an refers to Pharaoh and his followers:

'So when came to them Our clear signs, said they: "This is plain sorcery." They denied them in iniquity and arrogance while their hearts were convinced; See then how was the end of the mischief makers.' (27: 13 and 14)

An acknowledgement of God's divinity is also expressed in the following verses:

'And if you ask them: "Who created the heavens and the earth and made subservient the sun and the moon?" Certainly will they say: "God!" Whence are they then turned away? God (it is Who) makes abundant the sustenance for whomsoever he wills of His servants, and (similarly) He causes it to be straitened for him (whomsoever he wills); Verily God is Well-Cognizant of all things. And nothing is this life of the world but a vain sport and play; and verily the abode of the hereafter, is certainly the life: if they but know. And when embark they on ships, call they upon God sincerely vowing (only) unto Him, and when He brings them safe to land, behold! They associate (others with Him). (Then) Let them thank not for what We have given them, and let them enjoy; but soon shall they know.' (29: 61-66)

The last two verses mention the fact that disbelievers, as they are placed in a condition in which they are threatened from all directions and cut off from any means to save themselves from dangers, begin to reveal their inner or hidden acknowledgement (of God) and turn to God obediently and submissively to seek His help. But as soon as they feel that God has satisfied their needs and are no longer in danger, they revolt against God, take other creatures as their own deity, and make a great show of obedience to a tyrannical ruler or the rebels who have illegally captured the seat of power. It is worth mentioning that man's awareness of his true position and his inner acknowledgements of God's divinity constitute the essence or the reality of the invocation of God. The practice of *dhikr* or invocation comprises various levels or stages which, if passed through successfully, reach the higher stages of invocation, and the believer will attain to such a high degree of spirituality that his desires will be compatible to God's desires, and he will turn away from all that which God turns away from, eventually coming to love what God loves and hate what God hates. In other words, one's love, hatred and desire will become God's love, hatred and desire. This is actually the stage, or rather, the station (*maqām*) with which only the divine Prophets and a few chosen and spiritual masters are honoured.

The stages and degrees of invocation

The practice of invocation or *dhikr* involves various stages or degrees (*marātib*) each of which has certain effects and distinguishing features. Here we just touch on a few of them.

First stage

The first stage of the 'Invocation of God' is invocation with the tongue or with words. If invocation with the tongue (*dhikr-i lisānī* or *lafẓī*) is carried out in accordance with its rites and rules (*sharāyi' wa ādāb*) it can elevate man to higher stages or degrees, i.e., invocation with the actions *(dhikr-i 'amalī)* and then to invocation with the heart or the spirit *(dhikr-i qalbī)* or to what is termed by some as spiritual invocation *(dhikr-i ma'nawī)*. The most important rites and rules of invocation with the tongue are as follows:

1. Turning toward God, the Almighty, and turning (one's mind) away from everything other than God constitutes the first condition of the true invocation *(dhikr-i ḥaqq)*.

2. Purity is the essential condition for invocation. In other words, the invocation of God will be fruitless if it is not accompanied by pure intention. By purity we mean that the invoker (*dhākir*) seeks nothing but God's pleasure, and performs the invocation just for God's pleasure. Purity is of various degrees. In the higher stages of purity, man reaches and should reach the stations through the act of invocation, but not for the sake of his own wishes. In fact, in this stage he becomes aware of his nothingness and enters the battle against his own self so that he sees no reality for his self for which he seeks pleasure through the practice of invocation. His own self is annihilated in God's pleasures, he sees nothing other than God and thinks of nothing but the pleasures of God, and nothing remains within him save God's pleasure.

3. Entreaty (self-abasement) *(taḍarru')* and **broken-heartedness (humility)**. The invocation of God should be associated with broken-heartedness or humility. As God the Almighty addresses the Holy Prophet in the Glorious Qur'an:

> 'And remember thy Lord within thy self in humility and
> awe, and not in a loud voice, in the morning and evening;
> and be thou not of the negligent ones.'(7: 205)

Entreaty implies broken-heartedness along with the feeling of anxiety and helplessness. The one who suffers from this situation is the one who feels himself in great need of God and feels his need as urgent and all-embracing, and that nobody except God can save him from his miserable situation. He feels like a man surrounded by the roaring flames of a fire, and that there is nobody to help and grant refuge but God. Addressing those who have fallen into, and are threatened by serious dangers in wild deserts and seas and could find no saviour except God, the Glorious Qur'an says:

> 'Say thou: "Who delivered you from the (dread of the)
> darkness of the land and the sea, (when) ye pray to Him
> (openly) humiliating yourselves, and secretly (saying)"; "If
> He delivereth us from this, certainly we shall be of the
> grateful ones." Say Thou: "God delivereth you from them,
> and from every distress, yet again ye associate (others) with
> Him.' (6: 63 and 64)

In the Glorious Qur'an and the traditions *(ḥadīths)* related of the Infallibles (Shi'ite Imams), entreaty is termed as the spirit or the essence of supplication and the remembrance of God, and it is entreaty that brings the invocation of God and supplication to fruition. The tree of supplication and the invocation of God bears fruit when it is watered by entreaty or self-abasement. It is narrated by Imam Ṣādiq, the Sixth Imam of the Shi'ites, that God said to Moses:

> O the son of 'Imrān! Give me from your heart humility, and from your body submission, and from your eyes flowing tears and call me in the darkness at night when you will find my response and me so close to you. *(Wasā'il al-Shī'ah, Abwāb al-Du'ā, Bāb-i 30, Ḥadīth 2)*

And it is related in another *ḥadīth* that:

> Verily Allah revealed to Jesus (may peace and blessing be upon him): Call Me like the distressed flood-stricken person who has been carried away by water and there is nobody to save him! O' Jesus! Call no other one than Me till your prayer becomes worthy of being responded by me. *(Wasā'il al-Shī'ah, Abwāb al-Du'ā, Bāb-i 65, Ḥadīth 2)*

God, the Almighty, has repeatedly emphasized the attribute of entreaty and self-abasement in the practice of invocation and supplication:

> 'Call your Lord, humbly and secretly; Verily God does not love the transgressors.' (7: 55)

In many places the Glorious Qur'an insists on the point that most of the hardships and sufferings with which God has tried and tested mankind are intended to make man feel utter submission and humility before God, and then to reach the state of invocation and humble supplication and prayer. This verifies the fact that man's entreaty or self-abasement and humility before God are the means by which man can get rid of all sufferings, hardships and miseries he has fallen into; and that it is through entreaty and self-abasement before the Divine that man's prayer and supplication become worthy of response by God the Almighty and salvation is reached. This fact is referred to in many verses, as in the following:

> We sent [word] to nations before you and seized them suffering and hardship so that they might act submissively.

197

Why then did they not act submissively when our violence came to them, but instead their hearts were hardened and Satan made whatever they were doing seem attractive to them. So when they forgot what they had been reminded of, We opened up the doors to everything for them until just when they were happiest with what they have been given, We caught them suddenly and there they were confounded. The last remnant of the folk who had been doing wrong was cut off. Praise to God Lord of the Universe! (6: 42-45)

4. Fear and awe. In various verses the invocation of God is referred to in relation to fear and awe as in the following verse:

Remember thy Lord in thy soul, humbly and fearfully ...
(7: 205)

Fear of God the Almighty takes three forms:

Self-abasing fear *(khawf-i rahbah).* This refers to the kind of fear when one feels abased and humble before God and thinks one is failing to perform God's will which is incumbent upon mankind, and is represented in one's acts of submission and servitude. This is a real and genuine conviction and is not an illusion: as a matter of fact, man falls short of expressing his genuine obedience to God.

The fear of the Divine All-Knowing, All-Just Sovereignty *(khawf az ḥukūmat-i 'ālama wa 'ādila-yi ilāhī).* God the Almighty is the only and absolute ruler of the universe, who is just and His justice is infinite. In addition to being All-Just, God is Omniscient and nothing, seen or unseen, can fall outside his knowledge. Therefore, any grave sins or violations committed by human beings, whether deliberately or accidentally, whether within the heart or with the limbs, whether in public or in private, are not hidden from divine sight.

Naturally, the feeling of a man who is always subject to error and sin will logically be nothing but a feeling of fear and awe before a ruler like God who is at once Omnipotent and All-Just.

Fear of the self *(khawf az nafs);* anyone who becomes cognizant of his nothingness, deficiencies, unworthiness, guilt and misdeeds, finds himself shameful before God and His Divine Scales of Justice. Those who reassess their own selves will become aware of their own rebellion, grave sin and disobedience before God the Almighty. In this case, man naturally feels fearful of his sins and misdeeds. Thus, fear and awe before God is the most logical state a theist may experience. On the one hand, God has the great right that man show utter submission and obedience towards His just will and commandments. On the other hand, God is Omnipotent and Omniscient, aware of every aspect and detail of human existence, and has an all-embracing power. Man is always liable to grave sins before God.

5. Abundant invocation. One of the important rules and vows of invocation is the excess and continuity of invocation. According to the Glorious Qur'an, the excess of invocation is an indication of being a true believer, while the hypocrites are known for their lack of frequent invocation of God. The Glorious Qur'an says:

> 'Indeed, (there is) for you in the Apostle of God (Muhammad) an excellent pattern (of conduct) for him who hopes in God and the latter day (hereafter) and remembers God much.' (33: 21)

Elsewhere in describing the hypocrites, the Glorious Qur'an says:

> 'Verily the hypocrites strive to deceive God while He is deceiving them; and when they stand up for prayers, they stand up sluggishly (without earnestness), they do it only to be seen of men, and they remember not God save a little.' (4: 142)

First stage

Establishing the ritual prayers in conformity with their particular conditions is considered to be the first stage of the multitudinous character of the invocation of God, together with the degrees of multiple invocations through the supererogatory prayers *(nawāfil)* and some other rituals and other optional supplications which naturally add to the effects and qualities springing from them.

Second stage

The second stage of the invocation of God is said to be invocation with actions *(dhikr-i 'amalī)*. At this stage, the invoker *(dhākir)* goes beyond the invocation of God with the tongue and keeps invoking God in his conduct. Invocation with actions is meant to be the constant invocation of God in actions and conduct, which can be realized through submission and obedience manifested in human actions.

Hypocrites are characterized in the Glorious Qur'an as those who enjoin evil and forbid the performing of good, and as those who having forsaken God, have been forsaken by Him.

> 'The hypocrite men and the hypocrite women are one from another, they enjoin evil and forbid good and withhold their hands (from spending in the way of God); they have forsaken God, so He has forsaken them; verily the hypocrites, they are the transgressors.' (9: 67)

By contrast, believers are characterized as those who enjoin good and forbid evil and obey God and His Apostle (Muhammad):

> 'And the believer men and the believer women, they are guardians to one another; they enjoin good and forbid evil and they establish (the regular) prayers and pay the poor-rate and obey God and His Apostle (Muhammad). These, God will bestow on them His Mercy; verily God is All-Mighty, All-wise.' (9: 71)

The Glorious Qur'an frequently refers to the obedience to God not only as the most important attribute of believers but also as the criterion for making a distinction between believers and hypocrites:

> 'The Prophet believes in what has come down unto him from his Lord and (so do) the believers; all believe in God and in His Angels and His Book and His apostles; (they say) "We make no difference between His apostles;" and they say "We have heard and obeyed (and we implore) your forgiveness, O, Our Lord! And unto You is the end of all journeys." ' (2: 285)

Elsewhere the Glorious Qur'an addresses believers:

'And remember you the bounties of God on you, and His covenant He has bound you with, when you said "We have heard (your commandments) and we have obeyed (it sincerely)."' (5: 7)

Invocation with action is referred to in Qur'anic terminology as *true Islam*, and a *true Muslim* is introduced as the one who sincerely obeys the divine commandments and submits to Him in all conditions. Islam itself has various degrees and the great prophets of God throughout history are the divine leading figures who are the first people who have believed in Islam.

The Holy Prophet is addressed in the Glorious Qur'an:

'Say, "Verily my prayer and my sacrifice, my life and my death, (are all, only) for God, the Lord of the worlds."' (6: 162)

Ḥāfiẓ, the well-known Iranian poet and mystic, offers some lines in his poems in describing this invocation with action which is the very real or genuine Islam, as well as in describing the Holy Prophet (may peace be upon him and his household) as the excellent exemplar and manifestation of this sort of invocation:

بجز آن نرگس مستانه که حشیش مرساد
زیر این طارم فیروزه کسی خوش ننشست
جان فدای دهنش باد که در باغ نظر
چمن آرای جهان خوش تر از این غنچه نیست

Save that intoxicated flower—the (evil) eye reach him not!
None are seated happy beneath this turquoise vault (of heaven).
May my soul be the ransom of his mouth! For in the garden of vision,
The Parterre-arrayer (the Creator) of the world established no rose-bud more sweet than this rose-bud (of a mouth).

In these lines, Ḥāfiẓ, inspired by the holy verse mentioned above, describes the Prophet as a flower who has attained the station of perfection in loving God and mentions the fact that no human being under the azure sky has ever reached this stage of perfection as he has, the stage to which the Glorious Qur'an referred as 'the first Muslim'.

In the following lines, Hafiz has made an excellent mention of this station:

به حسن خلق ووفا کس به یار ما نرسد

تورا در این سخن انکار کار ما نرسـد

اگر چه حسن فروشان بجلوه آمده انـد

کسی به حسن وملاحت به یار ما نرسـد

بحق صحبت دیرین که هیچ محرم راز

به یار یك جهت حق گزار مانرسـد

To our friend in beauty of disposition and of fidelity, one—
　　reacheth not,
In this matter, to thee, denial of our work—reacheth not.
Although, into splendour, have come beauty-boaster,
To our beloved in beauty and grace, one reacheth not
By the right of old friendship (I swear) that any mystery
　　confident,
To our friend, of one way (sincere), thank-offering—
　　reacheth not.

Having referred to the Holy Prophet, Ḥāfiẓ describes him as *haqqguzār* (thank-offering), meaning someone who has performed his duties and has expressed his utter submission to the Divine and His commandments. Even his sincerity in submission to, and obedience of, God is described in these lines as one way or single-oriented to the beloved.

The higher degrees or stages of 'Islam' cannot be achieved except through spiritual journey and practising the invocation of God. Obedience to God in actions is claimed to be the first stage (true Islam or *Islām-i haqīqī*) which can be achieved through passing the stages of 'invocation with action' and then 'invocation with the heart', paving the way for man to traverse all the distances between the servant and God, and to reach the station in which he sees and wishes nothing but God.

Achieving the higher degrees or stages of invocation with action and invocation with the heart is not possible except through unconditional or utter obedience to the Holy Prophet and his divine teachings. As soon as one can attain this degree, one is apt to be placed in the station of 'the proximity of the Holy Prophet' *(jiwār-i Rasūl-i akram)* which is identical with that of the 'proximity of God' *(jiwār-i khudā-yi mutaʿāl)*. Those who can attain such a supreme station will be engulfed in the pleasure of (the station of) 'union with God' *(waṣl-i ilāhī)* and, while enjoying the noblest degrees of vision of God *(visio Dei)* or the vision of 'the Face of God' *(ruʾyat va naẓar bi vajh-i Llāh)*, which is not to be taken as a physical or bodily vision, can be endowed with the delights and pleasures of the universe as well, which is beyond the imagination and understanding of us who are imprisoned and captive in the fetters of this material world.

Third Stage

The third stage of the invocation of God is that of 'invocation with the heart' or 'spiritual invocation'. Turning toward God with the heart is the necessary condition of all forms of invocation, but is what we mean here by 'invocation with the heart' is different. It refers to a particular transformation that occurs in man's heart, turning the heart into a state which is called 'radiance' *(dirakhshandagī)* or 'purity' *(ṣafā)* or 'illumination' *(nūrānīyat)* and so on. This is what the great Muslim mystics call 'world-reflecting'. The awakened heart *(qalb-i bīdār)* is also referred to in mystical terminology as 'the reflecting cup' *(jām-i jahān namā)*.

Ḥāfiẓ, the great Muslim mystic says:

سالها دل طلب جام جم از ما مي كرد
آنچه خود داشت زبيگانه تمنا مي كرد

Search for the cup of Jamshīd (Divine knowledge) from me, years my heart made.
And for what it possessed, from a stranger, entreaty [my heart] made.

Invocation with the heart comprises various stages from which three general stages are mentioned below:

a. *Dhikr-i ḥālī* (invocation by state). At this stage, rust is removed from the mirror of the heart, the mysterious burden which, as a result of forgetfulness, prevents the heart ascending higher, disappears, and man feels as light as a feather, foresees future events, removes all the obstacles and veils which obscure the realities in the universe. He comprehends the transience of the world and the attachment to God of all things, witnesses God's domination of the world and all the things in it, becomes aware of his nothingness and unworthiness before the glory and majesty of God, and realizes his infidelity, deficiency and sins of omissions against the infinite love, mercy and grace of God. Therefore, his heart breaks and the dried fountain of tears bursts out again from his little eyes and signs of penitence, regret and repentance appear on his face. Invocation by state has a variety of forms some of which are referred to in the following:

a.1. Invocation by wakefulness *(dhikr-i bīdārī)*: this sort of invocation by state is experienced by those who have fallen into the darkness of forgetfulness and whose hearts have, all of a sudden, been illuminated by a flash of invocation, bursting into such roaring flames that captures all their existence and leads them to higher stages of invocation with the heart. A story related by the Glorious Qur'an is a case in point: magicians who were at the service of Pharaoh were awakened to the divine miracles accomplished by Moses, making them to turn their thoughts towards God.

a.2. Invocation by refraining *(dhikr-i bāzdārī)*: this form of invocation is often experienced by those who, despite having piety, are subject to certain illegal desires and tendencies, but before committing sins, the invocation of God comes upon them and restrains them from evil deeds. This kind of invocation is described thus by the Glorious Qur'an:

> 'Verily those who guard (themselves against evil) when an evil thought from the Satan afflicts them, they become mindful (of God and get awakened) then Lo! They see. (7: 201)

a.3. Invocation by return *(dhikr-i bāzāyī)*: this sort of invocation can be experienced by those who have been afflicted by sins, but on being afflicted, they suddenly become awakened and aware of the sins committed, turn to God and express their regret and repentance. This situation is clearly expressed by the Glorious Qur'an:

'and those, who when they do a shameful deed or commit
a wrong to their (own) selves, remember God and implore
for pardon for their sins; and who forgives sins except God?
And who persists not (intentionally), in what they have done
(amiss) while they know it.' (3: 135)

a.4. Invocation by vision *(dhikr-i dīdān)*. The invoker in this form of
dhikr-i ḥālī achieves the vision of God in his heart and experiences a state
of spiritual delight (ecstasy) which causes all the veils that prevent the
heart from having a vision of God to be removed, and the invoker no
longer sees veils and obstacles between himself and his God.

The most important veil which blocks the way for man to come
to the state of vision of God is the veil of his own self *(ḥijāb-i khudī* or
ḥijāb-i nafs). Fakhr al-Dīn-i 'Irāqī, the great mystical Persian poet, and
an intimate friend of Jalāl al-Dīn Rūmī, makes a reference to the veil of
the self saying:

در میان من ومحبوب همین است حجاب

وقت آن است که این پرده به یکسوفکنم

Between me and the Beloved is this very veil.
This is the time to remove this veil.

In the state of invocation by vision, the veil of the self *(ḥijāb-i
nafs)* is lifted up and man, becoming overwhelmed and illuminated by
the light which has captured all his existence, is drowned in the vision of
God. This condition rarely happens to the wayfarer *(sālik)*. Those who
have been endowed with God's grace will have the chance to have more
of such experiences, and for those who have achieved high degrees of
spirituality, this becomes as a state for them. Such people may experience
the vision of God most of the time or even permanently. A reference is
made to this state in the Glorious Qur'an:

'Verily the righteous ones shall be in bounteous bliss, On
exalted couches will they view. Thou (O, our Apostle
Muhammad) will recognize in their faces, the (delightful)
radiance of the bliss.' (83: 22-24)

This quality can be achieved in this world by those who have arrived at high stages of the knowledge of God. It is told of Imam 'Alī that he said:

If the veils are removed my certainty will not increase.

Imam 'Alī is also quoted as saying:

I was not to worship a lord whom I have not seen.

b. Invocation by quality *(dhikr-i wasfī)*. The stage higher and above that of invocation by state *(dhikr-i hālī)* is the one which is called invocation by quality. One who achieves this stage of the invocation of God is said to become mixed with His nature, and the invocation of God is never neglected by Him. Such a person is constantly in the state of the awareness of God and sees all things in God, and whatever he sees carries a sign of divine manifestation.

Referring to those who have attained this station (of invoking God), the Glorious Qur'an says:

'Verily, in the creation of the heavens and the earth and the alteration of the night and the day, there are signs for men who possess wisdom. Those who remember God standing, and sitting and reclining on their sides and think (seriously) in the creation of the heaven and the earth; saying "O, Our Lord! Thou hast not created (all) this in vain! Glory to Thee! Save us from the torment of the (hell) fire." O, Our Lord! Whomsoever Thou causeth to enter the (Hell) fire, surely Thou hast put him to disgrace; there is not, for the unjust, any of the helpers. "O, Our Lord! We have indeed heard the voice of a Crier (Apostle), calling (us) unto faith, saying "Believe ye in your Lord!" and we did we believe. O, Our Lord! Therefore "Forgive us then our sins and remove away from us our evil deeds, and cause us to die with the virtuous ones.' (3: 190-193)

Bābā Ṭāhir of Hamadan, the celebrated Iranian mystic and poet, refers to the same mystical station:

به دریا بنگرم دریا تو بینـــم

به صحرا بنگرم صحرا تو بینـــم

به هر جا بنگرم کوه ودر ودشت

نشان از قامت رعنا تو بینـــم

When I look to the sea, the sea I see is you;
When I look to the prairie, the prairie I see is you.
Wherever I look, at the mountains or the plains
I see nothing but signs of your lofty stature.

And also in these couplets:

خوشا آنانکه الله یارشان بی

به حمد وقل هو الله کارشان بی

خوشا آنانکه دائم در نمازنـد

بهشت جاودان بازارشان بی

O! Happy those whose friend is God
Their work is not but recitation of the Opening and the
Sincerity.
O! Happy those who ever are in prayer
Whose market-place is the everlasting Paradise.

Those who experience such an intense constant invocation of
God (exemplified in the above poem—a recitation of the 'Opening' and
the 'Sincerity' which are two chapters of the Qur'an that Muslims,
especially the Shi'a, recite in their ritual prayers) do not think about
food or sleep, and live in this world as a traveller who finds himself in a
state of passing on the Way towards God, his Beloved, as swiftly as possible
and yearns for the vision of the Beloved.

Imam Zayn al-'Ābidīn, the fourth Imam of Shi'ite Muslims,
describes certain attributes and states *(aḥwāl)* of the people who have
engaged in the practice of the invocation of God:

My God,
Inspire us with Thy remembrance

alone and in assemblies,
by night and they,
publicly and secretly
in prosperity and adversity!
Make us intimate with silent remembrance'
Employ us in purified works and effort pleasing to Thee,
And reward us with full balance,
My God,
Love-mad hearts are enraptured by Thee,
Disparate intellects are brought together by knowing Thee,
Hearts find no serenity except in remembering Thee,
Souls find no rest except in seeing Thee,
Thou art the glorified in every place,
The worshipped at every time,
The found at every moment,
The called by every tongue,
The magnified in every heart!
I pray forgiveness from Thee for
Every pleasure but remembering Thee,
Every ease but intimacy with Thee,
Every happiness but nearness to Thee,
Every occupation but obeying Thee,
My God,
Thou hast said—and Thy word is true—
O you who have faith,
Remember God with much remembrance
And glorify Him at dawn and in the evening!
Thou hast said—and Thy word is true—
Remember Me, and I will remember Thee,
And promised us that Thou wilt remember us thereby,
In order to ennoble, respect, and honour us.
Here we are, remembering Thee as Thou hast commanded
  us!
So accomplish what Thou hast promised,
O Rememberer of the rememberers!
O Most Merciful of the merciful![1]

---

[1] *The Psalms of Islam (Al-Ṣaḥīfāt al-Kāmilāt al-Sajjādiyya), The Whispered Prayer of the Rememberers*
  [81] XIII, 255, 256 (translated by William C Chittick).

As indicated in this whispered prayer, God the Almighty calls frequently in the Glorious Qur'an upon people to engage in constant invocation of God *(dhikr-i kathīr)*. The constant invocation of God implies the most important condition for the attainment of invocation by quality. Those who wish to attain this should engage in constant invocation of God and be adorned with the rules and rites of this sort of invocation.

Performing the (daily) ritual prayers and the recommended prayers *(nawāfil)* and reciting of the Glorious Qur'an in the morning and at night, and abundant and conscious recitation of *Allāhumma ṣall-i 'alā Muḥammad-in wa Āl-i Muḥammad* ('O God! bless Muhammad and his descendents!'), are considered to be the most important examples of constant invocation and the best means of achieving the stage of invocation by attribution.

One of the consequences of the abundant invocation of God, which is an inevitable implication of invocation by quality, is the burning flame of divine love within man.

In his reference to this quality of the invocation of God, Imam Zayn al-'Ābidīn in the prayer known as the Whispered Prayer of the Lovers *(Munājāt al-Muḥibbīn)* says:

> O God,
> place us among those
> whose habit is rejoicing in Thee and yearning for Thee,
> whose time is spent in sighing and moaning!
> Their foreheads are bowed down before Thy mightiness,
> their eyes wakeful in Thy service,
> their tears flowing in dread of Thee,
> their hearts fixed upon Thy love;
> their cores shaken with awe of Thee.
> O He
> the lights of whose holiness
> induce wonder in the eyes of His lovers,
> the glories of whose face
> arouse the longing of the hearts of his knowers!
> O Furthest Wish of the hearts of the yearners!
> O Utmost Limit of the hopes of the lovers!
> I ask from Thee love for Thee,
> love for those who love Thee,

love for every work which will join me to Thy nearness,
and that Thou makest Thyself more beloved to me
than anything other than Thee
and makest
my love for Thee
lead to Thy good pleasure,
and my yearning for Thee
protect against disobeying Thee!

c. Invocation by detachment and annihilation *(dhikr-i tajarrud wa finā)*

This is the highest or the supreme stage of the invocation or remembrance of God with which those stationed nearby *(muqarrabān)* in the divine Empyrean are adorned. In this stage of invocation the invoker is transformed into the pure remembrance or invocation of God. And all his existence is lovingly annihilated in the invocation of God and his words, his silence, his wakefulness, his sleep, his associations with others, his activities, his conduct, his sadness and delight, his laughter and cries, all become the invocation of God. The noblest example of such people who have attained this invocation of God is the holy being of the Prophet Muhammad. The holy Prophet of Islam is described in the Glorious Qur'an as *Dhikr* (Reminder):

> '... So fear you (the wrath of) God! O ye with understanding who believe! Indeed hath God sent down unto you a reminder, an Apostle who reciteth unto you the clear signs of God that he may bring out those who believe and do good deeds from the darkness unto light.' (65: 10 and 11)

Such people are considered to be not only the very invocation or remembrance of God but also the ones who, when they reside in a place or take part in an assembly, illuminate the place and the assembly with the light of invocation. Anyone who comes into contact with them can benefit from the light of the invocation of God, and if someone loves those stationed near to God, this, in fact, will constitute the remembrance and invocation of God. The divine light is illuminated in them and wherever they reside their existence will be the locus of the manifestation of God and His Grace. An outstanding example of such people is the Holy Prophet Muhammad and his family, who are explicitly characterized thus in the Glorious Qur'an:

> 'God is the Light of the heavens and the earth; the similitude
> of His Light is as a niche in which is a lamp, the lamp is in
> a glass; the glass is as it were a star shining bright, lit from a
> blessed olive tree, neither eastern nor western, the olive
> whereof almost gloweth forth (of itself), and (even) though
> fire toucheth it not. Light upon Light: God guideth unto
> his Light whomsoever he willeth; and God setteth forth
> parables for people; and God is All-aware of all things. (That
> Lamp is lit) in houses which God hath permitted to be
> exalted and His name be mentioned therein, therein declare
> glory unto Him in the mornings and the evenings. Men
> whom neither merchandise nor any sale diverteth from the
> remembrance of God and constancy in prayer and paying
> the poor-rate, they fear the day when the hearts and eyes
> shall writhe of the anguish.' (24: 35-37)

The most distinguished figures of this stage of the invocation of
God can serve as guides for those journeying towards God. This is not a
quality anybody can partake of. It is incumbent upon one who longs to
journey towards God and attain this station of invocation to follow the
spiritual teachings and guidance provided. These distinguished invokers
or reminders are characterized by their constant invocation of God,
which constantly invites others to follow their ways to which only a
chosen few can gain access. It is not the case that anybody can turn
hearts towards the remembrance of God and serve as a light which
illuminates neglectful hearts and awakens the clouded conscience and
purifies and washes away all internal impurities. This enterprise can be
accomplished by the constant invokers who, having been annihilated in
the invocation of God, have become the locus of the manifestation of
God and a radiation of His Divine Light.

As for the most outstanding quality of these invokers, one can
refer to the fact that not only do they illuminate individuals' hearts with
the Divine Light, but also that they provide assemblies, communities,
and nations all over the world and even the human race with illumination
throughout the ages. Furthermore, if people in all corners of the world
listen to their life-giving words and gain access to their spiritual teachings,

their lives will be totally absorbed in light for ever, the quality with which only the constant invokers are equipped.

In referring to this stage of constant and abundant invocation and the quality of invokers, Imam 'Alī ibn Abī Ṭālib says:

> Certainly Allah, the Glorified, has made His remembrance makes their hearts radiant which hear with its help despite deafness, see with its help despite blindness and become submissive with its help despite unruliness. In all the periods and times when there were no prophets there have been persons to whom Allah whispered through their wits and spoke through their minds. With the help of the bright awakening of their ears, eyes, and hearts they keep the remembrance of the days of Allah and make others fearful before the rigour and majesty of God as the guide-points in wildernesses. Whoever adopts the moderate way (of life) they praise his ways and give him the tidings of deliverance, but whoever goes right and left they vilify his ways and frighten him. In this way they served as lamps in the darkness and guides through these doubts. There are some people devoted to remembrance of Allah who have adopted it in place of worldly matters so that commerce or trade does not turn them away from it. They pass their life in it. They speak into the ears of neglectful persons warning against the matters held unlawful by Allah, order them to practise justice and themselves so and refrain them from the unlawful and themselves restrain from it. It is as though they have finished the journey of this world towards the next world and be held what lies beyond it. Consequently they have become acquainted with all that befell them in the interval during their long stay therein, and the day of judgment fulfilled its promises for them. Therefore they removed the curtain from these things for the people of the world till it was as though they were seeing what people did not see and were hearing what people did not hear. (*Nahj al-Balāgha*, Sermon 219)

Through following these chosen divine people, those who have attained the stage of the invocation of God, they are, in turn, capable of transferring the light and invocation of God to the other human beings, making use of the teachings and spiritual guidance of great invokers.

Today the healing solution for the wounded hearts of mankind is to make use of the spiritual teachings and guidance of these great invokers. These people can open up ways to the path of peace, friendship, love, compassion, equality, brotherhood, happiness, salvation and spirituality for modern societies which face serious spiritual crises.

THE PRINCIPLE AND THE PRACTICE OF THE REMEMBRANCE OF GOD: AN ISLAMIC PERSPECTIVE

Reza Shah-Kazemi

> *Verily the formal prayer keeps one away from lewdness and iniquity;*
> *and the remembrance of God is greater.*
> (Al-'Ankabūt, XXIX: 45)

This paper will explore the different dimensions proper to the notion of the 'remembrance of God' (*dhikru 'Llāh*) in the Islamic context. The principal argument is that this remembrance constitutes the very essence of religious devotion, both in principle and in practice. In principle, for the remembrance, understood as consciousness of the divine reality, is the goal of worship, in all its different forms; in practice, for the remembrance is also an activity, an all-embracing contemplative practice which is to be accomplished, and not merely thought about. This interplay between the principle and the practice of remembrance will be examined in relation to a series of key verses in the Holy Qur'an, and in the light of the sayings of the first Shi'i Imam, 'Alī b. Abī Ṭālib. These sayings go far in elucidating the meaning of the 'remembrance of God', and highlight the ways in which the inner realization of this remembrance transcends the plane on which formal prayer and outward action operate.

The verse cited in our epigraph above clearly establishes the principle that the remembrance of God is the summit of prayer, and thus of all religious practices; indeed, it is presented as the quintessence of all such practices, the remembrance of God being the very purpose for which the rites of religion have been instituted:

Establish the prayer for the sake of My remembrance (Ṭā Hā, XX: 14), Muslims are told. The very purpose and goal of the prayer, its spiritual value and substance, is thus the remembrance of God. It is therefore 'greater' than the prayer in the very measure that the goal transcends the means, the essence surpasses the form, and inner realization takes priority over outward practice. There is no prayer, no rite, no ritual that is separable from the remembrance; and this remembrance cannot be exclusively identified with any one of its possible modes.

This pre-eminence of the remembrance is affirmed by numerous sayings of the Prophet. To take just one as an example, he asked his companions: 'Shall I not tell you about the best and purest of your works for your Lord, and the most exalted of them in your ranks, and the work that is better for you than giving silver and gold, and better for you than encountering your enemy, with you striking their necks and them striking your necks?' Thereupon the people addressed by him said: 'What is that, O Emissary of God?' He said, 'The perpetual invocation of God—exalted and glorious *(dhikru'Llāh 'azza wa jalla dā'iman).'*

What, then, does the 'remembrance of God', the *dhikru'Llāh* mean? As regards the lexical meanings of the word *dhikr*, the most important, in the context of Islamic spirituality, are those of remembrance and invocation. The first relates to the principle of the awareness of divine reality, the only reality there is; the second pertains to the means by which this consciousness of God is to be attained, means which include prayer, supplication, glorification, praise, meditation, reflection, recitation of the Holy Qur'an, but which, in the context of Islamic contemplative discipline, is centred upon the continuous repetition or invocation of the Name or Names of God. *Dhikr* in the sense of remembrance, then, denotes spiritual consciousness, and *dhikr* in the sense of invocation refers to the central methodic practice that generates this consciousness. Both of these meanings must be borne in mind whenever the Arabic word *dhikr* is used. In what follows, we shall translate the word as 'remembrance' or as 'invocation' depending on the context, but each time one of these terms is employed, the other meaning should be understood as implicit.

★   ★   ★

The notion of the 'remembrance of God' takes us to the very heart of the Islamic message. This message, reduced to its most essential—hence, universal—dimensions can be summed up in the very word *dhikr* : for it is the purpose of divine revelation to 'remind' man, to make him recall that knowledge which is already ingrained in the depth of his inmost being, at the core of his intellect, woven into the very texture of his heart, the ultimate seat of consciousness. This knowledge of the reality of the Absolute has been clouded since the Fall, but not abolished by it; what is needed to revive this knowledge is not some extraneous item of information dictated from without, but a divinely revealed message which acts as a catalyst, a leaven for the raising up of the already extant knowledge within. Were it not for the existence of this innate and pre-personal knowledge of the Absolute, one would not be in a position to discern and affirm—to 're-cognize'—that the revelation is indeed a message from that self-same Absolute.

The Qur'an refers in several places to this innate knowledge of supernal realities within the human intellect. For example, we are told that, prior to the manifestation of creation, God took from the loins of Adam all the souls that would be born in the world, and asked them to testify: *Am I not your Lord? They said: Yea, we testify.* [This is] *lest ye say on the Day of Resurrection: Truly of this we were unaware.* (VII: 172)

Nobody, in other words, can plead ignorance on the Day of Judgement. Likewise these divine realities can be understood in reference to the divine spirit animating the human form, and articulating human consciousness: *Then He fashioned* [man] *and breathed into him of His Spirit* (Al-Sajda, XXXII: 9). This doctrine is also implied in the fact that God taught Adam the 'names'—the essences—of things: *And He taught Adam the names, all of them...* (Al-Baqara, II: 31). This divine spirit in man, together with the knowledge it contains, is the basis on which the angels are commanded by God to prostrate to Adam (Al-Ḥijr, XV: 28-29); it is also this spirit that defines the innermost, primordial nature of man, his *fiṭra*, patterned upon the divine nature itself: *... the nature of God (fiṭrat Allāh), that according to which He created man* (Al-Rūm, XXX: 30).

Each person's apparent lack of knowledge is the result, therefore, of the covering over of his heart by the 'rust' of worldliness, of egotism and of sin. *Nay, but what they have earned is rust upon their hearts* (Al-Muṭaffifīn, LXXXIII: 14). To remove this rust it is not only virtue but also, and pre-eminently, remembrance of the Real that is necessary. Moral conscience must be combined with spiritual consciousness if man's primordial nature is to be restituted. The necessity of these two dimensions, the horizontal and the vertical, is expressed in the following verses, which refer to the fallen state of humanity together with the means of overcoming it: *By the Age. Truly man is in a state of loss; except those who have faith and act virtuously ...* (Al-'Aṣr, CIII: 1-3). The vertical dimension is referred to in terms of faith, and the horizontal in terms of virtue. The last verse continues: *... and exhort one another to Truth and exhort one another to patience*; this reinforces the necessity of combining the two dimensions.

To focus more sharply on the vertical or spiritual aspect of the restitution of man's primordial nature, namely, the remembrance of God, we can turn to the following important exegesis by Imam 'Alī of the words of the Qur'an, *men whom neither commerce nor trade diverteth from the remembrance of God* (Al-Nūr, XXIV: 37). He comments: 'Truly God has made the remembrance *(al-dhikr)* a polish for the hearts, by which they hear after being deaf, and see after being blind and yield after being resistant. ... Indeed there is a special group *(ahl)* who belong to the *dhikr*, they have adopted it in place of the world, such that *neither trade nor commerce* distracts them from it. They spend the days of their life in it ... It is as though they had quitted this world for the Hereafter, and they are there, witnessing what is beyond this world ...'

The remembrance, then, is the principal means by which the revelation of God comes to be faithfully reflected in the mirror of the heart; the principles immanent within the intellect are brought to light by the message from the Transcendent—this being, precisely, one of the functions of revelation, according to the Imam. In one of his most important sermons, the Imam holds that God sent His prophets to mankind, 'to remind them of His forgotten graces ... to unearth for them the buried treasures of the intellects ...'

Thus, the purpose of revelation is not so much to teach man the principles that are essential for salvation, principles of which he is *a priori* ignorant; rather, it is to 're-mind' him of those principles which are 'buried' deep within his intellect, hidden behind clouds of forgetfulness, generated by egotism, vanity and pride. The process by which man comes to realize this innate spiritual knowledge—the 'remembrance of God' in the highest sense—can be referred to as the inner revelation of the intellect. For, according to the Imam, 'The prophet of a man is the interpreter of his intellect *(rasūl al-rajul tarjumān 'aqlihi).*'

Intellection from within reflects revelation from without. In the felicitous phrase of Frithjof Schuon, intellection is the revelation of the microcosm, just as revelation is the intellection of the macrocosm. This is the natural concomitant of the identification of revelation with remembrance, an identification made in the Qur'an itself in several places. For example: *Verily We have revealed the remembrance (al-dhikr) and verily We shall be its preserver* (Al-Ḥijr, XV: 9) ... *And God hath revealed a reminder (dhikrā), a Prophet reciting unto you the verses of God ...* (Al-Ṭalāq, LXV: 10-11).

This notion of remembrance, it is to be noted, embraces all previous revelations; it is not restricted to the Qur'an alone. For the essence of the revealed message is one and the same, however different be the outward forms by which it is enclothed, and however varied be the rulings, the rites and the rituals attendant upon the different revelations: *Naught is said unto thee* [Muḥammad] *but what was said unto the Messengers before thee.* (Fuṣṣilat, XLI: 43)

Just as the essence of the revelations is identical—the message of *tawḥīd*, to affirm the One Reality, and that of Islam, to conform to this One Reality—so one finds a remarkable unanimity within widely divergent religious traditions, as regards the quintessential means of performing this affirmation and realizing this conformity: the methodic invocation of a Name of the Absolute. The Names may differ but the Named is one and the same. This does not mean that any name we care to choose to refer to the Absolute becomes a valid name for it, but that any name of the Absolute *revealed* by the Absolute is a valid 'Name' of God, and its invocation, by man, leads to the realization of the Absolute, by virtue of the grace inherent in the Name—a principle to which we will return later.

This important point related to spiritual method is made clear in the Imam's supplication entitled *Du'ā' al-Mashlūl*—the supplication of the lame man. A dazzling array of divine Names and qualities are called upon in this supplication, and towards its end, one reads the following verse, which provides us with the key for the whole supplication, and also helps us to understand the efficacy of the invocation: 'I ask Thee by every Name with which Thou hast named Thyself.' The fact that God has named Himself imparts to the Names a theurgic power, that is, a power to make God truly present and active in one's consciousness and being. The Names are sacramental prolongations of the Named, charged with the divine presence, and thus with an infinite power of integration and attraction. They are not ordinary words or mere signs established by human convention, as modern linguistics and semiotics would have us believe. The Qur'an refers to such conventional names in the following verse, addressed to the pagan polytheists of Mecca who worshipped idols created by them and named by them: *These are but names which ye have named—ye and your fathers before you—for which God hath revealed no authority.* (Al-Najm, LIII: 23)

218

The divine authority *(sulṭān)* which invests a name with revealed substance is that which, alone, has the power to transform the soul; it is thus that the invocation of the Name leads to the Named. But for the invocation to have this ultimate transformative impact, three conditions are indispensable, one is methodic, another is liturgical and the third is moral. The first, methodic, condition is that the invocation be performed 'much'—in principle, always: *O ye who believe! Invoke God with much invocation* (Al-Aḥzāb, XXXIII: 42); *And invoke the Name of thy Lord morning and evening.* (Al-Insān, LXXVI: 25); *And invoke the Name of thy Lord, devoting yourself to it with utter devotion.* (Al-Muzzammil, LXXIII: 8) These verses are not to be taken in the abstract, but as concrete injunctions upon which the Prophet and his closest companions acted in earnest. We know from sound historical sources that the Prophet spent long hours each night in prayer, and the Qur'an likewise affirms: *Truly thy Lord knows that thou standest in prayer close to two-thirds of the night, and half of it, and a third of it—thou and a group of those with thee ...* (LXXIII: 20) While it is true that much of these night vigils would be taken up with recitation of the Qur'an—a form of remembrance, as we noted earlier—the practice of the invocation would also have been prominent as is obvious from the verses cited above.

The Imam makes clear, in disarmingly simple terms, why the invocation should be given such importance—why devotion to God should be expressed, among other things, through the invocation of His name: 'He who loves a thing dedicates himself fervently to its invocation.'This fervent dedication to the remembrance is well expressed in the following verses which describe the state of 'people of substance'. These are people who *remember God standing, sitting, and reclining on their sides and reflect upon the creation of the heavens and the earth ...* (Āl 'Imrān, III: 191)

This verse is also important in that it highlights the supraformal aspect of the invocation; the *dhikr* is presented here as the quintessence of all religious activity, or as the spiritual act *par excellence.* While the formal, canonical prayers are fixed in time, conditioned by various ritual requirements, and accomplished through specific movements and formulas, the *dhikr*, by contrast, is described as something to be performed at all times, in all places, in all postures; it is thus to be woven into the texture of everyday life, rather than super-imposed upon life as an extraneous, formalistic practice. The aim, then, of the methodic practice of the invocation is a condition in which the remembrance of God is uninterrupted.

As we saw earlier, the ideal state of the believer is that he is never distracted from the remembrance of God by outward activities; we are also told that the believers are those who are 'perpetually at prayer' *('alā ṣalātihim dā'imūn)* (Al-Ma'ārij, LXX: 23): they are not only regular in the performance of the canonical prayer at the appropriate times, there is no time when they are not 'at prayer', if one understands by 'prayer' the remembrance of God.

The following saying of the Imam is relevant here: 'Continuous invocation is the food of the spirit and the key to prayer *(miftāḥ al-ṣalāt)*.' One understands better in this light the reason why the Qur'an tells us, as was noted earlier: *prayer keepeth* [one] *away from lewdness and iniquity, and the remembrance of God is greater.* (Al-'Ankabūt, XXIX: 45) The formal, canonical prayer is described here in negative or constraining terms: it is a preventative. Its very formality is defined as a ritual necessity, but it is also, unavoidably, an existential limitation: it is performed and operative at one time and not another, expressed in certain forms and movements and not others, whereas the remembrance of God is greater in that it is the positive, enlivening substance of prayer, it is that which liberates consciousness from the limits—verbal, mental, existential—by which all formal prayer is defined. Since all formal prayer is thus inescapably defined, objectively, within certain limits, its *baraka* or blessedness, can all too easily become confined, subjectively, within those limits: one feels close to God only when praying, and not in one's every day life, outside the prayer-times. It is *dhikr*, in the sense of recollectedness, awareness of God, that allows prayer (or the consciousness conditioned by prayer) to open out into the intended essence of prayer, into an awareness of the unconditional presence of God.

From the point of view of this awareness, even the formal nature of the canonical prayer ceases to be a limitation: the reality of the divine presence bestowed by the remembrance comes to suffuse all of one's prayers, and eventually, with the grace of God, all of one's being. The prayers, then, are integrated within one's all-embracing remembrance, rather than simply being performed as a religious obligation. This leads to the second of the conditions for the efficacy of the *dhikr*, the liturgical. Despite the fact that the *dhikr* is 'greater' than the prayer, it cannot be performed except on the basis of the prayer, and all of the formalities that condition the prayer. It transcends these formalities, certainly, but without this liturgical framework, the performance of the *dhikr* becomes nothing more than an individualistic and subjective initiative, deprived of the grace—the Heavenly seal—that protects, stabilizes and strengthens all that the individual does by way of supererogatory practice. In the words of the *ḥadīth qudsī* (a 'holy utterance', by God, on the tongue of the Prophet):

> 'My slave draws near to Me through nothing I love more than that which I have made obligatory for him. My slave never ceases to draw near to Me through supererogatory acts *(nawāfil)* until I love him. And when I love him, I am his hearing by which he hears, his sight by which he sees, his hand by which he grasps, and his foot by which he walks.'

While the obligatory prayers initiate man's movement towards God, those prayers offered to God not out of religious obligation but spiritual aspiration, lead to the mystery of loving communion. Here are brought face to face with the ultimate degree of *tawḥīd*, mystical union, the *deificatio* or *theosis* referred to in the Christian tradition. But this mystical realization of *tawḥīd* cannot be attained without first accomplishing that prefiguration of effacement which *islām* is, the obedient conformity to the will of God. Conformity to the outward religious obligations is thus not so much a formal constraint that prevents one from realizing the essence, but the very ground upon which one ascends towards the essence.

This point of view is well expressed in the following saying of the Imam: 'Do not remember God absent-mindedly *(sāhiyan)*; nor forget Him in distraction; rather, remember Him with perfect remembrance *(dhikran kāmilan)*, a remembrance in which your heart and tongue are in harmony, and what you hide conforms with what you disclose. But you will not remember Him according to the true reality of the remembrance *(ḥaqīqat al-dhikr)* until you forget your own soul in your remembrance.'

The first part of this saying, stressing the need for harmony between the heart and the tongue, relates to the third condition for the invocation, that of virtue, to which we will turn shortly. The 'perfection' of remembrance refers to virtue—the harmony between the heart and the tongue, the intention and the action; the ultimate 'reality' of remembrance, however, is predicated on what appears to be its very opposite: the most radical 'forgetting'. But it is in the invocation itself that this forgetting of oneself takes place: you will not remember God according to the true reality of the remembrance 'until you forget your own soul *in your remembrance.*' The remembrance itself continues, but is no longer conditioned by individual consciousness. This can only mean that the seat of consciousness has shifted from the invoker to the Invoked: the reality, or *ḥaqīqa* of the *dhikr* is thus one with the object of Invocation, God Himself, al-Ḥaqq, the Real. Esoterically, then, it can be said that the true agent of the invocation is God Himself, the invocation by man being but an outward appearance—an appearance which is extinguished by the very act of the invocation itself. The Imam expresses this esoteric truth in the following saying: 'The invocation is not a formality of speech nor a way of thinking: rather, it comes forth, firstly, from the Invoked and secondly from the invoker.'

It is thus God Himself who performs the invocation, first and foremost; man's invocation is but a shadow, a reflection, or a consequence of this divine invocation. We shall return to this mystery below.

To return to the first part of the above saying, relating to virtue, or the harmony between the heart and the tongue, the need for sincerity or for integral virtue must be stressed as one of the conditions of the practice of the invocation: if one is invoking the divine Name, one's character must be governed by divine qualities—one must be as much 'like' God as possible, within the framework of one's creaturely possibilities, and this implies an active orientation towards all of the fundamental virtues, the reflections in the soul of the qualities of God. The Prophet instructed the Muslims: make your moral qualities those of God. If the tongue is invoking the divine Name, the heart must be assimilating the divine nature, only then is there harmony between the two, only then is the invocation 'perfect'.

Likewise, we have these verses from the Qur'an: *Successful indeed is he who purifieth himself; and invoketh the Name of his Lord, and prayeth* (Al-A'lā, LXXXVII: 14-15).

While the remembrance itself contributes to this purification in the most direct way, its efficacy will be deepened insofar as the soul is governed by virtue—or at least, by virtuous intentions—and correspondingly diminished if there be no active striving after virtue, and no effort to rid oneself of error, sin and vice.

The following Qur'anic verses should also be noted in this context. They link the invocation of the divine with a variety of moral qualities: *Call upon thy Lord in humility and in secret ... and call upon Him with fear and in hope* (Al-A'rāf, VII: 55-56); *And invoke thy Lord within thyself, in humility and awe, and beneath thy breath, in the morning and in the night* (Al-A'rāf, VII: 205).

In other words, a deep-rooted orientation towards all of the fundamental qualities of soul must accompany the invocation, the effectiveness of which is deepened thereby.

Finally, let us turn to another way in which the efficacy of the remembrance is enhanced, and this will take us back to the mystery touched upon above: the invocation comes first from God and secondarily from man. This can be understood not only as an expression of the truth that man can do nothing without the grace of God, but also in relation to the very process of creation, of divine existentiation.

The following verse serves well as a starting point for the reflection that will bring this talk to a close: *Hath there come upon man any moment in time when he was not a thing remembered?* (Al-Insān, LXXVI: 1) The time prior to man's creation is described as a 'moment' when he was not 'remembered' *(madhkūr)*. This implies that man's being 'remembered' is equivalent to his being created: thus, for God to 'create' man is tantamount to a divine 'remembrance' of man, creation equals remembrance. Man is summoned by the *fiat lux*, not from some forgetfulness within God, *quod absit*, but from that hidden, pre-existential state from which he emerges into the light of creation. The creative word uttered by God, 'Be!' *(kun)*, which brings into existence the possibilities of being, can be seen in this light as a form of *dhikr*:

> *His command, when he desireth a thing, is only that He saith unto it: Be! and it is* (Yā Sīn, XXXVI: 82).

If the divine *dhikr* is identified with creation, what does this imply for the human accomplishment of *dhikr*? It implies two processes, one affirmative and the other negative. As for the first, this is the active and conscious participation by man in the very reality underlying divine creativity—there is nothing more spiritually creative for man than performing the act which mirrors the divine act of creation. As for the second, this is the very opposite of creation: the effacement of the relative

223

in the Face of the Absolute, this stemming from the inverse analogy between man and God. As the Imam says, the individual is 'forgotten' in the very act of invocation, and only then is the *ḥaqīqa*, the ultimate spiritual reality, of the invocation attained. But attained by what or by whom, since individual awareness is no longer present? It can only be by God Himself, the true agent of the invocation: as the Imam put it, the invocation comes forth from the Invoked, from God Himself. The sole true agent of the invocation is also the only being in reality, and thus that which imparts to man whatever reality he possesses—or rather, is possessed by. Thus we arrive at the full metaphysical implication of the first testimony of Islam, *lā ilāha illa 'Llāh*, no god but God comes to mean: no reality but the one and only Reality. To realize—to 'make real' in the fullest sense—this one and only Reality is, by the same token, to realize the unreality, or the merely apparent reality of everything else. To remember God is thus to forget everything but God—and it means finding that in fact there is nothing but God in being. To return to the Imam's image of the heart 'polished' by the remembrance, the heart which 'sees' after being blind and which 'hears' after being deaf, we can conclude thus: the heart sees the Face of God wherever it looks, and hears the cosmic hymn of remembrance and praise chanted by the whole of creation. For, on the one hand:

> *Wherever ye turn, there is the Face of God* (Al-Baqara, II: 115).

And on the other:

> *...whosoever is in the Heavens and the earth praises God; and the birds in flight with outstretched wings—each knoweth its prayer and glorification* (Al-Nūr, XXIV: 41).

THE REMEMBRANCE OF GOD:
SOME ASPECTS OF CHRISTIAN PRAYER AND MONASTIC SPIRITUALITY

Wulstan Peterburs

Prayer, the remembrance of God, is essential for a Christian. Indeed, for a monk such as myself, it is the essence of my vocation, the very reason for my being a monk. Through prayer the believer is united with God the Father, and through the power of the Holy Spirit is transformed at the deepest possible level into the image of Jesus, the Son of God Incarnate, who came into the world to redeem sinners. From this it follows that fundamentally prayer is God's work in us. It is true that we have to make an effort, we have to say our prayers, but it is God who gives us the desire to pray, and it is God who works in us to enable us to live our lives in this world as a preparation for eternal life with Him in the next.[1] As St Francis de Sales (1567-1622) taught four hundred years ago in his *Introduction to the Devout Life*, true devotion to God:

> is nothing else than a true love of God. It is not, however, love as such. Insofar as divine love enriches us it is called grace, which makes us pleasing to God. Insofar as it gives us the strength to do good, it is called charity. But when it grows to such a degree of perfection that it makes us not only do good but rather moves us to do it carefully, frequently and promptly, it is called devotion.[2]

---

[1] So seems to be the import of the 'Our Father', the prayer that Jesus taught his followers when they asked him to teach them how to pray (Matthew 6: 7-15; Luke 11: 1-4). A number of spiritual writers, including St Augustine of Hippo (354-430) and St Teresa of Avila (1515-82) have offered commentaries on this prayer, showing how it is the summary of all prayer. This essay, rather than trying to emulate such spiritual masters, is concerned with only certain aspects of Christian prayer and monastic spirituality. Indeed, when placed in the context of the whole monastic tradition, even this is an ambitious project for one who has not been in monastic life for very many years.

[2] J F Power, ed., *Francis de Sales: Finding God Wherever You Are, Selected Spiritual Writings*, New York, 1993, 30.

Thus it is only over time, usually a lifetime, given to the loving remembrance of God, and to the love of enemies as well as friends,[3] that a person is able to begin to fulfil Jesus' command, 'Be perfect, as your heavenly Father is perfect.'[4]

So, on the one hand prayer is understood correctly as a Christian duty, but on the other it is a free and loving response to God's offer of salvation in Christ, the means by which a person grows in grace. But this does not mean that there is only one way for the Christian to pray. In fact, there are as many ways to pray as there are people, and as the former Benedictine Abbot of Downside, John Chapman, said, 'Pray as you can, and don't try to pray as you can't.'[5] Francis de Sales, albeit in the language of his time, is more specific:

> Devotion is to be practised differently by the nobleman, the worker, the servant, the prince, the widow, the young girl, the wife. Even more than this, the practice of devotion has to be adapted to the strength, life-situation and duties of each individual … Do you think … that it is suitable for a bishop to desire to live the life of a hermit like a Carthusian monk? If people with a family were to want to be like the Capuchins in not acquiring any property, if a worker spent a great deal of time in church like the member of a religious order, and if a religious was always subject to being disturbed in all sorts of ways for the service of his neighbour like a bishop, would not such devotion be ridiculous, disorderly and intolerable? It is an error, or rather a heresy, to try to exclude the devout life from the soldiers' regiment, the workers' shop, the court of rulers or the home of the married. It is true … that a devotion which is purely contemplative, monastic and religious cannot be practised in such occupations. However, besides these three sorts of devotion, there are many others suitable for leading to perfection those who live their lives in the world.[6]

---

[3] Matthew 5: 44; Luke 6: 27-9.
[4] Matthew 5: 48.
[5] J Chapman, *The Spiritual Letters of Dom John Chapman OSB*, edited and with an Introductory Memoir by Dom Roger Hudleston OSB, London, 1935, 25.
[6] Power, *Francis de Sales*, 31-2.

Accordingly, this essay cannot attempt to describe all the possible forms of Christian devotion. Rather it will first concentrate on some of the basic characteristics of Christian prayer, as found in the New Testament and exemplified in the life of Jesus, and then offer a few comments on monastic prayer and spirituality.

The Catholic Church teaches that God has revealed Himself in Christ and that 'no new public revelation'[7] is to be expected until Christ's Second Coming in glory at the end of time. Whilst this revelation is primarily a personal revelation, God revealing Himself to us, it is not only legitimate but necessary to articulate this revelation in propositional form.[8] The process by which this revelation is handed on from one generation to the next within the Church, and the meaning of it made more explicit, is called 'Tradition';[9] and the greatest 'monument' of Tradition is Scripture, the written Word of God.[10]

Thus the New Testament, the written record of Jesus' life on earth, is a particular source of inspiration and prayer for all Christians. Indeed, Jesus, chosen by God the Father before time began to be the priest of the new and everlasting covenant, who offered himself as a sacrifice to take away the sins of the world, provides a model of prayer and devotion for all Christians to follow. As the writer of the Letter to the Hebrews said of Christ:

> During his life on earth, he offered up prayer and entreaty, aloud and in silent tears, to the one who had the power to save him out of death, and he submitted so humbly that his prayer was heard. Although he was Son, he learnt to obey through suffering; but having been made perfect, he became for all who obey him the source of eternal salvation and was acclaimed by God with the title of high priest of the order of Melchizedek.[11]

---

[7] 'The Dogmatic Constitution on Divine Revelation', *Dei Verbum*, 4. Edition cited, A Flannery, ed., *Vatican Council II: Volume 1 The Conciliar and Postconciliar Documents*, New York, 1998.

[8] *Dei Verbum*, 6-7.

[9] Spelt with a capital 'T' and distinguished from individual traditions. J Ratzinger, 'The Transmission of Divine Revelation', in ed. H Vorgrimler, *Commentary on the Documents of Vatican II*, London, 1969, vol 3, 183-4.

[10] A Nichols, *The Shape of Catholic Theology: An Introduction to Its Sources, Principles and History*, Edinburgh, 1991, 177.

[11] Hebrews 5: 7-10.

This pattern of prayer and devotion, which in Jesus brings salvation to all who believe in him, is amply evidenced in the Gospels. As well as attending the synagogue and the Temple, Jesus is frequently portrayed as spending time in silent private prayer with God his Father, the source who sustains him; and at crucial moments in his ministry, the evangelists record that Jesus prayed. So, at the beginning of his public ministry Jesus spent forty days alone in the desert praying,[12] prayer accompanied the choosing of the Twelve,[13] prayer to the Father enabled the working of miracles, such as the raising of Lazarus from the dead,[14] prayer was his refuge when he had to resist the crowd's desire to make him king,[15] and as his earthly life neared its completion in his self-sacrifice on the cross at Calvary he went with his disciples to the Garden of Gethsemane to pray that ultimately he might do his Father's will:

> They came to a plot of land called Gethsemane, and he said to his disciples, 'Stay here while I pray.' Then he took Peter and James and John with him. And he began to feel terror and anguish. And he said to them, 'My soul is sorrowful to the point of death. Wait here and stay awake.' And going on a little further he threw himself on the ground and prayed that, if it were possible, this hour might pass him by. 'Abba, Father!' he said, 'For you everything is possible. Take this cup away from me. But let it be as you, not I, would have it.[16]

Moreover, Jesus' dying words were a prayer. As he hung on the cross,

> Jesus cried out in a loud voice saying, 'Father, into your hands I commit my spirit.' With these words he breathed his last.[17]

---

[12] Luke 4: 1-13.
[13] Matthew 9: 38 & Luke 10: 2.
[14] John 11: 41-4.
[15] Matthew 14: 22-3, Mark 6: 45-6, and John 6: 15.
[16] Mark 14: 32-6.
[17] Luke 23: 46.

In baptism the believer shares in this death, in Jesus' dying to pay for humankind the penalty for sin, and thus in Christ Jesus, the Christian finds the pattern of true devotion and submission to God, the exemplar according to which the believer's life will be conformed; and just as Jesus was raised from the tomb to complete the victory over sin and death and to reign with God in heaven, the believer too, through baptism and faith, has eternal life through him.

It is in this context that St Paul wrote to the early Christians in Colossae that they should:

> Let the Word of Christ, in all its richness, find a home in you. Teach each other, and advise each other, in all wisdom. With gratitude in your hearts sing psalms and hymns and inspired songs to God; and whatever you say or do, let it be in the name of the Lord Jesus, in thanksgiving to God the Father through him.[18]

When this is combined with Paul's advice to the Thessalonians to 'pray constantly',[19] it becomes clear that prayer is not an 'optional extra', but rather an essential part of human living. Prayer allows God into our lives, to work within and among us, so as to bring us to salvation; or to put it another way, it is through prayer that we may become all that God has created us to be, as we offer ourselves, whole and entire to Him. This happens most completely and effectively in the eucharist, the re-enactment and perpetuation of Christ's saving death and resurrection. As St Irenaeus taught in the second century:

> We must therefore, make an offering to God and show ourselves in everything grateful to him who made us, in the purity of our thoughts, the sincerity of our faith, the firmness of our hope and our burning charity, as we offer him the first fruits of the creatures that are his. This is the pure offering that the Church alone makes to her creator, presenting her gift to him gratefully from his creation.
> We offer him what belongs to him, as we appropriately recall our fellowship and union and confess the resurrection

---

[18] Colossians 3: 16–7.
[19] I Thessalonians 5: 17.

of flesh and spirit. For as the earthly bread once it has received the invocation of God upon it, is no longer ordinary bread, but the eucharist, and is made up of two elements, heavenly and earthly, so too our bodies, once they have received the eucharist, are no longer corruptible, but contain within themselves the hope of resurrection.[20]

Through faith and prayer, then, the Christian is alive to God, and so as St Paul wrote:

I have been crucified with Christ and yet I am alive; yet it is no longer I, but Christ living in me. The life that I am now living, subject to the limitation of human nature, I am living in faith, faith in the Son of God who loved me and gave himself for me.[21]

From this it follows that 'our homeland is in heaven'[22] and that the life we have 'is hidden with Christ in God',[23] animated by the gift to us of the Holy Spirit, through whom we become the inheritors of God's promised salvation. Thus St Paul wrote to the Romans:

Everyone moved by the Spirit is a son of God. The spirit you received is not the spirit of slaves bringing fear into your lives again; it is the spirit of sons, and it makes us cry out, 'Abba, Father!' The Spirit himself and our spirit bear united witness that we are children of God. And if we are children we are heirs as well: heirs of God and coheirs with Christ, sharing his sufferings so as to share his glory ...
The Spirit too comes to help us in our weakness. For when we cannot choose words in order to pray properly, the Spirit himself expresses our plea in a way that could never be put into words, and God who knows everything in our hearts knows perfectly well what he means, and that the pleas of

---

[20] Irenaeus, *Against the Heresies*, Bk 4, 18. 4 and 5.
[21] Galatians 2: 20.
[22] Philippians 3: 20.
[23] Colossians 3: 3.

the saints expressed by the Spirit are according to the mind of God.[24]

Christian prayer, then, is a uniting of the believer with the Trinitarian God, so that as the believer is conformed to Christ, God's power to save may become effective in his life, and through him in the world. This is the message of the prayer which St Paul taught the Ephesians:

> This, then, is what I pray, kneeling before the Father, from whom every fatherhood, in heaven or on earth, takes its name. In the abundance of his glory may he, through his Spirit, enable you to grow firm in power with regard to your inner self, so that Christ may live in your hearts through faith, and then, planted in love and built on love, with all God's holy people you will have the strength to grasp the breadth and the length, the height and the depth; so that knowing the love of Christ, which is beyond knowledge, you may be filled with the utter fullness of God.
> Glory be to him whose power, working in us, can do infinitely more than we can ask or imagine; glory be to him from generation to generation in the Church and in Christ Jesus for ever and ever. Amen.[25]

All that has been written so far about Christian prayer is necessarily true of the prayer of monks and nuns, who are called to give themselves to a life of seeking God in prayer, work and, normally, in community living. Furthermore, the three ways of praying that are often taken to typify monastic prayer and spirituality are not reserved to monastics alone, but can be practised by all Christians. Yet, in their combination, and as integral to a life lived according to a monastic rule[26] and dedicated to God through the three monastic vows of stability,

---

[24] Romans 8: 14–7; 26–7.

[25] Ephesians 3: 14–21.

[26] In the West the dominant influence upon monasticism has been the 6th century *Rule of St Benedict*. For the text of the *Rule* see ed. T Fry, *RB 1980: The Rule of St Benedict in Latin and English with Notes*, Collegeville, 1981; and for a study of its influence, J Leclercq, *The Love of Learning and the Desire for God: A Study of Monastic Culture*, New York, 2001.

conversatio morum and obedience,[27] these ways of praying come to be seen as characteristic of the monastic life. These ways are the divine office, called by St Benedict the *opus dei*,[28] the work of God; *lectio divina*, which is the prayerful reading of the scriptures and other spiritual works; and private, silent prayer, sometimes called 'mental prayer'.

The divine office, also called the 'liturgy of the hours', and sometimes 'choir office', is the prayer which a monastic community comes together in church at regular times during the day to pray, and is the most public and obvious way in which monastics are seen praying: it 'is the centre of the monk's life. All else flows out from it and leads back to it.'[29] This prayer consists mainly of the psalms, which are either chanted or sung, so as to heighten the sense of the sacred and to deepen the level of personal involvement in the prayer. With some modification to the timetable established by St Benedict,[30] a daily rhythm of communal prayer is followed in monasteries, the usual pattern being: matins, lauds, midday office, vespers and compline. The eucharist, which is the centre of the Church's liturgy, is also celebrated daily.

St Benedict's arrangement of the offices spaced regularly through the day builds on our natural experience of time,[31] linking this with the life and mission of Jesus. Thus matins, which begins before sunlight can be seen as reflecting the time of Christ's resting in the tomb and his descent to the dead. It can also be regarded as the 'eschatological office', the time of keeping vigil, according to the Gospel command to 'Stay awake!'[32] for the return of Christ at the end of time, when he will come to judge the living and the dead. Lauds consecrates the sunrise, which may be understood as a symbol of Christ's resurrection, whilst vespers, sung at evening is related to the crucifixion. Noon is celebrated by its own proper office, as is the time after sunset at the close of the day. As well as hallowing the day, the regular spacing of prayer during the day gives it a certain shape and rhythm, helping monastics to offer themselves, and all that they do and are, to God. This is also reinforced by the monastic

---

[27] *RB* 58: 17.

[28] *RB* 58: 7.

[29] C Smith, *The Path of Life: Benedictine Spirituality for Monks and Lay People*, Ampleforth, 1995, 122.

[30] *RB* 8–19.

[31] In St Benedict's day the times of the offices were set according to natural light and not according to clocks.

[32] Matthew 25: 13.

custom of turning the mind frequently to God throughout the course of the day with the aid of short, ejaculatory prayers, such as 'O God, come to my assistance' and 'Be merciful to me, a sinner.'[33]

The divine office is communal, rather than private, prayer, offered by members of the Church, the body of Christ.[34] Moreover, those who pray the divine office are participating in the prayer of Christ, who is constantly interceding for the salvation of all people. The significance of this is that the office is not so much concerned with one's own individual needs and desires, as with allowing oneself to become a channel for grace, so that Christ may pray in us. As St Augustine taught, Christian prayer is made to, through and in Christ.[35]

The vehicle for this universal prayer of Christ is the psalms. These originated as sung prayers, many composed for the ancient Jewish Temple liturgy, but 'the Church has always seen them as possessing a certain prophetic character, expressing (though sometimes in a veiled symbolism) the mystery of Christ, who he is, what he has done, and what he continues to do. We know that Jesus, during his earthly life, prayed these psalms daily, and it is in him that their full meaning emerges. It is in this sense that we should understand them and pray them.'[36]

The divine office, then, is a central feature of monastic prayer and spirituality. The office provides the day with its rhythm, hallowing its hours, and in these 'strong moments'[37] of the monastic day, those praying it are united with the prayer of Christ, interceding for the salvation of all. In this way, it is well named by St Benedict as the 'work of God'.

Also important, and equally characteristic of monasticism, is *lectio divina*, which St Benedict in chapter 48 of his *Rule* establishes as integral to monastic life. Although chapter 48 is actually entitled, 'The Daily Manual Labour', it is concerned with which portions of the monastic day should be assigned to *lectio* and work, the priority of *lectio*

---

[33] See John Cassian's *Tenth Conference* in John Cassian, *Conferences,* translated and with a preface by C Luibheid and with an introduction by O Chadwick, New York, 1985, 132-6; and also the anonymous, *The Way of Silent Love: Carthusian Novice Conferences*, London, 1993, 16-7.

[34] This remains true even when the office has to be celebrated in private.

[35] *Commentary on Psalm 85.*1.

[36] Smith, *Path of Life*, 133. On praying the psalms see also M Boulding, *Marked for Life: Prayer in the Easter Christ*, London, 1995, 44-57.

[37] A Field, ed., *Directory for the Celebration of the Work of God*, Riverdale, 1981, 24-5.

over work seemingly suggested in the command that, 'If anyone is so remiss and indolent that he is unwilling or unable to study or to read, he is to be given some work in order that he may not be idle.' [38]

The character of *lectio divina* was given its classic expression by the twelfth-century Carthusian monk, Guigo, in his *Ladder of Monks (Scala Claustralium)*. Guigo accepted a division of *lectio* into four stages:[39] reading, prayer, meditation and contemplation, which flow one into the next, and which he said constitute 'the ladder of monks by which they are raised up from earth to heaven'[40]. Guigo gives a brief definition of each of the four rungs:

> Reading is, as it were, the foundation and comes first; it supplies material and then refers us to meditation. Meditation earnestly enquires what we should seek, and, as it were, digs out and finds the treasure and shows it to us, but since it cannot obtain anything by itself, it refers us on to prayer. Prayer raises itself up with all its might towards God and asks for the desired treasure, the sweetness of contemplation. This, when it comes, rewards the labour of the preceding three ... Reading without meditation is arid, meditation without reading is erroneous; prayer without meditation is tepid, meditation without prayer is fruitless. Prayer with devotion wins contemplation, but the attainment of contemplation without prayer is rare or miraculous.[41]

This characterisation of *lectio*, however, if one is not careful to read it within the context of the monastic tradition, can seem to suggest that all one has to do to achieve a state of contemplation, and thus union with God, is to begin reading carefully. Furthermore, both reading and meditation, according to Guigo's presentation, can too easily be seen as purely intellectual exercises. The key to *lectio* is to regard the whole activity as prayer, and to remember that prayer is a gift from God. This means that it should be not a surprise if the gift of contemplation is only rarely

---

[38] *RB* 48: 1-2, and 23.

[39] S Tugwell argues that this division did not originate with Guigo. *Ways of Imperfection: An Exploration of Christian Spirituality*, Springfield, 1985, 93.

[40] Guigo, *Ladder of Monks*, 2, cited in Tugwell, *Ways of Imperfection*, 94.

[41] Guigo, *Ladder of Monks*, 12 and 14, cited in Tugwell, *Ways of Imperfection*, 99.

granted, except perhaps to those called 'mystics', and that for most an aspiration towards contemplation must suffice. The Fathers spoke of letting the mind descend into the heart, and, although St Benedict does not really say anything about 'prayer techniques' this seems to be close to what he understood *lectio* to be.[42] According to the Trappist Abbot André Louf what happens is that, 'the mind temporarily abandons its independent abstract explorations in order to arrive at union with the heart where the affective and intuitive faculties are hidden',[43] in other words, the prayer of *lectio* affects the whole person. Accordingly, meditation as part of *lectio* is not an active intellectual process whereby reading is fitted into a conceptual framework, but rather a process of allowing the Word of God to 'break open and reform' the reader.[44]

In the time of St Benedict, and into the middle ages, the reader actually pronounced the words of his *lectio* with his lips, albeit quietly, as part of memorising the text and allowing it to sink into himself. This reading and meditation,

> inscribes, so to speak, the sacred text in the body and in the soul ... To meditate is to attach oneself closely to the sentence being recited and weigh all its words in order to sound the depths of their full meaning. It means assimilating the content of a text by means of a kind of mastication which releases it is full flavour.[45]

Lectio divina, then, is a slow, meditative ruminating on the words of scripture, which allows Jesus, the Word of God, into both mind and heart, transforming the believer into his likeness. In short, it is 'prayerful reading',[46] and hence the advice given to the monk:

> When he reads, let him seek savour, not science. The holy scripture is the well of Jacob from which the waters are

---

[42] See for example *RB* 8: 3: 'In the time remaining after vigils, those who need to learn some of the psalter or readings should study them.'

[43] A Louf, *Tuning into Grace: The Quest for God*, London, 1992, 142.

[44] M B Pennington, *Lectio Divina: Renewing the Ancient Practice of Praying the Scriptures*, New York, 1998, 61.

[45] Leclercq, *The Love of Learning and the Desire for God*, 73.

[46] Leclercq, *The Love of Learning and the Desire for God*, 73. See also M Magrassi, *Praying the Bible: An Introduction to Lectio Divina*, Collegeville, 1998, for a careful discussion of *lectio*.

drawn which will be poured out later in prayer. Thus there will be no need to go to the oratory to begin to pray; but in reading itself, means will be found for prayer and contemplation.[47]

The third way of praying that has been characteristic of monasticism since its beginning, is private, silent prayer. This is often called 'mental prayer', and some Christian spiritualities, most notably those based on the *Spiritual Exercises* of St Ignatius of Loyola,[48] depend heavily on the imagination to picture and meditate discursively upon gospel images. The monastic tradition, however, is quite different from this. For monastics, private prayer is more a matter of just being silent and still in the presence of God. As the great 16th-century reformer of the Carmelites, St Teresa of Avila, taught, prayer is more a matter of love than of words or ideas.[49] Put a little differently, it is not so much a matter of talking to God, but of a 'deep, inarticulate longing for one in whom one's whole being can rest and be at peace. It is to do with leaving a space in which the silence of God can become real ... It is a question of getting out of the way and letting God take over.'[50] This type of private prayer, which originates in a desire for God, aspires to a wordless contemplation of Him, as is described, for example, in the anonymous fourteenth-century monastic classic of contemplative prayer, *The Cloud of Unknowing*.[51]

For St Benedict prayer should flow naturally from a (monastic) life well lived, and thus he says little specifically about private prayer, although what he does say gives some indication as to how he understood it. In his chapter on the 'Oratory of the Monastery', St Benedict teaches that the oratory is a place for prayer and nothing else, so that if 'someone chooses to pray privately, he may go in and pray, not in a loud voice, but with tears and heartfelt devotion,'[52] and when discussing 'Reverence in

---

[47] Arnoul of Boheriss, *Speculum monachorum* I, cited in Leclercq, *The Love of Learning and the Desire for God*, 73.

[48] *The Spiritual Exercises of Saint Ignatius of Loyola*, translated by W H Longridge, London, 1955.

[49] K Kavanaugh and O Rodriguez, eds., *The Collected Works of St Teresa of Avila: Volume 1 The Book of Her Life*, Washington DC, 1987, 94-100.

[50] D Morland, 'A Spiritual Jigsaw', ed. M Boulding, *A Touch of God*, Triangle, London, 1988, 71-2.

[51] W Johnston, ed., *The Cloud of Unknowing and the Book of Privy Counselling*, Fount, 1997.

[52] *RB* 52: 4.

Prayer', he says that, 'We must know that God regards our purity of heart and tears of compunction, not our many words. Prayer should therefore be short and pure, unless perhaps it is prolonged under the inspiration of divine grace.'[53] These short sentences touch upon the important monastic theme of compunction, sometimes called 'contrition of the heart',[54] and a discussion of this is perhaps a good way to understand private prayer.

The first aspect of compunction is contrition, which is a real piercing *(punctio)* of the heart with sorrow for sin, not just a generalised depressive sense of guilt. It is a matter of being aroused from complacency and being stimulated to action, and this leads to the second, arguably more important, aspect, namely being filled with an urgent desire to be possessed totally by God. As Michael Casey, the Australian Trappist monk notes, 'It is precisely the comparison between what we are and what we could be which constitutes the triggering cause of the experience of compunction.'[55] St Benedict's comments in the *Rule* on private prayer quoted above seem reflect this experience, and echo closely the teaching of Pope St Gregory the Great, who held that:

> There are two main types of compunction. First the soul thirsting for God is pierced *(compungitur)* by fear and afterwards love. In the beginning the soul is moved to tears at the remembrance of its evil deeds and fears the prospect of eternal punishment. But when, after a long and anxious experience of pain, this fear works itself out, then is born in the soul a calmness coming from the assurance of forgiveness and the soul is inflamed with love for heavenly joys. He who previously wept at the prospect of being led to punishment now begins to weep most bitterly because he is far from the Kingdom. For the mind contemplates the choirs of angels, the community of the blessed spirits and the splendour of the unending vision of God and then he is more downcast because he is separated from these eternal goods than he was when he wept because he was afraid of

---

[53] *RB* 20: 3-4.

[54] Louf, *Tuning into Grace*, 59-77.

[55] M Casey, *The Undivided Heart: The Western Monastic Approach to Contemplation*, Petersham, 1994, 51.

unending evils. When the compunction of fear is complete
it draws the soul into the compunction of love.[56]

So, from this it seems that private prayer may be described as
an urgent longing for God, inspired by a sense of one's need for, and
love of, Him. It opens the believer to God's action, so that He may
complete His work of creation by bringing His creature to salvation;
and this, of course, is the primary function of all Christian prayer. This
is exemplified in a story told of St Jerome, who tried his vocation as a
hermit in the Egyptian desert in the 4th century, but felt that all his
efforts counted for nothing:

> So Jerome worried and brooded, until suddenly he glimpsed
> a crucifix that had positioned itself between the dry branches
> of a dead tree. He threw himself on the ground, beating his
> breast with firm, sweeping movements …
> It was not long before Jesus broke the silence and addressed
> Jerome from the cross.
> 'Jerome', said he, 'what do you have to give me? What am
> I getting from you?'
> That voice alone put fresh heart into Jerome again and he
> immediately began to wonder what he could offer his
> crucified friend.
> 'The loneliness, Lord', he answered. 'I offer you the loneliness
> with which I am struggling.'
> 'Excellent, Jerome', replied Jesus, 'and thank you very much.
> You have certainly done your best. But have you anything
> more to give me?'
> Not for a moment did Jerome doubt that he had much
> more to offer Jesus.
> 'Of course, Lord', he resumed. 'My fasting, my hunger and
> thirst. I only eat after sundown.'
> Again Jesus answered: 'Excellent, Jerome, and thank you
> very much. I know it. You really have done your best. But
> have you anything else to give me?'

---

[56] Gregory the Great, *Dialogues*, 3.34, cited in Casey, *The Undivided Heart*, 51-2.

Again Jerome reflected on what he might be able to give Jesus. Successively he trotted out his vigils, his long psalmody, his study of the Bible night and day, the celibacy to which he devoted himself as best he could, the lack of conveniences, the poverty, the most unexpected guests he tried to welcome without grumbling and with a not too unfriendly face, and finally the heat of the day and the chill of the night.

Each time Jesus congratulated and thanked him. He had known for a long time that Jerome meant very well.

But with a half-smile on his lips, he also persisted with his questions, asking for more: 'Jerome, is there anything else you can give me? Or is this all?'

At long last Jerome had summed up all the good things he was able to scrape together from his memory. So when Jesus asked the question one more time he had no choice but, in great perplexity and almost total defeat to protest: 'But, Lord, have I not given you everything? I have nothing further to offer.'

Then Jesus replied—and it became deathly quiet in the hermitage and in the whole Judean wilderness—and said: 'But you do, Jerome. You have forgotten something: you must also give me your sins, that I may forgive them.'[57]

---

[57] Louf, *Tuning into Grace*, 146-8.

CONTEMPLATION IN ISLAMIC SPIRITUALITY

Mahnaz Heydarpoor

This paper engages with a very important subject in Islamic thought and particularly in Islamic spirituality, that is, "contemplation". In Islamic scriptures, there are some similar terms, such as *tafakkur, tadabbur, ta'ammuq* which approximate to contemplation.

Tafakkur means thinking, or reflection, or contemplation. It may even sometimes mean meditation. It is derived from the root *fikr* which means thought. *Tadabbur* also means reflection or pondering, and is derived from the root *dubur* which means back. Thus, *tadabbur* originally means to see or observe back or to the rear of the things existing before us. *Ta'ammuq* means deep thinking, and is derived from the root *'umq* which means depth. Thus, *ta'ammuq* involves going into depth and not just being satisfied with the superficial aspect of the realities. According to a well-known *ḥadīth*, God has revealed certain parts of the Qur'an, including Sūrat al-Tawḥīd (112) and the verses at the beginning of Sūrat al-Ḥadīd (57), because he knew that there would be a group of deep thinkers *(aqwāmūn muti'ammiqūn)* at the end of [or in the fullness of] time *(ākhir al-zamān)*.[1]

Thus, all these terms indicate nearly the same notion, namely contemplation. The emphasis upon this notion, as we will see in more detail later, is very significant and illustrates the weight that Islam gives to the intellectual aspect of human beings. According to the Qur'an, we are created to serve and worship God (51: 56) and 'the Right Path' is that of serving and worshipping God (36: 61). However, this does not just mean being involved in physical acts of worship. It would by no means suffice to be physically or even emotionally involved in physical prayers or recitations of the Book while forgetting God or not knowing Him properly. Of course, acts of worship are very important and some

---

[1] M Kulayyni, *Al-Kāfī,* 4th edition, Dar al-Kutub al-Islamiyah, Tehran, 1986 Vol. 1, 91; M B Majlisī, *Biḥār al-Anwār*, Mu'assisat al-Wafa, Beirut, 1404 AH, Vol. 3, 263, and Vol. 64, 371.

are compulsory, but the philosophy behind them is to prepare us for knowing and remembering God and then getting close to Him. The Qur'an says: 'Worship Me and establish the prayer for My remembrance.' (20: 14)

At the end of Chapter Three of the Qur'an, God praises a group of people who remember Him in different states and who are thoughtful. The verses read as follows:

> Verily, in the creation of the heavens and the earth and in the alternation of night and day, there are indeed signs for men of understanding.
> Those who remember God standing, sitting, and lying down on their sides, and think deeply about the creation of the heavens and the earth, (saying): 'Our Lord! You have not created (all) this without purpose, glory to You! Give us salvation from the torment of the Fire.' (3: 190 and 191)

Thus, people of understanding or thoughtful people are those who first remember God constantly, and second think deeply about the purpose of creation. Both facts can be found in many other verses or *ḥadīths*. According to a well-known divine saying *(al-ḥadīth al-qudsī)*, God says 'My remembrance is good in all circumstances.'[2] Therefore, Muslim jurists recommend the remembrance of God or mention of His names and attributes even at the most private moments during the day.[3] We also find in some *ḥadīths* that everything has a limit except the remembrance of God, which has no limit. For example, daily prayer, which is compulsory, consists of only 17 units. It is also recommended that we pray more. However, there are circumstances in which one may be asked not to say one's prayer, for instance, to save the life of an innocent person who is drowning. The extent of fasting is also clearly defined. In the month of Ramadan, fasting is compulsory and in ordinary days of the year it is recommended. However, there are circumstances in which one is not allowed to fast, as well as circumstances in which one is recommended not to fast. The same is true for all other acts of worship. It

---

[2] *Al-Kāfī*, Vol. 2, 497 and *Biḥār al-Anwār*, Vol. 13, 343.
[3] There are also specific supplications prescribed in Islamic hadiths for all these states, such as being in the bathroom or going into bed.

is only the remembrance of God which can and should be done in all circumstances.

It is of the utmost importance to be—in my words—spiritually alert, and not to let anything make us neglect or forget God. There are many people in society who look conscious but they are really unconscious and negligent. They are not alert. On the other hand, thoughtful people are those who are spiritually conscious and alert. The Qur'an speaks about a group of people 'whom neither trade nor sale (business) diverts from the remembrance of God, nor from performing prayer, nor from giving the alms. They fear a Day when hearts and eyes will be overturned (out of the horror of the torment of the Day of Resurrection).' (18: 37)

Thus, it becomes clear why Islam puts so much emphasis on qualities like knowledge, remembrance and contemplation. This is why we read in Islamic *ḥadīths* that 'contemplation for a while is more privileged than worshiping for a year'.[4] Therefore, a worshiper (*'ābid*) who worships God, for example, in a mosque or temple or in a desert or a cave for a year without thinking or contemplating is less privileged than a believer who contemplates for a much shorter period of time. There are also *ḥadīths* which state that contemplation for a while is more privileged than worshiping for sixty years.[5] It all depends on the quality of the contemplation and worship. Of course, this is not to underestimate the role of worship, but rather to emphasize the importance of contemplation. In other words, this is to show the importance of contemplation in contrast to mere physical acts of worship, that is, any sort of worship which is without the contemplation of the heart. Therefore, for someone who worships God and whose worship comes from and is accompanied by contemplation, the value of his worship is out of the question.

The recitation of the Qur'an, and even looking at its words, are highly recommended. However, it does not suffice to recite the Qur'an or even memorize it, if there is no awareness or contemplation of its contents. The Qur'an blames those who do not reflect on the Qur'an. For example, we read in the verse (47: 24), 'Do they not then reflect on the Qur'an, or are their hearts locked up (from understanding it)?' Either they do not reflect, or they may reflect but they can not come to a proper conclusion because their hearts are locked or sealed.

4 M Ayyashi, *Tafsīr al-'Ayyāshī*, Ilmiyah, Tehran, 1380 AH, Vol. 2, 208; *Biḥār al-Anwār*, Vol. 86, 129.
5 *Biḥār al-Anwār*, Vol. 66, 292.

If some one combines these two, i.e. worship and contemplation, with each other this will be very good. Indeed, one may worship God by contemplation and this is what we find about Abu Dharr, a well-known companion of the Prophet. According to a moving *ḥadīth*, 'Most of the worship of Abu Dharr was contemplation.'[6] We also find in Islamic *ḥadīths* that the most privileged form of worship is to continue thinking or constant contemplation about God and His power.[7] This is a very significant statement.

Thus, Islam gives such a high regard to contemplation that it considers contemplation for a while much better than mere worshipping for one year or sixty or seventy years, and then adds that (most of) the worship of some pious people is contemplation, or that the most privileged form of worship is constant contemplation.

Why is contemplation so important?

Having studied the importance of contemplation, we should now see why it is considered so important. Some of the benefits of contemplation are as follows.

1. Contemplation expands, deepens and stabilizes our understanding. In a very beautiful conversation with Hishām b. al-Ḥakam on the intellect (*al-'aql*), Imam Kāzim states, 'By contemplation, one believes in what he learns.'[8] One may know that God exists, or that there will be Heaven and Hell, but these beliefs may still be superficial or loose in one's heart. Such beliefs can easily be washed away or at least be ignored or neglected. Hence, one may know that God exists but one still may easily forget God or disobey Him. However, when you know an idea and then you contemplate and reflect on that idea, it is like pressing a seed deep into soil and then nurturing it till it grows and bears flowers. When that idea is well rooted and put in our heart then it will become stable. This is a very important idea.

Inspired by *ḥadīths* indicating the necessity of daily assessment of one's activities (*al-muḥāsabah*), Muslim scholars have suggested that an

6 M Amili, *Wasā'il al-Shī 'ah*, Al al-Bayt li Ihya al-Turath, Qum, 1409 AH, Vol. 15, 197.
7 *Al-Kāfī*, Vol. 2, 55.
8 *Ibid.*, Vol. 1, 17.

important step in getting close to God is to allocate some time each day for reflection, maybe in the early morning or before you go to sleep.[9] This can also be done before or after daily prayer or when one recites the Qur'an. So instead of having a fast recitation it is better to recite sentence by sentence and ponder on what you recite.

2. Contemplation brings harmony into one's soul: many of us have had the experience of knowing something but doing something else and, in this way, we suffer a lack of harmony. Many people know, for example, smoking is harmful but they still smoke, but if they think about it they may get the determination to do what they know to be right.

When you think about something you let the mental or the intellectual aspect of your being get control of the emotional aspect. Most people are easily moved by their emotions. But if we thought about our future, about our present state, about our desires, about our aims, about our origins and about what we should or should not do, this would make our mind and heart alert and let the intellectual aspect become superior to the emotional aspect. When we are not alert and we act automatically or quickly we lose our control. If you first think and then act or speak or write you will have a better control. This is why we read in the history that some people used to put some sand or small stones in their mouth to prevent them speaking quickly. So whenever they wanted to say something, they needed to take the sand or stones out of their mouth. This was the time when they could think whether or not to say something. This is not to endorse this practice, but I just want to appreciate the point beyond it. We read in *ḥadīths* that the heart of the fool lies behind his tongue. This means that the fool first talks and then thinks about what they have said, but the wise person first thinks and then talks.

3. Contemplation prevents self-admiration: in Islamic spirituality, self-admiration is considered to be one of the worst qualities of the human soul and very destructive.[10] Unfortunately, sometimes believers suffer from this ugly characteristic, especially when they have been able to perform a good service to the community or some difficult worship. Contemplation helps us understand that whatever we do has become possible only by

---

[9] It is narrated from Imam al-Kāẓim that 'whoever does not assess himself everyday is not one of us' (*ibid.*, Vol. 2, 453).
[10] For example, see *Al-Kāfī*, Vol. 2, 313-314.

Divine grace and is not valuable compared to the blessings that God has bestowed upon us. Moreover, although contemplation is the most privileged worship, it is far from self-admiration, since it involves no physical act. If you have physical worship then you may say, 'I am a very good person. I have said so many prayers or I have recited so many chapters of the Qur'an.' But if you are just sitting and thinking it is less likely to result in self-admiration, because you have done nothing, no physical activities. Contemplation usually is not considered by ordinary people as an act. Of course, it is really a very important act, but most people bedome self-admiring when they are involved in physical worship. There is also less chance for showing off in respect to contemplation, since contemplation is not visible. Of course, if a person is really wicked he may show off here as well.

Through contemplation, we understand that our acts are worthless compared to the blessings of God. This also helps to be safe from any sort of self-admiration.

4. Contemplation mobilizes our power: Each person is like a country with different resources and powers. Usually these resources are not optimally invoked and the powers are not maximally used. They may even be in conflict with each other, but when there is a wise leadership all of them can be oriented and mobilized for the interests of the country.

Something similar can be said about individual human beings. Through contemplation one can exercise a more conscious and enlightened control upon one's faculties and lead them towards one's ideals. Through contemplation, one fully observes the prospective consequences of every single action and, therefore, can make a wiser decision. We read in Islamic hadiths that 'Whenever you decide to do something contemplate upon its end.'

Objects of contemplation

Naturally the question arises as what to contemplate on. The most important objects of contemplation can be listed as follows.

1. God. The most precious object to remember and think about is God, the Almighty. We should reflect on God's creation of us, what He has done for us and what He expects from us. We should also think about the

Divine attributes so that we can get close to Him and resemble Him as much as possible.

2. Creatures. Thinking about God's acts, especially about His act of creation, we come to think about those created by God. As we saw earlier, the Qur'an says 'Those who remember God standing, sitting, and lying down on their sides, and think deeply about the creation of the heavens and the earth, (saying): "Our Lord! You have not created (all) this without purpose, glory to You! Give us salvation from the torment of the Fire."' (3: 191)

Among creatures, some are very outstanding like human beings. We should think about the creation of mankind and the purpose beyond their creation. We should think about people of good or bad character who lived in the past and then perished. We are recommended to recite the following verse whenever we visit historical places, such as palaces, houses, gardens and the like:

> How many of the gardens and fountains have they left!
> And cornfields and noble places!
> And goodly things wherein they rejoiced;
> Thus (it was), and We gave them as a heritage to another
> people. (44: 25-28)

We should take lessons from such visits and not just take photographs.

3. One's destiny. Everyone should always think about his future. This requires having plans for one's life and then always observing any success or failure that we make.

4. Death and the life after death. The remembrance of and contemplation upon death and the next world is highly recommended in Islam. The Qur'an in one third of its verses talks about resurrection and the Day of Judgement. Thinking about death is considered as a source of vitality, awakening and determination. It is told of the Prophet Muhammad that he said:

> 'The best worship is to remember death. The best
> contemplation is remembrance of death.'[11]

---

[11] H Niri, *Mustadark al-Wasā'il,* Al al-Bayt li Ihya al-Turath, Qum, 1408 AH, Vol. 3, 104.

5. Duties and responsibilities. One must always reflect on the circumstances in which one lives and the due responsibilities that one has in those circumstances. A believer does his best to discover his duties and perform them in order to please God. It is related of the Prophet Muhammad that he said: 'Contemplate in abundance on what you do!'[12]

6. Words of God and sayings of the Prophet and Imams. Describing the pious, Imam Ali says

> '... During night they are erect on their feet reading portions of the Qur'an and reciting it haltingly, creating through it grief for themselves and seeking by it the cure for their ailments. If they come across a verse creating eagerness (for Paradise) they lean towards it covetingly and their spirit turns towards it eagerly, and they feel as if it is in front of them. And when they come across a verse which contains fear (of Hell) they bend the ears of their hearts towards it and feel as though the sound of Hell and its cries are reaching their ears.'[13]

Some suggestions for better contemplation

1. Choose a proper time and place. Those who are strong in their faith or at least enjoy a strong concentration may be able to contemplate in different circumstances and various environments. However, it is better, and indeed for most people necessary, to choose a convenient place and suitable time. Regarding the place, it is better to choose a tidy and elegant place wherein nothing to distract our attention exists—of course, as far as possible.

Regarding the time, it is better to contemplate when we are not sleepy or very tired or very hungry or very thirsty. It would not also be fruitful, if we try to contemplate when we are full. There are many *ḥadīths* in this regard. For example, Imam Ali says

---

[12] *Ibid.,* Vol. 13, 143.
[13] 'Alī b. Abī Ṭālib, *Nahj al-Balāgha,*, trans Jafar Husain, Ansarian, Qum, 1989, Sermon 191.

'Whoever eats less his thought becomes clearer.'[14]

Imam Ali also says:

'Who can have clear thought while his stomach is full.'[15]

2. Regularity is also very important.[16] If we always contemplate in the same places or at the same times it will automatically help us to be better prepared for contemplation.

3. Continuity too is very important. It is much better to have a short period of contemplation on a daily basis than having much longer periods of contemplation once a week or several times a month.

4. Choosing some passages of the scripture relating to our present feeling or condition is very helpful and inspiring. There are also supplications specifically prescribed for different situations. There may also be personal attachments to certain passages or supplications. Of course, this selective reading and contemplation should be arranged in the way that one can also read and contemplate on the entire Qur'an now and then.

5. To observe presence of God. To be able to direct our heart and mind during our contemplation towards our supreme interests and higher desires and get rid of selfishness and short-sightedness, we should remind ourselves that wherever we are God is present. All our thoughts and decisions take form in the presence and full knowledge of God. To awaken our sense to the presence of God the Qur'an does not just say that God exists or knows us. The Qur'an emphasizes that God is present everywhere, He is always with us (29: 4) and He is 'closer to us than our jugular vein.' (50: 16) God sees and hears us. Indeed, He is the All-hearing (*al-samī'*) and the All-seeing (*al-baṣīr*). The Qur'anic verse, 'Does he not know that God does see?' (96: 14) suggests that human problems start when we forget this fact. The late Imam Khomeini used to say 'The universe is where God is present. Do not commit any sin in His presence.'

---

[14] A Amudi, *Ghurar al-Ḥikam*, Daftar-i Tablighat-i Islami, Qum, 1987, 7402.

[15] *Ibid.*, 8155.

[16] For example, see *Ghurar al-Ḥikam*, 11082 and 11080.

CHRISTIAN PRAYER
Ian Latham

Prayer is so simple and so profound! It is the breath of life: if we cease to pray, we die. For prayer is nothing else than the human expression of a living relationship with the living God.[1] And this relationship constitutes the essence of our being as Christians. It is a reality which, while using words, is in itself beyond all words, strictly ineffable. So it is only by a conscious reflection on this lived experience that we can talk about it and consider it. It remains that this reflective discourse is always, necessarily, defective: it falls short of the reality: a reality fully known only to God.

Christian prayer is, basically, a lived commentary on the prayer of Jesus. Jesus, 'one of us', prayed to God as Son to Father, and he invites us to enter into this same relationship[2] through the gift of his Spirit. So the one God becomes our God: 'my God and your God', as Jesus tells us (Jn 20: 17).

'He [Jesus] was praying in a certain place, and when he ceased, one of his disciples said to him, "Lord, teach us to pray" ' (Lk 11: 1). Here is the one foundation of all Christian prayer. Jesus' reply, 'When you pray, say "Father ... ,"' is the one model of how we can, and should, pray. As Jesus prayed, so the Christian is summoned to pray.[3]

Jesus' prayer is bound up with his human life. As a young man, he reached out to God as 'my Father' (Lk 2: 49). As a mature adult he heard

---

[1] *Catechism of the Catholic Church* (in brief, *CCC*), London, 1994, paragraphs 2558–2865. This is a masterful synthesis, centred on the '*Our Father*', of the key elements of Christian prayer. It begins by emphasizing that prayer is 'a vital and personal *relationship* with the living and true God' (2558: italics added).

[2] Cf. *CCC* 2780: 'The personal relation of the Son to the Father is something that man cannot conceive of ... , and yet the Spirit of the Son grants a *participation in that very relation*' (italics added).

[3] Cf. *CCC* 2601; 'By *contemplating* and hearing the Son, the master of prayer, the children learn to pray to the Father'. The theme of Jesus as *'the one model'* was particularly dear to Charles de Foucauld: '*Our Father*, teach me to have this name always on my lips with Jesus, in Jesus ...' ('Méditation sur "le Pater"', *Oeuvres Spirituelles*, ed. Denise Barrat, Paris, 1958).

the voice, 'You are my beloved Son' (Lk 3: 22). As his service as Messiah developed, he exclaimed, 'Father, I thank you, Lord of heaven and earth, ... all things have been delivered to me by my Father ...' (Lk 10: 21-22). As about to suffer and die, he cried out, '*Abba*, Father, ... not my will, but your will be done' (Mk 14: 36). And as he was dying, 'with a loud voice' he cried, 'Father, into your hands I commit my spirit' (Lk 23: 46).[4]

Always Jesus prayed 'in the Holy Spirit' (Lk 10: 21), and he gave the Holy Spirit, his Spirit and that of the Father, to his disciples after his resurrection from the dead and final ascension to 'the Father's right hand' (Lk 24: 49 and Ac 1: 4-5). His disciples, then, and in each now, are thus empowered to share in Jesus' own prayer as Son to the Father. Through the gift of the Spirit, they become 'sons in the Son',[5] as St Augustine puts it, following St Paul. They are no longer 'slaves' but 'sons', and as 'sons' they can and should enter with confidence into a simple and familiar dialogue with God, indeed with the familiarity of a 'little child'. For prayer is simply the explicit expression of our God-given relationship with God, and Jesus makes the little child the model of this relationship (Mk 10: 15).

Yes, Jesus himself, as he grew humanly into the perfect adult, became more and more this little child, reaching out to his Father's 'hands', as his last words indicate so well. In fact, we can justly see the trajectory of Jesus' whole life as the reaching out' of the son of Mary from his mother's womb and his mother's arms to the final fulfilment of his return as son of man to the loving embrace of his heavenly Father. And, as he was sent to do, he carried us all with himself,[6] to receive with him the same loving embrace: for he went, as he himself declared, 'to my Father and your Father, to my God and your God' (Jn 20: 17).

---

[4] The relationship of Jesus as Son to the Father as expressed in his prayer, while 'sensed' at times by his close companions, was rooted in a 'secret source' (*CCC* 2599). It was based on a growing awareness in his human mind and heart of his eternal relationship *in God*: '*In* me [is] the Father, and I [am] *in* the Father' (*Jn* 10: 38).

[5] 'Filii in Filio': St Augustine, *In Ps 8*; cf. *Gaudium et spes* 22 and *Rm* 8: 15. Our filial adoption is a source of 'confidence' in our access to God: *parrhasia* (Eph 3: 12; Heb 3: 6 etc.), a 'characteristically Christian expressions' expressing 'straightforward simplicity, filial trust, joyous assurance, humble boldness, the certainty of being loved' (*CCC* 2778).

[6] Cf. *CCC* 2602: 'He [Jesus] *includes all men* in his prayer, for he has *taken on humanity in his incarnation*, and he offers them [all] to the Father when he offers himself.' This key conception, dear to the 'Church Fathers', has been clearly affirmed at Vatican II: 'He himself, the Son of God, by his incarnation has in a way *united every human being* with Himself' (*Gaudium et spes,* 22; italics added).

We pray as we believe. As God has graciously made himself known to us, so His grace enables us to respond, in faith, to the *Mystery thus revealed.*[7] As God reveals his hidden inner Self in the human life of his Son, Jesus, so he invites us, through the free gift of his Spirit, the one Spirit of the Father and the Son, to communicate with Himself and to enter, trembling but confident, into his Presence.

The simplest Christian and the greatest mystic have the same fundamental relationship with the one God, the Most High. For this relationship, for each and every Christian, is God-given: as a seed, in baptism, but destined to grow through the exercise of faith, hope and charity. For these so-called theological virtues, freely given to us by God, are already a certain sharing in God's ways of knowing and loving, so that we can communicate with God as He is in Himself. We become, in St Peter's bold phrase, 'partakers of the divine nature' (2 *P* 1: 4). For to dialogue with the divine persons, we must become, in some measure, divine in our being. We are not only called God's children, we are in fact, or rather we are made, by God's free and unmerited gift, so to be. The mystics[8] are those who respond generously to this call of God, and who realize here and now, in many God-given various ways, something of God's infinite beauty. As the one who received the fullness of grace and the fullness of faith in her simple human self and life, Mary, Jesus' Mother,

---

[7] Christian prayer supposes the specifically Christian beliefs about the Trinity, the Redemptive Incarnation and our divine Adoption. These beliefs, for example that Jesus, son of Mary, is Son of God in the sense of being 'one' with the Father, are understood as going *beyond* what can be naturally and normally known about God, and as expressing *the secret of intimate divine mysteries* through the language and realities of *our ordinary human life*. This—for example applying the so human 'father-son' relation *in God*—can reasonably seem inappropriate, even shocking. Only faith, and the 'intelligence of faith', can enable us to see both the 'likeness' and the radical 'unlikeness' in these *'revealed analogies'* which, we believe, spring from, and lead us to, *'the heart of the deity'* (J Maritain, *Degrees of Knowledge,* London, 1959, 241-4).

[8] St John of the Cross, perhaps the most reliable 'doctor' of Christian 'mystical experience', teaches that this experience is the 'normal' fulfilment of the Christian life, which is the 'union of the human person with God *in love*'. The knowledge of faith tells us about the Trinity, but divine 'love' joins us to the reality of 'the Three' in their absolute Oneness, and so gives us a certain supra-conceptual awareness (an 'ignorant knowledge') of this ultimate mystery. 'The knowledge of the Trinity in unity is the fruit and end of our whole life' (St Thomas Aquinas, *In I. Sent.,* dist.2, *expos. Textus;* quoted Maritain, *Degrees,* 378). This 'mysticism' is clearly desired for his disciples, and offered to them, by Jesus himself in his *'last discourses'* (*Jn* chaps. 13-17, esp. 14: 21-23; 16: 13-15; 17: 20-26).

is the supreme example. Having accomplished her pilgrimage of faith,[9] she is ready and able, through God's favour, to support each of us on our journey of faith and life.

Christian prayer and life must go hand in hand. Inevitably there is, for most, if not for all, of us, a gap between the aspirations we express in prayer and our daily life! Charles de Foucauld[10] prayed, for example, 'My God, if you exist, make me know you'; a 'strange prayer' as he said, but it was answered, and he became an ardent disciple of Jesus. He later said, 'God is so great, I can only live for him,' and this implicit prayer was realized also, not at once but step by step until his death, the 'passage', as he hoped, to his 'glory', as a final gift of his 'Beloved Brother and Lord'. Most of us are less consequent in co-operating with God to effect in our attitudes and actions what we pray God to realize in us: we can only persevere in constantly asking God's pardon and the gift of continuous conversion.

We pray, more or less consciously but always in intention, in union with the human life and prayer of Jesus. For Jesus as son of man, and so as one of us,[11] shared all our human life: its stages from conception and birth to death; its ordinariness, monotony and daily work (as in Nazareth); its 'mission' to 'go out' to do God's will for the good of God's people; its many sufferings, frequent rejection and final death. It is in this human life that Jesus lived and expressed his unique relationship as Son with the Father, a lived relationship that was fully human, but one which purified our humanity and lifted it up to a new level of being and awareness. Through Jesus, our life and prayer, while remaining rooted in our humanity and human failings, becomes lifted up to the Father's Face.

---

[9] Cf. Vatican II, *Lumen gentium*, 58: 'The Blessed Virgin [Mary] advanced in her *pilgrimage of faith*'. It is as 'she who believed' (*Lk* 1: 45) that Mary, following Abraham, *'the father of all who believe'* (*Rm* 4: 11), is the chosen *'representative'* of the human race (cf. St Thomas Aquinas, *Summa Theologica*, III, 30,1) in her free and total 'submission' in faith to God's Word (*CCC* 144 & 511).

[10] Charles de Foucauld (1858-1916), having lost all faith in God, on meeting 'persons living in the continual presence of God' (Muslims in North Africa), was led to discover *'something greater* than all worldly concerns' (a reference to the Islamic prayer *Allahu akhbar*: Ch. de F.: *Lettres à Henry de Castries,* Paris, 1938, 89). Later, in the Algerian Sahara, he became, in the words of the Muslim scholar Ali Merad, 'a mystical witness for Jesus before Islam' (*Christian Hermit in an Islamic World,* Paulist Press, 1999, 44; translated from French, *Charles de Foucauld au regard de l'Islam,* Paris, 1975).

[11] This 'Nazarene' way of understanding Jesus' life and prayer is particularly dear to the followers of Charles de Foucauld (Cf. René Voillaume, *Seeds of the Desert,* Anthony Clarke, 1972, chapter 2).

Our prayer is therefore 'universal'. In praying 'Our Father', we are praying to the one God and Father of us all. And of course that commits us to live and work in the knowledge that we are all equally children of God, and so brothers and sisters of each and every human being, made to be friends not enemies, called by the same God on the same journey to the same 'end': the sharing of God's 'wedding feast', all together, and for eternity. For God's plan is to unite all humanity to Himself as his beloved 'Bride',[12] a destiny prepared by Jesus' ascension to the Father's side and signified by Mary's assumption, foreshadowing the joy of the whole people: the joy of the 'little bride', Mary in person, who will be the centre and joy of the all-embracing 'bridal people'.

So our Christian prayer is both personal and communal. It is personal, indeed intensely personal, because each of us as a person is unique: a unique subject with a unique life and a unique destiny; hence with a unique God-given way of praying to the one God of all. But it is also communal: we are made for 'togetherness', to receive from and give to each other, and so our praying must also be communal: the prayer of the community as such, both the local community and the wider community of the Christian assembly, the worldwide 'Church' with her 'liturgy'.[13] For we are and grow as persons only in community, and an authentic community is only realized in the unique and free persons who compose it. Experience shows that the given forms of liturgical prayer 'feed' our personal prayer, which, in turn, gives life and vigour to the liturgical celebration.

Along with the 'Our Father', the Psalms, the 'praises of God' of the Jewish people throughout their history, have always been 'taken up', assumed, by the Christian people, the 'Church'.[14] These ancient poetic songs express the many facets of universal human emotions in face of the

---

[12] God's covenant union with his people is often expressed under the symbolic imagery of the Ever-Faithful 'Bridegroom' seeking his unfaithful 'bride', a union that Jesus claims to 'fulfil', and which is understood as realized both in the church-community as a whole and in each particular member (Cf. *Ho* chap 2; *Mk* 2: 18-21; *2 Co* 11: 2). St John of the Cross, along with many contemplatives, has a special 'feeling' for this image (cf. *Spiritual Canticle,* stanza 40), as expressing the completion on earth of 'mystical union'.

[13] The 'liturgy' is the public worship of the Church. It is 'a participation in Christ's own prayer addressed to the Father in the Holy Spirit' (*CCC* 1073), offered both as 'blessing and adoration' to God and as supplication 'for the whole world' (cf. *CCC* 1083).

[14] The Christian is called to pray the Psalms 'in the name of the whole body of Christ, in fact *in the person of Christ'* (*General Instruction on the Liturgy of the Hours,* 1970, nn. 107-108).

mystery of life: its yearning for the God of 'life', its anxiety when experiencing God's apparent 'absence', its anger against enemies and its appeal for 'revenge' to the God of Justice, its cry for help in 'battle' to the God of Victory, its sense of being God's 'chosen people', its fear of death as radical loss and 'nothingness', its hope of 'eternal' life with the Eternal God. As we recite and pray these powerful songs, we both 'feel' these many emotions and so share in the universal human experience, and we enter the prayer of Jesus who gave these ancient psalms a 'new meaning, a fulfilment', through his own life and prayer. The 'battle' is no longer the crushing of enemies, but the defeat of evil, above all in ourselves, and the 'reign' of good, especially of self-giving love. The shadowy hope becomes the certainty of 'resurrection'. The experience of suffering is illuminated by the 'life-giving cross'. The pride in being 'chosen' is counter-balanced by the demand to be 'servants': humble servants of the temporal well-being and final destiny of all others.

The Eucharist is the 'source and summit' of all Christian prayer. This is not the place to describe and explain the great 'mystery' of the Eucharistic action and presence, where the risen Jesus invites his people to his 'table', to share his 'meal', to 'eat and drink' with him, in living 'memory' of his life-giving death and resurrection. Through these simple human actions, Jesus, as he promised, becomes 'present': present as the 'Host'[15] who invites his fellow guests to share their lives with His life, and so to 'pass' with Him from death to life. It is in the first place an act of God: God gives us, in a visible and social way, a living and effectual sign of his 'presence' with us and of his 'action' for us and in us. Our part is to be 'present' to that Holy 'Presence': first listening, attentive, receptive, then giving what we have, ourselves with our daily lives and relations, our hopes and prayers, our longings for fulfilment for ourselves and our world. Jesus, by his death and resurrection, makes us new persons, a new community, newly enriched with a greater share of his self-giving love, which is the one ultimate reality; 'for God is Love' (1 Jn 4: 8).

Christian prayer, then, is fundamentally an 'extension' of the prayer of Jesus. We pray, as St Paul says, as 'members of his Body', of which he is the 'Head'. So in prayer we open ourselves to the living action in us of the

---

[15] At the 'Last Supper' with his disciples, Jesus as 'Host' of the meal, made present symbolically the *meaning and value* of his death: 'dying you destroyed our death, rising you restored our life' (Eucharistic acclamation).

one Holy Spirit, the Spirit of Jesus, 'one and the same in the Head and in the members' (*Lumen gentium* 7, 7th para.). And so we pray to the *one God and Father of us all*, who is above all and through all and in all' (Ep 4: 6), saying, 'Hallowed [glorified] be thy Name'. To God alone be the Glory.[16] May we all share, as God wishes, in that one Glory.

[16] Cf. *CCC* 294: 'The ultimate purpose of creation is that God who is creator of all things may at last become "all in all", thus simultaneously assuring his own glory and our beatitude' (cf. *Ad gentes* 2; *1 Co* 15: 28).

PRAYER AND CONTEMPLATION IN ISLAMIC SPIRITUALITY

Mohammad Fanaei Eshkevari

The heart of spiritual practice is prayer. It follows the remembrance of God, which is the way to nearness to God, the essence of spirituality. To remember God is to have God in one's heart in the sense that one does not forget Him. Forgetting, or a negligence *(ghaflah)*, of God is being unaware of God, which paves the way to sin. But remembrance of God *(dhikr)* will give one the necessary resistance to avoid sin. God gives the human being desires or instincts and a right way to fulfil them, but the person has a tendency to follow his or her desires. This, combined with a negligence of God, leads to sin. Some attempt to refrain from sin by fighting or removing desire, but the desire itself is not a sufficient cause for sin; only the combination of desire and being negligent of God. The Qur'an states that, 'God knows what you reveal and what you hide' (24: 29). In the remembrance of God one has the awareness that God knows one's thoughts and intentions; nothing is hidden from Him.

Awareness of the presence of God prevents one from disobedience and encourages one to come into contact with Him, which is the real meaning of prayer. Both love and fear of God play such a role. The best news in the world is that God loves you. If you respond by loving God you will not want to jeopardize God's love by indulging in the very short-term benefits of this world. Remembrance of God gives vitality to love and fear. Accordingly, for mystics the practice of the remembrance of God is essential. They follow the Qur'anic teaching that states: 'remember God frequently' (8: 45). The remembrance of God not only protects from sin, but also intensifies our love for God. Sometimes love comes as a gift without our intention, but one can also initiate love and improve it. For example, a husband may neglect his spouse and his love for her fades, but if he would remember her devotion to him, her choice to be married to him, he might buy her flowers or with a clean heart, practice remembrance of her, and his love for her may be renewed. God commands human beings to love and this means they have the ability to love. Even regarding nature, some have a love of nature and some do not, but this can be developed or improved upon. When we see nature as a work of God it becomes beautiful; this may be easier amidst forests and mountains, but with the use of the intellect even the desert becomes beautiful. Seeing the desert as a collection of random effects is different from seeing it as an overall part of God's plan. With regard to people one should not compare between one and another; each has a different and special gift to be appreciated.

Remembrance is in our heart, but God encourages us to speak our memory of God; this makes our remembrance more alive and vital. In praying we usually pronounce the remembrance of God which is in our heart. Prayer has four aspects and the following order is important.

First, prayer is praise *(hamd)* of the beauty and magnificence of God; one uses one's blessings from God in a way which honours God paying attention to God's greatness and magnificence.

Second, prayer is thanksgiving *(shukr)*. In prayer we thank God for what we receive from Him. What we receive from God is endless and we are unable to count it as the Qur'an says: 'If you count God's blessing, you will never number it; surely man is sinful, unthankful' (14: 34). In his book of prose and poetry, *Gulistan*, Sa'di begins his introduction in thanks to God. In wanting to thank God in completeness he is frustrated because of needing to thank God for the previous breath which he used in thanking God; therefore he was always a breath behind in complete thankfulness. It is impossible for the human being to give complete thanks to God; one must do what one can; God does not expect more than that.

Third, prayer is asking for forgiveness *(istighfar)*. The famous formula for this is 'I ask forgiveness from God and do repentance before God'. In one of his prayers, the fourth Imam 'Ali ibn al-Husayn Zayn al-'Abidin cries: if I sin once and pray for a lifetime I cannot make up for the sin; only your blessing can clear and forgive me.

Fourth, prayer is petition, asking for what we want from God, material and spiritual, individual or social. In the Qur'an and the *hadiths* we are ordered to ask for the good things of this world and the next and not to be bashful with God. We are encouraged to ask for the needs and welfare of others along with our own. In many prayers the words 'we' and 'us' are used, indicating our awareness of being a part of a larger community and acknowledging that God's care extends beyond me. A frequently recited prayer in the Qur'an says: 'Our Lord, give to us in this world good, and good in the world to come, and guard us against the chastisement of the Fire' (2: 201). The above order respects the 'politeness of obedience'.

Two representative examples of prayer from two holy books can bring us closer to the nature of prayer. The opening chapter of the Qur'an is a prayer, which is recited by a Muslim at least ten times a day. It reads:

> In the Name of God, the Merciful, the Compassionate
> Praise belong to God, the Lord of all Being,
> The All-merciful, the All-compassionate,
> The Master of the Day of Doom.
>
> Thee only we serve; to Thee alone we pray for succour.
> Guide us in the straight path,
> the path of those whom Thou hast blessed,
> not of those against whom Thou art wrathful,
> nor of those who are astray.

Now we look at a prayer from the Bible. Matthew in the Holy Bible records this teaching from Jesus about praying. (Matthew 6: 9-15)

> 'Pray then in this way:
> Our Father in heaven,
> Hallowed be your name.
> Your kingdom comes.
> Your will be done,
> On earth as it is in heaven.
> Give us this day our daily bread.
> And forgive us our sins,
> As we also have forgiven those who sin against us.
> And do not bring us to the time of trial,
> But rescue us from the evil one.'

Remembering God and praying is talking to God, being with God, and living with God. When reciting the Qur'an, it is as if God is talking directly to the person reciting. In prayer one is talking to God. In this way of thinking about reciting scripture, revelation is alive and related to one's own life. Different persons can look at scripture differently. An unbeliever may read scripture as literature to be understood and to learnt from. An ordinary believer will read scripture with the understanding that it was revealed by God to the prophet. However, in an alive reading of scripture, the verses are taken as if they are revealed to one personally. In reciting prayers one has the same feeling. It is a live contact, and conversation with God in which the servant is the initiator.

Prayer in its higher form comes with contemplation. God is always present. Contemplation brings an awareness of the presence of God, not through speculative reason but through a feeling of heart. This awareness is more the result of love than discursive thinking. In discursive thinking there is a gap between the subject and object, whereas direct awareness shortens the distance and tends toward unity, and in a sense toward the dissolution of individuality. I, as a separate, independent, self-subsistent entity, disappear *(fana)*. I find my true self in God *(baqa)*. I am not God, nor a part of God, but at the same time not apart from God. This paradoxical mystery is the essence of mystical metaphysics.

Prayer and contemplation *(dhikr* and *fikr)* should not be separated. Prayer without contemplation is not worth much. It is related that the Prophet said that thinking for one hour is better than 70 years of worshiping without thinking. By thinking one may realize that God is the source of everything; the combination of prayer and contemplation leads to enlightenment.

The real ideas of mysticism are in the prayers of the mystics, which come from their hearts following their face-to-face communication with God. The books written by mystics are like a translation of the real language of mysticism into the language of common people. The prayers of the mystics are God-centred and are filled with the praise and glorification of God, and then praise for the prophets, who carry the message of God, and the angels and sages. Their primary respect is for the message of God and then the servant who brings and/or teaches the message. Ordinary believers have a direct relationship with God, but do not receive revelation from God as the prophets did. For those close to God and who love God, their prayer expresses this love and a respect for what belongs to God.

From the prayers of the saints one learns about the relationship between the servant of God and God, in a language which is not that of the mere 'brain/mind' and the book, but a language fresh and close to one's heart. This teaches not only a kind of metaphysics but also a way of life, morality, dealing with self and others. The language is a language of asking, not only for worldly things, but for what one needs for the development of body, soul and personality in its totality; not only for individual and private needs but also for social and public needs. One asks for what makes the world a better place to live in, what one needs for perfection and spiritual development and for a good world according to the plan of God in dealing with the rights and dignity of others. One prays for what one can obtain by choice, and also for what only God can provide.

Prayer and the remembrance of God should always be in one's heart, but, in addition, according to Islamic teaching, there should be daily time for this alone and some time for audible prayer. An example would be paying attention to one's health. There must be some specific time for exercise but throughout the day one must use one's back and one's knees in right ways. Exercise if done to the exclusion of other activities may be harmful. All of life is lived within balance; the body with the spirit and this world with the world to come. One must not live in this world in a way that would result in harm for eternal life. Care of the body should not be done in a manner that harms the soul. For example, one needs to eat, but to steal food would be harmful to one's spirit.

The heart of all prayer is the awareness of a God-centred world in which one asks for everything from God, but at the same time remains active, doing one's best. Some say that one should do what one can and then pray to God for what one cannot do. This is a separation of prayer from action. God wants both: for one to act within one's responsibility while at the same time praying for God's help even with small tasks. One needs to guard against the danger of one's spirituality when it is separated from action and life within the world. We have a responsibility to others here on earth. We are encouraged to act and pray with the understanding that all we do is a part of our relationship with God. We are alive and able to act and pray by God's help; apart from God's grace we can do nothing, and apart from God we are nothing.

Prayer has the benefit of peace of mind in this world, but it is not only for peace of mind. It must encourage love. At the heart of spirituality is the motivation of love; the practice of spirituality from the motivation of fear is good but not enough. Loving God brings a love for others and caring for them. One should see others not as a means to an end, someone instrumental to meet one's needs, but consider others as an end in themselves. A self-centred world-view is to love someone as long as one needs them. For example, one is encouraged to love one's parents as long as they live, not only as long as they are of benefit to one. As one improves intellectually and spiritually, one's needs and one's attention change; one's attention gradually moves from that of personal desire for wealth, fame and other this-worldly privileges, to a concern for all of humanity.

In prayer one is not only asking but one is teaching one's self how to act and, more importantly, how to be. The best manner of moral education is self-education and each person has his own teacher. In the language of prayer, one can be honest in conversation with God and thus be active in moral self-education. Preachers talk to others, but they need time to listen as well. A good example of self-educating prayer is what Imam Sajjad cries in his prayers. Reflecting on a prayer or section of a prayer can be done anywhere and for as long as time allows. Isolated spirituality, when one goes to a mosque or church one day and on other days acts like a non-believer, is of not much benefit, therefore it is not enough. Real spirituality must be present always and everywhere.

Prayer is the product of knowledge and brings awareness. This type of awareness that we are by ourselves nothing, dead, empty and dark, brings humility and this type of knowledge brings obedience. But one, who has a self-centred pride, is ignorant, does not know reality, forgets where he came from and thinks he is his own, disregarding what God says, and commits proud disobedience. For example, a child may grow and become a successful person and then only see his present situation, forget his past, become ungrateful toward his parents and those who have helped him on his way. In one's relationship with God the situation is magnified because God has created everything for one's use. The child does become independent of its parents, become stronger and more knowledgeable than its parents but not so with God; one is always dependent on God. But if one begins to develop self-knowledge, realizing one's nothingness apart from God's grace, this will result in obedience.

Knowledge or insight that follows prayer, referred to by discovery *(kashf)*, witnessing *(shuhud)* and seeing *(ru'yah)*, here meaning internal seeing, seeing with the heart, it is knowledge not gained by external sensation, rational thought or indirectly through scripture. It is gained when a person touches truth directly, without mediation. The highest form of this type of knowledge is revelation *(wahy)* received by one of the prophets. This knowledge is not the result of discursive thinking or life experiences but what the prophet directly receives from God, either via an angel, an audible voice or is placed directly in the heart. According to Islamic teaching, revelation will not be received after the death of the Prophet Muhammad, but mystical knowledge which is at a lower level of importance will continue to be received; for God is always ready to give this knowledge to anyone who is properly prepared. A form of mystical knowledge is inspiration *(ilham),* the voice of God in one's heart; the prophets also share in this type of knowledge. Mystical knowledge is hidden from many people and not acquired through ordinary ways of knowing, even if one is a genius; human faculties alone cannot gain this type of knowledge. The person is almost passive in receiving such illumination. Only God decides to whom to give this illumination, even though one needs to prepare oneself for this. Other kinds of knowledge gained through history, the senses, or thinking are available at some level to all, some more and some less depending on their capability and attempts.

Mystical knowledge requires along with prayer the presence of moral or spiritual values in the life of a person, and not everyone deserves to receive this type of knowledge. This knowledge is a reward that the virtuous person may receive on earth. One's inner eye is opened and one may see. This is God's best and most pleasurable reward, that of seeing truth and reality directly. As the spirit and soul become more settled they enjoy more mystical knowledge or things of the heart. This is God's gift, giving special attention to a person. Of course, spirituality must not be sought for the sake of mystical experience or any inner pleasure; rather it must be sought only out of one's love for and obedience to God.

The Qur'an says that God gives knowledge to whomsoever he wants. One receives mystical knowledge on the condition of faith and the cleansing of one's soul. The Qur'an states: 'Whosoever believes in God, He will guide his heart' (64: 11). One may take from this that God's guidance is the way for receiving this knowledge. The Qur'an also says that if you are pious, God will give you the insight and wisdom to distinguish between truth and falsehood (8: 29). So one learns that practising a pious way of living is a way which may enable one to receive mystical knowledge. Those who live better and are closer to God will receive more illumination from God. This is consistent since God is the light of the heavens and the earth; the closer one is to the light the more one will receive.

THE WORD OF GOD AND THE IDEA OF SACRAMENT: A CATHOLIC THEOLOGICAL PERSPECTIVE

Michael Kirwan

Introducing sacraments

Christian sacraments are 'sacred signs, instituted by Christ, to give grace'.[1] This succinct description, however, is prefaced by a reminder that sacramentality is not a monopoly of Christianity, but rather is basic to all human experience. The problem for an adequate sacramental theology is how to negotiate this tension: between what appears as revealed within a particular religious tradition (Christianity), and at the same time describes a universal anthropological reality. As we shall see, contemporary theologians are readier than their predecessors to acknowledge this second, human perspective, an emphasis which, however, (for some other theologians at least) runs the danger of neglecting what is distinctively Christian about sacraments and sacramentality.

This paper will attempt to describe and explore these tensions. It will do so by means of a broad definition of sacrament, one which will indicate the key historical shifts which have shaped present discussions of this theme. The issues at stake are crudely but adequately delineated by Louis-Marie Chauvet's terms 'objectivist' and 'subjectivist'; the balance between these tendencies achieved by the Second Vatican Council (1961–65) coincides with a growing acknowledgement that the dichotomy between 'Word' and 'Sacrament' which has dominated since the Reformation no longer has significant theological relevance.

It is hoped that this summary will serve as an adequate preparation for the second part of the paper: an explication of some current themes in Eucharistic theology, more precisely the Eucharist as political theology. Cavanaugh and others delineate the Eucharist as a 'truly Catholic practice of space and time', one which is resistant both to the oppressive and destructive practices of the nation-state (modernity),

---

[1] Bernard Cooke, 'Sacrament' in *New Dictionary of Sacramental Worship*, ed. Peter E Fink SJ, Gill & MacMillan, Dublin, 1990, pp. 1116.

and to the hyperextension of these practices in globalizing post-modernity. Cavanaugh's approach is associated with 'Radical Orthodoxy',[2] a theological project which is not without its problematic aspects; nevertheless his reflections may provide a point of common interest for anyone concerned about how religious traditions are to survive under contemporary conditions.

To begin, therefore, with a working definition. For Cooke, the notion of Christian sacrament involves three elements: the ultimate meaning of human experience; the divine saving presence; and the transformation of humans, individually and communally. Because men and women live self-consciously, each of the experiences through which they live is what it is because of the meaning it has. Religious sacramentality concerns itself with the '*ultimate* meaning of people's experience, that which confirms or challenges all other meaning';[3] this ultimate meaning comes from the presence of God, the result of divine communication through God's word of revelation and the response in faith. The relationship thus set up is what brings about the transformed world view and life of the believer, a transformation which technically we refer to as 'sacramental grace'.

That such a transformation of experience was at stake in the life and teaching of Jesus Christ is clear, even if it only became manifest to the disciples of Christ after the 'Easter experience', which convinced them of his mysterious and powerful, continued living presence among them. This awareness dawned above all in the communal meals which they celebrated together, and at which they shared their memories; as well as in the practice of Baptism as the form which initiation into the community took for those who accepted the gospel message. 'Though Jesus did not himself leave these rituals as such to his followers, it was his life and particularly his death and resurrection that "instituted these sacramental rituals" by being the mystery the rituals celebrate.'[4]

Just as in Baptism the believer enters into the death and resurrection of Christ, so in the Eucharist the changing of the bread and wine into the body and blood of the risen Lord proclaims an existential

---

[2] William T Cavanaugh, *Torture and Eucharist*, Blackwell, Oxford, 1998. See bibliography for related works: Catherine Pickstock, *After Writing*; and Graham Ward's contribution to the *Radical Orthodoxy* volume, 163–181.

[3] Cooke, *loc. cit.*.

[4] *Ibid.*, 1116–7.

reality. Five other rituals were given similar sacramental status in the Catholic tradition: reconciliation, confirmation, ordination, marriage, the sacrament of the sick. Each of these rituals is both a gesture of faith, and a pledge to lead a particular kind of life: hence the term *sacramentum* meaning 'an oath or solemn promise'.

Historical overview

From the outset of Christianity, therefore, there was a sense of how God's grace is 'mediated' by means of specific ritual actions. There followed an unfortunate development, however, as an alternative way of looking at the sacraments gradually took root: what is usually referred to as the 'instrumentalist' approach. According to this view, these ritual actions are means used by God to give grace to believers, who were now seen as merely passive recipients. This downgrading of the human pole of sacramental action was evident by the 9th century, as both a marginalization of the community's participation, and a loss of understanding as to what was going on.

The Protestant Reformation of the 16th century was a dramatic reaction to this double alienation. Positively, it drew attention to the importance of personal faith and of active participation in the celebration; negatively, the rituals themselves were downgraded by the reformers, in favour of personal reflection on the Bible. A dichotomy between 'Word' and 'Sacrament' opened up, which will be explored in more detail below. In terms of the Catholic response to the Protestant innovations, the Council of Trent (1545-1563) represented the first systematized statement about Christian sacraments, one which provided the basic framework for thinking about the sacraments up to the 20th century. The Council insisted that the sacramental actions were initiated by Christ, and that the other five ritual celebrations were to be included in the definition of sacraments, as well as Baptism and Eucharist (a point disputed by the reformers).

Above all, there was controversy about the efficacy of the sacraments: the reformers denied that the sacraments had the kind of transforming power described above; they were merely a promise that such a transformation would take place in the future. They proclaim an assurance of salvation, but do not bring it about. Trent's Catholic response was to insist on the intrinsic, grace-giving power of sacraments which derives from the death of Christ. This is what is intended by the crucial term *ex opera operato*: that is, simply by virtue of their being carried out, the sacramental actions are efficacious.

It is with the Second Vatican Council that something of a correction to this imbalance occurs, with a renewed understanding of the need for 'full, active and conscious participation' of the faithful in what is happening in the sacraments, and an appreciation of the early Church synthesis that had been lost by subsequent developments. L-M Chauvet[5] expresses this tension between sacrament as 'instrument' and as 'mediation' by means of three theoretical models: the first, which he calls the 'objectivist' model, is principally attributed to the 13th century and to Thomas Aquinas, though subsequent uses of this model lack Thomas' subtlety and flexibility. On this model the *ex opere operato* dimension of sacraments is stressed; they are viewed more as the operative means by which salvation is brought about, while their revelatory sign value is comparatively neglected. A sacrament is seen as 'instrument', 'remedy', 'channel' etc,, in a perspective which can also be very individualistic; the celebrating community, as noted above, fades into the background.

The second model for Chauvet, the 'subjectivist', represents an understandable reaction to the problematic aspects of the first. It finds its expression in Protestant theologians (Karl Barth is the example cited), for whom any efficacy attributed to the sacraments can only take away from the sovereign freedom and power of God to save as and how God wants. Nothing in the Church must be allowed to hinder or obscure God's autonomy: the only possible significance for sacraments is that they are the community's acts of thanksgiving and recognition towards God. Chauvet also outlines a number of contemporary Catholic understandings which are similar in essence to Barth's position, but much less theologically acute. These stress the 'subjective' human response in such a way as to confuse authenticity with human sincerity, and run the risk of elitism, rigorism, or an anti-institutional hostility towards the Church. According to this model, grace is conferred anthropologically, to be 'transmitted' (as thanksgiving) from the human community back

---

[5] Louis-Marie Chauvet, *The Sacraments: the Word of God at the Mercy of the Body.* Liturgical Press, Collegeville, Minnesota, 2001.

to God; in fact this second model is just as 'instrumentalist' as the first, but the direction has changed.

With the third model, typified by Vatican II itself, some balance is achieved by correcting the one-dimensionality of the first. This is done in large part by recognizing the layered nature of sacramental reality:

> —firstly, in Christ we have the source-sacrament of God's encounter with humanity;
> —secondly, the community of believers is explicitly articulated as the 'sacrament of humanity' or 'sacrament of the reign of God';
> —thirdly, the Church is therefore the foundation on which the understanding of the seven specific sacramental actions is to be constructed.

This reassertion of the Church itself as a sacrament enables a more flexible and inclusive approach, one that is more alert to the anthropological context in which God and humanity encounter one another:

> All the basic experiences that comprise the fabric of people's lives—birth, growth into adulthood, sickness and suffering, love and friendship, caring for one another, sin and reconciliation, and in a special way death—are meant to be transformed by what has happened in the life and death and resurrection of Jesus. In all these areas, ritual has an important, indispensable role to play; but effective rituals do not function apart from that which they symbolise. It is the entire experience with a particular focus on the ritual moment that deserves the name 'sacrament'.[6]

Three truths, therefore, need to be kept in view at the same time: that God's action is sovereign, involving all human beings, and not just within the framework of Christian sacraments; that the sacraments are nevertheless a means or cause of sanctification for believers; that the

---

[6] Cooke, *op. cit.*, 1119.

sacraments are also revelatory or expressive signs of this sanctification. In this way there is a 'healing' of the split between sacrament as sign and sacrament as cause. As the history of the Church has shown, however, it is possible for this sense of balance and synthesis to be lost, and Chauvet's book undertakes what he sees as a still essential theological clarification. Nevertheless, the Vatican II position outlined here allows us to see with greater clarity what has been at stake in the tension or dichotomy between 'Word' and 'Sacrament'.

Word and sacrament

'Word' and 'Sacrament' are connected by virtue of an understanding of God's word as 'more than mere external utterance or intellectual discourse. It is, rather, the efficacious self-communication of God to creation. For God, to speak is to do. The word of God is an event of encounter.'[7] It is in Christ that the Word of God is made incarnate, an enfleshment which, as suggested toward the end of the last section, is continued in the existence of the Church and in its celebration of sacraments.

In other words, there is a complementarity of 'Word' and 'Sacrament', expressed in Augustine's understanding of a sacrament as a 'visible word'. During the history of Christianity, however, and in tandem with the instrumentalization of the sacraments which we examined above, the sense of this unity became lost; greater attention was given to proclamation of the Word as a matter of communicating and maintaining intellectual truth. The importance of preaching declined, as the proclamation element came to be a non–essential prelude to the celebration of the sacrament. Once again, the emphasis of the 16th century Reformation is a reaction to this imbalance, one which initiates a debate which continued until the Second Vatican Council. Polemically, the Protestants were seen as a 'Church of the word', while the Catholic emphasis made it a 'Church of the sacrament'. This dichotomy is now much less evident, largely as a result of biblical and patristic studies which have allowed the relationship between Word and Sacrament to be formulated once more in terms of their complementarity. There is a

---

[7] Andrew D Ciferni, 'Word and Sacrament' in *New Dictionary of Sacramental Worship*, ed. Peter E Fink SJ, Gill & MacMillan, Dublin, 1990, pp. 1318-9.

renewed appreciation of the scriptural understanding of God's word as a saving event, rendering present the grace of God which it announces.

This makes it possible for Karl Rahner to propose that while this reality (God's saving word) is found throughout the Church, its supreme and most intensive realisation is precisely the sacramental word. The Church itself is the primary sacrament: in celebrating these solemn actions, especially the Eucharist, God's word is addressed to human beings in decisive situations of human salvation. 'All other acts of the Church are ordered to the sacraments and all the sacraments to the Eucharist where Christ is present by the power of his own word.'[8] For Rahner, the word is permanently constitutive of the sacrament.

The most immediate outcome of this renewed understanding on the life of the Church has been the encouragement of Vatican II towards greater reading and appreciation of the Bible among Catholics, and better preaching, as ways of restoring the mutuality of 'word' and 'sacrament'. This is now something which characterizes nearly all Christian Churches, so that the split between the two is no longer an operative factor. From a Catholic perspective, Paul Janowiak traces the connection, made explicit by post-Vatican II theologians (Karl Rahner, Edward Schillebeeckx), between the proclamation of the Word of God, the preaching of the homily, and the consecration of the bread and wine. Taken together, these constitute 'the one whole word of God' (Karl Rahner), with the whole of the Eucharist, including the preaching, being regarded as a single, transformative, sacramental event. As summarized by Timothy Radcliffe, this single Eucharistic action has a threefold dynamic: firstly, Jesus reaches out to disciples in their puzzlement and disorientation (we may think here of the Easter story of Jesus meeting the disciples on the road to Emmaus); secondly, he gathers them into community; thirdly, there is an opposite movement of breaking out beyond this community, in order to reach for the fullness of the Kingdom of God:

> There is a rhythm to these moments, like the tempo of breathing. We reach out to the people, gather them in and then reach out into the Kingdom, like lungs that are emptied, filled and then emptied again. Humanity's history is breathing, from the gift of breath to Adam, to Christ's

---

8   *Ibid.*, 1319.

yielding of his last breath on the cross, to the breathing into us of the Holy Spirit. Our preaching will be sacramental, efficacious if it reflects the rhythm and measure of humanity's breathing, gathering in and expelling out, giving us life, and oxygen for our blood.[9]

Recent eucharistic theology

Janowiak's recovery of the relation between Word and Sacrament is developed using contemporary literary theory; Chauvet draws on contemporary insights into human communication through language and symbol. In each case the author is exploring what I have expressed above as the 'anthropological' pole of current reflection on sacraments.

In fact Chauvet's extensive study goes even further, since as well as analyzing the sacramental action itself he offers a moving reflection[10] upon the 'pastoral interview'. Here Chauvet uses communication theory and the anthropology of 'rites of passage', to ask what is happening when Christians approach the priest or pastoral worker to request marriage, or the baptism of their child. As often as not, in the post-Christian French context out of which Chauvet is writing, this conversation is a delicately-poised affair, a negotiation of power relations, an inchoate faith which may or may not find its way to explicit awareness. 'Interviewers and requesters are in the same boat,'[11] traversing a rough sea—but it is the responsibility of the interviewer (priest, pastoral worker) to bring the boat safely to port. When both parties to this conversation are able to go beyond evasion and power games—when real communication takes place concerning the things of faith—this can be truly 'the moment of grace'. An interesting suggestion, in other words, that the moment of sacramental significance may occur in the preparation for the ritual as well as in the ceremony itself.

Such insights are made plausible, as we have seen, because of the transformed theology of the sacraments since Vatican II, resulting in

---

[9] Timothy Radcliffe OP, 'The Sacramentality of the Word', in ed. Keith Pecklers, *Liturgy in a Postmodern World*. Continuum, NY, 2003, 146-7.

[10] Chauvet, *op. cit.*, 184–200.

[11] *Ibid.*, 192.

what Chauvet describes as a distinctive but unstable theological synthesis. The council stresses the ecclesial foundation of the sacraments (i.e. the Church is the primary sacrament, within which the seven traditional sacraments have their meaning), and by so doing is better able to articulate the anthropological as well as the religious significance of sacramental action. However, Chauvet also indicates why this synthesis is a tentative one, in particular highlighting the temptations of an over-enthusiastic embrace of the anthropological perspective. For Chauvet, many contemporary believers have (over-)reacted to the earlier 'objectivist' model by adopting modern versions of the 'subjectivist' attitude. Accordingly, orthodoxy is identified with orthopraxis (good conduct), and the qualities of subjective sincerity and generosity are valued over those of truth and faith.[12] On this account, sacraments are regarded as celebrations of 'the Kingdom of God', here identified with an unproblematic human nature, imbued with the presence of God. The Church disappears from the picture.

I would like to highlight one author's recent attempts to challenge this deviation, and the allegedly distorted theology from which it derives. William Cavanaugh seeks to recapture an authentic understanding of Eucharist, the sacramental action towards which, as we have seen, the other sacraments are ordered. An extraordinary text in this regard is Cavanaugh's *Torture and Eucharist*, which draws on sacramental theology as part of a case-study of Chile under the Pinochet dictatorship during the 1970s and 1980s. Cavanaugh builds up his argument as a contrast between the use of torture by the regime as a sustained attack upon the social body as well as individual bodies, and the Church's resistance to this. Paradoxically, the function of torture in this regard is the creation of individuals—as atomized and powerless units—at the same time as they are prevented, by fear and widespread mistrust as well as physical coercion itself, from grouping together and challenging the state's authority. Because torture (and the fear it engenders) scatters individuals, it is described by Cavanaugh as an 'anti-liturgy' or 'perverted liturgy'.[13] This he opposes to the Church's celebration of true liturgy, or 'Eucharist', understood broadly as a series of practices intended to gather individuals into a collective, which can challenge and denounce the state's practices

---

[12] *Ibid.*, xvii.
[13] William T Cavanaugh, 'The World in a Wafer: A Geography of the Eucharist as Resistance to Globalisation', *Modern Theology*, 15.2 April 1999, 181-196.

(various examples of the Church's defence of human rights are cited here, such as establishing the Vicariate of Solidarity and threatening torturers with excommunication).

Cavanaugh's fascinating study indicates a broadening of the term 'Eucharist' to include faith-inspired social action. What concerns us more immediately is his contention that the Church had to *learn anew* how to 'celebrate Eucharist' in this fashion, because it had become politically 'invisible' in the Chilean social context. The reasons for this, he alleges, are contained in the complex history of Church-state relations in Chile, and the deviated theological perspective which they brought about; in the process he denounces the kind of 'subjectivist' deviation adverted to above, where a particular kind of well-intentioned blurring of the line between 'liturgy' and 'politics', or between 'Church and kingdom/world', has taken place. Too many Latin American theologians, he suggests, have asserted enthusiastically that the barriers between sacred and secular have been broken down; that the whole world is 'graced', and that the Church is no longer a separate sanctuary, but totally bound up with the world's politics and economics. The Eucharist as 'sign' therefore points to the political process, imbued with the presence of God.

> However, if the Eucharist is only a sign and has no content of its own, then the divide between liturgy and politics is only exacerbated. The Eucharist can embody no 'politics' of its own but can only point to something other, and other signs might do the pointing just as well. In Leonardo Boff's book on the sacraments, one finds chapters entitled 'Our Family Mug as Sacrament' and 'My Father's Cigarette Butt as Sacrament'. Although Boff considers the Eucharist to be one of the 'special' sacraments, he contends that anything on earth can be a sacrament for a particular individual, provided she look through the object itself and see the presence of God. God is always present in everything, he argues, but the person of faith must learn to read the deeper meaning behind the signs. This attempt to re-enchant the secular world, however, only leaves the world more bereft of God. If God always stands 'behind' signs, then signs become interchangeable, and God never truly saturates any particular sign. This approach easily flip-flops into the modern post-

Kantian suspicion of all representation as unable to reveal
the transcendent.[14] (Cavanaugh, 1998: 13)

What is being commemorated in the Eucharist, Cavanaugh
insists, is not merely the 'incarnation' of God, omnipresent in the created
world, but also the death and resurrection of Christ. A Eucharistic
'counter-politics', such as he describes took place in Chile under the
dictatorship, is 'in sharp discontinuity with the politics of the world which
killed its saviour. The point is not to politicize the Eucharist, but to
"Eucharistize" the world.'[15] (13-14)

This Cavanaugh proceeds to do in a later article which concerns
itself with Eucharist and globalization.[16] The structure of the argument is
strikingly similar to that of *Torture and Eucharist*: in this work, as we have
seen, he contrasts the anti-liturgy of state torture (which he investigates
as part of a wider critique of the modern view of the nation-state) with
Eucharistic practice. In the later article, Eucharist is similarly seen as a
source of resistance, this time to globalization. The paradox is only
apparent, since Cavanaugh argues that globalization does not signal the
demise of the nation-state, rather it is 'a hyperextension of the nation-
state's project of subsuming the local under the universal.'[17] (Cavanaugh,
1999: 182) The changes brought about by globalization do not end the
state project, rather they generalize it across space.

What Cavanaugh seeks to establish is a recovered understanding
of the Eucharist as a source of a 'truly Catholic practice of space and
time', one which contrasts with globalisation's destructive discipline or
'mapping' of space and time, insofar as the Eucharist does not simply
prescind from or flatten out the local. On the contrary:

The true catholicity produced by the Eucharist, however,
does not depend on the mapping of global space ... the
Eucharist overcomes the dichotomy of universal and local.
The action of the Eucharist collapses spatial divisions not

---

[14] William T Cavanaugh, *Torture and Eucharist. Theology, Politics and the Body of Christ*, Blackwell, Oxford, 1998, 13
[15] *Ibid.*, 13-14.
[16] 'The World in a Wafer: A Geography of the Eucharist as Resistance to Globalisation', *Modern Theology* 15.2 April 1999, 181-196. This special issue of *Modern Theology* contains the proceedings of a conference on the Eucharist, held at Duke University, April 1998.
[17] Cavanaugh, 1999, 182

by sheer mobility but by gathering in the local assembly. The *Catholica* is not a place, however, but a 'spatial story' about the origin and destiny of the whole world, a story enacted in the Eucharist.[18]

It is in the gathering of the community that the distinctive spatial character of the *Catholica* becomes evident, not as a gathering into a particular space to be defended, but as a collapsing or concentrating of the whole:

> By the same liturgical action, not *part* but the *whole* Body of Christ is present in each local Eucharistic assembly ... Catholic space, therefore, is not a simple, universal space uniting individuals directly to a whole; the Eucharist refracts space in such a way that one becomes more united to the whole the more tied one becomes to the local. The true global village is not simply a village writ large, but rather 'where two or three are gathered in my name' (Mt. 18.20).

In setting the 'logic' of Eucharistic gathering over against the practices of secularism in both its modern and post-modern forms, Cavanaugh is aligned with the project of 'Radical Orthodoxy', a theological movement emerging from Cambridge in the 1990s, whose productions include the writings of John Milbank, Catherine Pickstock and Graham Ward.[19] These theologians assert that the logic of secularism, which has defined and constructed the world for several centuries, is finally imploding. In response, Radical Orthodoxy:

> attempts to reclaim the world by situating its concerns and activities within a theological framework. Not simply returning in nostalgia to the premodern, it visits sites in which secularism has invested heavily—aesthetics, politics, sex, the body, personhood, visibility, space—and resituates

---

[18] *Ibid.*, 189.

[19] Catherine Pickstock, *After Writing: On the Liturgical Consummation of Philosophy*. Blackwell, Oxford, 1998; Graham Ward, 'Bodies. The Displaced Body of Jesus Christ', in *Radical Orthodoxy: a New Theology*, eds. John Milbank, Catherine Pickstock, Graham Ward. Routledge, London 1999, 163-182.

them from a Christian standpoint; that is, in terms of the Trinity, Christology, the Church and the Eucharist.[20]

It may be asked whether the Radical Orthodoxy programme raises more questions than it answers, and in any case it is one that by its high level of conceptual engagement is unlikely to attract the attention of the majority of ordinary believers. Nevertheless, an excursus into consideration of the theology of Eucharist is justified, insofar as it allows some of the features of contemporary sacramental theology to be depicted with especial clarity. Pope John Paul's recent Encyclical Letter, *Ecclesia de Eucharistia*,[21] opens with the assertion that 'The Church draws her life from the Eucharist', and refers to the teaching of Vatican II that the Eucharistic sacrifice is 'the source and summit of the Christian life'. The letter is a powerful Christocentric expression and rekindling of Eucharistic 'amazement' at this reality which embraces all of history as the recipient of God's saving grace.

The Pope notes shadows also: in particular, a devaluation or reductionism of Eucharistic devotion, which he attributes to a neglect of its primary significance: 'Stripped of its sacrificial meaning, it is celebrated as if it were simply a fraternal banquet.' The document as a whole insists on this sacrificial understanding, rooting the Eucharist very firmly in the selfless death and resurrection of Christ, events which it 're-presents' continually. It also stresses the essential nature of the Eucharist as the foundation of the community of Christian faithful: 'the Eucharist builds the Church and the Church makes the Eucharist'; the Pope draws from this intimate connection a number of conclusions about the status of the ministerial priesthood, and about the unacceptability of inter-communion with those other Christian denominations which lack the fullness of unity of Catholic belief and ecclesial discipline.

Conclusion

It is fair to say that, however painful they may be, the controversies over Eucharistic discipline which the pope seeks to address in *Ecclesia de*

---

[20] *Radical Orthodoxy*, Introduction, 1.

[21] Pope John Paul II, *Ecclesia de Eucharistia*, 111.newadvent.org.

Eucharistia are of more immediate relevance and accessibility to the majority of Catholic believers than the stimulating but largely inaccessible assertions of the Radical Orthodoxy theologians. With the Pope's encyclical we return to the concerns expressed at the beginning of this paper, namely the tension between sacramentality as a human reality and the need to preserve the contours of a specifically Catholic identity and purpose.

It should be evident that each side of this tension finds itself articulated in contemporary Catholic sacramental theology. Writers like Chauvet and Janowiak[22] see Word and Sacrament rooted in the *humanum*, in the linguistic, symbol-making faculties of human beings; to use Chauvet's beautiful sub-title, 'the Word of God at the mercy of the Body'. At the mercy, therefore, of meaning and interpretations which cannot be controlled. Lieven Boeve insists that '[I]n the postmodern context the Christian narrative can regain contextual plausibility only by re-textualising and reconstructing itself as an open narrative:'

> In this regard, it must be able to take distance from premodern and modern ontological foundations, as well as from the modes of legitimation offered by modern philosophies of history. The sacramentality of life, clarified and celebrated in the sacraments, is no longer considered as participation in a divine being, nor anticipation of a self-fulfilling development, but as being involved in the tension arising from the irruption of the divine Other into our human narratives, to which the Christian narrative testifies from of old.[23]

Such a 'retextualised' understanding could not, apparently, be further away from the insistence of the Pope, and for that matter the Radical Orthodox theologians, upon the need for a recovery of a clear and authentic doctrine of the Eucharist, both as to its meaning and to its practice and discipline. 'The Eucharist is too great a gift to tolerate ambiguity and depreciation' (*EDE*: 10):

---

[22] Paul Janowiak, *The Holy Preaching: Sacramentality of the Word*, Liturgical Press, Collegeville, Minnesota, 2000.

[23] Lieven Boeve, 'Postmodern Sacramento-Theology: Retelling the Christian Story', *Ephemerides Theologiae Lovanienses*, LXXIV, 1998, 343.

The mystery of the Eucharist—sacrifice, presence, banquet—*does not allow for reduction or exploitation*; ... These are times when the Church is firmly built up and it becomes clear what she truly is: one, holy, catholic and apostolic; the people, temple and family of God; the body and bride of Christ, enlivened by the Holy Spirit; the universal sacrament of salvation and a hierarchically structured communion. (*EDE:* 61)

It is beyond the scope of this paper to explore this tension further, but the solution to this apparent dilemma would appear to be a diachronic one: the Eucharist, along with the other sacraments, is both gathering and dispersal, a place where Christian identity is both lovingly built up and prophetically undermined, an action which 'reflects the rhythm and measure of humanity's breathing' (Radcliffe). As I hope I have indicated in this paper, contemporary sacramental theology seeks to preserve and do justice to both these 'moments', and to steer us away from a dual temptation: of a nervous desire to control meanings on the one hand, and a misplaced enthusiasm for a false 'anthropological' inclusiveness on the other.[24]

---

[24] The following works have also been referred to: eds. Lieven Boeve and Lambert Leijssen, *Sacramental presence in a postmodern context*. Peeters, Leuven 2001; eds. Lieven Boeve and Lambert Leijssen, *Contemporary sacramental contours of a God Incarnate*. Peeters, Leuven, 2001; David Brown and Ann Loades (eds), *Christ: the Sacramental Word*. SPCK, London, 1996; Louis-Marie Chauvet, *Symbol and Sacrament: A Sacramental Reinterpretation of Christian Existence*. Liturgical Press, Collegeville, Minnesota, 1995; Bernard Cooke, *The Distancing of God: the Ambiguity of Symbol in History and Theology*. Fortress Press, MN, 1990; Peter E Fink SJ, *Worship: praying the sacraments*, Pastoral Press, Washington DC, 1991; Michael G Lawler, *Symbol and Sacrament: a Contemporary Sacramental Theology*. Creighton University Press, Omaha, Nb, 1995; Joseph Martos, *Doors to the Sacred: A Historical Introduction to Sacraments in the Christian Church*, SCM, London, 1981; Kenan B Osborne, *Christian Sacraments in a Postmodern World: a Theology for the Third Millennium*, Paulist Press, NY, 1999; Karl Rahner, 'The Word and the Eucharist', *Theological Investigations*, Vol IV, Helicon, Baltimore, 1966.

WORD OF GOD AND REVELATION:
A SHI'A PERSPECTIVE
Mohammad Jafar Elmi

The communication between God, the Infinite Being, and the human being, this finite being, is a well known phenomenon in Islam. At the advent of Islam, the Qur'an was introduced, and Muslims have considered the Qur'an as an instance of this phenomenon (Qur'an 2: 23; 4: 82; 11: 13; 52: 34).

According to Islamic beliefs it is not just the Qur'an but other Divine books such as the Torah, the Gospels and the *Zabūr* of Prophet David that are other examples of this connection between the Divinity and mankind (Qur'an 3:3 and 48 and 65; 4:163; 5: 46 and 110; 17:55; 21:105).

There are different terms used in the Qur'an that refer to this occurrence: *kalāmu-llāh, waḥy* and *qawl*, which respectively mean the word of God, revelation and speech.

A full understanding of the revelation can be known in relation to the divine attributes. According to the Qur'anic perspective there is a relationship between the creation on the one hand and the revelation on the other. The argument used here by Muslim scholars is in relation to the absoluteness of the nature of God's essence and his divine attributes.[1]

Divine guidance and revelation

In brief, this means that God has absolute knowledge of the needs of His creatures and knows how these needs can be fulfilled. Moreover, He has absolute power to actualize His knowledge and to fulfil these needs, and there is nothing that can prevent Him from making that happen. In addition, as one of His divine attributes, He has absolute generosity. In other words, there is no obstacle, either external or internal, to prevent

---

[1] This argument is known as the 'best choice'. For more explanation, see Mullā Ṣadrā, *Al-Asfār al-'Aqlīyah al-Arbi'ah*, vol. 7, 244-76.

Him from fulfilling the needs of His creatures in their journey toward their final goal of existence, i.e. perfection.

Therefore, He is always in a position of bestowing his guidance on His creatures in different ways depending on their needs.[2] And this is the meaning of God as the Lord *(Rabb)* of creation. *Rabb* in Arabic means nourisher, cherisher, and sustainer. According to Raghib, the great Arab etymologist, the word *rabb* signifies 'the fostering of a thing in such a manner as to make it attain one condition after another up to its goal of perfection'.[3] The process by which this 'guidance' reaches created beings is known as 'revelation'. In this way revelation is not confined to normative realms such as ethics and legislation, but rather it has a notion of a universal divine guidance which includes all entities. This type of guidance may differ from one being to another, depending on their peculiarities. However, the common point between these different types of revelation is a sense of communication between God and His creatures. Verses of the Qur'an speak, in this way, of the revelation to the skies[4] and to the bees,[5] as well as to mankind.

The divine guidance which all creatures, except human beings, receive is related to the realm of creation. They are created and also guided by the natural instincts that every creature is endowed with. Human beings on the other hand are created with free will and the ability to choose. Therefore, divine guidance for mankind has taken place in a different way, which has come to be known as religion. In that way, man by his own choice has to turn to religion for guidance. To provide and present this divine guidance, God has sent different prophets (Qur'an 4: 163-5). As man expresses his thoughts through the medium of signs which might be in its usual form (i.e. voice or some other form), he has to make various combinations of signs to describe different ideas which are in his mind. In the same way, God has used different signs to communicate with mankind, and these signs are known as the Word of God.

[2] Qur'an 20:50: 'Our Lord is He Who gave to each (created) thing its form and nature, and then, gave (it) guidance.'
[3] A M Pūyā, *The Holy Qur'an*, Karachi, 1991, 19-21.
[4] Qur'an 41:12: 'and He revealed to each heaven its duty and command.'
[5] Qur'an 16:68: 'And your Lord revealed the Bee to build its cells in hills, on trees, and in (men's) habitations.'

The Word of God

One of the expressions used in the Qur'an to address this divine communication is *kalimatu-llāh*. In Arabic, *kalimatu-llāh* means the word of God. In spite of the customary usage of this term which is the utterance or speech of God, according to Islamic teaching the Word of God is not confined to this commonly known notion; rather it has a wider usage in the Qur'an.

'The word of God' in Qur'anic terminology includes all acts of God. In this way the Qur'an conveys to mankind that creation in its totality has a meaning in itself. In other words, when God explains His Will by communicating to mankind, this divine manifestation could be in different ways and not just by speaking to it, as long as these signs can express the divine will and present the intended meanings.

In that way, in the verses of the Qur'an all aspects of creation are considered as the Words of God (Q 18:109; 31: 26-7).[6] Therefore, it can be seen that in many verses of the Qur'an man is asked to contemplate different parts of creation, and he is invited to read and understand this most important divine book (Qur'an: 13: 3; 16: 11; 30: 8; 45:13).

In the same way, the Qur'an addresses the events in the life of the Prophet Moses (Qur'an 7:137) and more specifically the Prophet Jesus as the Word of God as well. In several verses of the Qur'an, Jesus is referred to as the Word (*kalimah*) of God.[7] It shows that there is a message embedded in his existence and because of that he deserved to be named

---

[6] Qur'an 18:109: 'Say: If the ocean were ink (wherewith to write out) the words of my Lord, sooner would the ocean be exhausted than would the words of my Lord, even if we added another ocean like it, for its aid.'

Also Qur'an 31:26-27: 'To Allah belong all things in heaven and earth: verily Allah is He (that is) free of all wants, worthy of all praise. And if all the trees on earth were pens and the ocean (were ink), with seven oceans behind it to add to its (supply), yet would not the words of Allah be exhausted (in the writing): for Allah is Exalted in Power, full of Wisdom.'

[7] Qur'an 3:39: 'While he [Zachariah] was standing in prayer in the chamber, the angels called unto him: 'Allah doth give thee glad tidings of Yahyā, witnessing the truth of a Word from Allah, and (be besides) noble, chaste, and a prophet, of the (goodly) company of the righteous.'

Qur'an 3:45: 'Behold!' the angels said: 'O Mary! Allah give thee glad tidings of a Word from Him: his name will be Christ Jesus, the son of Mary, held in honour in this world and the Hereafter and of (the company of) those nearest to God.'

Qur'an 4:171: 'Christ Jesus the son of Mary was (no more than) a messenger of Allah, and His Word, which He bestowed on Mary, and a spirit proceeding from Him.'

the 'Word of God'. The appellation of Jesus as the Word of God is rooted in the fact that Muslims fully accept the virgin birth of Jesus (Qur'an 19:16-33), a unique occurrence that had never before happened in the world.

However, the common usage of the 'Word of God' alongside the above-mentioned instances is the speech of God, or divine revelation and communication with mankind as will be explained in the following section.

Revelation

It was explained earlier that according to the Qur'an all aspects of creation benefit from the divine revelation *(waḥy)* and that through that they are guided toward their final goal. However, the specific usage of the word 'revelation' is about the communication between the God and prophets. According to the Qur'an, there are different ways in which God manifests His will, as the following verse demonstrates:

> 'It is not fitting for a man that God should speak to him
> except by revelation, or from behind a veil, or by the sending
> of a messenger to reveal, with God's permission, what God
> wills: for He is Most High, Most Wise.' (Qur'an 42:51)

The Qur'an, in this verse, says that God's communication with mankind takes place in three ways. The first one is the direct communication between Him and His apostles without any intermediary. The other method of divine utterance is communication with prophets from behind a veil. The last channel between God and man is through the intermediary called the Archangel Gabriel. The common point between these three methods, is that in all of them God speaks to the prophets and teaches them divine knowledge which they could not obtain otherwise.

Two modes of communication

In Islam, a clear distinction is made between revelation *(waḥy)*, which is applied to the verbatim transmission of the Qur'an to the Prophet Muhammad, and inspiration *(ilhām)*. The difference between these two modes of divine communication is that in revelation, such as in the case of the Qur'an, its meaning and wording are directly revealed to the Prophet Muhammad and he has merely transmitted the message without making any changes to it.

However, in inspiration the concepts perceived by the Prophet were divine and from God, but the words and the language used in expressing them were that of the Prophet himself. That is to say the divine communication through revelation in essence was devoid of the spoken word. The Prophet then conveyed this divine understanding to the people through the mediation of the Arabic language.

This situation is found in the case of the category of the Prophetic traditions classed as divine statements *(al-aḥādīth al-qudsiyyah)* in which the communication is in the form of guidance through revelation but transmitted in the form of the words chosen by the Prophet.[8] It shows the importance of the Qur'an in the eyes of the Muslims, even in comparison to the sayings of the Prophet.

Revelation immune to distortion

Another point about the divine revelation is that in its communication to human beings it is protected from any mistakes or alterations. This notion which is known as the infallibility of the prophets, *al-'iṣmah*, means that the role of the prophets in receiving, preserving, and delivering the divine revelation is to transfer the message of God as it has been revealed to them (Qur'an 72:26-8). 'Allāmah Ṭabāṭabā'ī, a great contemporary Shi'a exegete, explains this point by saying:

> '[Prophets] are as instruments at the disposal of the Creator's wisdom. Were they to make an error in receiving or teaching the message of the revelation or be led astray by whispering of evil persons, were they themselves to commit wrong or deliberately change the message they had to deliver, then the wisdom of God would be unable to perfect its programme of guidance.'[9]

---

[8] Ṭabāṭabā'ī, *Al-Mīzān fī Tafsīr al-Qur'ān*, al-A'lamī, Beirut, 1974, vol. XI, 75.

[9] Ṭabāṭabā'ī, *The Qur'an in Islam: Its Impact and Influence in the Life of Muslim*, A Yates, tr., Zahra Publications, Blanco, 1987, 80.

Man: an active agent in the process of interpretation

Having received divine guidance through revelation, man begins to play a more active role, from a passive recipient of the message of God to a more active participant in the interpretive process. Therefore, it can be seen that the Qur'an has been the subject of interpretation from the time of its revelation to the Prophet up to the present day. During the time of the Prophet, Muslims used to go to him to seek explanations, so as to gain a greater understanding of the verses that he would recite to them. The Qur'an has noted that that Prophet was not simply the 'transmitter' but also 'the explainer' of the divine message (Qur'an 16:44).

One of the issues in understanding any written work in general, and scriptural texts such as the Qur'an in particular, is this: How is it possible to discern 'the authorial intention' in the text itself? The importance of this question is clearly manifest in regard to religious scriptures, which have been with us now for many centuries. The circumstances in which these were revealed is not always clear to us. Moreover, we do not have the authority of the Prophet in our time to tell us, as he did during his life, whether our understanding of the text is accurate or inaccurate.

When we look at different interpretations of the same scriptures, it can be seen that each explicitly or implicitly presents itself as one true understanding of the scripture in question. Then, the issue that immediately arises is: which of these different, and in some cases contradictory, understandings of the same text is the true understanding of the text as intended by God?

In addition, it can be seen in our times that some philosophers have denied *ab initio* any possibility of discovering the authorial intention with any degree of objective verifiability. According to them 'understanding' is the act of the reader; the meaning which is presented by the interpreter has to be considered as his or her own production, not the author's actual intention.[10]

---

[10] E Palmer, *Hermeneutics*, Northwestern University Press, Evanston, 1969, 181-19. K J Vanhoozer, *Is there a meaning in this text?* Apollos, Leicester, 1998, 44-99.

Islam's opposition to subjective interpretation

Islamic teachings on the science of interpretation of the Qur'an are in direct opposition to this approach in interpretation. From the time of the emergence of Islam and the Qur'an, there has been a strong warning issued to Muslims, to those who would be interpreters of the revealed text, that in their effort to obtain divine guidance, they must at all costs avoid super-imposing their own unsubstantiated opinions on the objective meanings of the text.

One of the interesting issues which can be seen in the field of Qur'anic studies in the last few decades is the classification of different approaches in understanding the Qur'an.[11] Essentially there has been a number of well-established approaches to the interpretation of the Qur'an. These include the theological, philosophical, mystical and scientific approaches.

Thus, it seems that an element of subjectivity does exist in understanding the Qur'an. It shows that interpreters of the Qur'an have not always been able to prevent themselves from reading and interpreting this book according to their unsupported presuppositions. This issue can be viewed in relation to different interpretations which are written on the Qur'an. In the words of al-Zarqānī, who is one of the authorities in this field:

> All different groups [of interpreters] interpret the Book of God more or less subjectively according to what pleases them [and is accepted by them]. Consequently interpretation becomes the mirror which shows the reflection of the [ideas of] interpreters according to their different methods.[12]

Having studied different schools of interpretation, 'Allāmah Ṭabāṭabā'ī refers to the same conclusion:

> Most of the Muslim sects are not free from subjectivity in [interpreting] the verses of the Qur'an, especially in those

---

[11] A Rippin, 'Tafsir', in ed. M Eliade, *Encyclopedia of Religion*, New York,1987, vol. XIIII, 236-244. J Burton, 'Qur'anic Exegesis', in ed. M J L Young, *Religion, Learning and Science in the Abbasid Period*, Cambridge University Press, Cambridge, 1990, vol. I, 40-55.

[12] M Al-Zarqānī, *Manāhil al-'Irfān fī 'Ulūm al-Qur'an*, vol. 1, Beirut, 1999, 380.

verses whose apparent meaning goes against their beliefs. They seek refuge in wrapping such verses with meanings of their own choice, and their so-called arguments boil down to this: 'The apparent meaning of this verse is contrary to what has already been established by rational proofs; therefore, it must be given a new meaning, against the apparent one.[13]

Pitfalls of the scientific approach

Among the different methods of interpreting the Qur'an is the method of interpretation which is known as the 'scientific approach'. The interpretation of the Qur'an using scientific findings has a long and established history. It goes back to the early 2nd century of Islam when Muslim scholars, through translation of Greek scientific works, became familiar with this field.[14] Some examples of this approach can be seen in the works of Ibn Sīnā who interpreted the verses of the Qur'an pertaining to the sky and the earth, and some other natural phenomena according to Ptolemaic astronomical theory.[15]

In recent centuries, and after the massive scientific achievements and discoveries, it became clear that some of the scientific theories that had been used to interpret the Qur'an were wrong. This put the interpreters of the Qur'an into an awkward position and forced them to rethink the relationship between the Qur'an and the sciences, and to reinterpret those verses relating to scientific fields. They aimed to maintain the validity of the Qur'an by showing that what had been mentioned by previous interpreters was invalid. In addition, they tried to show the miracle of the Qur'an by presenting the compatibility of the Qur'an with modern sciences.[16]

---

[13] Ṭabāṭabā'ī, *Al-Mīzān: An Exegesis of the Qur'ān*, tr. S S Akhtar Rizvi, World Organization for Islamic Services, Tehran, 1984-1992, vol. 5, 119.

[14] M A Rezā'ī, *An Introduction to Scientific Interpretation of Koran*, Oswih, Tehran, 1375 AHS., 21.

[15] For example, see Ibn Sīnā, 'Tafsīr Sīrah al-Falaq' in Ibn Sīnā, *Al-Rasā'il*, Bīdār, Qum, 324-329.

[16] For some thematic commentaries with this approach see S Abdul Wadūd, *Phenomena of Nature and the Qur'an*, Khalid Publishers, Lahore, 1971, and S Ahmad Mahmud, *Scientific Trends in Qur'an*, Taha Publishers, London, 1985.

This approach was used widely in the late 19th and the first half of the 20th century by Muslim scholars. But thereafter it faced some strong criticisms and accusations due to what was regarded as the materialistic interpretation of the metaphysical aspects of the Qur'an.

A case in point: al-Quṭb's critique of scientific exegesis

Here we might consider the interpretation of Muhammad 'Abduh, a late 19th/early 20th century Egyptian scholar, of Sura 105. In this chapter, the Qur'an narrates the story of the 'companions of the elephant' and says, 'Do you not see how your Lord dealt with the companions of the elephant? Did he not make their treacherous plan go astray, and send against them flights of birds called *Abābīl*, striking them with stones of baked clay, making them like straw eaten up?'

This chapter refers to the story of the attack on Mecca in the same year that the Prophet Muhammad was born. Abrahah, king of Yemen, marched on Mecca with an army including elephants. But before he could reach this sacred city, God sent birds of Abābīl against him and his army. Through this miracle worked by the Lord, Abrahah and his army were destroyed and the sacred city remained intact.

'Abduh in his interpretation suggests that Abābīl is the name of some flying insects that carried microbes of some illness that caused leprosy. It was clear that this interpretation was formulated as pure conjecture and could not be derived from the apparent text of the Qur'an.

Al-Quṭb, a 20th-century Muslim scholar and activist, criticized this explanation and said:

> These kinds of attempts cannot be fruitful since the miracle of swarms of insects is no less striking than the stones themselves, or, in other words, God's words need not be necessarily experimented with in order to quench man's quest for understanding them. In fact in some ways it is better left as an unknown mystery … We should just accept it in all humility. If the Qur'an or the traditions refer to a miracle, we should not attempt to change the meaning of the verse and then to interpret them.[17]

---

[17] S M Quṭb, *Fī Ẓilāl al-Qur'an*, tr. M 'Ābidī, Nashr Inqilāb, Tehran, 1361 Sh., vol. 1, 537.

The question that must be asked here is how is it possible to interpret the Qur'an in a manner that is devoid of the interpreter's own views and is derived exclusively from principles of interpretation that can be attributed to God.

The Qur'an interprets itself

The solution which was presented by Ṭabāṭabā'ī for this problem, and highly supported by other Shi'a scholars,[18] is interpreting the Qur'an by the Qur'an itself.

Ṭabāṭabā'ī believed that it is with the reader that this unwarranted mixing-up of meanings—the subjective with the objective—takes place; and it is with this factor that the distortion of the meaning intended by the author—in this case God Himself—takes place. Therefore, the chief concern here is to limit, as much as possible, the interference of the reader in the intended meaning of the author.

According to this method, in order to obtain an objective meaning from the verses of the Qur'an, the interpreter has to put all his or her own ideas and views aside, and make an effort to understand and to interpret the verses of the Qur'an in the light of the other verses of this book. This method had been partially used by different schools of interpretation, but Ṭabāṭabā'ī, in his seminal commentary *al-Mīzān*, has applied this method as the very cornerstone of his interpretive hermeneutic. Explaining the main differences between his preferred method and other methods, he says:

> There are three options available to us when trying to provide a commentary for the Qur'an. First, by using knowledge, scientific or unscientific, that one already possesses. Second by way of the traditions of the Prophet or the Imams. Third, by way of contemplation, *tadabbur*, upon the Qur'an, and by allowing the verses to become clarified by comparing them to other verses, in addition to using traditions whenever possible. The third method is [...] the method that the Prophet

---

[18] A Jawadī Āmulī, *Tasnīm: Tafsīr-i Qur'an-i Karīm*, Isrā', Qum, 1378 Sh, vol. 1, 61-75.

himself and the Imams of his family have indicated in their teachings.[19]

From Ṭabāṭabā'ī's point of view, the difference between different interpretations lies in the preconception of interpreters. Accordingly, the interpretation of the Qur'an, even by the Qur'an, in the light of these preconceived notions falls under the category of subjective interpretation, because interpreters are trying to interpret the verses, and in doing so, are using their own preconceptions.

What Ṭabāṭabā'ī says about the role of the presuppositions of interpreters can be clearly gauged from the conflicts that exist in their interpretations, which arise as a consequence of the preconceptions of the different schools. To express his dissatisfaction with these methods of interpreting the Qur'an, Ṭabāṭabā'ī in his introduction to the *al-Mīzān* says:

> If you look at all the mentioned schools of interpretation, you will find that all of them have a very bad defect, which is that they impose the results of scientific or philosophical discussions on the meaning of the Qur'an.[20]

He further mentions that the appeal of the method he is using lies in the fact that the interpreter looks at the Qur'an without having any preconceived notions. He states about his commentary and writings:

> We have not based the explanations on any philosophical theory, scientific idea or mystical inspiration. We have not based on anything extraneous to the Qur'an, except for some fine literary points on which the understanding of Arabic eloquence depends, and self evident premises which can be understood by one and all.[21]

---

[19] Ṭabāṭabā'ī, *Qur'an Dar Islam*, 53.
[20] Ṭabāṭabā'ī, *Al-Mīzān*, vol. 1, 8.
[21] Ṭabāṭabā'ī, *Al-Mīzān*, vol. 1, 12.

Conclusion

By way of conclusion, and to summarize the points that have been discussed, we can say that there is an unavoidable interaction between the interpreters' ideas and modes of cognition, and their interpretation of the verses of the Qur'an. Sometimes this interaction results in contradictory interpretations.

Furthermore, interpreters often adopt a subjective approach and render the verses of the Qur'an in such a way as to make it compatible with their own viewpoints. It can be said, therefore, that their interpretation is not a true interpretation of God's aims and intention in revealing this Book, but only expresses their own understanding.

The method of interpretation of the Qur'an by the Qur'an as presented by Ṭabāṭabā'ī is considered to be the ideal method for interpreting the word of God. It is the most promising method for uncovering the objective meanings enshrined within the divinely revealed text.

IN CHRIST WE DIE

John McDade

In her study of Johann Sebastian Bach's six sonatas and partitas for solo violin, Professor Helga Thöne proposes that these works progress thematically in pairs according to the great feasts of the Christian year: from Christ's birth (Christmas) to his death and resurrection (Good Friday and Easter) and finally to his sending the Holy Spirit upon the Church (Pentecost):

Christmas:	Sonata no 1 (G minor)	Partita no 1 (B Minor)
Passion/Easter:	Sonata no 2 (A minor)	Partita no 2 (D Minor)
Pentecost:	Sonata no 3 (C Major)	Partita no 3 (E Major)

Her argument that a religious structure underpins these purely instrumental works is based upon the large number of chorale quotations in the movements, their relationship to the liturgical calendar and the numerological analysis (*gematria*) of notes and letters in the works. In particular, the Chaconne of the Partita in D Minor, which she interprets as Bach's musical epitaph in memory of his first wife, Maria Barbara, and appropriately one of the Passion/Resurrection works, evokes the melody and text of Martin Luther's Easter hymn, *Christ lag in Todesbanden*:

'Christ lay in death's bondage/Given up for our sins.
He is raised/ And has brought us life ...
No one could subdue death/ Among all the children of men.
Our sin caused this./No innocence was found then.
That is why death came so quickly to dominate us
And hold us captive in its power.'

If Professor Thöne is right, the instrumental music of the Chaconne, dependent upon coded religious meanings, is a transcription of teachings about Christ, sin and death that come to light only when the invisible and inaudible religious structure, the template which Bach devised first and then concealed, is restored to the music. This is music that was heard only once before: in the mind of Bach as he composed it. What Bach gives us in the score is a concealed theology in notes and numbers inspired by orthodox Christian teaching about Christ's death and us. In the resultant music religious insights are hidden, coming to light only when its religious structure and character are made explicit for the hearer. [1]

Before that point, one is aware only of an astonishing violin piece (the Chaconne is one of the most remarkable of Bach's compositions), but once the elements of its underlying religious structure are restored, the music is then heard in relation to the creative intelligence which produced it and hid itself within it. Like God and the creation, one might say: the creation does not give irrefutable signs of divine presence—the world conceals at the same time as it manifests God—but there are moments in the world's history when the truth about God's action towards us is glimpsed, in ways which, preserving the mystery of the oneness of God, compel faith and submission as the proper human responses. When those moments happen, a yoke is laid upon human beings, the yoke of obedience and submission before the ineffable and merciful God, because we are then in touch with how God has chosen to bring us into contact with himself. To this, Islam and Christianity bear witness. We are communities created by God's address to humanity, by God's Word spoken to all.

The Christian and Muslim traditions have different accounts of the underlying structure of the divine action in the light of which the world is to be 'heard' or interpreted. Our linked traditions are ways in which we express how we see the divine action that makes possible the 'music' of the world. What is worth noting is an isomorphism in both Catholic Christianity and in Shi'i Islam, a similarly shaped account of the death of a holy man for the sins of others. There are significant parallels between Jesus and the grandson of the Prophet, Imam Husayn who, faced with a battle at Karbala with fellow Muslims which he could not avoid, accepted his fate for the sins of those who had been unfaithful

---

[1] Thöne's research has been dramatically presented on *Morimur*, a recent CD by the Hilliard Ensemble and Christoph Poppen of the chorales and the D Minor Chaconne: singers intone the single verses of the 'hidden chorales' and hymnic fragments alongside the virtuoso violin part (ECM New Series 1765 461 895-2). The accompanying booklet introduces the theories of Helga Thöne which I present here.

to the teachings of the Prophet. For both traditions, the self-sacrifice in death of a holy man for the sins of others is a central feature of how divine mercy comes to the world. This is brought out in a recent book:

> Jesus and Husayn each can be described as the 'martyr of martyrs' in their respective religions. It is in this sense that Husayn, not the Prophet Muhammad or Imam 'Ali, is best compared to Jesus Christ. As martyrs par excellence, Jesus and Husayn offered themselves for the reception of sinners. Each hero foresaw his fate as martyr. Each had the choice of passing up this painful role. Each feared the suffering that such a role entailed. And each chose death, apparently for similar reasons. Each understood that this kind of gesture, the ultimate sacrifice, would leave a lasting legacy while serving to atone for humanity, which had lost its way ... Both Jesus and Husayn stand as central suffering figures whose violent deaths at the hands of ruthless temporal adversaries have been interpreted by their followers as universal redemptive acts. Both deaths represented the climax of a terrible period of passion and suffering that helped cleanse the world of injustice, tyranny, and corruption and set a great example to their followers ... Each is a powerful intercessor: Jesus, 'seated at the right hand of the Father, receive our prayers,' and Husayn dispenses the waters of the Pool of Kawthar and is grated the keys of the treasury of intercession.[2]

If I have understood the parallel correctly between Jesus' death and Husayn's death, both offer themselves for those who are caught in their sinfulness. Imam Husayn, as one of the Twelve Imams, and Jesus are sinless: only a person who is not as divided and affected by sin as we are can act effectively on our behalf. The themes of sacrificial death, intercession for sinners and the power of martyrdom as a witness to God's truth are features common to both traditions. Finally, it may be no accident that the day on which Imam Husayn died, 10 Muharram 61 (10 October 681), was also the date of the Jewish Day of Atonement, the

---

[2] J A Bill and J A Williams, *Roman Catholics and Shi'i Muslims: Prayer, Passion & Politics,* University of North Carolina Press, Chapel Hill, 2002, 49-50.

Muslim and Jewish calendars being still aligned with each other.[3] If so, then the themes of the Day of Atonement shape Muslim interpretation of the death of Imam Husayn, and as we shall see, those same Atonement rites flow into Christian interpretation of Jesus' death. These parallels are important and will be the focus of further discussion between Catholics and Shi'i Muslims. My role here is to offer some reflections on how these themes of death, sacrifice and sin are dealt with in how Christians understand Christ's work.

I return to the analysis which Helga Thöne gives of these Bach violin pieces. She also proposes that, in addition to the Christ-focused sequence of Christmas, Easter and Pentecost, the violin pieces also relate to a Latin Trinitarian formula found on German tombstones:

> *Ex Deo nascimur* (From God we are born)
> *In Christo morimur* (In Christ we die)
> *Per Spiritum Sanctum reviviscimus* (Through the Holy Spirit
> we live again)

The prepositions carry all the weight in this sequence: *from, in, through,* all of them applied to different aspects of God's action towards us and all three of them having an irreplaceable significance in this formula of who we are in relation to God. There is also the sequence of verbs: being born, dying, living again. In the first phrase, there is a double reference: first of all, to our coming from the creative source of divine life, the Father, 'the fountain and source of divinity' (*fons et origo deitatis*) from whose expressiveness all things come.[4] The second reference is to the spiritual rebirth that Christ brings: in the Gospel of John, it is said that 'to all who received him (Christ), who believed in his name, he gave power to become children of God; who were born, not of blood nor of the will of the flesh nor of the will of man, but of God' (John 1.12-13). It is as though we come afresh from God in a 'second birth' that completes the dynamic of creaturely identity: it is what we are made for.

---

[3] Bill and Williams, *op. cit.*, 39.

[4] Christian theology strongly affirms the direct connection between God and the world he sustains. St Thomas Aquinas speaks of God being directly present to the creation 'by essence, presence and power': in other words, no intermediary stands between God and the world he makes; our existence is directly contingent upon God's continuing to make us be.

The third phrase relates us to the work of the Holy Spirit in raising Jesus from the dead. The important teaching, of course, is given by St Paul:

> If the Spirit of him who raised Jesus from the dead dwells in you, he who raised Christ from the dead will give life to your mortal bodies also through his Spirit that dwells in you. (Rom 8.11)

We can understand the verse in these terms: since the power and love of God has taken Jesus from death into the life of God, there is sure hope that this same power will bring us too into the divine life. We too will 'live again' in the second birth that is the resurrection. So both the first and the third phrases refer to a second birth, the first of which follows on faith and the second of which follows on death.

The central phrase will be our concern: 'In Christ we die.' I take it to mean that all human death takes place in the context which Christ creates, a context so intimately determinative of human identity that our deaths—the deaths of all—can be regarded as taking place *in* Christ. His mission is 'for all', culminating in his self-offering to God in death; he died and was raised from death 'so that he might establish his Lordship over both the dead and the living' (Rom 14.9). The value of his death is particularly for those who have set themselves against God; it is a sacrifice 'for sinners' or 'for sins'. We shall come back to this theme when we consider how Christ understood his death, but for the moment, let us keep to the theme of being 'in Christ'.

This phrase is the Christian equivalent of the *umma*, the community of believers in Islam. It identifies who you are, where you are, where you belong, where your identity is most deeply established. Before I am a member of a particular political community or nation, my primary identity is that I am 'in Christ'. The theme of being 'in Christ' occurs most strongly in the letters of St Paul:

> In Christ Jesus you are all sons and daughters of God, through faith. There is neither Jew nor Greek, there is neither slave nor free; there is no male and female; for you are all one in Christ Jesus. (Gal 3.26ff)

Being in Christ means the dissolution of the distinctions between Jews and non-Jews, the elimination of the hierarchical division of social power and powerlessness and the abolition of the Adamic burden of being men and women subject to futility and death. Christ changes everything by being the one in whom human identity is reconfigured and fulfilled in relation both to God and to others.

I want to approach this theme with the help of a comment by Michel de Certeau: 'Christianity was founded upon the loss of a body, the loss of the body of Jesus Christ' after his burial.[5] Because the body of Christ is lost in the resurrection, de Certeau suggests, the early believers in Christ are pressed to recover, find, construct a body that will be the focus of their newly emerging religious identity. They come to be excluded from the body of Torah-observant believers in Israel and they establish the conditions of their survival as a different community by creating a body, the body of the Church, that is configured as the spiritual body of the physically risen Christ.

No longer needing the rituals of the Temple because Christ himself is now their Temple (Jn 2.21; 1 Cor 3.16), the early Christians construct their life as a body of believers around a baptismal ritual that they interpret as a symbolic immersion into Christ's death and resurrection (Rom 6.3; 1 Cor 12.13) and an atonement ritual that is a contact with the body and blood of Christ offered to God on the Cross. Within a few decades of Christ's death, Paul can write about the significance of this ritual:

> The cup of blessing which we bless, is it not a participation
> in the blood of Christ? The bread which we break, is it not
> a participation in the body of Christ? Because there is one
> bread, we who are many are one body, for we all partake of
> the one bread. (I Cor 10.16-7)

The Eucharistic acts of drinking the covenantal wine and eating the sacred bread give the Christian a share in the blessings of Christ's death. It is difficult to exaggerate the continuing importance of these themes for the Church because the Church is constituted by the rituals of sharing in Christ's life, death and resurrection. The Catholic

---

[5] M de Certeau, *The Mystic Fable*, Vol. 1, University of Chicago Press, 1992, 81.

concentration on the sacramental celebration of Christ's presence flows from the sense that both the Church and its Eucharist are the modes in which the body of Christ continues to be formed as the body of believers. Christ dies for sinners, and the effect of this is that sinners, called to be believers, come to be part of him. The word 'incorporation' ('inbodying') of sinners into the body of Christ describes it simply and perfectly, and that is why, if our human life is now 'in Christ', our death too is 'in Christ'. No one dies alone: all who die are touched by Christ's presence in death.

This brings us to the question of how Jesus interpreted his death. At the heart of Christian faith is the belief that Jesus willingly offered himself to God in death for the sins of humanity. He charged his death with meaning, a universal and decisive meaning. In the earliest traditions Jesus refers to the oracles of two prophets in relation to his death. 'The Son of Man', Jesus says, 'came not to be served but to serve and to give his life as a ransom for many' (Mk 10.45). With this phrase, he evokes the suffering of the Servant of God who 'has borne our griefs and carried our sorrows; smitten by God and afflicted, he was wounded for our transgressions and bruised for our iniquities; upon him was the chastisement that made us whole ... and the Lord has laid on him the iniquity of us all ... he bore the sin of many, and made intercession for the transgressors' (Is.53.4ff, 12). Every Christian, hearing these lines, sees the face of Christ.

At the final meal with his disciples, Jesus evokes Jeremiah's oracle about the new covenant that God will make: the wine that they will drink will be his blood of the new covenant that will bring God's love to climactic realization. Before this, in the cryptic riddle, 'Destroy this temple and in three days I will rebuild it,' he identifies his mission as that of building the Temple, the dwelling place of God, that will replace the Jerusalem Temple which is about to be destroyed. Jesus conducts his mission with a prophetic sense that judgement is coming upon Israel and that Jerusalem and its Temple will be destroyed, but also with the conviction that through him God is acting to make Israel the light of the world, the Temple and dwelling place of God to which all the nations of the world will come in pilgrimage to worship God. His summons to Israel is to become the eschatological Temple, the final dwelling place of God in the world, the definitive community of salvation.

It is intriguing is to ask about the connection between Jesus' understanding of his mission as the building of the final Temple and the theme of making atonement for sins. After all, the Jerusalem Temple was the location of the ritual sacrifice on the Day of Atonement when the high priest entered the Holy of Holies to atone for sins. This ritual rendered the Temple, the land and the people holy to God. It seems to me that Jesus consciously understood his death as the sacrifice that rendered the community he was gathering holy and worthy of bearing the divine glory. He was to enter the divine presence bearing not of the blood of sacrificed animals, but offering himself 'for all', so that all would become the holy dwelling place of God. This flows into the Church's sense of being made holy by the self-sacrifice of Christ in death: that is why Catholics go to mass.

We do know that in a creative interpretation of profound importance for subsequent Christian belief, the earliest Christian community came to understand that the events on the Mount of Calvary should be viewed in the light of the priestly atoning ritual on the Mount of the Temple. The earliest testimony to this insight probably comes in Paul's quotation from an earlier, presumably Jerusalem, tradition: he speaks of

> Messiah Jesus whom God put forward as the expiation *(hilasterion)* in his own blood for the remission of sins committed in the time of God's forbearance. (Rom 3.25)

The Greek word *hilasterion* translates the Hebrew *kapporeth*, the 'mercy seat', the throne of the divine presence, the place where the Lord appeared (Lev.16.20), which is sprinkled with blood by the high priest. In Paul's dense formula, the implication is clear: the blood of the crucified Messiah on Golgotha is to be viewed as the blood shed in the presence of God for the atonement of sins. The crucified Messiah, who has entered behind the veil of creation into God's presence, is now the mercy seat, the true locus of expiation, prefigured in the atoning rites of the Temple. It is only a short step from this to the Epistle to the Hebrews which presents Jesus as the high priest who enters the divine presence, taking with him his own blood as an offering to God, there to be received by God and to become the source of the world's final atonement. Christ's self-offering in death comes to be seen as the unique and unrepeatable priestly atonement at the heart of human history, endowing all human beings with mercy. This insight, relating Jesus' death to Temple ritual, more than any other, is the generative core of Christian faith.

Catholic Christianity is a conscious affirmation and transformation of these features of Temple religion in which the Jewish tradition of sacrificial offering for sins is not abandoned but re-worked and reinterpreted in relation to Christ and his continuing presence in the Church.[6] Catholic Christianity retains a stronger legacy of Biblical and 1st-century Jewish religion than Rabbinic Judaism which focuses on Torah-study, prayer and works of charity as ways in which Jewish life without a Temple was to be lived. It is a culmination of the religion of Biblical Judaism in which priestly access to the divine presence is extended to all by their Eucharistic union with the sacrificial death of Christ.

The effect is to flood the practices and imagination of Catholic Christianity with religious categories drawn from the Temple: the Eucharist becomes indelibly sacrificial; a spiritual participation in Christ's atoning sacrifice for sins becomes a core feature of Catholic spirituality; priestly mediation, intercession, a ritualized pattern of worship, blessings, sacred space and cultic ministry come to characterize Christian ministry; it retains in its churches an altar (not a table) on which the sacrifice of Calvary is re-presented; medieval piety will develop a worship of the Blessed Sacrament, the sanctified bread of the divine presence, and revere it as the presence of the Risen Christ in ways which evoke the Biblical Ark of the Covenant and the Holy of Holies. Catholics have a deep sense of themselves as defined by Christ's sacrificial death. This theme is the invisible structure, like Bach's template for the Chaconne, which makes the world a place of wholeness, defined ultimately not by its sin and evil, but by divine mercy. Only God resolves the enigmas of human freedom, and God uses the self-sacrifice of Christ for all as the medium by which mercy and truth come to the world.

When a Catholic discovers that in Shi'i Islam, within the proper boundaries of the great Islamic religious tradition, what Christians say

---

[6] The religious category of priesthood and high priesthood, redundant in post-70 Judaism, is boldly revivified by Christian Jews who apply these roles to Christ himself, even they know that he is not of a priestly family (Heb 7.14). No less boldly, Catholic Christianity revives cultic terminology in applying the category of 'priest' also to those who minister liturgically and pastorally in the church as presbyters, co-workers with bishops. Like Christian life as a whole, ministry in the name of Christ comes to be seen as a 'ministerial priesthood', a participation, centred on the Eucharist, in Christ's priestly work.

about Jesus is echoed in what is said about Imam Husayn, it is as though one discovers an unknown brother whom one recognizes as within the same family of faith. Recognition of a bond, certainly, but also a question about what purpose there might be within God's guidance of our communities that there should be such resonances and similarities. We can ask such a question and with God's help we may answer it.

ABRAHAM, MAN OF FAITH:
A SHI'A PERSPECTIVE
Morteza Sanei and Mohammad Soori

In the Holy Qur'an, God says: 'You have a fine model in Abraham and those with him.' For Muslims, the Qur'an is the most important source that embodies the final message of God for entire mankind. The Qur'an has a unique way of dealing with things. For example, the Qur'an does not usually tell a story from the beginning to the end in one place. One should study all the verses about a subject and put them together in some way or another to understand and draw a complete picture of the whole story. The reason for this is that the Qur'an is not a book on history; rather, the aim of the Qur'an is the training and guiding of mankind, and guiding them to draw nearer to God. In these cases, we should use the same method that the great commentators of the Qur'an, like 'Allāmah Sayyid Muḥammad Ḥusayn Ṭabāṭabā'ī in his commentary *Al-Mīzān fī Tafsīr al-Qur'ān*, have adopted, which is to interpret the Qur'an by the Qur'an *(tafsīr al-Qur'ān bi'l-Qur'ān)*.

There are more than 170 verses in the Qur'an about the Prophet Abraham. In what follows, we first try to offer an account of his life in a chronological order based on these verses which are spread put throughout the Qur'an.

Abraham's life in the Qur'an
Beginning of the appeal

After Abraham had been dispatched to the people as a prophet, he called them to turn towards God. He began this with Āzar, one of his nearest kinfolk (6: 74) and told him gently: 'Why do you worship something that neither hears nor perceives anything, and does not benefit you in anyway?' (19: 42) This was a weight on Āzar's mind and heart and he got confused at what Abraham said. Āzar also wondered where Abraham could have obtained this from. Abraham told him that he had been given

300

some knowledge which had not come to Āzar. (19: 43) This means that this came from God, not from himself. Abraham wanted him not to serve Satan, so as to prevent himself being punished by God. Although Āzar had no convincing responses, he did not believe in God and threatened Abraham with stoning and exile. Abraham withstood his threats and said softly: 'Peace be upon you! I will seek forgiveness for you from my Lord; He has been so gracious towards me.' (19: 46) But when it became clear to him that he (Āzar) was God's enemy, he declared himself to be clear of him. (9: 114)

Then he said Āzar and his people: 'What are these statues (images) to whose worship you cleave?' They answered: 'We found our forefathers worshipping them.' He told them that their forefathers had been in obvious error, and that their being in error was not a good reason for them to remain in manifest error. But it did not work (21: 52-54) and so Abraham decided to do something against their idols. (21: 57) Once, all of the people of the city went out for a ceremony. Before departure, they put some food in front of idols to be blessed. Abraham was ill, so he did not go with them, but shifted his attention to their false gods and said: 'Don't you eat? What is wrong with you that you do not utter a word?' (37: 88-92) He broke them into pieces except for the biggest one, so that when the people returned they question it. When the people returned to the city and realized what happened to their idols, they became angry and said: 'Who did this to our gods? He must be some evildoer.' Some people said: 'We heard a young man mentioning them; he is called Abraham.' They arrested Abraham and brought him before the people so they might witness it. They said: 'Is it you who has done this to our gods, Abraham?' He said: 'The chief of them is this, therefore ask them, if they can speak.' Since they did not have any reasonable response to give him, they turned to one another and said: 'You yourselves are the evildoers!' Then they hung their heads in wonder: 'You knew that those things do not utter a word. So why you want us to ask them.' Abraham, who had achieved his goal, said: 'So, do you worship something instead of God that neither benefits you in any way nor you any harm? Shame on you and on whatever you worship instead of God alone! Don't you use your reason?' They could not answer Abraham, so they sentenced him to death saying: 'Burn him up and support your gods if you must be doing something.' But by the order of God, the fire became cool and safe for Abraham and this turned them into the greater losers. (21: 58-70) It was a good time to believe, so some people believed (40: 4) and Lot was the pioneer in believing in God. (29: 26)

Arguing with the king

After the fire, the king realized that threatening and intimidation would not work with Abraham. Therefore, he called Abraham and argued with him about his Lord. The king asked: 'Who is your Lord?' Abraham replied: 'My Lord is the One Who gives life and brings death.' The king said: 'I too give life and bring death;' meaning that he could say, kill one prisoner and release the other. It is clear that this was a fallacy, so Abraham replied: 'God brings the sun from the East, so you bring it from the West.' The king was dumbfounded. (2: 258) Then, under pressure fromthe king and unbelievers, Abraham decided to migrate with his wife (37: 100) and Lot to the Blessed Land, Palestine (17: 1) in order to rescue themselves from their injustice (21: 71) and to pray and perform their holy rites freely.

Arguing with the star-worshippers

On the way to the Blessed Land, Abraham crossed an area whose people were star-worshippers. Abraham spent a while there to guide them. He went to them and mixed with them to make the task of guiding them much easier. When night came, he saw a star and said: 'This is my Lord.' But when it set he said in a way that everyone could hear him: 'I love not the setting ones.' At the second time, the same thing happened about the moon. Finally when he saw the sun rising, he said: 'This is my Lord. This is even greater.' But as it set, he said: 'O my people, I am free from giving partners to God. I have turned my face to Him who originated heaven and earth. I am not of the polytheists.' The people argued with him and frightened him with their gods (the Sun, the Moon and the stars). He said: 'Are you arguing with me concerning God, while he has guided me? I do not fear what you associate with Him, unless my Lord should wish for something else. My Lord embraces all things in His knowledge. Will you not remember? How can I fear what you associated with Him, while you do not fear having associated something with God for which He has not given you any authority? Those who believe and do not mix up their faith with iniquity, those are they who shall have security and they are those who go aright.' (6: 76-82) After these arguments, Abraham continued his journey to the Blessed Land, Palestine.

The birth of Ishmael and leaving him in Mecca

At the beginning of his migration, Abraham asked God for a child; so God gave him good news about a wise boy (37: 99-101) and Ishmael was born from Abraham's second wife.[1] In Palestine, Abraham received an order from God to settle Ishmael and his mother in Mecca which was then a valley without any crops and to return to Palestine. In return, Abraham called upon his Lord and said: 'Our Lord, I have had some of my offspring reside in a valley without any crops alongside your Hallowed House, our Lord, so that they may keep up prayer. Make the hearts of some people yearn towards them and provide them with fruit so they may be grateful. (14: 37) My Lord, make this countryside safe and provide any of his people who believe in God and the Last Day with fruits.' God said: 'And whoever disbelieves, I will let enjoy things for a while, then I will drive him to the chastisement of the Fire. How awful is such a destination!' (2: 126)

Sacrificing his son

From time to time, Abraham would go to Mecca to meet his family.[2] Once, when Ishmael reached the age of maturity, God ordered Abraham in a dream to sacrifice his son.[3] He said to his boy: 'My son, I saw in my

---

[1] This is expressly mentioned in the Qur'an, but since the good news of the birth of Isaac was after sacrifice of Ishmael (see 37: 99-101) and happened in Palestine (See 11: 71), we can conclude that Abraham has another wife and it was she whom Abraham settled in Mecca with Ishmael. Of course, this can clearly be understood from *hadiths*.

[2] At least this is mentioned twice in the Qur'an: sacrifice of Ishmael (37: 102) and restoration of the foundations of the House (2: 127). From these two we can drive that he was going to Mecca from time to time.

[3] The Qur'an does not specify the name of the sacrifice, but the context of verses in *Surat al-Ṣāffāt* (37) as well as the later news of Isaac and Jacob determine that the sacrifice was Ishmael.

dream that I must sacrifice you. Look for whatever you may see in it.' He said: 'My father, do anything you are ordered to; you will find me to be patient, if God so wishes.' When they both committed themselves peacefully to God, and Abraham had placed him face down, God called out to him: 'You have already confirmed the dream! Thus We reward the doers of good. This was an obvious test. We ransomed him with a great sacrifice.' (37: 102-107)

News of Isaac and Lot's people

After this event, Abraham returned to Palestine. At this time, Lot, the first believer in Abraham (29: 26), was a prophet in another land, but near Palestine.[4] One day, Abraham had some guests. They were originally angels but they visited Abraham as human beings (15: 51) and said: 'Peace!' He said: 'Peace!' and immediately set about bringing in a roast calf. But he saw their hand did not reach out towards it, so he deemed them strange and became fearful of them. They said: 'Do not fear; surely we have been sent to Lot's people.' His wife was standing by and she laughed, so the angels informed them about the good news of Isaac. (11: 69-70) He said: 'Have you brought me word like this once old age has set in on me? What sort of word do you want to spread?' They said: 'We have brought you word of the truth, so do not act so discouraged.' He said: 'Who despairs of his Lord's mercy except the erring ones?' (15: 54-56) His wife was surprised too and said: 'O wonder! Shall I bear a child while I am an old woman and this husband of mine is elderly? That would be an amazing thing!' They said: 'Do you marvel at God's command? God's mercy and blessing are on you people in this house. He is Praiseworthy, Glorious!' So when the fear had gone away from Abraham as the good news came to him, he pleaded with the messengers about Lot's people so that they might intercede on behalf of them, because he was so lenient, forbearing, tenderhearted and oft returning. They said: 'Abraham, leave off this! It is merely that your Lord's command has come to pass, and torment which cannot be averted has come to them' (11: 71-76) He said: 'But yet Lot is in it.' They said: 'We are quite aware as to who is in it. We will save both him and his household, except for his wife; she is one of those who will stay behind.' (29: 33)

---

[4] We know that because the angels on their way to Lot visited Abraham as guests.

Rebuilding God's House

During Abraham's last journey to Mecca, when Ishmael was fully-grown, God ordered them to build the House once again and clean it out for those who circumabulate it and secluded pray there, and who bow down their knees in worship. (2: 125) When Abraham, along with Ishmael, laid the foundations for the house, they said: 'Our Lord, accept this from us! Indeed you are the Alert, the Aware! Our Lord, make us both submissive to You and raise from our offspring a nation submitting to You, and show us our holy rites and turn towards us. You are so Relenting, the Merciful. Our Lord, bring forth a messenger from among them who will recite Your verses to them and teach them the Book and wisdom and purify them, for You are the Powerful, the Wise.' (2: 127-129) After finishing the rebuilding, God told Abraham to 'proclaim the Pilgrimage among mankind: they will come to you on foot and on every lean camel,[5] coming from every remote path to bear witness to the advantages they have, and mention God's name in appointed days over such heads of livestock as he had provided them with ... Then let them attend to their grooming, fulfill their vows, and circle round the Ancient House.' (22: 27-29)

Then Abraham prayed to God: 'My Lord, make this countryside safe and keep me and my sons away from worshipping idols. My Lord, they have led so many men astray. Anyone who follows me belongs to me, just as anyone who disobeys me will still find You Forgiving, Merciful. (14: 35-39) Our Lord, You know whatever we hide and whatever we display; nothing on earth, nor in the sky is hidden from God. Praise be to God Who has bestowed Ishmael and Isaac on me in my old age. My Lord is so alert to anyone's appeal. My Lord, make me persevere in prayer, and have my offspring do so too. Our Lord, accept my appeal. Our Lord, forgive me, my parents and believers on the Day when the Reckoning will be set up.' (14: 38-41)

Abraham the Imam

Abraham returned to Palestine. Now he had performed, in the best way possible, all the duties that God had asked of him and he had triumphed

---

[5] They are lean because of the long journey.

in the tests God had set for him. Therefore God appointed him as Imam (leader) and said: 'I am going to make you an Imam (leader) for mankind.' Abraham asked: 'What about my offspring?' God replied: 'My pledge does not apply to evildoers.' (2: 124) Abraham lived a long life. Before death, he enjoined his sons that 'my sons, God has selected your religion for you. Do not die unless you are submissive [to God].' (2: 132)

Lessons from Abraham's life

As we saw at the outset of this paper, God considers Abraham as a fine pattern and example for us. Abraham's lifestyle offers some lessons for mankind. In what follows we refer to just two of them.

Submission to God

The outstanding point in Abraham's life is said to spring from his utter submission and devotion to God. He showed his complete submission to God, even offering his son as a sacrifice at God's command. We think that this is the main trait of Abraham's conduct. Abraham showed his utter commitment and submission by responding to God's calling him towards the right path. He showed this in practice as the Qur'an explicitly indicates: 'When his Lord told him to surrender, he said: I have surrendered to the Lord of all things.' (2: 131) And we noticed this in the case of Abraham when he was put into the fire and when he scarified his son and left his family alone in a dry arid land, and in many other cases.

Love for people

In spite of the fact that Āzar and the idol worshippers were cruel to Abraham, he kept on being kind and courteous towards them and wished them God's blessing, since he knew that calling people to God should be done by awakening their conscience. Turning towards God, according to the Qur'an, lies in our nature and does not involve undergoing changes, but sometimes the rust of forgetfulness covers it and it requires some Divine instigation to make it return to its origin, as we saw that overthrowing the idols awakened at least for a moment the idol worshippers' hearts. So why did not they believe then? One answer might be that narrow self-interest sometimes prohibits man from responding the inner call of the heart. This is why Abraham left his people, because there was no hope for the people whose hearts were hardened to belief. Therefore, Abraham decided to emigrate to the Blessed Land, since he had accomplished his mission.

Abraham was not only courteous and kind to people, but also loved everyone, even those who worshiped idols. A good example is his intercession on behalf of Lot's people, although he was informed of their evil deeds and of God's order. That is why God calls him lenient, forbearing and tenderhearted. Abraham's love for people comes from his love for God and this causes people to turn towards God after they have forgotten him.

ABRAHAM, MAN OF FAITH:
A CATHOLIC PERSPECTIVE
Mary Mills

'Thus Abraham "believed God, and it was reckoned to him
as righteousness". So you see that it is men of faith who are
the sons of Abraham.' (Galatians 3:6-7)

From this passage the reader of Paul's Letters can derive a religious
paradigm, that of Abraham—man of faith. This paradigm takes the biblical
character, Abraham, and constitutes him as a religious and cultural icon
of what it means to be a person of religious faith. The contents for this
modelling of a faithful human being come from Genesis 12-22, where
Abraham's story is told. In Paul's Letter Abraham has moved from the
hero of a biblical narrative to a timeless theological construct. Based on
this model Abrahamic Christian behaviour consists of trust in God to
complete His promises of future life. The idea of being son relates to
being 'homely', being accepted by God as part of His divine household
in heaven. How can a Christian achieve that 'at-homeness'? Abraham
trusted that God would give him a promised son; by derivation all who
share Abraham's attitude of trust will become 'sons' both to Abraham and
to God. Here the function of Abraham as human father is extrapolated
to create a moral paradigm for readers of the Old Testament. This New
Testament usage forms a basis for an exploration of aspects of the 'mapping
and mything' of Abraham in Christian thought. [1]

How is the content of the term 'religious icon' to be defined in
the context of reading Abraham? This concept is derived from the work
of R Barthes, in his examination of social symbols. [2] Barthes argues that

---

[1] This term refers to a recent work of biblical scholarship by R Walsh, which explores the
concepts of 'myth' and 'map' as proper tools for the task of biblical scholarship. Walsh
argues that the concept of myth provides a good basis for describing the work of biblical
interpretation since all exegesis involves an imaginative response by the reader to the
metaphoric language of text. See R Walsh, *Mapping Myths of Biblical Interpretation*, Sheffield
Academic Press, Sheffield, 2001.

[2] R Barthes, tr. A Layers, *Mythologies*, Hill and Wang, New York, 1972.

literary and visual images become signifiers of wider cultural values, thus turning into the category of 'myth'. Myth denotes the underlying cultural significance of the surface image which acts as a medium for sharing and endorsing the cultural values involved. For Barthes a social myth floats free of literal, historical truth, though still materially tied to the culture producing it. One of Barthes' most famous examples is the *Paris Match* photograph of a young Negro officer saluting, against the backdrop of the tricolour.[3] Barthes argues that this picture is to be interpreted as signifying 'that France is a great Empire, that all her sons, without any colour discrimination, faithfully serve under her flag.'[4] What is being endorsed through the photograph is national honour, but this has a shadow side, since it also endorses the colonial aspirations of French society. Barthes states the need for a self-critical stance with regard to the impact of social myth.[5] For the myth draws the reader into its value system.[6] Barthes' paradigm of social mythology can be applied also to religious models of meaning drawn from biblical texts.

Barthes' somewhat critical stance can be put alongside the rather more positive approach of Timothy Luke Johnson to biblical imagination.[7] Johnson argues against the hegemony of historical criticism in biblical exegesis on the grounds of its restriction of possible meaning. The move to scriptural imagination invokes the "appropriate apprehension of Scripture as itself a body of literature that does not primarily describe the world but rather imagines a world and by imagining it, *reveals* it".[8] For Johnson, to live within the imaginative world is not an escape from reality but a commitment to live within the alternative reality of Christian tradition.[9] Pursuing the exegetical tool of scriptural imagination requires an engagement with the world of metaphor and linguistic images found in biblical books.[10] Applying this perspective to the Abrahamic story

---

[3] Barthes, 116.

[4] *Ibid.*

[5] Barthes argues for the role of mythologist: someone whose task is to take a suspicious approach to social myths in order to uncover their ideological basis. For reference to the work of such a figure in interpreting social symbols and the means of communication, see Barthes, 128-131.

[6] Barthes, 124.

[7] T L Johnson, 'Imagining the World Scripture Imagines' in eds. L Jones and J Buckley, *Theology and Scriptural Imagination*, Blackwell, Oxford, 1998.

[8] Johnson, 10.

[9] *Ibid.*

[10] Johnson, 12.

means taking seriously the potential of textual presentation of character and plot to offer images of personhood, the paradigm of a human existence as a 'myth' or 'icon' of theological, moral seriousness. Social myth-making and scriptural imagination work together in the act of reading. [11]

Reading Abraham as an 'icon' means finding religious messages in the life of a family man, largely in his actions in the domestic sphere of relations with wives, sons and kin—since these are the constitutive elements of the story of Abraham. As W Janzen argues, moral teachings in the Old Testament stem from the stories themselves. 'These stories tell of events, but perhaps more impressively, of characters who act.'[12] Like other literary stories they offer the reader a sense of relationship with their heroes and heroines.[13] It is Genesis 12-22 which is the heart of the iconic Abraham, telling his story from the command of '*Lek leka*' in chapter 12, God's command to migrate, to the repetition of this command in chapter 22, this time to take Isaac for sacrifice. In between there are two stories of Abraham and Sarah in trouble in a foreign land, two scenes with Abraham and Lot, two scenes with Abraham, Sarah and Hagar. These scenes balance out to leave the hinge of the story as the theme of covenant. In this over-arching perspective the story of Abraham concerns the God of Abraham's demands of his worshipper (submission to divine will), while a subplot also highlights the link of trust between two males (Abraham and God). The characterization of the human protagonist produced in this plot sequence is one which is both clear and ambiguous. The clarity of the covenantal plot is delivered within the frame of a narrative which has gaps and silences with regard to recounting Abraham's reactions to events. Even where there is direct speech dialogue it is terse and an aura of silence hangs over the character of Abraham. When God speaks he does not always reply. He acts as God wants but offers little comment on what that action implies.

Gathering together the overall plot line with the manner of the narrative voice and balancing these out, it is possible to create a picture of a noble, dignified Abraham who does not cry out loudly and constantly

---

[11] The development of Abraham as religious icon in this paper owes much of its thought to a larger work on biblical symbols: M Mills, *Biblical Morality*, Ashgate Publishing, Aldershot, 2001. In that volume the exploration of Abraham is set within the framework of narrative criticism.

[12] W Janzen, *Old Testament Ethics*, Westminster John Knox Press, Louisville, 1994, 7.

[13] Janzen, 7-8.

against his lack of a promised child, but who goes on with the daily business of living in silent trust that God will indeed redeem his promises. The textual silence about Abraham's motives could be read to indicate his deep religious commitment. Abraham goes in search of the God whom he has heard speaking and in search of his own human destiny. Similarly, the repetition of the command to go in chapter 22, together with Abraham's acceptance of it, allows us to assume that Abraham's motive for the sacrifice of Isaac is his genuine religious observance, his loyalty to God even in the face of life's appalling paradoxes. Thus is created an Abrahamic symbol of action which is that of solemn, self-possessed, silent and resourceful living. This profile is not necessarily comfortable to relate to, but is to be respected for its faith keeping with a personal understanding of God.

Such a reading creates the Abrahamic symbol of 'pious personhood' and this model is key for most mainstream commentaries on Genesis, as in the recent work by K-J Kuschel.[14] In this particular religious myth Abraham's worth is linked to monotheism, the quality of single-minded attachment to a given deity. For Kuschel this produces not only religious meaning but also a potential cultural tool for bridging real political and social gaps and hostilities between three of the world's religions. Not only is Abraham personally an ethical being but also he showed the way of being truly religious to later generations. In this interpretation Abraham, for Kuschel, sums up the key tenets of Judaism and produces a model of religious trust.[15] For Kuschel this provides the basis for an anthropology of faith, a faith based on total trust in God even when this is problematic. The possibility of authentic religious dialogue is forged by the fact that Abraham is an iconic figure in each separate tradition.[16]

Kuschel can be said to be both describing and developing an Abrahamic icon in his treatment of the story. He notes, for instance, Philo of Alexandria's idealising of Abraham as migratory. This is a philosophical expansion of the Genesis text. Abraham is a migratory seeker after truth, and this meant a search for the absolute deity.[17] Furthermore the Book of Jubilees adds in the element of Abraham as an idol-hater to this single-minded search, an aspect reinforced by Rabbinic

---

[14] K-J Kuschel, *Abraham*, SCM Press, London, 1995.

[15] Kuschel, 26.

[16] Kuschel, 28.

[17] Kuschel, 42-3.

tradition.[18] From these elements was forged an Abraham who is a Jewish religious icon, 'a theological-political figure with the help of whom creative theological attempts were made to react to ever-new challenges of history.'[19]

One central moment in Abraham's story, here, is the promise made in Genesis 22 that Abraham's trust in God would make him the father of a nation, and a source of blessing to all nations. This can be interpreted in line with Abraham's monotheism, to make his an abstract fatherhood of all believers in a single absolute deity, linked to ancient Semitic traditions. The Letter to the Hebrews, for example, posits Abraham as a model of a faithfulness which endures incomplete return on promises preached in God's name, such as an imminent parousia, alongside an Abraham of story who waited for his promised son.[20] The story of Abraham is quarried by the writer of Hebrews to show how, in Genesis 14, Abraham submits to the authority of Melchizedek, himself the forerunner of the true king and priest, namely Jesus Christ. Thus Abraham and his son are re-sited as Abraham as a type of son to Christ who is himself the heavenly Son.

Kuschel argues that, for Islam, the religious insights offered in the model of Abraham the monotheist are central to true belief and should be strengthened and protected. It is important for human beings to free themselves from the false religious views which have come down to them.[21] Christian readers also can relate to an Abrahamic rejection of idolatry which both stresses loyalty to the One God and demands reflection on what the current faces of false religion might be, in terms of practical social experience. Although this image of Abraham makes him a foundational figure for religious belief it is, not, for Kuschel, a simplistic viewpoint in which all Abraham's acts are equally deserving of moral praise. Abraham is capable of cowardliness which injures others. Mixed into the story of religious growth are flawed human situations, such as the stories of jealous tension between Abraham and his wives, leading to

---

[18] Kuschel, 58-9. See also the article by G Nickelsburg, 'Abraham the Convert' in eds. M Stone and T Bergren, *Biblical Figures outside the Bible*, Trinity Press International, Harrisburg, 1998. In this paper Nickelsburg focuses on traditions which developed regarding Abrahams's role as idol hater and how he thus came to be viewed as patriarch. In particular Nickelsburg discusses the presentation of Abraham in the Book of Jubilees and how the traditions used there may have influenced Paul's preaching.

[19] Kuschel, 64.

[20] Hebrews, chapter 6: 13-18.

[21] Kuschel, 143.

a brutal expulsion.[22] However, for Kuschel this behaviour is explicable since Abraham is a model of piety and not of perfection.

This Abrahamic icon has a moral vision in which the basis of religious thought is the theological teaching of the unity of the Godhead. It is a myth which promotes both religious freedom and religious duty. Abraham is called to be free of surrounding cultural values, to go out from a polytheistic culture and to live by the vision of monotheism. At the same time this freedom involves a clear line of duty—to undertake whatever that belief binds on a person. Abraham, having chosen freedom, now serves the God of his faith to the point of sacrifice. There are boundaries to his possible freedom to act, since loyalty requires him to listen for God's purpose in the new experiences of his life, both in life and in death situations. This Abrahamic religious myth is used by Paul, for instance, to call early Christian communities to change their social and cultural patterns in order both to come out of the Hellenistic culture of their day and to engage in the discipline of the bond of community, since all are one in Christ. It is a model envisaged by scriptural imagination in the service of cosmic and community ends.

The trajectory of an Abrahamic icon focusing on faith in God is towards the global, universal dimensions of human existence and imagines Abraham as a universal religious paradigm. But this image is derived from stories told largely about a man and his extended family. Another facet of Abrahamic moral vision emerges when this family loyalty is examined. In Genesis 13-14, and again in chapter 18, issues arise with regard to Abraham and Lot. In Genesis 13 a tense situation over land usage is resolved by Abraham's suggestion that he and Lot choose different areas for herding their flocks, allowing Lot to take the fertile plain. In chapter 18 Abraham's pressure on God not to destroy Sodom and Gomorrah if just a few just persons are there is to be read in the wider narrative context of the Abraham/Lot scene, since Lot chose the plains for his portion and is therefore under threat of annihilation, a plot interest played out in the subsequent scene. Meanwhile Genesis 14 sees Abraham concerned to rescue Lot from his captors.[23]

---

[22] Kuschel, 27-8.

[23] J Lundblom, 'Parataxis, Rhetorical Structure and the Dialogue over Sodom in Genesis 18' in eds. P Davies and D Clines, *The World of Genesis*, Sheffield Academic Press, Sheffield, 1998, makes the point that the narrative between Abraham and God makes sense in the light of Abraham's underlying concern for his kinsman, Lot. This point is also addressed by D Fewell and D Gunn, *Gender, Power and Promise*, Abingdon, Nashville, 1993, chapter 3.

Janzen views this paradigm of brotherly loyalty as central to a vision of Abraham as source of moral identity.[24] Abraham seeks to avoid conflict with Lot at all costs and is careful of his kinsman's interests when these are threatened by hostile forces. In Genesis 13 Abraham's 'non-assertive and peaceful disposition makes him willing to yield the choice to Lot, even at the cost of personal disadvantage.'[25] Thus Janzen builds up an image of Abraham as exemplifying Christian virtue and posits the view that 'such a "Christlike" readiness for self-denial is welcomed by the Christian reader.'[26] The basis for the Christian virtue, though, is not abstract ethical commands but action generated through a narrative in which Abraham's aim is to restore harmony within the kinship group.[27] The self-denial of Abraham's acts works towards the fulfilment of that specific aim.

Theology and moral values are interwoven; moral meaning and thus Abraham as moral icon, cannot be separated from plot and characterization. Janzen notes that it is the 'same' Abraham who is the supreme monotheist on the one hand and the loyal family member on the other. The Abrahamic icon is developed from the inter-relationship of these two layers, wider story and particular scene.

> A story presenting an exemplary action is not a self-contained whole yielding an encapsuled and timeless ethical people. Instead, the exemplary action emerges from a situation shaped by a preceding story and in turn contributes to the ongoing movement of that story.[28]

This icon is in harmonious dialogue with the picture of Abraham presented in the pious Abraham model. Abraham acts justly with regard to God and to his brother. Thus the universal Abraham image is fleshed out by acts on the local scene of the family interests. This in turn links the Abraham, man of faith icon, with Abraham as man of justice. But to this latter image there are several, contradictory layers.

---

[24] Janzen, 10.
[25] *Ibid.*
[26] *Ibid.*
[27] *Ibid.*
[28] *Ibid.*, 11.

Family loyalty and just relationships within the human community open out to wider issues of Abraham's status as a paradigm of righteousness on a global level. The Abrahamic icon of a hero who is a migrant, converted to monotheism, ties the reader of Genesis to a fairly static view of the narrative in which this ordering model takes over the story's other elements and subordinates them to a moral vision of trust and faith in God as the key to life's meaning. The story of Abraham, though, consists of many scenes each of which can be interpreted and its meaning read against the whole. What emerges from the text then is a multi-layered set of meanings.

J Magonet's book, *The Subversive Bible*, takes account of this structure and its impact on reading the narrative for its moral vision.[29] Magonet explores the ways in which scenes produce different and even opposing views, thus providing a form of Abrahamic icon which is a tool for destabilizing as well as for fixing, moral meaning.[30] One of Magonet's illustrations of this argument is his treatment of the subversive role of the Abraham story in relation to justice. He contrasts the Abraham who pleads with God over justice in the Sodom and Gomorrah case with the Abraham who is willing to suppress justice when he offers Isaac as a sacrifice to God. Magonet suggests that the contradictions are the work of 'the subversive hand of a single author'.[31] Positing the view that these ambiguities are deliberate creations allows the reader to engage with an Abraham who is himself ambiguous, in turn offering ambiguity as a possible model for moral vision.

Genesis 18 shows God choosing Abraham to be the father of a great nation and to educate them in the principles of justice. Because of this God decides to teach Abraham the nature of good and evil by revealing his judgement on the two towns. But Abraham turns the situation around by querying divine justice, thus producing a new form of moral vision, according to Magonet. God and human being now stand on equal terms, both looking for true justice.[32] 'In a culture where gods are supreme powers and human beings are totally subordinate [this] is an outstanding reversal of roles.'[33]

---

[29] J Magonet, *The Subversive Bible*, SCM Press, London, 1997.

[30] Magonet, 3f.

[31] Magonet, 21.

[32] Magonet, 23.

[33] *Ibid*.

Yet this same character is willing to sacrifice his own son to God without arguing his case for justice expressed through mercy. Read literally the event contradicts the image of a man of moral vision found in chapter 18. Only by shifting the context of the event, by describing it as a supreme test of loyalty, can the two images of Abraham be reconciled. For then there is no actual sacrifice involved. The use of two names for God enables this reading. Elohim tests Abraham, but YHWH stops him.[34] Yet the essential difficulty remains, as Magonet acknowledges.

> Abraham remains a riddle in the complexity of his character captured by these accounts. At the moment when we might domesticate Abraham we find his dark side, the single-minded fanaticism that would allow him to sacrifice his son.[35]

It is only a short step from the recognition of Abraham's dark side to a tragic approach to the narrative, producing an Abrahamic icon of violent action. J Miles, for instance, views the Abraham stories as scenes in which God and man struggle for mastery over life and death.[36] The vehicle for this struggle is the human power of procreation, which God had freely given his creature in Genesis 1-11. God now reclaims control over human life by limiting Sarah's fertility to divine control. Only if Abraham obeys God will life come. Abraham does migrate but then hands Sarah over in Egypt, showing a lack of full trust in divine word. Later God demands submission through the sign of circumcision.[37] Abraham responds suitably, but his conversation with God is marked by underlying hostility, according to this reading.[38] The climax of the struggle between God and Abraham comes in Genesis 22, where God demands full control over the powers of life and death. Abraham is prepared to call his bluff (would he really have killed his own son?). Both protagonists admit defeat here, without an actual death but a heavy shadow hangs over the scene and Isaac emerges as a tragic pawn in the bitter contrast between two males.

---

[34] Magonet, 27-8.
[35] Magonet, 36.
[36] J Miles, *God—A Biography*, Simon and Schuster, New York, 1995.
[37] Miles, 52.
[38] Miles, 55.

P Trible takes the theme of violence which demands sacrifice one step further, in tragic terms.[39] She points to hidden violence in the repeated Hebrew word *laqach* ('seizure' or 'grasping') in Genesis 22 and notes how in the dialogue of Genesis 22 Abraham evades truth, both with his servants and his son.[40] It can be argued that although the final use of 'took' is the replacing of the child with a ram, there is an aura of tragedy here. An anomaly in the text highlights this reading, for Abraham comes down from the mountain alone, gathers his servants and departs.

These tragic themes pave the way for the production of an Abrahamic icon which offers a role model of accepted violence, whose impact is to endorse child sacrifice and a deity who can desire such a thing. If the reader is to follow the lead of Abraham here it will be into behaviour with violent undertones, argues C Delaney.[41] She recounts a story from the contemporary world in which a man has religious hallucinations where he is told to cut his daughter's throat and does so. Is this murder, proper religious faith, insanity …? The issues raised at the court hearing ask the essential questions about moral vision and led Delaney to focus on an Abraham who stands for savage parenting.[42]

> In all three monotheisms the story has been a primary structuring force. It has figured in notions of faith and steadfastness, sacrifice and love, authority and obedience. On the stage of history it figures in conflicts over territory, cities and shrines.[43]

Even secularized society in Europe shares this inheritance, for Delaney, since it comes under the influence of Freudian psychology. Although Freud looked to the murder of the father by the sons, nevertheless there is a residual sense of the father's hold over the son. Delaney suggests that Freud's view that the concept of God was a projection of the feared and admired qualities of the human father still endorses the underlying fascination with parental figures.[44] In this

---

[39] P Trible, 'Genesis 22: the sacrifice of Sarah' in ed. A Bach, *Women in the Hebrew Bible*, Routledge, London, 1999.

[40] Trible, 274-6.

[41] C Delaney, *Abraham on Trial*, Princeton University Press, Princeton, 1998.

[42] Delaney, Part I, chapter 2.

[43] Delaney, 184.

[44] Delaney, 180.

perspective the Abrahamic myth fits Barthes' category of a symbol which oppresses rather than frees.[45]

The key question is whether the *akedah* theme is comic or tragic in mood, whether life or death dominates the episode. Reading the story as comedy would not detract from the seriousness of the issues involved but would move the trajectory of the story from death to life. As Gellmann points out, it is possible to view Abraham's sense of being called to sacrifice as evidence rather for his own exalted sense of religious vocation than for divine intention.[46] This constitutes a cosmic joke for the idea that Abraham can contribute something to divine existence, even by killing his cherished son, is absurd.[47] To view the scene as comic is to move it out of the realm of human design and to reveal, by contrast, the divine realm of unfathomable infinity in which death and life converge.

For Gellmann, Kierkegaard also contributes to this shift of meaning by suggesting that the story involves setting the religious above ethical human behaviour. God does not command evil as such, but calls Abraham to a further plane of meaning in which religion stands higher than human order as the source of ultimate worth. Gellmann wants to read the story as a parable of the family as the highest ethical expression, thus producing a further Abrahamic icon.[48] In this mode, unlike that offered by Janzen's reading, family is not the ultimate expression of truth. Instead the group must be set aside so that the individual can emerge to full growth.[49] In this view the voice of God constitutes the process of an internalization of values, a turning aside from conformity to social systems as the highest form of duty.[50] Abraham is now the symbol of individual religious faith, the call to be free, to stand before God with infinite possibilities. For Gellmann this means viewing Abraham, rather than Isaac, as the type of Christ in the story.[51]

---

[45] Barthes makes the reader aware that social myth serves ideological purposes, endorsing the views of an elite. Thus, the image of the negro officer serves imperialist concerns of French policy. See Barthes, 124, where Barthes notes the way in which myth itself seeks to take the reader over in an oppressive manner.

[46] J Gellmann, *Abraham! Abraham!*, Ashgate Publishing, Aldershot, 2003.

[47] Gellmann, 24.

[48] Gellmann, 33.

[49] Gellmann, 34.

[50] Gellmann, 35-6.

[51] Gellmann, 53.

A further slant on the ambiguities of meaning to be found in Genesis 22 has been offered in the commentary by D Fewell and D Gunn, who read the scene in line with previous scenes.[52] Abraham is called to sacrifice here as a balance to the times when he has escaped from sacrifice earlier on by sacrificing the interests of other members of his family.[53] Whereas Gellmann's version of the Abraham myth envisages it as a sign of growth to human freedom, Gunn and Fewell's approach stresses the contradictions and narrowness of human behaviour. Yet, in the end, their version, too, produces an iconic Abraham who is called via sacrifice of his own interests to a wider human identity. It is God who walks with Abraham along the path of growth here, since God continually restores the life and rights of those whom Abraham has sacrificed.[54] Yet even at the point of sacrifice, forced to admit the reality of loss of his hopes for descendants through Isaac, does Abraham really grow? Or is his falling into line with divine command simply forced upon him unwillingly? God has made a divine point but what has Abraham made of it? Fewell and Gunn, like Trible and Delaney, find hints of violence in the story which leave their traces in the future applications of the Abrahamic myth to historical claims to land and inheritance.[55]

Interpreting the scene of the binding of Isaac, imagining it scripturally, is central to the process of constructing icons of Abraham, man of faith. The scene can be read as part of Abraham's monotheism, without complication. But this may gloss over the darkness of the narrative. If it is read more ambiguously, Abraham emerges as a suitable religious icon, but the reader is made aware of the tensions within the myth between comic and tragic elements. Abraham emerges as a man on a journey towards God. From his first call to his last he is continually moved to go beyond his current understanding of his life and his accepted values. On the way he makes human decisions which change the story, adding in human complications such as a larger family unit. But God makes sense of it all, providing for wives and children, for instance. From death God provides life, though not without a sacrifice.

For the Christian understanding the resolution of these elements is found in the Christian mysteries of the Paschal events, the death and

---

[52] D Fewell and D Gunn, *Gender, Power and Promise* (see above).
[53] Fewell and Gunn, 53.
[54] Fewell and Gunn, 54.
[55] Fewell and Gunn, 55.

rising to life of Jesus Christ. Here too human approaches to the deeper meaning of existence are challenged by the seemingly inexplicable requirement of a death. Violence and death are named for what they are, but their capacity for destruction is negated and what follows is a more powerful life-force. The Abraham/Christ icon thus reads the stories in Genesis 12–22 as a parable connected with the reversal of life and death themes. This religious myth balances the simplicity of single-minded worship of the deity with the complex and often messy human events which are the mirror of that faith and are its practical expression. As Abraham both sets out on a specific journey and yet wanders and strays, so also human beings seek the face of God in scenes of doubt and uncertainty. It is both through clarity and unclarity of vision that the blessing of God is to be found.

GLOCAL SPACES: GLOBALIZATION AND THE POWER OF RELIGION

Saied Reza Ameli

Introduction

The globalization of space as an outcome of simultaneous communication has changed the concept of space in the arenas of culture, politics and economics. Within the contemporary disciplines of sociology, geography and international relations, therefore, the theme of space has become a key concept for any critical discussion.[1] The theme of many sociologists today is the dislocation of place and space.[2] In the era of globalization, space is located in 'deterritorialized' channels of communication: Delanty[3] states that 'space is no longer dominated by the space of the state; other deterritorialized spaces have emerged along with the break-up of national society as the privileged codifier of social space.'

'Glocal' space refers to a concept coined by Roland Robertson, who suggests that 'glocalization' describes more accurately the simultaneously enlarging and telescoping influence of global and local forces.[4] This new concept was introduced by Robertson for two reasons. Firstly, the analysis of the processes of globalization has hitherto neglected local influence to a large degree, and has been constructed on largely trans- or super-local bases.[5] The glocal factor therefore takes into consideration both local and global factors. The inter-relatedness of world society, mediated by the global communications industry, synthesizes the local and global spheres into one space. This not only results in a one-way flow of the domination of indigenous

---

[1] G Delanty, *Citizenship in a Global Age: Society, Culture and Politics*, Open University Press, Buckingham and Philadelphia, 2000.

[2] R Robertson, *Globalization*, Sage, London, 1992; M Waters, *Globalization*, Routledge, London and New York, 1995; M Featherstone, *Undoing Culture: Globalization, Postmodernism and Identity*, Sage, London, 1995; M Castells, 'The Information Age: Economy, Society and Culture', Volume I: *The Rise of the Network Society*, Blackwell, Oxford, 1996.

[3] Delanty, 129.

[4] Robertson, 28.

[5] S R Ameli, *Globalization, Americanization and British Muslim Identity*, ICAS, Press, London, 2002, 24.

cultures by trans-national values, cultures, and civilization, but also creates a flow in the opposite direction. It is thus relative, and not absolute. It is relative due to the fact that globalization can work in so many different ways: as a wake-up call, or a reflective mirror for cultures to see themselves, their history and their national identity more clearly then ever before; as a force that weakens cultures and attitudes by showing their relativity. This process is thus a relatively introspective ground for crystallizing binary opposites, such as self-identity vs the identity of the other; indigenous vs alien culture; national vs trans-national values. The outcome of such oppositions is never easily predictable.

Divinely-revealed religion in general, and Islam and Christianity in particular, as trans-space religions addressed to all people of the world regardless of differences in gender, race, civilization and nationality, have a very important position in this world created by a single space environment. At the same time, the position of religion as a source of individual, social and political power is subject to critical changes. The establishment of the Islamic revolution of Iran;[6] the emergence of Islamic Republics in Sudan and Pakistan; conflict in the Balkans and Chechnya; the expansion of religious fundamentalism, whether Islamic,[7] Christian,[8] or Jewish all over the world; and the increasing characterization of Europe and the United States as distinctively Christian territory, together with the on-going secularization and relativization of religion in the public as well as in the private sphere, all form the background against which the implicit and explicit power and powerlessness of religion in contemporary world society must be viewed. Such circumstances overtly and covertly illustrate many different kinds of globalizations[9] around the world. We can identitfy four discernible trends in the globalization overwheliming world society today: non-ideological and ideological globalizations on the sender side and cognitive and non-cognitive on the receiver side.

[6] N R Keddi, *Roots of Revolution: An Interpretive History of Modern Iran*, Yale University Press, New Haven and London, 1981; A Jabbari, and R Olson, *Iran: Essays on a Revolution in the Making*, Mazda Publishers, Lexington, 1981; D Hiro, *Iran under the Ayatollahs*, Routledge & Kegan Paul, London and New York, 1985; M Kamrava, *Revolution in Iran: The Roots of Turmoil*, Routledge, London and New York, 1990.

[7] J G Mellon, J G, 'Islam and International Politics: Examining Huntingtons Civilizational Clash Thesis', *Totalitarian Movements and Political Religions*, Vol. 2(1), 2001, 73-83.

[8] L L Streyffler, L L and R J McNalhy, 'Fundamentalists and Liberals: Personality Characteristics of Protestant Christians', *Person, Individual Differences*, Vol. 24(4), 1998, 579-580.

[9] P L Berger, and S P Huntington, *Many Globalizations: Cultural Diversity in the Contemporary World*, Oxford University Press, Oxford, 2002.

It is also important to take into account the impact of 11 September as an accelerating factor for the articulation of the ideological response to the domination by the West of the rest, in particular for Muslims and Islam. Such a situation brought about astonishing statements from politicians of the West; for example, Silvio Berlusconi, the Italian prime minister, asserted publicly that Islam was the main enemy of Western civilization.[10] One can observe clearly the rule of religion as a means and source of power in the current dialogue in the political and cultural spheres of global society.

Based on such a theory, this paper will try firstly to give a conceptual definition of globalization, power and the power of religion; and secondly, to look at the relationship between non-ideological and ideological globalization and religion as an agency of power alongside non-cognitive and cognitive globalization power. Throughout this paper, fundamental elements of religion's power will be considered as a dependent variable in the context of globalization, to discover any critical shift in terms of reconstruction, reformation or boomerang responses of religion to new glocal spaces.

Conceptual definitions

There are three inter-related concepts which construct the theoretical dimension of this paper. Firstly we need to review the concept of globalization and establish a conceptual typology which formulates our perspective on the power of religion. Secondly, we need a proper definition of the concept of power, which gives an introduction to theorizing about the concept of the power of religion as a central theme of this paper.

Globalization

To understand the concept of globalization, one needs to know why globalisation is considered to be a new phenomenon. There have always been global networks of power, and imperialist regimes, often accompanied by fierce local resistance from the colonized entities. Globalization is new,

---

[10] A S Ahmed, *Islam Under Siege: Living Dangerously in a Post-Honor World*, Polity Press, Cambridge, 2003.

both in terms of the speed at which it occurs, and of the involvement of communication technology, which appears to shrink geographical distance and time.[11] Communication occurs beyond time and space. The message arrives at the destination a thousand times more quickly than if the sender of the message delivered it him or herself.

Instantaneous communication through a variety of media has changed our experiences of time and space. They have become distantiated—where we experience distant events unfolding instantaneously on the screen in our homes—or 'compressed'—where spatial and temporal differences are radically undermined.[12] Gillespie[13] has suggested that this speeding up, or growing intensity, of time-space compression, has created significant effects on social, economic and cultural processes. Society has been subjected to a constantly accelerating pace of change.

According to Falk,[14] the fundamental aspect of globalization is the pervasive compression of time and space. This affects the way we think, feel and act, introducing speed and proximity as defining and inherent characteristics of our daily human experience. For instance, the visual presentation of world news, even including wars, in real time is abolishing our sense of distance, compacting space while intermingling virtuality with reality.

Morley and Robins[15] suggest that the new information and communication technologies have played a powerful role in the emergence of new spatial structures, relations, and orientations. Corporate communications networks have also produced a global space of electronic information flows. The new media conglomerates have created a global image space. What is particularly significant is the transformed relationship between boundary and space that this entails. Things are no longer defined

---

[11] A Cvetkouich and D Kellner, 'Introduction: Thinking Global and Local', in eds. A Cvetkovich and D Kellner, *Articulating the Global and the Local: Globalization and Cultural Studies*, Westview Press, London, 1997.

[12] M Gillespie, *Television, Ethnicity and Cultural Change*, Routledge, London and New York, 1995, 3.

[13] Gillespie, *op. cit.*.

[14] R Falk, 'The Monotheistic Religions in the Era of Globalization', in *Global Dialogue*, No. 1, 1999, 139.

[15] D Morley and K Robins, *Spaces of Identity: Global Media, Electronic Landscapes and Cultural Boundaries*, Routledge London and New York, 1995, 75.

and distinguished in the ways that they once were: by their boundaries, borders or frontiers.

The cultural and cognitive consequences of this new relationship between time and space in the age of instantaneous communication are of critical concern for the present research. The concept of 'time' and 'space', being 'far' or 'near', 'in here' or 'out there', 'alien' and 'compatriot', the meaning of 'citizenship' and 'diaspora' and finally the concept of 'society' and 'community' have been partially changed. This has changed our social understanding of our sense of belonging and therefore our identity. For instance, the concept of citizenship does not necessarily mean the sense of belonging to the country of which one is a citizen. People may live and be citizens in a particular country and yet not have any patriotic feeling towards it. That is why the concept of diaspora, which originated with the Jewish displacement, has extended today to any type of homelessness 'at home'. The concept of nostalgia 'at home' reflects the same meaning.

In this paper four types of globalization should be distinct, which will help us to elaborate its implementation in relation to the power of religion within the individual, society, and the institutional, political and civil arenas.

Non-ideological globalization: Non-ideological globalization has arisen from normal globalization, which historically goes back to the exchange of civilization, culture, knowledge, information, money and goods in the past. Non-ideological globalization defines globalization as a natural trend which occurs in different processes of interconnection between the peoples of the world. The only difference between the typical globalization of today and that of the past is the advance of communications technology, which has demolished the obstacle of place and time. People can access each other immediately without any time-lag. If one compares the world of the ideological management by a superpower with the world in a natural process without any ideological imposition on the peoples of the world, then the typical globalization will be more transparent and understandable.

Ideological (dominated) globalization: Ideological globalization can be seen as a programme for changing the world according to world superpower interests. Such an understanding of the world will create two simultaneous orientations: exclusive orientation which arises from a mono-centric perception of the world as a whole; and inclusive orientation, which is more based upon the mutual support between members of the community. This type of orientation has arisen from the motivation for more expansion and domination.

Non-cognitive (light) globalization: While non-cognitive globalization is very light and sprawling, it is indeed overtly very superficial in nature. One could argue that light globalization can be a result of the natural process of compressing the world into a single world society, and it does indeed portray the apparent compacting of ideological globalization in everyday life in the form of consumerism. Non-cognitive globalization induces non-cognitive changes, which is a result of Western consumerism turning every day life, in all its different forms of fashion, entertainment, and lifestyle, into a commodity modelled on Western standards.

Cognitive (powerful) globalization: Cognitive globalization introduces an inward and deeper aspect and a more powerful effect of globalization. This powerful globalization is not very extensive but it is covertly very influential, significant and directive. It is more powerful than non-cognitive globalisation, as its effects remain more permanently on those who are penetrated by it.

Power

Power, in a very narrow perspective is equivalent to politics, but in a wider view it includes many other dimensions. The Marxist theory of domination articulates a more economic aspect of power, but according to Mann[16] and Giddens,[17] it is not possible to understand the nature of power or the roots of change in society unless we move away from the idea that economic power and economic class are the basis of power. This is why Poggi[18] emphasized four sources of social power: political, ideological/normative, economic and military power. He ignored, however, the power of culture. One can argue that power as a concept is fundamental to the analysis of both political affairs, and different forms of the cultural arena.

---

[16] M Mann, *The Sources of Social Power*, Vol. 1, Cambridge University Press, Cambridge, 1986.

[17] A Giddens, *Sociology*, 4th edition, Polity Press, Cambridge, 2001.

[18] G Poggi, *Forms of Power*, Polity Press, Cambridge, 2001, 24.

Bertrand Russell[19] suggests that power is to culture what energy is to physics. But it is important to realize that 'neither power nor energy is an object of the sensate world; both are hypothetical constructs. One does not see or touch energy as such, but one may observe its manifestations in heat, light, motion, growth, and decay. Thus we say that energy has been expended when in fact what we see is a bird taking flight or a rock falling. So with power: it is a construction of the mind introduced because it is useful in describing and explaining important empirical phenomena. One cannot actually reach out and touch power but one observes its manifestations in every human relationship and social arrangement.

This is why the concept of power is so elusive and it has been defined in so many different ways. As Thomas Hobbes (1588-1679) suggested: 'the power of a man, to take it universally, is his present means, to obtain some future apparent good'. Bertrand Russell[20] saw power 'as the production of intended effects'. These definitions, while containing some value, are not so relevant for our purposes. Hobbes and Russell define power more in terms of political resources, which is a sort of institutional definition and thus delimitation of power. Our concern, on the other hand, is with power in a more non-restrictive sense, such as it operates within the arena of culture.

Power of religion

The power of religion is a multi-layered concept which can generally be divided into the political, economic and cultural arenas. One can conceptualize the power of religion in relation to the entity of religion itself, to the individual and to society as six distinguishable layers. These include the message of religion, the individual as a carrier of religion, the public sphere as a place of social demonstration of religion, the political space as a site of power, the civil law in terms of the legitimatized implementation of religion, and the institutional elements of religion which explain its organizational and networking aspects.

Generally speaking, culture was used as an attachment of religion, and religion is indeed an attachment to culture. Religion at a practical

---

[19] Bertrand Russell, *Power: a new social analysis*, Norton, New York, 1962.
[20] Russell, *op. cit.*, 35.

level cannot be understood with cultural considerations, and culture cannot be examined at a deeper level unless religion is studied in its own context. Based on such an assumption, one could argue that the power of religion would be relatively allied to the power of culture, and vice versa. Today the cultural background in general, and particularly with regard to religion's power, seems more extensive and demonstrative then ever before. This is because firstly during the era of modernization, many circumstances intervened to segregate religion from the political and economic spheres, and secondly, in the era of globalization it seems that individuals have much more opportunity to shape their own everyday life than was once the case,[21] and this greatly expands the cultural grounds from which an individual can choose. Thirdly, while the colonization of culture has become predominantly professional, cultural awareness has made culture more non-normative then ever before. All these developments have made cultural power worthy of considerable academic attention. Many sociologists now emphasize the centrality of culture compared to politics and economics.[22]

There are different approaches to the power of culture.[23] Classical sociologists like Weber[24] show how the struggle for power has shaped ideas and values, arguing that the interests of powerful groups have exercised a lasting influence on the shape of a culture. Contemporary theorists like Foucault,[25] on the other hand, see culture as itself a form of power. He argues that new kinds of knowledge and associated practices in effect construct new sites where power can be deployed. New disciplines, such as psycho-analysis, construct new loci such as the unconscious; new

---

[21] Giddens, *op. cit.*, 61.

[22] Robertson, *op. cit.*, 1992; Featherstone, *op. cit.*

[23] See J Lears, 'Power, culture, and Memory', *The Journal of American History*, Volume 75, Issue 1, June 1988, 137-140; A Kane, 'Cultural Analysis in Historical Sociology: The Analytic and Concrete Forms of the Autonomy of Culture', *Sociological Theory*, Volume 9, Issue 1, Spring 1991, 53-69; M R Somers, 'What's Political or Cultural about Political Culture and Public Sphere? Towards an Historical Sociology of Concept Formation', *Sociological Theory*, Volume 13, Issue 2, July 1995, 113-144 and 'Narrating and Naturalizing Civil Society and Citizenship Theory: The Place of Political Culture and Public Sphere', *Sociological Theory*, Volume 13, Issue 3, November 1995, 229-274; V Bader, 'The Cultural Conditions of Transnational Citizenship: On the Interpenetration of Political and Ethnic Cultures', *Political Theory*, Volume 25, Issue 6, Dec. 1997, 771-813.

[24] M Weber, *Economy and Society: An Outline of Interpretive Sociology*, University of California Press, Berkeley, 1968.

[25] M Foucault, *Power/Knowledge: Selected Interviews and Other Writings*, 1972-1977, ed. C Gordon, Pantheon, New York, 1980.

subjectivities where power can be exercised (and also where resistance can emerge). Foucault[26] eliminates the question of who has power, leaving aside the role of interested agents, to emphasize instead that each cultural formation, each technique of power, has a history of its own, and that different actors adopt these techniques for different purposes. Since cultural practices, categories, and rules are enactments of power, Foucault does not think of culture as being pursued by the powerful to maintain their power; rather, he thinks of power itself as embodied in the practices which deploy knowledge, as well as constituting the ground upon which human beings operate as the subject of that knowledge.

Pargament[27] reviewed empirical studies assessing the independent predictive power of religion. According to his study, religion is a unique source of motivation and values, a unique form of coping, and a unique source of distress. He also attempted to make a connection between religion and health and well-being, not to explain away religion, but to gain a more complete understanding of religion and human nature generally. For him, religion represents not only a resource for psychological well-being and physical health, but a distinctive human dimension that carries meaning and power in and of itself.

One theorist whose work is relevant to our concern here is Pierre Bourdieu. Bourdieu[28] shows how deeply inequalities between the more and less privileged penetrate persons, constituting the fundamental capacities for judgement, aesthetic response, social ease, or political confidence with which they act in the world. Actors use culture in creative ways to forward their own interests in a system of unequal power, but the effect of that struggle is to reproduce the basic structure of the system.[29]

Based on the cultural perspective of religion, the relationship between power and religion can be discussed. The interaction between religion and power has been studied in the different disciplines of

[26] M Foucault, *Discipline and Punish*, Vintage, New York, 1997.
[27] K I Pargament, 'Is Religion Nothing But ...? Explaining Religion Versus Explaining Religion Away', *Psychological Inquiry*, Vol. 13 (3), 2002, 239-244.
[28] P Bourdieu, 'The End of a World', in P Bourdieu *et al.*, *The Weight of the World: Social Suffering in Contemporary Society*, trans. Priscilla Parkhurst Ferguson *et al.*, Polity Press, Cambridge, 1999, 317-320.
[29] A Swidler, 'Cultural Power and social Movements', in ed. L Spillman, *Cultural Sociology*, Blackwell, Oxford, 2002, 314.

sociology, politics, anthropology and theology.[30] Ali (2003)[31] examines religion as power in terms of knowledge controlling education. Bugra and Lieu[32] look at religion more in terms of a political force. Galloway[33] explains the relationship between religion, power and wealth in the medieval town. Martin and Barnes[34] explore the relationship between religious traditions and empire as initial constructs, analytical descriptions, and, in some cases, implications for praxis. They addressed methodological issues such as typologies, category crossing, and the fluidity of types, as well as the decentring of older foci. They also examined themes such as state and religious power, conflict, and pluralism, responses to pluralism and multiple sites of authority; and religious and political agency. Horsley[35] in his recent work has also briefly examined ancient and modern examples of three different patterns of relations between empire and religion: (a) the imperial elite's construction of the religions of the subject people; (b) the subjected peoples' revival of their own traditional ways of life in resistance to imperial rule; and (c) the development of the religious practices that constitute the imperial power relations. These cases raise key issues for religious and biblical studies, such as the modern Western reduction of religion to individual belief, the relationship between the religious and the secular domains, and, particularly, the relationship between religion and power.

Duja[36] has also worked on the meaning of religious affiliations and their use in the re-definition of social identities, leading to the transformation of Albanian identity and ethnicity, and re-establishing traditions of political, social and national history.

---

[30] B H Raven, 'Kurt Lewin Address: Influence, Power, Religion, and the Mechanisms of Social Control', *Journal of Social Issues,* Vol. 55(1), 1999, 161-186.

[31] K Ali, 'Controlling Knowledge: Religion, Power and Schooling in a West African Muslim Society', *The Muslim World,* Vol. 93(2), 2003, 348-349.

[32] A Bugra, 'Labour, Capital, and Religion: Harmony and Conflict among the Constituency of Political Islam in Turkey', *Middle Eastern Studies,* Vol. 38(2), 2002, 187-204; J Lieu, 'Religion and Power: Pagans, Jews and Christians in the Greek East', *Journal of Theological Studies,* Vol. 53(1), 2002, 309-311.

[33] J Galloway, 'Religion, Power and Wealth: Reappraisals of the Medieval Town', *Journal of Urban History,* Vol. 28(6), 2002, 793-801.

[34] J M Martin, L L Barnes, 'Introduction: Religion and Empire', *Journal of the American Academy of Religion,* Vol. 71 (1), 2003, 3-12.

[35] R A Horsley, 'Religion and Other Products of Empire', *Journal of the American Academy of Religion,* Vol. 71(1), 2003, 13-44.

[36] A Duja, 'The Politics of Religion in the Reconstruction of Identities: The Albanian Situation', *Critique of Anthropology,* Vol. 20(4), 2000, 421-438.

Ali, Camp and Gibbs[37] discussed power and authority in terms of the Ten Commandments (TCs). The paper reviews the TCs in Christianity, Judaism, and Islam to discover the treatment and basis of power and authority in each religion. It was suggested that in today's business environment, people tend to be selective by identifying only with those elements of the TCs which fit their interests and that the TCs should be viewed as general moral guidelines in everyday life and even in the political sphere.

Clear and his colleagues[38] emphasise that in the promotion of the expansion of religious programmes in prisons lies the claim that faith in a higher power prevents relapse into criminal activity better than secular strategies. The continued focus on religion's use in preventing future criminal conduct diminishes religion's immediate value to the inmate during the term of incarceration. With this latter function in mind, Clear *et al.*[39] also reflected findings from qualitative research conducted in several prisons nationwide. Designed to reveal the meaning of religion to inmates, the study calls attention to the role of religion in preventing devaluation and fostering survival.

Religion, culture, race and even nationality become interlinked features of social life. Religion has sometimes become a powerful force for the unification of one nation within a state against the majority of society, such as Elijah Muhammd's Nation of Islam (NOI), which crystallizes the distinctions between the black and white populations in society. Curtis[40] shows how the ritual 'islamization' of the black population by the NOI was a central feature of the life of the movement from the 1950s through to the 1970s. Adopting some theoretical tools from Catherine Bell's *Ritual Theory, Ritual Practice*, Curtis also explores the relationship between ritual and power within the organization itself and in its interactions with the larger social worlds of which it was a

---

[37] A J Ali, R C Camp, M Gibbs, 'The Ten Commandments Perspective on Power and Authority in Organizations', *Journal of Business Ethics,* Vol. 26(4), 2000, 351-361.

[38] T R Clear, P L Hardyman, B Stout, K Lucken, H R Dammer, 'The Value of Religion in Prison: An Inmate Perspective', *Journal of Contemporary Criminal Justice,* Vol. 16(1), 2000, 53-74.

[39] *Ibid.*, 61.

[40] E E Curtis IV, 'Islamizing the Black Body: Ritual and Power in Elijah Muhammad's Nation of Islam', *Religion & American Culture,* Vol. 12 (2), 2002, 167-196.

part. For Curtis,[41] in creating and sustaining the NOI rituals, Elijah Muhammad and his followers depicted the black population as a battleground for the souls of black folk, a site of contest where members of the NOI would save themselves from white violation, poison, and in the case of men, emasculation.

In a more theoretical and practical step, it is possible to identify the major elements of the power of religion. The power of religion is a multi-layered phenomenon which can be transparent in six different arenas:

1. *The power of the religious message:* not all religions have the same power and influence in society and over individuals. In the majority of cases, the power of the religion is related to the message of the religion. Some religions have multi-dimensional aspects, which include individual, social and political life, while others may emphasize only a particular aspect of life, the spiritual, or individual behaviour. This is why, among the thousands of religions in the world, only a few, such as Christianity and Islam, have become globally popular across different societies.

2. *The individual power of religion:* the individual power of religion is examined in an individual believer's practice and values. To understand the strength of the religion's influence among individuals we need to find out how an individual practises, believes in religion and avoids religion's permissiveness in the personal domain.

3. *The public power of religion:* religion also can be discussed as a source of power which affects the masses and the public sphere. This will happen when religion becomes a popular value, belief and practice among people.[42]

4. *The political power of religion:* the political power of religion is illustrated through the influence its discipline has on the political decisions and policy–making of a country, both internally and internationally. It can also be demonstrated by the employment of ministers of religion in political positions. The political power of religion is also formed in the constitutional aspect of politics.

5. *The civil power of religion:* civil religion is associated with non-supernatural religious objects whose existence promotes solidarity for

---

[41] *Ibid.*, 172.

[42] M J Mejido, 'The Illusion of Neutrality: Reflections on the Term "Popular Religion"', *Social Compass*, Vol. 49(2), 2002, 295-311.

the group and a sense of belonging for the individual.[43] This comes through the combination of the religious tendency with national orientations in the field of culture and economics, and particularly in the political arena. According to Andrew Shanks,[44] civil religion is related to civil theology which explains the interplay between politics and religion. The civil power of religion, according to the secular perspective, should not be involved with normative politics in such a way that either politics becomes religious or that religion becomes politicized.

6. *The institutional power of religion:* the institutional power of religion here means the power of religion to captivate the masses. Power here is a form of organizational activity to support the community of believers and reject non-believers. The institutional power of religion can be allied to religious organization in social demonstrations of religion through collective religious ceremonies, pilgrimages and prayers.

Non-ideological globalization and the power of religion

Globalization as a natural process of the interconnection of world society has a great potential to reduce or increase the influences of religion in the public and political as well as the individual domain. It is also full of global energy to reformulate organizational networking in terms of movement and organization. From this perspective, globalization is a global communications industry which creates an extensive socio-cultural and religious basis for social interaction based on common values, ideas and belief in world society. Such circumstances detach culture and religion from indigenous spaces, and merge the global and the local, hence glocal space. A glocal space's religion is not considered necessarily part of a national resource, but as belonging to transnational community of believers.

If we imagine globalization without a dominant ideology/ideologies, then world religion would be disseminated among individuals cognitively and non-cognitively according to individual choices and interests. As long as the world's religion, in terms of influence and social position, can be divided into central religion and peripheral religion, it is to be expected that the central religion of the world will both expand

---

[43] T Bilton, P Jones, T Lawson, D Skinner, M Stanworth, A Webster, *Introductory Sociology*, 4th ed, Palgrave, New York, 2002, 428.

[44] Andrew Shanks, *Civil Society, Civil Religion*, Blackwell, Oxford, 1995.

and be more internally connected internally then ever before. The central and peripheral nature of the world's religion would be re-constructed according to the global nature of sacred messages and the universality of religious values.

It is important to note that, while trans-religion or universal religion, universalism is emerging in a world society based on the common values of all religions, such as the respect for justice and the rejection of injustice in a non-dogmatic form, for example embodied in the supportive campaign of the Christian and Muslim worlds for the Palestinians, it seems that the local orientation of religious and national cultures will again reproduce in response to the impact of globalization. While this reproduction might be ended by the domination of one culture over another, it can also relatively empower the home religion and culture.

It is also central to this issue to consider not one, but many globalizations taking place around the world. This diversity of globalization makes relatively national culture multi-layered. Culture will become multi-layered, and therefore in some aspects will induce a very religious/nationalistic orientation. To some extent this might establish two different affiliations, one religious, which is universal in nature, detached from any sort of national particularity; and the second highly nationalistic, promoting the particularity of religion within the national context. Accordingly, one might also observe two different types of citizenship in the era of globalization: official citizenship and cultural citizenship. Official citizenship recognizes the person as a member of a particular nation-state; he/she can benefit accordingly and is responsible and accountable to the state and *vice versa*. Cultural citizenship explains rather an individual cultural and religious interest, which also creates a new type of social responsibility. The cultural orientation within a glocal cultural environment is also the locus of the emergence of a new nostalgia. Nostalgia, which Stuart Hall[45] described as 'we are all immigrant today', in such a glocal space, leads to feelings of isolation and alienation, not only in alien space but also within the home culture; this trend seems inevitable in our future life.

Globalization, as a non-ideological process which should be seen more as a process which relies upon the improved advancement of the communications industry, will induce the expansion of the institutional

---

[45] S Hall, 'The Local and the Global: Globalization and Ethnicity', in ed. A D King, Culture, *Globalization and the World System: Contemporary Conditions for the Representation of Identity*, SUNY Press, Binghamton, 1991, 20-39.

power of religions, in particular central religion backed by a strong institutional base with a global reach. The diasporic follower of such a religion will be more in contact with central institutions around the world. Such demands do not follow the same models in differing cultures and societies. One can argue that global particularization will deepen the demand for communication between followers of the same religion around the world to create a strong global power; protecting the society of believers from other types of globalization. The follower of religion, especially in a country where national citizenship is weak, has more to gain from being in contact with trans-national religious organization.

Ideological globalization and power of religion

Ideology can be defined as 'shared ideas or beliefs which serve to justify the interests of dominant groups'. The concept of ideology, therefore, is closely connected with that of power and domination, since ideological systems serve to legitimize the different powers held by groups.[46] Globalization and ideology are discussed from different perspectives.[47] The relationship between ideological globalization and the power of religion is also a critical discussion which is more related to the political and economic aspects of religion, and globalization which is also a fundamental part of the economic and cultural domain of globalization. Here we need to discuss first the relationship between power and religion in relation to politics and economics, and secondly we should find out how globalization as a domination ideology of exclusion and inclusion can effect or create defensive, assimilative or reproductive reactions on the receiver sides of globalization.

The power of religion as a source for political movement has been emphasised by many studies.[48] This is why studies on the contemporary

---

[46] Giddens, *op. cit.*, 691.

[47] R S Spich, 'Globalization folklore problems of myth and ideology in the discourse on globalization', *Journal of Organizational Change Management*, Vol. 8(4), 1995, 6–29; V Birchfield, 'Contesting the hegemony of market ideology: Gramsci's "good sense" and Polanyi's "double movement"', *Review of International Political Economy*, Vol. 6(1), 1999, 27–54; B Gao, 'Globalization and Ideology: The Competing Images of the Contemporary Japanese Economic System in the 1990s', *International Sociology*, Vol. 15(3), 2000, 435–453; M Rupert, *Ideologies of Globalization: Contending visions of a New World Order*, Routledge, New York & London, 2000.

[48] Bugra, *op. cit.*, Lieu, *op. cit.*, Martin, *op. cit.*

relevance of religion in general, and Islam in particular, often emphasize an embodiment of the power of religion to unify aspirations and behaviour across social classes. This emphasis sometimes leads to the minimization of the role of different life experiences that reflect class and social positions in determining the nature of social projects designed around religious themes.[49] Brett also shows how different denominations such as Protestantism and Catholicism make different contributions in political activity. Brett[50] described the Australian party system's historic link between religious identification and party support in terms of overlapping gaps, with the coincidence of Catholicism and working-class socio-economic status given greatest agency. The evidence, however, is questionable for working-class predominance amongst Catholics at the time of fusion. For Brett, non-labour's easy slippage between the vices of Labor and those of the Catholic Church explains why Catholics preferred Labor more convincingly than does the accepted class-based justification.

Haddorff[51] attempted to formalize religion's power in relation to the market by proposing three basic paradigms, and then applying them to contemporary Christian social thought (or social ethics). The first conflicting model is related to the Max Weber and Karl Marx thesis, that views religion and the market in opposition, which results in greater secularization. The second paradigm, influenced by Emile Durkheim, proposes a 'functionalist' model of society, in which the market itself becomes sacred. The third, following Karl Polanyi, claims that the two are more dialectical, in that both are affected by the power of the other; they remain in an ambiguous relationship. Haddorff argues that the third model is the most coherent description of this complex relationship as well as the one most consistent with the convictions of Christian social thought.

Banerjee and Linstead[52] critically examined different discourses of globalization and explored how concepts of globalization have been ideologically represented in organizational theory. They argue that, despite

---

[49] Bugra, *op. cit.*

[50] J Brett, 'Class, Religion and the Foundation of the Australian Party System: A Revisionist Interpretation', *Australian Journal of Political Science*, Vol. 37(1), 2002, 40.

[51] Haddorff, 'Religion and the Market: Opposition, Absorption, or Ambiguity?', *Review of Social Economy*, Vol. 58(4), 2000, 483-504.

[52] S B Banerjee, S A Linstead, 'Globalization, Multiculturalism and Other Fictions: Colonialism for the New Millennium?', *Organization*, Vol. 8(4), 2001, 683-722.

its celebratory rhetoric of 'one world, many peoples', notions of globalization are inextricably linked with the continued development of First World economies, creating new forms of colonial control in the so-called 'post-colonial' era. Therefore, globalization increasingly becomes the new global colonialism, based on the historical structure of capitalism and is a process that executes the objectives of colonialism with greater efficiency and rationalism.

Globalization as a global ideology takes place in the form of American exclusivism and inclusivism. This dominated orientation is an attempt to isolate the power of religion in an individual, public, political, civil and institutional domain. Ideological domination even looks at the message of religion from a particular angle. From this perspective, religion is not rejected or accepted as a whole, but its message is articulated or demonized according to the ideologies' interests. From the perspective of the dominant ideology, religion with no power is not a problem, but it is indeed serious problem, when it comes as source of power in the public, political and institutional area, and it is in serious conflict with the possession of power in a global area.

Exclusivism implemented in the form of hard power and soft power

While secular and liberal religion is absorbed by the liberal democratic system, totalist religion, which looks for the domination of religion in all aspects of life including politics, economic and everyday life, will be rejected systematically and ideologically. The stronger religion becomes in terms of political participation, the more it is rejected by the liberal democratic system. This process is in general an outcome of the secular orientation in world politics and a particular orientation of American power in relation to Islam. Such an orientation causes the isolation of religion in the political, civil and public spheres as well as a great loss of religious self-confidence among individuals.

Theoretically, exclusivism is taking place as a hard power in a militant system with extensive demonization of the enemy, which causes the threat of war and mass destruction of world society. It is also implemented in the form of soft power, in which people do not feel they are involved in war, but it is indeed another way of the mass cultural and political destruction of a society.

Although three types of exclusion have been so far identified — economic, political and social exclusion[53]—nonetheless the majority of 'exclusion studies' are economics oriented.[54] Economic exclusion explains inequality in terms of production and consumption, such as people lacking a permanent place of residence or lacking enough food to survive. Political exclusion is regarded as a prohibition of political participation, the latter being a foundation stone of the liberal democratic doctrine. Social exclusion is considered as formed by the ways in which individuals may become cut off from full involvement in the wider society, which can be experienced in the realm of social and community life such as facilities like parks, sports fields, cultural centres and theatre halls. These three types of exclusion mainly indicate tangible and physical aspects of exclusion in the local sphere, but what remains mysterious here is the intangible dimension of exclusion which might be distinguished in three different arenas in the local as well as global domains which potentially refer to religious exclusion as well:

1. *Recognitional Exclusion*: Many citizens of world society feel isolated and prohibited from being considered as ordinary members of the local and world society. This is due to the fact that either the local state does not recognize all members of the society as citizens—citizenship in such a society is so stratified that only high class members are regarded as citizens and the rest of the society is left unrecognized; or a lack of recognition refers to the classification of the world into first, second and third world countries; or classification related to the religious orientation of the world society, as a result of which people are excluded from social, political and even cultural position because of their faith. Consequently those who are not members of the so-called first world are left unrecognized, feeling thereby deprived and marginalized. The first explains the local sense of exclusion through the lack of social intangible recognition, the second clarifies the position of individuals within world society in terms of exclusion and inclusion, and the third describes the current secular orientation of the liberal political system.

---

[53] Giddens, *op. cit.*

[54] I G Begg and J Berghman, 'Introduction: EU Social (Exclusion) Policy Revisited?', *Journal of European Social Policy*, vol. 12(3), 2002, 179-94; C Mayes, 'The Teacher as Archetype of Spirit', *Journal of Curriculum Studies*, vol. 34(6), 2002, 699-718.

One way of recognitional exclusion is the exclusion of a great religion. After 11 September many tendencies towards hatred of Islam appeared among politicians and religious ministers. Akbar Ahmad[55] noted that:

> Certain Christian groups launched an offensive to 'eliminate Islam' altogether (see 'False Prophets: Inside the Evangelical Christian Movement That Aims to Eliminate Islam' by Barry Yeoman in *Mother Jones*, June 2002). Richard Lowry, the editor of *National Review*, created a storm of controversy when he came up with a 'final' solution to the Muslim problem: 'Nuke Mecca' and force the remaining Muslims to accept Christianity (see National Review Online, 'The Corner', March 7, 2002).

Fox Television commentator Bill O'Reilly equated the holy book of the Muslims, the Qu'ran, to Hitler's *Mein Kampf*— so much for the channel's self-description as offering 'fair and balanced' coverage. The Reverend Jerry Vines, former leader of the Southern Baptist Convention, the largest Protestant denomination in the United States, denounced the Prophet of Islam as a 'demon-possessed paedophile'. To the Reverend Jerry Falwell, the Prophet was a 'terrorist'. The Reverend Franklin Graham, who offered the invocation at Bush's inauguration, called Islam 'a very wicked and evil religion'. Islam's God was not the God of Christianity, declared Graham, the son of Billy Graham. Pat Robertson said much the same thing.[56]

These types of reaction are more related to the power of Islam as a religion. The actual message and messenger of Islam is in serious question.

2. *The need to share an equal standard of living*: this is a need to look for justice and equality in the standard of living; scarcity is not necessarily only real or absolute poverty, but it is the feeling of being poor in relation to others or to one's own standards. Scarcity in rich societies is the result of the growth of expectations about assets, wealth and success, and hence it is possible to date this form of scarcity to the rise of mass consumerism

---

[55] Akbar Ahmad, *op. cit.*, 37.
[56] *Ibid.*, 36.

(Turner, 1999: 268) alongside the hegemonic presentation of goods. Globalization as a process of global transnationalization expands all the boundaries of the economic, cultural and political arena, and has brought the entire world into a 'single space'.[57] Such integration has created a serious gap between poor and rich, westerner and easterner, which will result in very painful nostalgia for society and individuals while they live at home. Having said that, religion, in particular divine religions such as Islam and Christianity, play an important role in promoting the idea of 'justice for all' and the necessity of creating convenient ground for access to justice in a society. Such a principle will cause rejection and exclusion in the majority of political systems, in particular in the capitalist system of thought.

3. *Communicational exclusion and the needs of co-existence through local and global interactions:* when ways of communication are flowing smoothly, but are predominated by a one-way flow of information, culture and civilization, one feels even more humiliated and mortified. Co-existence requires co-operation, co-ordination and mutual respect. Co-existence requires respect for the neighbours at the same level of respect for house members. Communicational exclusion can also related to the level of involvement of an individual with religious values. In a secular society dominated by secular system, one can not feel happy unless one has oneself adopted the actual secular norm of the society; someone with considerable religious involvement will, therefore, be confronted with many communicational rejections in the society. This refers to the dialectical interaction between normal and abnormal behaviour supported and encouraged by the liberal political system, which induces the rejection and exclusion of the religious norm, in particular political, social and economic religious norms.

Inclusivism implemented through soft power

To understand the mono-centric imposition of a one-way flow of culture, civilization, religion, value and information, one needs to understand 'Dominated symbolic cultural dialogue' in which, while individuals

---

[57] Robertson, 1992, *op. cit.*

subjectively feel they are involved in a 'dialogue circle', they are dominated objectively by a mono-centric discourse which violently misleads them, and transfers the determinative elements of cultural autonomy from the home culture to the dominant culture.

When power and political systems target culture, one can observe the place and value of 'soft power' for penetrating the public sphere locally and globally. A vastly increased sense of individual awareness in global terms first changed the nature of social stratification, and secondly created new political forces among lay society— the source of power in international affairs as well political security. Therefore, culture plays a significant role and is making a comeback in international relations practice and theory. For a long time, culture was discredited as a soft, immeasurable, and (perhaps therefore) unscientific ingredient in the study of global politics. In particular, the discipline of strategic studies, which dealt with military relations between states, was dominated by realist thinking, in which cultural aspects hardly played a role. But today, students of security studies are more interested in the role of norms, values, and culture, having agreed among themselves that the concept of security should be contested and made 'insecure'.[58]

Constructivist scholars now argue that 'ideas and discourse matter' and that norms, values, and identity heavily influence political life. Constructivism implies that normative factors shape the behaviour of states and that such factors may serve as road maps or focal points for them, as well as for other international actors. By linking 'civilization' to 'conflict', Huntington made it clear that major facets of international politics cannot be fully understood without an analysis of the impact of norms and values. He argued that conflict is most likely, if not inevitable, in regions where the tectonic plates of 'we' and 'them' overlap and clash.

American cultural inclusion here takes place through the modernization of the cultural values of world society, which is equally closely linked to the exclusion orientation policy. Although this process is very complicated and requires much clarification, it is important to realize that it is intrinsically problematic to make the attempt to embrace Western

---

[58] B McSweeney, *Security, Identity and Interests: A Sociology of International Relations*, Cambridge University Press, Cambridge, 1999; eds. M A Smith and P Kolloc, *Communities in Cyberspace*, Routledge, London and New York, 1999; M Ronnei, *Cultural Politics in Latin America*, Macmillan, Basingstoke, 2000.

technology without Western values. Sociology has suggested that you cannot have modernization, technology, urbanization and bureaucratization without the cultural baggage that goes with it, and this baggage is essentially a post-Enlightenment system of thought. One can suggest that modernization does not have the same meaning for all nations and cultures. Different historical backgrounds can affect the perceptions and implications of modern technology in the everyday life of individuals and societies. For example, while the process of modernization in Turkey has resulted in deep and extensive secularization, the same cannot be said of Saudi Arabia where outwardly it is not inherently secular but secular tendencies may manifest themselves within the inner structure of society.[59]

Cognitive globalization and the power of religion

Cognitive globalization explains the deeper influence of a transnational ideological world view upon an individual, public sphere, political and civil dimension of religion as well as the institutional implementation of religion.

Although today's world is a world of many new religions and cults, according to Dawson[60] one must learn to accept that most new religious movements differ very little in their nature and operation, and in their moral and social failings, from more conventional or mainstream religions (e.g., the Catholic Church or Methodists). Yet the controversy surrounding the cognitive of religion is not only related to reformation inside the religious body, but also to two structural changes, which mainly result from the cognitive modernization that has been accelerated by globalization as means of the distribution and development of Western enlightenment values. These two are secularism and relativism. Secularism and relativism can cognitively and non-cognitively change the direction of an individual, the popularity of religious values, and civil and political orientation as well as the institutional aspect of religion's power.

---

[59] B S Turner, *Orientalism, Postmodernism and Globalism*, Routledge, London and New York, 1994.

[60] L L Dawson, *Cults and New Religious Movements*, Blackwell, Oxford, 2002.

Secularism

Secularization is one of the consequences of the process of modernization in the West and essentially entails the separation of Church and state and, by extension, the exclusion of religion from social and political institutions and its confinement to the private domain. Protestant movements are regarded as the epistemological driving force behind the evacuation of social consciousness from religion. Robinson[61] refers to and creatively applies, the important analytical distinction drawn by Berger between structural and subjective secularization. Structural secularization is a process that evacuates religion from society's institutions. This means that religion is driven out of the frameworks of law, of knowledge, and of political power. Subjective secularization is a cognitive evacuation of religion from the consciousness of man, which disentangles the religious vision from the consciousness of human beings. However, Giddens[62] has suggested that secularization does not seem to result in the complete disappearance of religious thought and activity. While this is no doubt true—religious consciousness has not disappeared, but simply taken on different forms—it cannot be denied that, as regards public 'space' within society, religion has been effectively excluded. Most of the situations of modern social life are manifestly incompatible with religion as a pervasive influence upon day to day life.[63]

Shepard[64] believes that the Muslim world has witnessed a relatively moderate secularism, which seeks to separate religion from politics and other areas of public life. The most extreme case of secularism in the Muslim world is Turkey, which in 1928 removed from its constitution the clause that made Islam the state religion. At present the relevant article reads: 'The Republic of Turkey is a democratic, secular and social state governed by the rule of law ... loyal to the nationalism of Ataturk and based on the fundamental principles set forth in the Preamble' (Article 2).

In the era of globalization, the secularization model has been developed in different modes and degrees all over the world. While in some parts of the world religious movements and revolutions are taking

---

[61] Robinson, *op. cit.*
[62] Giddens, *op. cit.*
[63] See Cassell, *op. cit.*, 301.
[64] Shepard, *op. cit.*

place,[65] secularization has expanded such that it now penetrates nearly all aspects of life structurally and subjectively in many parts of the world. This process has become increasingly similar across the world through, for example, the influence of secular education. Similar course syllabus and content, comparable term units and semesters and increasing professorial similarities are part of the global homogeneity in the education system. Also, the process by which society is 'rationalized' according to the programme of conventional modernization, through the democratization, liberalization, and bureaucratization of the political and social system, has successfully 'evacuated' religion from the whole social system—that is, from the domains of law, education and power as well as art, broadcasting, and the media. The whole way of life in Islamic countries has been influenced by this secularizing process. Although most policy-makers in Muslim states have actively participated in this process, they have been opposed by significant numbers of Muslims who have tried to uphold Islamic values and laws, seeking to apply the *Shari'ah* in all aspects of social and political life.

In the type of society in which a multitude of choices in diverse domains is available, it might be argued that individuals are deprived of that mental 'space' that allows them to focus on religion. In other words, religious consciousness has, traditionally, functioned within a social and psychological framework that was less cluttered by multifarious items, all seeking attention and consuming time. Traditional rhythms of social life and intercourse were modulated according to religious norms, whereas the rhythms and demands of modern life, on the contrary, relativize religious practices by relegating them to the margins of social and professional interaction.

Accordingly, in the era of globalization, what has been called 'subjective secularization' is much stronger and more influential than ever before. Today, people have access to hundreds of global television channels, and millions of internet sites, which connect them to the news, economics, music, fashion, sports, sciences, pornography, the different religions and cults, and forms of entertainment found throughout the world. It is not just global television and the internet which have given

---

[65] For example, the Islamic Revolution in Iran, and the Islamic movements in the Lebanon, Egypt, Algeria, Sudan, Pakistan, Nigeria and many other Muslim countries, taking place and gradually expanded around the world.

consumers the opportunity to access images or texts visually: all these materials have been repackaged in the form of videos, CDs, journals, and books, and are available in the cities and even villages of the world.

Britain, which is considered by some as the upholder of Christian values, is also regarded as the vanguard of secularism. This paradoxical state of affairs has left little room for the direct role of religion within social and political institutions, the media, the educational system and the law. In this context, the local environment, and not just the global one, plays a highly significant role in influencing or changing the views of British citizens, including British Muslims, *vis-à-vis* the construction of a secular identity. Therefore, global Western culture and local British forces have come together to create conducive conditions for the secularization of British citizens. Needless to say, however, this has caused its own reaction: young Muslims in Britain are clearly resisting the tide of secular and modern forces, or as Robertson[66] termed it 'anti-globalization'.

Secularity itself can be examined from a subjective and objective perspective in its relationship with individual and social life, but the main characteristics of the secularists can be subjectively examined as regards their attitudes and behaviour in everyday life and objectively portrayed as one that involves the applicability of religion in social and political institutions and processes.[67]

Relativism—end of fixed ideas and certainty

One can also argue that in the age of globalization, ethical and religious values have lost their absoluteness and have been turned into relative concepts. This in turn has led to the adaptation of pluralistic attitudes towards religion as well as the generation of extreme conflicts between religions and other by-products of cultural globalization.

---

[66] R Robertson, 'Globality, Global Culture and Images of World Order', in eds. Hans Haferamp and Neil Smelser, *Social Change and Modernity*, University of California. Berkeley, 1992.

[67] Robinson, 'Secularization, Weber and Islam', in ed. T Huffed, *Weber and Islam*, Transaction, New Brunswick, NJ, 1999.

Robertson,[68] as one of the leading contributors to a growing sociological discussion of globalization and religion, has explained religious identity from the relativist point of view. Featherstone,[69] Beyer[70] and Eade[71] have also made important contributions in this regard.

Robertson[72] in his representation of 'the model: the global field', has emphasized a number of processes of relativization. Relativization is meant to indicate the ways in which, as globalization proceeds, challenges are increasingly presented to the stability of particular perspectives on, and collective and individual participation in, the overall process of globalization. As Robertson highlights, this picture of the global field indicates overall processes of differentiation of the main spheres of globality, which have increased over time. He points out that 'thus differentiation between the spheres was much lower in earlier phases of globalization; while the effects of such differentiation have been encountered unevenly and with different responses in different parts of the world.' [73] For him, an important aspect of the process of differentiation is depended on the ways in which school, college and /or 'multicultural' lines have interacted.

Robertson's most pervasive theme clusters around issues of identity-formation or reformation. This is the process by which, because of the compression of the world into such a small place, many groups and individuals are forced to interact at new levels of intensity. Hence they re-formulate their identity with respect to one another. This involves the alteration, retrenchment, or invention of new social identities and transformation of symbolic boundaries.

Robertson[74] explains the reformation of identity in relation to the dialogical process between local and global—universal and particular. The most important aspect of Robertson's work on globalization relates to the dichotomies of universalism-particularism, or globlism-localism. These tensions have become part of the global-human condition, and

---

[68] Robertson, 1991 and 1992.

[69] M Featherstone, 'Global Culture: An Introduction', in ed. Mike Featherstone, *Global Culture: Nationalism, Globalization and Modernity*, London and New Delhi, 1990 and 'Undoing culture'.

[70] P Beyer, *Religion and Globalization*, Sage, London, 1994.

[71] J Eade, 'Introduction' in ed. John Eade, *Living the Global: Globalization as Local Process*, London and New York, Routledge. 1997.

[72] Robertson, 1992.

[73] Robertson, 1991, 29.

[74] Robertson, 2000.

have constituted a global-cultural form, a major axis of the construction of the world as a whole.[75] Robertson does not see them as states of being, but as a process. Actors negotiate and reformulate their identity as part of the process of managing the tensions between the universal and the particular. In this dialectical tension, universal processes impact on particular identities such as Muslim identity, and particular identities promote universalization. Robertson[76] has named this process: 'the universalism of particularism' and 'the particularization of universalism.' In the first case, particularistic identities (national, ethnic, religious, etc.) are reinforced by universalizing processes which relativize any one given identity. The second process involves giving socio-political concreteness to universal symbols, processes, or meanings.

Featherstone[77] points out that the closeness and proximity of cultures and religious thinking have made the process of decision-making more difficult. Intercultural communication is one of the phenomena of globalization which makes people more and more involved with a variety of cultures, which alter the fixed culture to the relative culture—an absolutism to a relativism.

On the other hand, Featherstone[78] has looked at relativism from the post-modern perspective. He suggests that consumer culture and postmodernism are both taken as signs of dramatic changes which are altering the nature of the social fabric as a result of a double relativization—of both tradition, and the tradition of the new (modernism). The latter results in a questioning of all modes of fundamental values—a transvaluation of values has not only moved humankind beyond the possibility of constructing a moral consensus and the good society, but has also caused some to see the only solution as being the rejection of all forms of subjective identity construction in favour of immersion in the various sensual flows of the body without organs.[79]

Beyer[80] has explained the relativist point of view from a different perspective: the 'Rushdie affair exemplifies the point that globalization

---

[75] A D King, Culture, *Globalization and the World System: Contemporary Conditions for the Representation of Identity*, SUNY, Press Binghamton, 1991.

[76] Robertson, 2000.

[77] Featherstone, 1990, 8.

[78] Featherstone, 1995, 72-85.

[79] Featherstone, 1995, 86.

[80] Beyer, 1994, 4.

brings with it the relativization of particularistic identities along with the relativization and marginalization of religion as a mode of social communication.' On the other hand, Beyer has pointed out that globalization has also created a situation in which the revitalization of religion is a way of asserting a particular identity, which in turn has been a prime method of competing for power and influence in the global system. But this is to a large extent according to the fact that religion has an affinity for particularistic identities and because it, like so many groups in our world, has become somewhat marginalized as a consequence of globalization.

Eade[81] indicated that 'the multiplication of social and cultural worlds encourages an increase in individualism and the relativization of Identity.' Eade has suggested that the multiculturalization of the world has been erected by the global mass communication network. Multiculturalization has encouraged and increased the processes of the relativization of identity. Plurality within the domain of culture, religious thinking and beliefs has been a further by-product of the relativism that globalization has generated. This mode of thinking totally rejects the absoluteness of any values and questions the monopoly of truth being in any one particular kind of thinking.

Non-cognitive globalization and the power of religion

Turner[82] posed the question: What is the main reason for religious change in response to the impact of globalization? Are the changes cognitive and/or ideological? He believes that specific types of cognitive change, that is, those within the structure and style of globalization which tend to commodify everyday life, do not undermine religion. He suggests that the main threat to the Islamic character of knowledge is not cognitive. The main threat to religious faith, he argues, is in fact the commodification of everyday life. People do not adopt or reject belief systems simply on the rationalistic grounds that they are not intellectually coherent. Beliefs are adopted or rejected because they are relevant or irrelevant to everyday needs and concerns. For Turner, what makes religious faith or religious

---

[81] Eade, 'Introduction', 1997, 2.
[82] Turner, *op. cit.*

commitment problematic in a globalized post-modern society is that everyday life has become part of a global system of exchange of commodities, not easily influenced by political, intellectual or religious leaders.[83]

In such terms the 'corruption of the pristine faith is going to be brought about by Tina Turner (head of CNN) and Coca-Cola and not by rational arguments and the rational inspection of presuppositions that are the basis of Western secularism'.[84] For Turner, 'this is what is wrong fundamentally with Ernest Gellner's book *Postmodernism, Reason and Religion* (1992) and Akbar Ahmed's book on *Postmodernity and Islam* (1992). They are both talking about intellectual cognitive problems of religious leaders and intellectuals, not the problems of everyday life. What they both fail to emphasize is that the Ford motor car did more damage to Christianity than any type of argumentation.'[85] In other words, people do not stop believing in God merely as a consequence of rational criticism; rather they stop believing in God when religious belief is eroded by the transformation of everyday life, which makes belief either irrelevant or impossible.

According to Turner, then, globalization has driven the effect of religion out of the social domain into a personal environment consequently changing human societies' way of thinking. Of course what has been said should not be taken to mean a general decline in religious tendencies. It means that there is a reduction within the sphere of religious influence. For example, a brief look at society's collective conscience would show that there is no decline in the belief in God within Western societies, especially that of North American; on the contrary, there is a marked increase in religious belief. There is, however, a marked decline in the belief that religion is an ideology with its own way of thinking, social structure and system of education. The change within religious motivation does not stem from changes within deep-rooted ideological perceptions, like dialectical materialism replacing metaphysics. Rather, there has been a profound shift in people's disposition towards the day to day realities of mankind. The change is primarily due to people being preoccupied or dazzled by colourful pictures of daily living and the range of attractions they generate.

---

[83] *Ibid.*, 9–11.

[84] *Ibid.*, 10.

[85] *Ibid.*, 10.

Conclusion

Generally speaking one could conclude that globalization, not only in the form of ideology and cognitive penetration, but also in terms of informational and non-cognitive determination has reformulated the structure of power, including that of religion. That is why for Castells[86] power is no longer concentrated only in local institutions (the state), organizations (capital firms), or symbolic controllers (corporate media churches). Power is diffused in global networks of wealth, information, and images, which circulate and transmute in a system of variable geometry and dematerialized geography. Although power still rules, shapes and dominates local society, it is now more diffused in global structures. Accordingly, global spaces or more precisely, glocal spaces can be understood as a locus for religions power. Religion's power from this perspective is a transnational power, which enforces religious networked relationship all over the world. This is a type of global consciousness based on people's shared mind, and so people according to their historical experiences and religious orientation support justice and reject injustice. In a more particular conclusion one can argue that the two religions of Islam and Christianity, in terms of social power, should see clearly that the forces of globalization have produced two new threats which should be considered as the dangers of globalization, and one major advantage. The two new threats are fundamentalism from within, articulated by a religio-phobic presentation of global dominated powers, and atheism from without.

As regards the first, it is clear that the essential dignity and beauty, not to mention the ethics and the spirituality, of the two faiths are under attack by those who are using the new forms of communication to 'fundamentally' alter the message of religion. That is, they attempt to convert what has hitherto been a fringe phenomenon—extremism, militancy, bigotry, chauvinism, violence in the name of religion—into a global threat. Now the extremist form of religion is being presented as the 'true' or the 'authentic' religion. It is the duty of all those who understand that the authenticity of religion resides in its essential humanity, dignity, and inclusiveness to combat this poison that is ruining religion from within. They must reassert all the ethical and the spiritual values

---

[86] M Castells, *The Information Age: Economy, Society and Culture, Volume II: The Power of Identity*, Blackwell, Oxford, 1997, 359.

that bring the religions closer together, and that bring out the best of humanity in terms of inclusivity; rather than allow the fundamentalists to succeed in hijacking religion and converting it into a means of achieving political and ideological goals. In this connection, what these religions share needs to be stressed more than ever before; and the means of promoting these shared features have never been more powerful and global in their reach than they are today. It is important to bear in mind that the media presentation of religion, in particular Islam, in a very phobic way plays fundamentally to change the picture of religion in the world society or create a fundamentalist reaction to such orientation.

On the other hand the internal threat to religion can be discussed when religion is enforced by political power. From this perspective religious authority can become a critical force for the powerlessness of religion in society if the politicization of religion creates a new secularity. The recent work of Pyle and Davidson[87] shows how religious power turns out to be motivation source for social stratification and social division in a society. They believe that religious stratification occurs when religion is institutionalized in the laws and/or customs of a society as a criterion for the allocation of social positions and their attendant rewards. According to such a theory, religion becomes a dangerous power for the disintegration and fragmentation of the society, when religion advocates the relatively stable ranking of religious groups in terms of their access to power, privilege, and prestige.

As for the second threat, atheism from without, this is taking increasingly aggressive forms, both explicit and implicit. The first threat is explicit in the many groups, intellectuals, etc. that openly refer to religion as a vestige of the past, seeing religion as a regressive force, and one that ought to be abolished. The threat is implicit in the multifaceted forces of commercial and materialistic globalisation, advertising, promotion of lifestyles, etc. that do not necessarily attack religion head-on; rather, the cumulative impact of these forces is to make religion appear either to be irrelevant or to marginalize it altogether as a wholly individualistic pursuit, having no social significance whatsoever. In a certain sense the New Age religions also promote this marginalisation of authentic religion, and are to be resisted.

---

[87] R E Pyle, J D Davidson, 'The Origins of Religious Stratification in Colonial America', *Journal for the Scientific Study of Religion*, Vol. 42(1), 2004, 57–75.

As regards the major advantage that globalisation has produced for religious believers: the upholders of religion must be creative in meeting these challenges, and take full advantage of the very forces that are creating the challenges and dangers in the first place. That is, they must adapt their traditional pastoral,[88] and in the idea of *qut al-qulub* techniques to the new environment, and use such things as the internet to promote the values of their religion. To be conservative means to be creative, and not merely reactionary. All religious believers should 'globalize' both in the technical sense, of using the new technologies, and also in the spiritual sense: they must realize that, together, as believers, they form one global community against those who attack religion from without, and those who would in the very name of religion destroy religion from within.

Religion can and should be a global force which interiorises cognition at the same time as universalizing it. That is, it can turn consciousness inward, towards the spiritual roots of the religion, and at the same time, by stressing the commonalities of the faiths of all believers, universalize our cognitive attitudes to other religions. This is the very opposite of the current trends, which accentuate specificity and exclusivism in order to uphold a particular religion. What we should argue for, on the contrary, is an upholding of the specificity of our faith, as being one expression of the universal principle of religious belief. The particularity of religion can be upheld without detriment to the principle of the universality of its essence.

Finally, glocalization can apply to religion's power. This is because according to our religious orientation, followers of religion have to be global in their outreach, and local in their promotion of the particularities of their own religious culture. All the uniqueness of their faith must be preserved at the same time as emphasizing the values they all share in common: this is the real meaning of religious pluralism: that differences are respected and valued, not that differences are ironed out for the sake a flat mediocrity, the lowest common denominator, or a meaningless monotony. The very diversity of divinely revealed religions and cultures is the expression of the divine will for humanity, as this verse of the Qur'an says:

---

[88] This is a key word, which means, 'taking spiritual and moral care' of one's flock, from which the words 'pastor' or priest come. It clearly relates to the notion of 'pasture' of 'feeding' the believers with spiritual sustenance. In Islam the same idea is expressed in *rizq*.

For each We have ordained a Law and a Path. And had God willed, He would have made you one community (but He made you as you are) in order to test you in what He gave you. So vie with one another in good works. Unto God is your return, all of you, and He will tell you about those things in which you differed.

A CATHOLIC THEOLOGICAL AND POLITICAL READING OF CHURCH

Patrick Riordan

The relationship of religion with secular society was a frequent topic during the Catholic-Shi'a Encounter in the summer of 2003. In this paper I address elements of this topic from the perspective of Catholic Christianity. I note first the various ways in which the topic of the relationship between the religious and the political arises today, usually in relation to liberalism, the dominant political philosophy in the West. Second, I sketch various stances taken by believers as they struggle with the tensions generated by living in liberal political systems within pluralist societies. Third, I outline elements of the Catholic accommodation, whereby the Church has found a way of living within and alongside liberal polities.

First, a clarification about the use of the term 'liberalism'. It is useful to distinguish liberal philosophies, liberal institutions, and the liberal popular culture which animates and sustains the life of the institutions. The point of distinguishing them is to avoid the error of assuming an identity of philosophy, institution and culture. While there are influences in various directions, there are also distinctive features of each which are not reducible to the other two.

As a political philosopher I tend to focus on the philosophies of particular liberal thinkers such as John Stuart Mill, or John Rawls. Ideas generated by such thinkers have greatly influenced both the political institutions and the popular culture of Western states. But the structures of government of the UK, the USA, or European states are products also of their individual histories and transmit values from sources other than liberalism.

Popular culture, influenced by and expressed in print and broadcast media, tends to reduce the ideas of the philosophers and the values sustained by the institutions to slogans which find ready recognition, but which are often distortions of the original ideas. The freedoms which people claim for themselves in the name of liberty may often be incompatible with the kinds of concerns which led political thinkers to elaborate a philosophy of liberalism. So while this essay notes the tensions which religious thinkers experience, it should also be remembered that many liberal philosophers take a critical attitude to the excessive trends they observe in liberal popular culture.[1]

There are many different liberal philosophies, and to date there is no agreement among philosophers as to which one is best. Critics of liberalism such as Alasdair MacIntyre exploit this lack of consensus.[2] Liberal institutions can function and be accepted by their citizens even in the absence of a coherent justification. A liberal in politics is one who contributes to the maintenance, support and development of political institutions that respect human freedom. To be rational and consistent as a liberal citizen in this sense is not conditional on the success of some philosophical theory to justify and explain the liberal polity. One can be a liberal in politics without endorsing any particular theory.

The problem

There are many elements of contemporary life in the Western democracies with which people of faith are uncomfortable. Many of these elements have to do with practices that are incompatible with the moral standards espoused by faith communities. In many cases, the discomfort experienced is not due to the idea of individual liberty as such, but to the use to which this idea has been put in shaping institutions and forming popular culture.

There is another source of discomfort, which is the sense of being unwelcome or out of place in the kind of society in which the values of self-expression and gratification dominate popular culture. The shift within liberal polities to an acceptance of multiculturalism and pluralism has meant that the usual suspicion of communities of faith has been abandoned. But it is worth recalling that at its origins, liberal political thought rejected the possibility of accommodating Catholics and Muslims. There is a danger that this situation will recur. Liberal fears of religion have been reawakened by recent developments. The religious origins of various types of terrorism, the emergence of Christian fundamentalism

---

[1] M A Glendon, *Rights Talk. The Impoverishment of Political Discourse*, The Free Press, New York, 1991, is a case in point.
[2] A MacIntyre, *After Virtue*, 2nd edition, University of Notre Dame Press, Notre Dame, Indiana, 1984.

with its political ambitions, the role of Islam in international affairs and the political significance of the New Right in America have drawn attention to the relationship between religion and politics and the possible dangers associated with religious involvement in public discourse.

John Locke must be counted as one of the original liberal political thinkers. Although he favoured liberty and toleration, he also expressed concerns about the dangers of unrestricted religious expression.[3] For instance, he included Catholics and Muslims among the categories of people who could not be tolerated as citizens of the political communities in which rights would be secured by limited government. Catholics ought not to be tolerated, Locke thought, because in a position of power, perhaps being a majority in a democracy, they themselves would not be tolerant of the religious views of others. Their performance in history as well as their espoused doctrine confirmed him in this view. Muslims, on the other hand, believed by Locke to owe allegiance to a foreign prince, the Mufti of Istanbul, could not be tolerated as fellow citizens engaged in rule of the polity on a basis of equality. The same argument was also used against Catholicism, which was accused of owing allegiance to the Pope, a foreign prince. It should also be mentioned, however, that atheists could not be tolerated either, according to Locke, because of their inability to take an oath.

The liberal maintains that the governing of human societies must be with the consent of the governed. For the liberal, theocracy must always be suspect, because of the fear that the will of God (as interpreted by the powers that be) will be imposed on those who do not share the faith of those in power. This fear is warranted historically, and John Rawls, for instance, makes a great deal of the history of religious persecution, and the turmoil caused by the wars of religion in Europe as the background to his political liberalism.[4] Robert Audi, in his listing of aspects of religious (as distinct from secular) reasons in politics includes the following features: 'infallible supreme authority', 'condemnatory tendencies', 'threat of religious domination', 'cults and the spectre of fanaticism', 'dangers of an inflated sense of self-importance', and 'a

---

[3] J Locke, 'An Essay on Toleration', in *Political Essays*, ed. M Goldie, Cambridge University Press, Cambridge, 1997, 151ff.

[4] J Rawls, *Political Liberalism*, paperback edition, Columbia University Press, New York, 1996.

passionate concern with outsiders'.[5] This list indicates the liberal's perceived grounds for anxiety.

Given the sense of discomfort on both sides, the question whether people and communities of faith can live comfortably within pluralist societies with liberal democratic forms of government is urgent.

The debate

This question stimulates debate at the margins of Theology on the one hand and Political Philosophy on the other. I note some of the trends in this debate.

a) Communitarian critique and the cultivation of virtue
b) Eberle and the philosophical critique of liberalism in the name of theism

The cultivation of virtue

Many critics of liberal political philosophy have been linked together under the label of communitarianism. While the critique of liberalism can be identified as common to the work of the authors so linked, it is not a shared project, and different thinkers focus on different issues. Typical criticisms are that the liberal sees persons as 'unencumbered' so that their social involvement is not part of the constitution of their identity, that inherently communal goods are overlooked in the liberal view of the individual as asocial, that individuals' choices of ends and goods are assumed to be a matter of arbitrary preference, and that liberalism avoids a thick conception of the good, aiming at a neutrality which it cannot attain.[6]

There is also a positive version of communitarianism which presents a political programme to restore a concern for fostering community, family values, and a vision of the good life to the centre of

---

[5] R Audi, *Religious Commitment and Secular Reason*, Cambridge University Press, Cambridge, 2000, 100-3.
[6] S Mulhall and A Swift, *Liberals & Communitarians*, Blackwell, Oxford, 1992; M J Sandel, *Liberalism and the Limits of Justice*, Cambridge University Press, Cambridge, 1982.

political life.[7] But many thinkers who are labelled communitarian content themselves with the criticism of liberalism and do not attempt to formulate an alternative. One theme, however, which is common to several in this group, is the commitment to fostering virtue. This represents a shift of focus from the institutions of the liberal state to the formulation of standards of excellence which might be realised in forms of life confined to small-scale community. Alasdair MacIntyre gave the lead on this strategy with his appeal to St Benedict and new forms of community at the end of *After Virtue*.[8] John Milbank echoes this solution at the end of his recent article in *New Blackfriars*, in which he exposes once again the hollowness at the heart of liberalism. He writes that

> we need to surpass liberal democracy and search again for the common good ... (W)e should both locate and form real groups pursuing real goods and exchanging real gifts among themselves and with each other according to measures judged to be intrinsically fair. We need to acknowledge the place and point of families, schools, localities, towns, associations for genuine production and trade ...[9]

This strategy appears attractive to some faith communities. It confirms them in the sense of preserving values and visions of the good which are absent from, and even denied by the political institutions. It reinforces their sense of providential selection, being different, and chosen to be apart from the world. On the other hand, it does mean that the polarisation between the religious and the political is exacerbated. Political institutions and their sustaining culture are denied the exposure to debate with religious world-views and do not have the opportunity to develop accordingly. Religious groups fail to find theological meaning in political institutions and in political life, and this weakens the comprehensiveness of their theological vision.

---

[7]   A Etzioni, *The Moral Dimension. Toward A New Economics*, The Free Press, New York, 1988.

[8]   A MacIntyre, *After Virtue*, 263.

[9]   J Milbank, 'The Gift of Ruling: Secularization and Political Authority', *New Blackfriars*, 2004, 212-38, 237-8.

Eberle and the philosophical critique of liberalism in the name of theism[10]

Christopher Eberle is unusual as a critic of liberalism on religious grounds. He wishes to defend a strong form of theism, namely the belief that the obligation to obey God's command overrides all other obligations. He challenges all forms of justificatory liberalism, because of their conviction that 'a responsible citizen in a liberal democracy ought not support (or reject) a coercive law on the basis of religious convictions alone.'[11] However, his challenge is formulated in terms of typically liberal arguments and he attempts to show that the liberal position is untenable.

Eberle explains that there are two requirements expressed in this common position of justificatory liberalism. The first is the requirement that those wishing to support or reject a coercive law should pursue public justification for their favoured position. This is the requirement of pursuit. The second requirement is restraint: that a citizen should restrain from supporting a coercive law for which no public justification is available, or that a citizen should not rely exclusively on religious grounds for supporting or rejecting a coercive law.

Eberle maintains that justificatory liberals succeed in grounding the obligation of pursuit in the duty of respect. However, he thinks that their efforts at grounding the obligation of restraint are less successful. He challenges the liberal consensus that the requirement of restraint is justified. His thesis is: 'a citizen has an obligation sincerely and conscientiously to pursue a widely convincing secular rationale for her favored coercive laws, but she doesn't have an obligation to withhold support from a coercive law for which she lacks a widely convincing secular rationale'.[12] In other words, against the liberal consensus he argues that there are circumstances in which a citizen is morally permitted to endorse a coercive law even if she only has religious grounds for doing so.

Eberle focuses in particular on the liberal philosophy of John Rawls.[13] He uses Rawls's own argument used in generating his principles of justice to challenge Rawls's assumption that the requirement of restraint

---

[10] This section draws on material published in Patrick Riordan, 'Permission to Speak: Religious Arguments in Public Reason', *Heythrop Journal*, XLV, 2004, 178-96.

[11] C J Eberle, *Religious Conviction in Liberal Politics*, Cambridge University Press, Cambridge, 2002, 12.

[12] C J Eberle, *Religious Conviction*, 10, emphasis in original.

[13] J Rawls, *A Theory of Justice*, Oxford University Press, Oxford, 1972, and *Political Liberalism.*, Columbia University Press, New York, 1996.

is justified. Rawls's argument relies on the device of the original position. The original position is a hypothetical choice situation, in which choosers are imagined to choose principles to regulate society's main institutions so that a just society would be achieved. To ensure that no one will be unfairly advantaged or disadvantaged the choosers are described as choosing behind a veil of ignorance. That means that they are assumed to be without all that particular information about themselves which might influence them to choose in their own favour. They do not know what family or social class they belong to, they do not know what their ideal of the good life is, or what their guiding values are. At the same time they are assumed to have sufficient general information about psychology and society, economics and politics, to be able to choose principles for a society. Using this device, Eberle asks if the requirement of restraint would be acceptable to the choosers in the original position.

Retracing the steps of Rawls's argument he proceeds as follows. Behind their veil of ignorance, the choosers in the original position do not know if they are theists or not. But from their general knowledge, they know what theists are, and what they believe. They know, for instance, that theists consider that their obligation to obey the will of God overrides all their other possible obligations. Accordingly, they know that if they were to choose the principle of restraint in the original position, and then subsequently discover their religious commitment as theists, they would not be able to sustain the undertaking given in the original position. This is the 'strains of commitment' argument which Rawls relies on in his discussion of the principle of average utility. Eberle formulates the question: 'given that the parties in the original position might turn out to be theists, and given that they might take themselves to have an overriding and totalizing obligation to obey God, can they commit themselves in good faith to the liberal principle of legitimacy?'[14]

The core of Eberle's criticism of Rawls is a powerful and telling argument. It exploits a strength of Rawls's powerful device of the original position and uses it to endorse the requirement of pursuit while at the same time showing that the requirement of restraint does not enjoy the same foundations in the duty of respect. If Eberle's description of the theist is accepted, then it seems that the citizen of a liberal democratic

---

[14] C J Eberle, *Religious Conviction*, 146.

polity is not bound to restrain herself from reliance on exclusively religious reasons when deliberating about coercive law.

The Catholic accommodation

There are several elements in the Catholic Church's adaptation to political institutions which rely on liberal political ideas for their justification. It should be noted that liberal thought has also undergone some development, so that it now appears much more hospitable to people and communities motivated by religious faith. Three points warrant attention.

a) The rejection of coercion
b) The distinction between common good and public order
c) The Church's role in public political culture

The rejection of coercion

Eberle's argument relies on the view that the theist recognizes an overriding and totalising obligation to obey God. This premise in the argument is only relevant to the conclusion, however, if it is also assumed, first, that God may command something which would require of the believer that fellow citizens be coerced so that God's will may be done, and second, that there are instances in which no public justification would be available for that which God commands. Both of these assumptions are contrary to Catholic convictions.

    Catholics traditionally understand natural law as God's law in the human itself. As created, human nature has an exigency and a teleology, and these reveal God's will for His creature, as imprinted in what He has made. God's will for His creature, as revealed through Scriptures and Church teaching, cannot be inconsistent with God's will for His creature, as revealed through the creature's created nature. At the same time, for those matters in social and political existence for which coercion is required, the Catholic tradition conveys a confidence that appropriately non-religious arguments can be found. A classic example is Aquinas's discussion of the natural law bases of civil law, and the question whether the civil law ought to command or prohibit all that natural law commands or prohibits. For Aquinas, whether or not some activity, known to be immoral, should be prohibited in the civil law, depends on the impact that activity has on society. So he maintains that certain actions like murder and theft could not be tolerated, not because of their wrongfulness, but because they would make social existence impossible.[15] What is necessary for the security and survival of society is a matter of practical judgment and can be deliberated upon without any reference to revelation.

Catholic tradition has developed a sophisticated position concerning the impact of moral teaching on political and legal order. The Second Vatican Council in its 'Declaration on Religious Freedom', *Dignitatis Humanae*, insisted that no one should be coerced in the matters of religious belief and practice. This teaching marked a significant development from the previously accepted position in the Church, according to which error had no rights, and the good state was one in which Catholic moral norms were enforced in civil law. While abandoning neither the claims of the Church to truth, nor the assertion of the duty of all to seek the truth and the true Church, the Council acknowledged that even an erroneous conscience possessed dignity and ought to be respected.

> Freedom of this kind means that all should be immune from coercion on the part of individuals, social group and every human power so that, within due limits, nobody is forced to act against his convictions nor is anyone to be restrained from acting in accordance with his convictions in religious matters in private or in public, alone or in association with others.[16]

This principle of religious liberty has been applied in the Church to the question of the appropriate attitude of the state to moral matters.[17] This is the significant area in which Catholics have been faced with the

---

[15] '… human laws do not forbid all vices from which the virtuous abstain but only the more grievous vices from which it is possible for the majority to abstain and chiefly those that are to the hurt of others, without the prohibition of which human society could not be maintained; thus human law prohibits murder, theft, and suchlike'. Aquinas, *Summa Theologiae*, trans. by Dominicans of Blackfriars, Eyre and Spottiswoode, London, 1966, Vol. XXVIII, IaIIae.96.2.

[16] A Flannery, ed., *Vatican Council II. The Conciliar and Post Conciliar Documents*, Dominican Publications, Dublin, 1975, 801.

[17] P Hannon, *Church, State, Morality & Law*, Gill and Macmillan, Dublin, 1992, especially chapter 7.

question whether they are required by their faith commitment to coerce fellow citizens into abstaining from activity which Catholics hold to be immoral. Transposed from the arena of religious freedom to that of morality, the principle requires that state law on moral matters should not coerce anyone to act against their conscience, nor should the law prevent anyone from following their conscience, within due limits. This applies even in cases in which one might rightly hold the view that people were acting immorally. Note that the due limits refer to those requirements mentioned by Aquinas as necessary for the existence of society, and include the protection of human life in all its stages.

Common good and public order distinguished

On the traditional Thomist understanding, those with authority in the state hold responsibility for the common good. Traditionally, the 'common good' is understood to include the complete flourishing of every human being. And since moral integrity is an element of complete flourishing, responsibility for the common good would require the state to ensure that its citizens achieve complete flourishing including moral uprightness. This echoes Aristotle's dictum that the political community has concern for the goodness of its citizens, and this distinguishes it from other forms of association such as mutual non-aggression pacts, or contracts for the supply of goods and services.[18] The development in the Church's position in relation to liberty required a refinement also in this view of the duty of the state with regard to the common good. The implication of the new understanding is that although the state does have its own interest in the flourishing of individuals as part of its responsibility, this is not to be understood as an unrestricted interest. The state's interest is not in the 'common good' in the full sense, but in 'public order', that dimension of the common good which is of particular relevance to the well-being of society, and which it is able to affect through its appropriate instruments, including coercive law.

The treatment of the topic of the common good in the Vatican Council's *Gaudium et Spes* exemplifies this new qualification in the different levels of good and the different responsibilities. *Gaudium et Spes* §26 describes the common good as:

---

[18] Aristotle, *The Politics*, Book III, chap. 9.

the sum total of social conditions which allow people, either as groups or as individuals, to reach their fulfilment more fully and more easily. The whole human race is consequently involved with regard to the rights and obligations which result. Every group must take into account the needs and legitimate aspirations of every other group, and still more of the human family as a whole.[19]

A similar definition is offered in the context of a discussion of the nature and purpose of political community, in §74 of the same document.

The political community, then, exists for the common good: this is its full justification and meaning and the source of its specific and basic right to exist. The common good embraces the sum total of all those conditions of social life which enable individuals, families, and organizations to achieve complete and efficacious fulfilment.

These passages distinguish means and goals, conditions for the realizations of ends and those final purposes themselves. The complete fulfilment of every individual and of every group is understood by the Church in terms of life with God in the Resurrection. It is not the business of the state or of any human institution to specify for people what their ultimate good consists of. On the other hand, the meaning and purpose of state institutions is to provide for people the political, legal, social and economic conditions which will allow them to pursue freely their own good.

Since the Council, commentators have introduced a distinction into the notion of the common good, in order to accommodate the differentiation achieved in these passages. The term 'common good' is used analogically. It refers to God himself as humans' common good achieved in their ultimate fulfilment in the beatific vision. At the same time, the term also refers to the means and conditions on which people rely in pursuing their good through their life histories. In order to be able to pursue their good, people must be able to enjoy the kind of

---

[19] A Flannery, ed., *Vatican Council II.*

liberty which is ensured for them in a liberal polity. As a result, the achievements of the liberal state with its institutions in securing peace and stability, the rule of law with its guarantee of rights, and the functioning of the market in providing for material needs are valued from the theological perspective as providing conditions for the pursuit of ultimate good. These conditions, as secured by the state, can be referred to as public order, a more restricted category than that of the common good.[20]

The Church's role in public political culture

There has been a noticeable development within John Rawls's liberal political philosophy acknowledging the liberal credentials of the Catholic Church's position.[21] In his later work, *Political Liberalism*, he presents a political conception of justice which could be accepted by many different groups holding a variety of reasonable comprehensive doctrines, but which would not require them to compromise their commitment to those doctrines. Each position would have its own reasons, in terms of its comprehensive doctrine, for supporting the content of the overlapping consensus. It is noteworthy that Rawls in this discussion lists secularist doctrines alongside religious ones as examples of comprehensive doctrines which could coexist in supporting a political conception of justice. Secularism is not the stance from which religious world-views are to be adjudicated; rather it too is a comprehensive doctrine which must find accommodation in a situation of reasonable pluralism.

Rawls refines the traditional distinction between public and private. Where formerly in liberal thought the 'public' identified the arena of politics from which religious arguments were to be excluded, Rawls now recognizes a much more complex notion of public reason. He identifies public reason narrowly understood as that which applies to the deliberation about and implementation of coercive law, and in this context the principle of restraint is applicable. But as well as the narrow definition, he provides a broad understanding of public reason as that

---

[20] I have argued this at greater length in P Riordan, *A Politics of the Common Good*, Institute of Public Administration, Dublin, 1996, especially chapters 5 and 6.

[21] J Rawls, 'The Idea of Public Reason Revisited', *University of Chicago Law Review*, 64 1997, subsequently reprinted in J Rawls, *The Law of Peoples*, Harvard University Press, Cambridge, Mass., 1999. Citations are from this last edition.

which operates within the political culture. Here he welcomes the contribution of the Catholic Church and positively evaluates its language of solidarity and common good.

Rawls quotes the Catholic theologian, David Hollenbach SJ, to support his encouragement of an open and free communication of ideas in public political culture.

> Conversation and argument about the common good will not occur initially in the legislature or in the political sphere (narrowly conceived as the domain in which interests and power are adjudicated). Rather it will develop freely in those components of civil society that are the primary bearers of cultural meaning and value—universities, religious communities, the world of arts, and serious journalism. It can occur wherever thoughtful men and women bring their beliefs on the meaning of the good life into intelligent and critical encounter with understandings of this good held by other peoples with other traditions. In short, it occurs wherever education about and serious inquiry into the meaning of the good life takes place.[22]

Acknowledgement of the importance of this forum and of the role of the Church within it is the key to the exercise by committed Christians of their mission in politics. This is not a watering down of the Church's mission. There is no abandonment of the task of evangelization. The public role of the Church and of Christians in public life is articulated by Pope Paul VI in his apostolic exhortation *Evangelii Nuntiandi*: '... the Church evangelises when she seeks to convert, solely through the divine power of the Message she proclaims, both the personal and collective consciences of people, the activities in which they engage, and the lives and concrete milieux which are theirs'.[23] The central important condition making it possible for Christians to play this role, and to be accepted in the public space as legitimate participants, is the renunciation of reliance

---

[22] D Hollenbach SJ, 'Civil Society: Beyond the Public-Private Dichotomy', *The Responsive Community*, 5, 1994/95, 22, quoted by Rawls, 'The Idea', 135.

[23] Pope Paul VI, *Evangelization in the Modern World*, Catholic Truth Society, London, 1975, §18.

on coercion. Rawls recognised this shift away from the willingness to impose Christian norms and values in the Church's acceptance of the basic value of human freedom rooted in the dignity of persons as created in God's image and as called to communion with God.

> A persecuting zeal has been the great curse of the Christian religion. It was shared by Luther and Calvin and the Protestant Reformers, and it was not radically changed in the Catholic Church until Vatican II. In the Council's Declaration on Religious Freedom—*Dignitatis Humanae*—the Catholic Church committed itself to the principle of religious freedom as found in a constitutional democratic regime. It declared the ethical doctrine of religious freedom resting on the dignity of the human person; a political doctrine with respect to the limits of government in religious matters; and a theological doctrine of the freedom of the Church in its relations to the political and social world. All persons, whatever their faith, have the right of religious liberty on the same terms. ... As John Courtney Murray, S.J., said:'A longstanding ambiguity had finally been cleared up. The Church does not deal with the secular order in terms of a double standard—freedom for the Church when Catholics are in the minority, privilege for the Church and intolerance for others when Catholics are a majority.[24]

---

[24] J Rawls, 'The Idea', 166, n.75.

THREATS TO CERTAINTY:
A SHI'A PERSPECTIVE ON EXTERNAL CHALLENGES OF THE CONTEMPORARY AGE

Muhsin Javadi

Religious life

One of the main ontological teachings of the Abrahamic religions is that God created the world for a true purpose. He was not simply idling: 'We did not create Heaven and Earth and anything in between just for playing around. We have created them not save in truth; but most of them do not realize it' (44: 38-9). Surely humankind as part of this world is also created for a true purpose: 'What did you think that we created you only for sport, and that you would not be returned to Us?' (23: 115). The idea of the return to God is repeated frequently in the verses of the Qur'an; 'To Him shall you return, all together—God's promise, in truth. He originates creation, then he brings it back again' (10: 4).

The return to God can be taken as a metaphor to refer to human responsibility in this worldly life. He returns to God to be questioned about his endowed abilities and how he has used them. On the Day of Judgment God will command: 'Stop them! They must be questioned' (37: 24). We are obliged to live only in accordance with knowledge and not illusions. God says: 'And pursue not that which you have no knowledge of: your hearing, eyesight and vital organs will be questioned' (17: 36).

The urgent problem for us is how can we use our abilities properly so that we can answer God's question rightly? To know this we must know the purpose of the creation of mankind. The Noble Qur'an says, 'I have not created jinn and mankind except to serve Me' (51: 56). To serve God is the only true purpose in the creation of the rational beings and forgetfulness of the service of God makes one forget oneself. The Noble Qur'an says, 'Be not as those who forget God, and so He caused them to forget themselves; those they are the ungodly' (59: 19). God endowed us with everything to enable us to serve Him, so He certainly will question us about those things. It is only by using our abilities in the way of service to God that we can find an answer to God's question about our life. Indeed, according to the Noble Qur'an the common content of all prophetic messages was the invitation to mankind to this real end of creation: to serve only God. 'And we sent Noah to his people: and he said; O my people, serve God' (7: 56), 'And to 'Ad their brother Hud: he said, 'O my people, serve God! You have no god other than He; will you not be God-fearing?' (7: 65), 'And to Thamud their brother Salih; he said, O my people, serve God (7: 73), and so on.

What is service of God? Usually people take this word to mean worship, the performance of rituals, but it must have a more inclusive meaning. Certainly the end of the creation of mankind is not just the performance of rituals, although they are important elements of that service. Indeed, the Qur'an sometimes refers to the importance of prayer by mentioning that it results in avoiding bad actions; 'Recite what has been revealed to you of the Book, and perform the prayer; prayer forbids indecency and dishonour' (29: 45). Then we can conclude that avoiding indecency, or generally speaking, the observance of moral rules, that is, to do good actions and avoid bad actions, is also one of the most important elements of the purpose of creation of mankind which can be acquired also by the way of rituals. The life of service is the life of reason, and using reason in the correct way is better than performing some rituals. The Prophet Muhammad addressing Imam 'Ali says:

> 'In the competition of service, if you concentrate on thinking,
> you will win those who concentrate on performing different
> forms of good actions such as prayer and fasting.'[1]

Service is a form of life that we can call a religious form of life that has two parts: believing and doing righteous deeds. Many verses of the Glorious Qur'an explicitly assert that only those who live in this way avoid wretchedness. 'By the age! Surely man is lost, save those who believe, and do righteous deeds' (103: 2-3). Indeed, all religions in different ages and by different names came to affirm this reality, that the beatific vision or salvation can be acquired only by having faith and good deeds together. The Glorious Qur'an says: 'Those who believe and those who are Jews, Sabeans and Christians—anyone who believes in God and the Last Day and acts honourably, should have no fear nor will they be saddened' (5: 69).

---

[1] Abu 'Alī Sīnā, *Mi 'rāj Nāmeh*, Āstān-i Quds-i Raḍavī, Mashhad, 1996, 94.

In addition to the verses of the Qur'an, we can find many *hadiths* that explain service or religious life. For example, concerning the importance of faith, Imam Ali says: 'There is no salvation save by faith,'[2] and elsewhere he stresses that faith which does not bring good deeds is not sufficient: 'Do not be of the people who hope for good in the hereafter without doing something.'[3] We can find the same idea in the Bible:

> 'What [doth it] profit, my brethren, though a man say he
> hath faith, and have not works? Can faith save him? If a
> brother or sister be naked, and destitute of daily food, And
> one of you say unto them, Depart in peace, be [ye] warmed
> and filled; notwithstanding ye give them not those things
> which are needful to the body; what doth it profit? Even so
> faith, if it hath not works, is dead, being alone.' (Jas 2: 14-8).

In brief, religious life or the service of God comprises faith and the performance of righteous deeds. Faith is based on knowledge, but it is more than the mere acceptance of a proposition to the effect that God exists. Faith includes the submission of the whole of one's mind and heart to God.[4] The emotions of a believer must fit in with his knowledge and must not direct him against his knowledge. We can conclude that faith has a twofold character that includes knowledge and the wholehearted commitment to the truth which is known. Imam Ali says: 'The most knowing of you is the most believing'[5] and on the other hand he says: 'Is religion other than love for the sake of God and hatred [of evil] for the sake God?'[6] Since faith is a rational commitment, it is not contrary to reason or knowledge. Indeed, faith implies both reason and knowledge. Imam Sadiq says: 'Whoever will be rational will be religious too.'[7] Indeed, it is only by possessing reason that we can be addressed by revelation. Reason is a pre-established messenger of God which makes us ready to

2 Khānsārī, *Shar'-i Ghurar al-Ḥikam wa Durar al-Kalim*, ed. 'Amūdī, Tehran, 1373/1994, Vol. 3, No. 4206.

3 Abu Muḥammad al-Ḥasan ibn 'Alī ībn al-Ḥusain ibn Shu'bah, *Tuḥaf al-Uqūl*, Qum, 2001, 180.

4 Mohsen Javadi, *Naẓarīya-ye Imān*, Qum, 1377 (1998), 155.

5 'Allāmeh Majlesī, Mohamad Baqir, *Biḥār al-Anwār*, Beirut, 1983, Vol. 3, p. 14.

6 Al-Kulayni, Muhammad b. Ya'qūb, *Al-Kāfī*, Dar al-Uswah, Tehran, 1376 (1995), Vol. 2, 154, No. 1873.

7 *Op. cit.*, Vol. 1, 28, No. 6.

accept revelation. Only by taking account of the teachings of revelation and reason together can we find the way of service.

The life of service may increase or decrease in degree depending on the degrees of knowledge and love and also on the number of the righteous deeds by an individual or society. It is important to know the causal and evidential elements for the strength or weakness of religious life. To discuss the threats to the life of service we must consider each level of service separately, although they are in practice related to each other.

Before considering the threats to religious life in modern times we must remember that according to the verses of the Glorious Qur'an man is free and may easily accept false propositions and desire to do evil. Indeed, this natural tendency, which is the requirement of both the twofold character of humanity, body and soul, and his free will, is the root of his being misled. In other words, without man's own consent no one, or more precisely, no external factor can force him to go astray. Thus external elements as such are not a threat to the religious life of the individual; they can work only when one is prepared to be misled. The Qur'an says: 'He [Satan] has no authority over those who believe and trust in their Lord. His authority is over those who take him for their master and ascribe associates to God' (16: 100).

Thus, human misfortune, which is the result of his neglect or denial of religious life or service of God is due to a person himself. However, there is no doubt that the external elements, of course to differing extents, are also important, since they may have a role in stimulating the internal element. Different ages and different cultures may represent different external threats, while the internal grounds of these threats do not differ. People differ in their abilities to resist these threats, depending on the purity of their hearts, but the threats always remain to be faced by humans as a result of their essential humanity.

Certainly there are varieties of threats to religious life that need to be addressed. However, in what follows I will concentrate only on the threat to the core of religious life: certainty.

Certainty

Faith cannot be alive without certainty and as soon as doubt begins to grow, faith will decrease. Imam 'Ali explicitly asserts, 'Doubt foils faith.'[8] It is evident that doubt cannot coexist with faith; faith and doubt are mutually exclusive.[9] To grow the tree of faith in the soil of the heart we need to water it with certainty. Imam Ali provides a good analogy to explain the role of certainty in relation to faith. He takes faith as a city and certainty as its walls (fortifications). The city is safe as long as its walls are in good shape. As soon as the walls of a city are damaged, the city itself will be subject to damage. Describing the barbarism of pre-Islamic times in the Arab peninsula, Imam 'Ali says:

> At that time people had fallen into vices whereby the rope of religion had been cut off, the pillars of belief had been shaken, the system had become topsy-turvy, openings were narrow, the passages were dark, guidance was unknown and darkness prevailed, Allah was disobeyed, Satan given support and belief forsaken. As a result the pillars of religion fell down, its traces could not be discerned.[10]

Doubt fights against faith, and so we must keep our faith at a distance from doubt. According to Imam 'Ali, certainty is not only the root of faith but is also its guard from dangers. No doubt the enemy of certainty directly challenges faith and the life of service. Unfortunately, the spread and depth of scepticism concerning religious matters today is not comparable to any other times.

Before discussing the matter I must mention that doubt *per se* is not a threat to faith, but on the contrary it sometimes improves our understanding of religion. Imam Ali himself was engaged in a religious battle when suddenly one of his soldiers raised a question about the meaning of monotheism. Some people became angry, but the Imam began to reply in detail and told the people around that they were fighting only to provide good conditions for keeping the faith.

What is dangerous is to remain in doubt, as opposed to making doubt a means to arrive at certainty. We can say that doubt is a good road, not a good house to rest in. In explaining the danger of doubt, the Imam says: 'Who doubts much, his faith will be corrupted'[11] and

---

[8] Khānsārī, *op. cit.*, Vol. 1, 189, No. 722.

[9] See 'Doubt' in *Catholic Encyclopedia*, internet.

[10] *Nahjul Balāghah*, Ahl ul-Bayt Assembly of America, 1996, 5.

[11] Jalāl al-Dīn, *Muḥaddith*, Vol. 5, 205, No. 7997.

'Continuing to doubt will result in the denial of faith.'[12] The problem in our modern world is that we are living in doubt and sometimes we are told that certainty is the sign of simplemindedness, while doubt is a sign of sophistication. This is the problem, but what is the solution? To solve the problem we must consider the factors that result in doubt about religious matters in our private or social life.

The evidential challenge

According to natural theology, which is accepted by to most religious traditions, our natural light of reason can prove the existence and some basic attributes of God, and also some other basic articles of faith. Modern thought, mainly under the influence of the empiricism of Hume and his positivist successors, and on the other hand under the influence of the transcendental idealism of Kant and the growth of modern science, denies the power of reason to prove articles of faith. This denial has resulted in the spread of doubt and a lack of certainty, and has led to questioning the veracity and authenticity of faith and religious life.

Some theistic philosophers have tried to bring back the previous laws of reason by showing the errors of empiricism and transcendental idealism and proving that science by itself not only does not rule out faith but also can help us in proving some articles of faith. In opposition to them, Kierkegaard and other fideists properly understood the threat to certainty from the objective claims of empiricism and modern sciences, but unfortunately they tried to find a subjective basis for faith. By placing certainty inside the human mind, they sought to keep it safe from any challenge of scepticism. Not only did they think that an objective attack on faith would pose no real threat to religious life, but they even considered an objective scepticism to have the advantage of making clear the subjective character of faith.[13] But this subjective certainty cannot long be maintained without objective evidence. If subjective certainty did not find objective support it would easily be eliminated, or else turned

---

[12] *Op. cit.,* Vol. 3, 220, No. 4272.

[13] Terence Penelhum, 'Fideism' in eds. Philip L Quinn and Charles Taliaferro, *A Companion to Philosophy of Religion*, Blackwell, Oxford, 2000, 377.

into blind fanaticism. We cannot live in this state of paradox: a wholehearted commitment to God whose existence our reason denies. Penelhum says: 'If I myself think that something I believe is truly paradoxical, then, although I may indeed come to believe it from a variety of causes (including the encounter with someone I think has divine authority), I will also have come to believe in its falsity. I will then have a conflict of beliefs ... The radical fideist evinces an inner conflict but mentions verbally that it is resolved.'[14]

Subjective certainty without objective support will be reduced to mere emotion and lose its inter-subjective character and we cannot defend it in a society in which certainty can be defended only in the language of objectivity. The Glorious Qur'an teaches us that we can find God's signs in everything through the use of our reason. Repeatedly when the Qur'an mentions something about creation, it immediately asserts that there are many signs of God there. 'Surely in that are signs for a people who reflect'(39: 42). I am not saying that every person can see these signs, but I only want to assert that one who has a reflective mind and is ready to see the truth can find objective evidence for his faith. We must not lose or even neglect our reason's ability to support faith, because by this denial or neglect we are disarmed in the struggle with the atheist and sceptic. Although I am sure that mere scientific knowledge as such does not contradict religious certainty, it is our duty to defend religious objective certainty in the face of every misguided interpretation of science that conflicts with faith. In summary, we must resist in the face of the evidential challenge[15] to faith and try to make the tradition of natural theology more vital and vigorous.

Causal threats

The evidential challenge of modern thought is important, but more important than this, I think, are the causes that give rise to religious skepticism and atheism today, such as poverty, the decline in morals and the abuse of religion to justify everything from terrorism to hedonism.

---

[14] *Op. cit.*, 380.
[15] For a full discussion of this challenge, see Alvin Plantinga, 'Reason and Belief in God', eds. Alvin Plantinga and Nicholas Wolterstorff, *Faith and Rationality*, University of Notre Dame Press, Notre Dame, Indiana, 1983, 17-39.

According to Islamic teaching, the external actions of humanity are not included in the essence of faith but have an inevitable influence upon it.[16] The Noble Qur'an concerning the relationship between faith and the performance of good deeds says: 'To Him good words go up, and the righteous deeds uplift that' (35: 10). On the contrary, doing evil results in a failure to see the signs of God and consequently in denying His signs. The Qur'an says: 'Then the end of those that did evil was evil: they denied the signs of God and mocked at them' (30: 10).

Thus, it can be said that the relation between faith and good deeds is like the relation between a tree and its fruits. Sometimes the tree is healthy, but for some reason does not bear any fruit. But if it never or hardly ever bears fruit, we say that the tree has died. Likewise, if one hardly ever performs good works, it would seem that one's faith has died. As believers, we have a duty not only to support faith by reasoning against sceptical challenges, but also to defend it against causes of scepticism. Here I cannot enumerate all the causes of scepticism but only refer to some important ones.

The absence of morality

Morality is usually related to controlling our emotions by our reason, a view accepted within the world's major religions. According to religious traditions, the moral life is not possible without one paying attention to purifying the soul and controlling our desires. We must try to be content with taking up the burden of purifying our souls in the way of salvation. Unfortunately, we are living in an age in which it is difficult even to speak of controlling our desires in accord with reason. Indeed it is commonly accepted that we not only have no duty to restrict our desires in accord with reason or religion, but also, on the contrary, many believe that our duties are established through the coordination of our desires. Religions teaches us that our emotions must be under the control of our reason to help us in the way of salvation. The Noble Qur'an says:

Have you seen him who has taken his wishes to be his God, and God has knowingly led him astray and set a seal upon

---

[16] Mohsen Javadi, *op. cit.*, 119-59.

his hearing and his heart, and put a covering on his eyes? Who shall guide him after God? Will you not remember? (45: 23)

Contrary to this teaching, modern culture teaches us that our reason must serve our desires; we must take our desires as our guide in life. Accordingly, we must not think about our desires, but only think about how we can satisfy them. There is no doubt that if our desires are not under the control of reason, they will lead us to deny those truths that are not compatible with our desires. The Noble Qur'an teaches us that some cases of denial of the Day of Judgement are not evidence-based but depend on some human desires:

> We are able to shape again his fingers, nay, but man desires to continue on as a libertine, asking, 'When shall be the Day of Resurrection?' (75: 4 and 6)

Poverty

According to religious teaching, poverty can be a cause for atheism. A person or a society that needs food and other basic necessities such as shelter, will not be in a good condition for observing moral rules and has no time for thinking of religious matters. They will be ready to sacrifice their human dignity to satisfy their urgent needs. The spread of prostitution and other vices are mainly the results of poverty. A religious scholar not only has a duty to answer theoretical problems challenging faith, but also has a duty to fight against poverty. Aristotle says:

> Happiness extends, then, just so far as contemplation does, and those to whom contemplation more fully belongs are more truly happy, not accidentally, but in virtue of the contemplation; for this is in itself precious. Happiness therefore, must be some form of contemplation.[17]

---

[17] Aristotle, 'Nicomachean Ethics' in *The Complete Works of Aristotle*, ed. Jonathan Barnes, Princeton University Press, 1863, Vol. 2, 1178b28.

However, religions urge us to struggle to provide good conditions of life for the majority of people. Facing demands from the people for his leadership, Imam Ali—who is famous for his private prayers and contemplative life—said that if God did not forbid scholars from neglecting the poverty of the majority while a minority is rich, he would have abandoned the leadership of the people.[18] The Imam knew that the poverty is the nearest thing to atheism and scepticism.

Conclusion

As religious believers, we must try to keep the fortification of the city of religion, that is certainty, safe from the various threats to it. We must try to use natural reason to prove or support the articles of faith in order to show that religion is not contrary to reason. On the other hand, we must try to provide a good context for religious life, by trying to expand morality in its correct meaning and by removing poverty and the different forms of discrimination from the society.

---

[18] See Imam Ali, *Nahj al-Balāgha*, Sermon Al-Shiqshiqīyah.

A CHRISTIAN REFLECTION ON WORK, CULTURE AND SOCIETY

Catherine Cowley

If an employee, faced with an ethical issue at work, were to propose a solution based on religious belief and conviction, it is increasingly possible that her colleagues would be surprised. Indeed, some of them would go further and be offended. It would be argued that, whilst such reasoning might be appropriate for her private life, it has no place in a public context. It is, of course, not only religiously based personal morality which is expected to defer to public morality; but it is especially vulnerable to this sort of exclusion due to the widespread notion of privatized religion.

Many factors contribute to this situation. This paper will concentrate on a few of those which are heightened in the context of economic activity, factors which present particular challenges to uniting faith and daily activity. These challenges are simple to list. They include postmodernism, especially its rejection of grand narratives of knowledge and emancipation; secularism, or perhaps a better term is de-traditionalization;[1] reductionistic materialism; the arguments of many theorists that religion has no place in the public forum as it is inherently divisive.

It is not so simple to see how they can be responded to. As Christians we have absorbed and contributed to these social conditions. We accept, sometimes unthinkingly, sometimes not, the presuppositions of those around us. The increasing attenuation of the Christian social heritage means that the common Christian horizon has more or less vanished in many areas. Thus, culture and society no longer intrinsically support being a Christian.

---

[1] This term may be preferable as the secularisation thesis is placed under increasing doubt. See D Herbert, *Religion and Civil Society: Rethinking Public Religion in the Contemporary World*, Ashgate, Aldershot, 2003; ed. P L Berger, *The Desecularization of the World: resurgent religion and world politics*, Eerdmans, Grand Rapids, Mich., 1999. It is also preferable as it points to the increasingly 'free-floating' nature of much religion and spirituality.

Following the Second Vatican Council (1963-65), particularly under the influence of *Gaudium et spes*, there was what appeared to be a successful attempt to reconcile culture and faith. With a renewed articulation of Catholic social teaching and the development of liberation theologies the notion of privatized religion seemed to be countered. There was the presumption that the values of Christian faith and modern culture shared the same dynamics and therefore should not exclude one another. What was considered good in human terms was identified in Christian terms as part of God's plan. Christians, by their manner of living and participating in modernity, strove to provide a constitutive place for modern rationality and its thirst for knowledge and emancipation in their faith reflection.

The cultural shift from modern to postmodern, however, means that today the very possibility of shared discourse about meaning, values, purposes, is being challenged. Postmodern theorists assert that we can no longer seriously pursue questions of purpose and objective meaning. Others may not go quite so far, but it is difficult to deny that fewer and fewer convictions are held in common, and public discourse suffers increasing fragmentation as subjectivism and relativism increase. In a pluralistic context Christian faith is seen as just one option among many. Life and faith no longer simply overlap. Life is seen as a highly multi-interpretable concept, and beliefs about the world must be explained in terms of their social, political or psychological usefulness to human beings. 'God' only 'explains' anything for 'those who believe in God.'

Christians today are also postmodern people. We participate in a culture in which God's role has been obscured and in which profoundly human or religious experiences no longer refer us directly and automatically to the God of Jesus. Instead it is often argued that appeals to God only reveal the psychological needs of those who continue to believe in God. Religion has been described as 'less a public affirmation of faith than a private consolation, along with philosophy, literature and cricket, against the cruel indifference of the world, personal failure and inevitable death.'[2] In such circumstances, it can seem foolhardy to suggest that there can be unity between faith and daily activity.

Furthermore, postmodern theorists would argue that such an aim must fail. The self, they suggest, is inescapably multiple and fragmented.

---

[2] D J Goldberg, *The Independent*, 26 April 2003, 24.

This is due, amongst other things, to the diversity of roles which people inhabit, the complex, numerous relations we have, the multiple forms of discourse in which we take part and the social construction of gender. Therefore to attempt to live an integrated life would be either illusory or oppressive; illusory because such an attempt would need to deny the multiplicity of the self, or oppressive because it would have to impose a false unity.

Yet such unity of life is integral to the Christian vision. The Christian tradition, with its strong emphasis on the active presence of God in the world insists that the whole of life is to be lived in conformity to God's will. Therefore all aspects of our existence should be ordered to serve the end of virtuous and pious living. This includes economic activity. Unlike some other religious traditions, Christianity has never held that an escape from the economic realities of life is the ideal for a religious person. Rather, the religious relationship with God comes in the midst of the living of daily life, and economic dimensions of that life are as religiously significant as any other. Justifying the claim that unity of faith and life is still possible requires examining in more detail some features of contemporary culture. The connection between faith and life means that theological ethics must respond in a Christian manner to the basic moral question of how we should live. It is this question which is at the heart of moral reflection. It is not a question about the immediate. Neither is it a question about what I should do now or next. Rather it is about a manner of life.

The rise of modern thought—and particularly modern science with its abstraction from questions of purpose—sundered fact from value and left us with the challenge of finding a ground for ethics that could not be reduced to individual preference or social convention. Postmodernity, with its rejection of the credibility of modern master narratives intensifies this challenge. Contemporary culture increasingly lacks orientating patterns of integration. We move quickly among so many different experiences, contexts and value schemes that the question, 'Who am I?' becomes hard to answer. Many experience their self as fragmented, dispersed through a multiplicity of roles, purposes, and values. The narratives which served to keep the many fragments together in a meaningful cohesion appear to have been lost.

All except one. There is one narrative which increasingly assumes the mantle of master narrative, which establishes patterns of integration, meaning, and identity. It has become so all-encompassing that we increasingly fail to notice it. It has become 'the way things are.' It is the narrative of economism: the narrative that forces everything and everyone into the perspective of the market. It is the running of society as an adjunct to the market, with profit the only standard of excellence.

Economics, through its role as master narrative, operates as a secular religion. I do not think that our theological reflection adverts sufficiently to the religious nature of economics. I am here going beyond the commonplace of seeing shopping as a religion. This is merely a symptom of something far deeper and more pervasive. When theologians engage with economics we tend to deal with it as a technical subject, with technical phenomena as its outcomes. We see it as an empirical science which can, or cannot, be refuted using the standard analytic and evaluative tools of modernity. For example, we ask if this form of the economy can deliver social justice; or does this example of economic practice exploit the poor or not. These are obviously important points, but in responding in this way we miss its most significant and powerful level. As a secular religion it is extremely successful. It utilises the techniques of both modernity and postmodernity; and in its neo-conservative, free-market form it is, I suggest, one of the most significant challenges that theistic religion faces.

Its nature of secular religion is expressed, for example, in the religious characterisation of the market. Capitalism operates within a perception of the market as having the status of an external, independent, transcendental sphere, separate from society but imposing fixed and eternal laws on all people, at all times, in all places. Its implicit value system is, in essence, another formula for saving the world, this time through economic progress.[3] It contains an implied theology to explain how evil can be banished from the world. In broad brush terms that theology runs something like this. Evil exists because people are driven to it by their material circumstances—the very struggle for survival forces people to lie, steal, cheat and so on. In this way material scarcity functions as original sin. If scarcity forces people to sin, secular salvation will come from a world of material abundance through devotion to economic efficiency. Economic expertise will guide people to this abundance, freeing

---

[3] For the interpretation of modern economic analysis as a secular religion, see R H Nelson, *Reaching for Heaven on Earth: Theological Meaning of Economics*, Rowman & Littlefield, Savage, Md, 1991.

them to realize their true and uncorrupted natures. Thus economists must be the 'priesthood' as they have the knowledge to save humanity.

Not least among the attractions of this approach for many people is the way that the root cause of evil is placed nicely outside our responsibility. It plays to our instinct to claim that 'it's not my fault.' This leads to an attitude whereby moral and individual problems are subordinated to the collective problem, to the total economic system. This leads to the displacement of all responsibility for the problems of greed, envy, theft, covetousness, injustice and so on, onto what are presumed to be the objective interplay of economic operations. This, in turn, leads to the tendency for ethics to 'disappear', apart from questions such as distribution, due to the assumption that, whatever the problem might be, I, the individual, can do nothing until the 'system' is perfected. All I have to do is to campaign for socialism, or free-market liberalism (or whatever), and as soon as society's problems are solved, I shall be just and virtuous—effortlessly.

Within this secular religion advertising assures me that by submitting to the embrace of the market I will find myself, whole and entire. It is through consumption that the individual receives identity. It is conferred through the market. Ultimately what is bought is unimportant. It is the purchasing process itself which becomes central and which clothes itself in religious features: the wide airy spaces of shopping malls are our new cathedrals, temples to consumerism and places of pilgrimage.

Religion itself becomes functionalised by the market. As Taylor has noted, the modern world is a disenchanted place.[4] With postmodernity, however, there is a re-enchantment—although this time an enchantment which the market has moved in on.[5] De-traditionalized and stripped of its classic integrative dimension by the continued assertion of the primacy of choice, religion becomes a commodity on the market, to be chosen (arbitrarily) by the consumer. People are still free to believe what they like; in fact, the need for some sort of spiritual life is increasingly recognised. The market is quite capable of meeting the needs generated

---

[4] C Taylor, *Sources of the Self: the making of modern identity*, Cambridge University Press, Cambridge, 1989.

[5] This re-enchantment is not limited to a market phenomenon, but goes much wider. For example, see J D Caputo, *The Prayers and Tears of Jacques Derrida*, Indiana University Press, Indianapolis, 1997.

by such a spiritual life. Demand can be met through a welter of artefacts, rituals and experiences under both generic and brand names. Thus the 'religious' person is presented with all the necessary items to compose their religious identity according to their own choice of 'pick-and-mix' components. The illusion is fostered that individuals are capable of giving themselves an identity, whereas the reality is that it is the market which has given it.

It is not surprising, therefore, that an employee's colleagues find the proffering of religiously-based moral reasoning somewhat bizarre. Religious identity is increasingly seen as a life-style choice which speaks of our personal development and personal fulfilment: religion as personal hobby. In the public world, religious identity is not considered either primary or necessary. It is, therefore, not a valid basis for coming to decisions in a public context. To suggest otherwise might well be viewed as intolerant of other people's valid choice of lifestyle.

This subverts one of the most basic moral questions of human life—the question of what identity-conferring commitment(s) ought to characterize and guide our lives. It is not the commitments which I have (some given, some chosen), commitments which carry values through time, which ground and guide my choices. Now it is my consumer choices, whimsical, arbitrary, fleeting, which bestow my identity, an identity which, apparently, can be taken up and discarded at will. We can reinvent ourselves continuously. To quote an advertisement for a watch, 'Who will you be for the next 24 hours?' Choices are only a matter of what works, and therefore have no existential or ethical meaning. Increasingly, expediency becomes the only viable option for my moral decisions, as principle cannot operate in the world of the arbitrary. This, then, reveals the first of the great challenges: how can my personal identity be grounded so as to enable me to come to moral identity?

The arbitrary nature of a market-conferred identity, if it does not lead to expediency, will increase relativism. The usual definition of relativism is well known: the belief that there are no objective moral values that transcend either culture or the individual. Equally well known are the standard objections to it, developed in innumerable articles and books. It is not less culturally pervasive for all these refutations. The standard objections will not be repeated here. Instead, I will note a couple of features which bear particularly on the situation of the employee.

Persons act in diverse social roles in numerous social practices which seem to have their own local moral rationality. No values are superior to other values, because there is no such thing as truth. In the public sphere the space left by the absence of a comprehensive notion of truth will be filled by power and vested interests. The interests of dominant groups will come to dictate the events of daily life and instead of independent criteria for truth, group biases will be considered sufficient. This renders opposing perspectives impotent. This is particularly marked in the sphere of work. Economic groups and interests exert considerable political and social power, not least by the way in which economic, instrumental rationality has contributed to the privatization of other modes of truth. In addition, the work environment will be affected by two particular features.

The first relates to morality of the specific organisation within which the person works. Some commentators suggest that business organisations are not proper subjects for ethical enquiry; only individuals are. Ladd asserts

> We cannot and must not expect formal organisations or their representatives acting in their official capacities to be honest, courageous, considerate, sympathetic, or to have any kind of moral integrity. Such concepts are not in the vocabulary, so to speak, of the organisational language game.[6]

The second is the question of the morality of the market itself. Hayek, whose influence remains enormous, suggests that it is no more sensible to discuss the morality of the market than it is to discuss the morality of the climate.[7] He bases this on the assertion that market outcomes are not directly chosen or intended by the individual. Rather they are the cumulative result of a multiplicity of separate, individual decisions. Paradoxically, then, the market, rather than being a social

---

[6] Quoted in R C Solomon, *Ethics and Excellence: Cooperation and Integrity in Business*, Oxford University Press, Oxford, 1992, 132.

[7] F A Hayek, *The Constitution of Liberty*, Routledge, London, 1960. There are, of course, many economists who adopt a different approach, but within business corporations, especially transnational ones, many elements of Hayek's analysis, and those of his followers, remain operative.

practice with its own, relative, moral rationality, is presented as a social practice with no moral rationality.

However, those who believe that they can dispose of ethics and the posing of value questions overlook the fact that economic activity places enormous moral demands on individuals. It requires a moral attitude that the economy alone cannot produce. Whilst the economy can show the individual the relative prices and the optimal allocation of his or her resources for certain goals, it cannot relieve that individual of the choice between goals and values. Ladd's view requires that the employee live his or her life in discrete compartments, operating as a different type of moral agent in different contexts.

However, the extensive literature on corporate culture makes clear that the working environment is not neutral. Any organisation quickly evolves some sort of corporate culture which will contain either implicit or explicit moral expectations. Schein[8] describes culture as a model of basic assumptions—invented, discovered or developed by a particular group as it learns how to confront its problems of external adaptation and internal integration—that have been influential enough to be considered valid and consequently taught to new members as the correct way of perceiving, thinking about and experiencing these problems.

Study of these cultures has verified that many of the thoughts and actions of individuals in organisations are culturally influenced. Individuals can act and operate according to different standards and criteria depending on the context. In addition, socialisation processes in organisations are usually aimed at shaping individuals to fit into a normative structure.[9] The values of the organisation shape the expectations of managers and staff and their views about 'right' and 'wrong' behaviour in a corporate context. The question then arises of how the members of that organisation can evaluate the demands of the culture in which they find themselves. Ladd's perspective would not allow for this to happen. What it would entail, however, is that the role of business practitioner must take precedence over all other roles.[10] In this view, if one's personal

---

[8] E H Schein, *Organisational Culture and Leadership*, San Francisco, 1985.

[9] See, for example, A Kennedy and T Deal, *Corporate Cultures*, Addison-Wesley, Reading, Ma, 1982; L K Trevino, 'A Cultural Perspective on Changing and Developing Organizational Ethics', *Research in Organizational Change and Development*, Vol. 4, 1990, 195-230.

[10] This is explicitly the case in A Carr's classic article 'Is business bluffing ethical?', 1968, reprinted in eds. G D Chryssides and J H Kaler, *An Introduction to Business Ethics*, Chapman and Hall, London, 1993, 108-18.

morality is such that it conflicts with business practice, that person either has to suppress that morality or give up business. Once again we see the assertion of a necessary distinction between public and private morality.

The position adopted by Ladd, Hayek, and many others, masks the place of the market as ideology. As with all successful paradigms, its fundamental assumptions tend to be taken for granted, no longer to be questioned, no longer only one possible alternative among different types of economy and behaviour. What happens is that it claims to prove what it in fact assumes, namely the Smith/de Manville dictum that pursuit of self-interest via the market processes serves the common good.

Both Ladd and Hayek display an unjustified faith in the mechanical workings of the market. As long as it is believed that the invisible hand of the market leads to beneficial results, the question of the morality of the market, and therefore of institutions operating within it, is avoided. As long as it is believed that only impersonal market forces guide the economy, no moral decisions have to be made. The invisible hand makes all decisions and choices; nobody is supposed to have any market power. The striving for profit maximization is all that is required, both of firms and of individuals.

When questions of morality are relevant only for individuals, not for institutions, these institutions tend to become ends in themselves and cannot accurately be described as morally neutral.[11] However, if there is market power, if business practitioners are making deliberate choices and decisions that influence others' lives, there must be guiding norms for such decisions. If the market is a mere social fact, as Hayek maintains, just as the climate is a natural fact, then it is beyond the control of those who work in it. But, if the market is not totally beyond our control, if we can—at least to some extent—influence the circumstances within which we act, then the question of the morality of our decisions and actions does arise. We are back with our opening problem.

I said earlier that the heart of ethics is about a manner of life. I have also suggested that it is identity-conferring commitments capable of carrying values through time which should ground and guide moral choices. It follows, then, that ethics addresses the question of the project to which we ought to commit our lives. For theological ethics this is the

---

[11] Kathryn E Kuhn 'Social Values and Bureaucratic Reality', eds. Gerard Magill and Marie D Hoff, *Values and Public Life: an interdisciplinary study*, University Press of America, London, 1995.

question of the moral meaning of Christian faith. This moral meaning cannot be restricted to the purely personal (if there is such a thing.) There is a false dichotomy between public and private morality—they are both on the same continuum. Conscience cannot be privatised. As Tracy puts it, no Christian 'alert to the radical theocentrism at the heart of theology can rest content with the fatal social view that religious convictions are purely "personal preferences" or "private opinions."'[12] All very well, but if it were as simple as that, we would not have the problems we do.

Part of our problem arises from the schematic way that morality is often handled in the Catholic tradition, at least at the pastoral level. The *Catechism of the Catholic Church*[13] adopts a typical approach. When it treats the practical outworkings of morality, it does so by examining the Ten Commandments which it divides into two blocks corresponding to the two great commandments of Christ (Mark 12: 29-30). The first block, consisting of commandments one to three, is discussed under the heading 'You shall love the Lord your God with all your heart, and with, all your soul, and with all your mind.' These deal with what the *Catechism* describes as 'our duties towards God'. The second block, consisting of commandments four to ten, is discussed under the heading 'You shall love your neighbour as yourself' and deals with our relations with one another.

In general, moral reflection in the Catholic tradition flows from this second block. It is where the overwhelming majority of the Church's moral teachings is located. It also forms the basis of most ethical discussion with those of other beliefs or none. It is not hard to see why it is much easier to confine ethical discussion in the public sphere to this second block, which is more likely to be accepted as being relevant to daily life. There exist some areas of commonality across a wide spectrum of groups and beliefs. It is possible to find at least some common ground on which to build, such as 'does this action/this type of action lead to human flourishing?' It is an approach which is, however, quite inadequate to address the challenges identified here. Because the tendency is to look at discrete acts or types of act, it can quickly reduce the moral life to quandary ethics: specific actions viewed from the minimalist perspective

---

[12] D Tracy, 'Defending the Public Character of Theology' in *Christian Century*, 1 April 1981, 350-6, 351.

[13] *Catechism of the Catholic Church*, Geoffrey Chapman, London, 1994.

of being right or wrong. Vision, moral imagination, virtue, goals and many other aspects of the moral life do not easily find a home in such an approach. Such aspects become subordinated to an understanding of morality based primarily on a legal model. It reduces Christianity to moral precepts.

In the face of such a situation there is no one solution which will solve all the issues, no magic bullet. But there is one ingredient which, I believe, could make a significant contribution. It is one which is deceptively simple sounding. I say 'deceptively' because it is, I suggest, rather like Wendell Holmes's 'simplicity on the far side of complexity'. It is based, not on the morality of acts, but rather in the universal call to holiness outlined in *Lumen Gentium,* which reveals the exalted vocation of all the faithful in Christ. The suggestion is that the question of the 'project' to which we commit our lives, a commitment which both grounds our identity, and is capable of carrying values through time, and removes the false dichotomy between public and private, is the project contained in the first commandment: 'I am the Lord your God … you shall have no other gods before me.'

My core identity can be summed up in the statement, 'I am the person I am because God is *this* God.'[14] If I am created in the image and likeness of God, and if God creates *ex nihilo*, then I am constantly held in being by God; I continually emerge from out of the creative impulse of God. My identity as me is being continuously confirmed, rooted and strengthened. It is embodying an aspect of the infinite, inexhaustible God. Nothing can remove this identity; no matter what I do I cannot discard it. It is not arbitrary, not re-inventable. It is given. This choice, because it is God's choice, has both existential and ethical meaning.

It might be objected that this notion is still a privatised one, a variation on 'me and Jesus'. It lacks a social dimension. This can be answered in several ways. It is true that there is an intensely 'private' dimension, if by that is meant intimacy. This God is, as Augustine put it, 'nearer to me than I am to myself.' Faith, seen as participation in God means that one identifies with God because that is where one's focus is fixed. Life then becomes a continual interaction with God, fed by God.

---

[14] I am here pointing to a Trinitarian understanding of the creating God. See, for example, I Delio, 'Does God "Act" in Creation? A Bonaventurian Response', *Heythrop Journal*, Vol. 44, no. 3 (July 2003), 328–44.

Aquinas, in his theory of charity, which is both theological and ethical, conceives the union between the human being and God as one of friendship,[15] a conception which indicates the threadbare nature of considering the first commandment solely under the heading of 'duty'. However, alongside this is Aquinas' treatment of the inner unity between the love of God, self and neighbour,[16] which he develops from the New Testament presentation of *agape*. There it has the constant meaning of the creative love of God for human beings, the responsive love of human beings for God, and included in that love, the love of human beings for one another. Many today would wish to add here that it includes the love of human beings for the whole of God's creation. The moral life is seen in terms of the person's multiple relationships with God, self, neighbour and the world.

So here we can see the beginnings of how this notion can provide a basis for our social morality. It provides motivating reasons, as well as justificatory ones. The source and ground of moral values is not social convention, human creativity or personal preference. The source and ground of value is God. '"My God" is not a name that provides for a good night's sleep, but a passion that disturbs our rest and keeps us on the alert.'[17] Morally and religiously serious people are interested in transforming the world, making it better. And this faith in God can be united with daily life, as moral injunctions may be unified as distinguishing characteristics of a single way of life, the life of living the first commandment. The demands of discipleship are based on the uniqueness of God before whom everything else disappears. Everything is an application of the first commandment.

A second answer, which highlights the indivisibility of the personal and the social, lies precisely in the identity of the 'we' of the Church. If I, as an individual Christian, have my identity because of who this God is, then so do we, who are the People of God. It liberates us from the modern myth that we are really solitary beings, each pursuing his or her own private good in fierce competition. The deepest truth of our human nature is that we are not, as the market insists, selfish and greedy, but rather that we hunger and thirst for God and in God we find each other, for we meet others at the depth at which we allow ourselves

---

[15] *Summa Theologica*, II–II, q. 23 ff.

[16] *ST*, II–II, 25–26.

[17] Caputo, *The Prayers and Tears of Jacques Derrida*, 334.

to be met by God. Human life finds its unity in adoration of the one God. The commandment to worship the Lord alone integrates us and saves us from endless disintegration.

Another objection is that, due to its particularity, this approach will be divisive. To take the first commandment as a main foundation for social ethics will lead to a return to the ghetto. Catholic social teaching seeks to engage in dialogue with 'all people of good will' and it has done so on the basis of human reason. However, I would argue that this objection is based on an overly optimistic view of what Catholic social teaching achieves. Despite a move away from an organic vision of society to one which more readily acknowledges the reality of conflict, Catholic social teaching still assumes that religion should ultimately serve a unifying function for the culture and society.[18]

Such an assumption claims too much. We cannot ignore the boundaries separating moral communities. Sometimes they are irreducible. Acknowledging these boundaries, however, does not mean that discourse between different communities is impossible. What it does require is that we avoid trying to find and impose an illusory semblance of commonality. I am not seeking to dismiss the value of the search for commonality, indeed it is vital, but to suggest that we must allow for moral differences. If Christians do not, why should others? Pluralism is real, and cannot be airbrushed out of the picture by attempting to present differences as largely superficial, merely different ways of expressing a common experience.[19] Commonality and consensus are not to be so easily found. Moral particularity is not something to be afraid of; rather it is the place where we must begin our moral and ethical reasoning. The Church either subordinates its witness to an externally defined agenda or it identifies from within its own tradition its own authentic social mission and the grounds of its own identity.

It might still seem that this notion only worsens the problem with which I began. I do not think so, and I believe that there is no alternative. We communicate the integrity or fragmentation of our lives

---

[18] This is true not only at the level of official magisterial teaching. Theologians such as David Tracy share the same fundamental assumption. See, for example, D Tracy, 'Theology, Critical Social Theory and the Public Realm', eds. D S Browning and F S Fiorenza, *Habermas, Modernity and Public Theology*, Crossroad, New York, 1992, 19–42.

[19] This is one reason why the search for a 'Global Ethics' is problematic. See, for example, H Kung, *A Global Ethic for Global Politics and Economics*, SCM Press, London, 1997.

in the manner of our responding to the questions which life poses us. One of the myths of modernity is that the good is a matter of choice and that such choice is an exercise of objective, uninvolved reason. In the Christian tradition, however, the moral self is characterized by the radical willingness to be open to God implied by the first commandment, leading to involvement. Engagement, not retreat, is the real possibility and demand of faith. We must live the expectation, the hope, 'the hope against hope' in a transforming future. Without that hope we are reduced to the present, the immediate and to mechanistic rationality

In the context of postmodernism, truth cannot be claimed merely on the basis of the authority of institutions or institutional leaders. This will be resisted as an imposition. Not only must we live the hope, we must also live the truth, do the truth. Truth is not a claim, it is witnessed to by how we live. Our relationship with truth is personal, not abstract. When that truth is God, we do not possess it but love it. As Rahner said, 'the Christian of the future will be a mystic or will be nothing at all.'[20] A Christian, like other people, tends to see the world initially with him or her self at the centre. We ask: 'What place does God have in my life?' We need constantly to re-learn that the question is: 'What place do I have in God's life?' This leads to seeing, evaluating and judging all things in relation to God, to unifying all our actions into the one project to which we can commit ourselves—God's project for us as individuals and for the world. We lose our very selves if we concentrate our ethical reflection solely on actions.

---

[20] K Rahner, *Theological Investigations*, Vol. 7, 15.

THE VALUE OF LIFE IN ISLAM
Mohammad Ali Shomali

There is no doubt that life in all its forms enjoys a very high status in Islam. Life is a divine quality and a gift of God. It is only God who can bring to life and again it is only He who can put an end to the life of living beings. Human life is one of the most sacred entities created by God. Therefore, it must be appreciated, respected, protected, and taken care of. Human life must not be manipulated, neither in its beginning, nor in its end. Reproduction must occur in the context of a legitimate and stable family. Human life must be regulated according to divine instructions, that is, to its best and towards a fully human one. Abortion, euthanasia and suicide demonstrate a lack of respect for human life and are morally wrong.

Among God's attributes and names in the Islamic scriptures, 'the Living' (*al-Ḥayy*) is one of the most obvious and outstanding ones. The Qur'an says:

> And put your trust in the Living one who dies not, and glorify His praise... (25: 58)

> He is the Living, there is no god but He, therefore call on Him, being sincere to Him in obedience. All praise is due to God, the Lord of the worlds. (40: 65)

Who is the giver of life and death?

This is one of the basic questions in bioethics which can entirely influence one's approach towards life and its treatment. If one believes that life is created by chance or that it can be created by man himself then it loses its sanctity and the result would be that it can also be destroyed by chance or by man. But if life is a gift of God who are we to take it away?

God is the only source of life. In other words, all forms of life are originated by Him. This is an idea on which special emphasis has been put in the Qur'an. For example, we read:

> Verily, it is God who causes the seed-grain and the fruit stone (like date-stone) to split and sprout. He brings forth the living from the dead, and it is He Who brings forth the dead from the living. Such is God, then how are you deluded away from the truth? (6: 95)

> And a sign for them is the dead land. We give it life, and we bring forth from it grains, so that they eat thereof. (36: 33)

Thus, life is a gift of God, for which we are held responsible. Not only is it only God who gives life, but also it is only God who brings life to an end. For example, we read in the Qur'an:

> There is no god but He. It is He who gives life and causes death—your Lord and the Lord of your forefathers. (44: 8)

> …You bring the living out of the dead, and you bring the dead out of the living. And You give sustenance to whom You will, without limit. (3: 27)

> It is He Who gives life and causes death. And when He decides upon a thing He says to it only: 'Be!'—and it is. (40: 68)

> Say (to them): 'God gives you life, then causes you to die, then He will assemble you on the Day of Resurrection about which there is no doubt. But most of mankind know not.' (45: 26)[1]

The Qur'an blames those who attribute death to things like travelling or fighting or illness or to people.

---

[1] There are many more verses referring to the fact that life and death are exclusively created by God, e.g: 3: 156, 9: 117, 10: 31, 22: 6, 30: 4, 50: 43, 53: 44, 57: 2, 67: 2.

O you who believe! Be not like those who disbelieve and
say about their brethren when they travel on the earth or
go out to fight: 'If they had stayed with us, they would not
have died or been killed,' so that God may make it a cause
of regret in their hearts. It is God that gives life and causes
death. And God is All-seer of what you do. (3: 156)

According to the Qur'an, refuting Nimrod's claim of deity, the
Prophet Abraham said [to him]: 'My lord is He Who gives life and causes
death.' (2: 258) Nimrod said: 'I give life and cause death.' *(Ibid.)* Then he
asked for a prisoner who was supposed to be executed to be released and
another prisoner who was not supposed to be killed to be executed.
When Abraham saw the depth of Nimrod's ignorance or deception
concerning the real meaning of giving life and causing death and the
acceptance of the people who were present, he said to Nimrod:

'Verily, God causes the sun to rise from the east; then cause
it you rise from the west.' So the disbeliever was utterly
defeated. And God does not guide the unjust people. *(Ibid.)*

Now, let us reflect on the real meaning of giving life and causing
death. Does it mean that nothing other than God can bear on or become
involved in the process of giving life or causing death? Obviously, not.
For example, reproduction is certainly a form of involvement in the
process of life. It is also true about feeding and catering. Children feel
indebted towards their parents for their life. On the other hand, a murderer
is held responsible for—in a sense—causing death to his victim.[2] It is
true that Nimrod or even his agents could have a significant role in the
death of the victim. However, it is still true that 'it is God that gives life
and causes death.' (3: 156) So was Abraham's argument against Nimrod
that 'My lord is He Who gives life and causes death.' (2: 258)

The great Shi'a exegete of the Qur'an, Sayyid Muhammad
Husayn Tabataba'i writes:

When Ibrāhīm [=Abraham] mentioned life and death, he
meant life and death as we find them in living things. His

---

[2] Even more, whoever can save an innocent life but stays indifferent and lets the person die
is morally responsible.

argument was that these living things could only be created
by One who was the source of life. Lifeless nature cannot
bestow life on others when it has no life itself …

If Namrūd [Nimrod] had interpreted Ibrāhīm's argument
honestly, he could not have refuted it at all. But he resorted
to deception, interpreting life and death with an allegorical
meaning. 'To give life' really means, for example, to create
a living foetus; but it may be used equally correctly (but in
a metaphorical way) if you rescue someone from an
extremely dangerous situation. Likewise, 'to cause to die'
really means the act of God by which a soul departs from a
body; but metaphorically it may be used for murder, etc.
(*Mīzān*, 1982, vol. 4, p. 184)

Thus, it is possible to suppose that man and natural environment
can have a role in the process of giving life and causing death. The
reason is this: in this world God usually acts through natural rules and the
cause-effect system.[3] It is also possible to suppose that natural factors and
circumstances may have a role in something being created or brought
into existence.[4] However, it is only God who truly and genuinely brings

---

[3] Of course, there have been miracles and extraordinary acts performed by the Prophets or
holy people. These may seem to contradict the general rule mentioned above: 'In this
world God usually acts through natural rules and cause and effect systems.' However, it
must be noted first that miraculous and extraordinary acts do not represent the *usual*
procedure, and second, that even in the case of such acts there is no exception to the
cause-effect system. The only difference is that instead of natural causes supernatural causes
are used. Just as there are natural causes, say, for the treatment of an ill person, there may be
supernatural causes, such as prayer and giving charity.

[4] Muslim philosophers divide beings into two main groups: beings of the Universe of
Command (*'Ālam al-Amr*) and beings of the Universe of Creation (*'Ālam al-Khalq*). For
the existence of the first group, there is no need for material conditions. This is related
to abstract beings (*al-mujarradāt*) whose creation only depends on God's command, that
is, 'Be!' For the existence of the latter, material conditions are needed. This is related to
material beings (*al-mādīyāt*), whether they be material just at the beginning or they
remain material forever. Here the Divine command for their existence is not issued
before that completion of necessary conditions, such as the existence of an apple after
the existence of natural conditions like water, heat and light or after the existence of
supernatural conditions. In other words, for the creation or existence of the first group
it is only an originating cause (*al-'illah al-fā'ilyah*) which is needed, but for the creation
of the latter group both an originating cause and a material cause (*al-'illah al-mādīyah*) are
needed.

into existence or gives life.[5] We humans have no control or even complete knowledge of our existence or life. So how is it possible to suppose that we can grant existence or life to something else?

The sanctity of life

All forms of life are precious and are considered as signs (sing. *al-āyah*) of God. However, among all forms of life in the material world, human life is the most outstanding and the most precious. Referring to different stages of the creation of mankind, the Qur'an says:

> And certainly We created man of an extract of clay. Then We made him a zygote in a firm resting-place. Then We made the zygote a clot, then We made the clot a lump of flesh, then We made (in) the lump of flesh bones, then We caused it to grow into another creation, so blessed be God, the Best of creators.' (23: 14)

The above verse refers to different phases of the creation of man. The first part, i.e. creation from soil, refers to the creation of the first man, that is Adam. The next part refers to the creation of Adam's offspring, generation by generation. Human life is so important that God mentions its development step by step and finally after reference to the creation of spirit—which is considered as *khalqan ākhar*—says: 'Blessed be the Best of creators!' (23: 14) If the Creator of man is the best of Creators, man himself must be best of creatures—at least potentially.

Life is one of the greatest gifts and blessings of God and must, therefore, be appreciated and respected. Killing an innocent person is not only considered as a criminal act (i.e. murder), but also represents an underestimation of and insult to human life as a whole. This fact is interestingly expressed in the following verse:

> For this reason We prescribed to the Children of Israel that whoever slays a soul, unless it be for manslaughter or for

---

[5]   It has to be noted that God may revive something in hand with which He is pleased. For example, the Qur'an talks about Abraham who was practically shown how God gives life to the dead. (2: 260) Another example is Jesus who was able to 'bring the dead to life with God's permission'. (3: 49)

mischief in the land, it is as though he slew all men; and whoever keeps it alive, it is as though he kept alive all men; and certainly Our messengers came to them with clear proofs, but even after that many of them certainly act extravagantly in the land. (5: 32)

One may conclude from the above verse that:

a. Causing death to one person unjustifiably is like causing death to all people. In other words, lack of respect for an individual life demonstrates lack of respect for life as such and, therefore, for all individual lives.[6] This is in addition to the fact that whoever commits a murder is likely to murder more people and endanger all people.[7]

b. Giving life to one person or more precisely saving one person out of one's respect for life is like saving all people (from dangers that kill).

c. Causing death to a murderer or someone who does mischief on the earth is permitted since it demonstrates respect for the lost life and prevents further dangers and damage to life as a whole. This is why the Qur'an considers necessary legislation on retaliation and even regards it as a

---

6   Commenting on the above verse, 'Allamah Tabataba'i writes:
    The Divine words: 'whoever slays a soul, … it is as though he slew all men,' are an allusion to the fact that all men have one single reality, that is humanity in which all are united, and one and all are equal in it; whoever attacks the humanity found in one of them, attacks the humanity found in all of them'. (*Al-Mīzān*, trans. Sayyid Akhtar Rizvi, 2001, vol. 10, 146) It is narrated in both *Al-Kāfī* and *Ma'ānī al-Akhbār* that the fifth Imam of the Shi'a, Imam al-Bāqir, was asked: 'How can it be as though he slew all men, while he had slain a single soul?' The Imam replied: 'He will be put in a place in Jahannam (Gehenna) where the punishment of the people of the Fire reaches its utmost limit; if he had killed all men, he would have entered the same place.' The narrator again asked: 'Then if he killed another (man)?' Imam replied: 'The punishment will be increased for him.' According to the verse, this *hadith* and other *hadiths*, 'Allamah Tabataba'i concludes that 'equality is in the nature of punishment and difference will be in intensity of punishment and the effect it will have on the killer.' (*Ibid.*, 152)
7   According to a *hadith* from the Prophet Muhammad, the heart of man admits aspiration and fear unless he sheds blood unjustifiably. When he sheds blood unjustly his heart becomes perverted and very dark so that he does not recognize the good. Nor does he condemn the evil. (*Kanz al-'Ummāl*, no. 39951)

source of life, though it prefers pardon when there is no
fear of threat to the security of the public.[8]

In Islamic law and morality, murder in general and the murder
of believers in particular, is very severely treated to the extent that the
Qur'an sets out an everlasting punishment of hell for those who deliberately
commit such an act. We read also in Islamic *hadith*s that the destruction of
the whole (non-living) world is less vicious in the eyes of God than the
murder of an innocent person.

Animal life

We also find in Islamic *hadith*s that even the killing or destroying of
animals unjustifiably is very severely treated. For example, Imam Sadiq,
the sixth Imam of the Shi'a, referes to the divine punishment of a woman
who had tied up a cat with a rope so that the cat could not move and
died of thirst.[9] A typical view among the Shi'a jurists can be found in
the following passage by 'Allamah Mohammad Taqi Ja'fari:

> Consideration of all the sources of Islamic jurisprudence
> (*fiqh*) leads to the conclusion that animals must not be killed
> unless there is a legal permission [from God] such as
> benefitting from them or being safe from their harm. There
> are adequate reasons prohibiting the hunting of animals for
> sport and one can argue from these reasons for the
> prohibition of killing animals without having a permitted
> cause.[10]

The above idea is part of a broader Islamic perspective on animal
life. According to Islamic law, there are many rights for animals that
must be observed. Consideration of those rights shows that not only their
life must be protected, but also the quality of their life must be observed.
For example, animals must not be burdened by forcing them to carry

---

[8] For example, see the Qur'an (2: 178 and 179).

[9] Muhammad Baqir Majlisi, *Biḥār al-Anwār*, Beirut, 1983, Vol. 76, 136.

[10] *Rasā'il-i Fiqhī*, Tahdhib va Mu'assasah-yi 'Allamah Ja'fari, Tehran, 2002, 250. Elsewhere he
writes: 'Hunting animals for amusement and without need is prohibited. Therefore, if
someone makes an excursion for such hunting, his hunting is a sinful hunting'. (*Ibid.*, 118)

heavy goods or to move faster than they can tolerate. Neither can animals be cursed or sworn at. It is reported that Imam 'Ali said: 'Whoever curses an animal he himself will be cursed by God.'[11]

The beginning of human life
Human life must not be tampered with in its beginning

Owing to the high value of human life, Islam attaches a very special regard to it before it starts and this continues after it ends with death. The only proper and legitimate way for having a child is through marriage. In other words, a male and female may have a child only when they appreciate the value of human life and therefore are committed to take the full responsibility of bringing up a child in the sacred institution of the family. Marriage is not just a financial or physical arrangement for having sexual relations or living together. Nor is it just a legal contract between a man and woman. Marriage is a sacred covenant between the two and God is the witness of it. Marriage is a gift of God for human beings to complement each other and to console each other. The Qur'an says:

> Among His signs is [the fact] that He has created spouses for you from among yourselves so that you may console yourselves with them. He has planted affection and mercy between you; in that are signs for people who contemplate. (30: 21)

> God has granted you spouses from among yourselves, and granted you children and grandchildren by means of your spouses. He has provided you with wholesome things. So will they still believe in vain things and be ungrateful to God's favour? (16: 72)

The violation of this sacred covenant by adultery or by homosexual relations is unlawful and is unanimously rejected by all Muslim scholars. It seems also immoral to use modern biotechnology to bypass

---

[11] *Ibid.*, cited from *Wasā'il al-Shī'ah*, Vol. 8, 356.

marriage and reproduce human beings artificially and out of the context of the family. Of course, a married couple may use legitimate biomedical techniques for parenting. The Qur'an says:

> He is the One Who created humanity from water. Then he established blood ties as well as in-laws. (25: 54)

Human life must be respected from its beginning

On the beginning of life, a typical Islamic point of view can be found in the following statement by the Islamic Organization for Medical Sciences:

> *One:* The inception of life occurs with the union of a sperm and an ovum, forming a zygote which carries the full genetic code of the human race in general and of the particular individual, who is different from all others throughout the ages. The zygote begins a process of cleavage that yields a growing and developing embryo, which progresses through the stages of gestation towards birth.
>
> *Two:* From the moment a zygote settles inside a woman's body, it deserves a unanimously recognized degree of respect, and a number of legal stipulations, known to all scholars, apply to it.
>
> *Three:* When it arrives at the spirit-breathing stage, the time of which is subject to controversy, being at either 40 or 120 days, the foetus acquires greater sanctity, as all scholars agree, and additional legal stipulations apply to it.[12]

When does human life start?

Islam considers having children as a great gift of God and highly recommends people to get married and establish family ties and have

---

[12] The full minutes of the Seminar on 'Human Life: Its Inception and End as Viewed by Islam', held on 15 January 1985, in Kuwait. (http://www.islamset.com/bioethics/incept.html)

It has to be noted that this organization is not a Shi'a organization. However, what has been mentioned above is in general acceptable to both Sunni and Shi'a Muslims.

children. However, Islam does not compel people to get married or have children after marriage unless there is an overriding (secondary) reason which makes marriage and the formation of a family or having children necessary. For example, if the only way to protect one's piety and chastity is to get married or, if the protection of the people of faith from the attacks of enemies depends on the increase in the number of the members of the society, it becomes compulsory to get married and have children.[13]

Thus, Islam allows family planning to prevent pregnancy, but does not allow its termination.[14] Now, naturally the question arises as to when pregnancy starts and whether the beginning of pregnancy coincides with the beginning of human life or not.

Regarding the beginning of pregnancy from a religious point of view, the question is whether pregnancy begins

1) with the entering of semen into the uterus or
2) with the fertilization of an ovum by a sperm in the fallopian tube or
3) with the implantation of a fertilized ovum in the uterus?

As we saw above, 'from the moment a zygote settles inside a woman's body, it deserves a unanimously recognized degree of respect, and a number of legal stipulations, known to all scholars, apply to it.' In other words, it is the combination of the above three things that constitutes religious pregnancy. The Qur'an uses the word *haml* to describe pregnancy (see the Qur'an, 19: 22; 31: 14; 46: 15). In Arabic, the term *haml* means 'to carry', and this starts when the zygote is implanted in the uterus and not before it. The late Ayatollah Khu'i said: 'The criterion in applying the [word] "pregnant" for a woman is correct only after the settling

---

[13] In his *Marriage and Morals in Islam*, Chapter Four, Scarborough, S M Rizvi writes:
According to the Shi'ah *fiqh*, family planning as a private measure to space or regulate the family size for health or economic reasons is permissible. Neither is there any Qur'anic verse or *hadith* against birth control, nor is it *wajib* [obligatory] to have children in marriage. So basically, birth control would come under the category of *ja'iz*, lawful acts. Moreover, we have some *ahadith* (especially on the issue of *'azl*, *coitus interruptus*) which categorically prove that birth control is permissible. Later he adds that 'the majority of our mujtahids believe that coitus interruptus is allowed but *makruh* [disliked] without the wife's consent' (*Sharh al-Lum'ah*, vol. 2, 28; al-'Urwah, 628; *Minhaj*, vol. 2, 267).

[14] Family planning in itself is not forbidden, but there are methods of family planning which are not allowed. The details are discussed by Muslim jurists.

down *(istiqrār)* of the sperm in her womb because just the entering of the sperm in her womb does not make her pregnant.'[15]

Thus, from the very beginning of the pregnancy its termination is prohibited and the zygote must be protected. The respect shown to the zygote at this early stage does not necessarily mean that it is a real human being.[16] The zygote is in a state of active potentiality to become a human being with the full genetic code of the human race in general and of the particular individual. As we saw above in verse 23: 13, the implantation of the ovum in the uterus constitutes the first stage of the creation of man. According to a *hadith*, Isḥāq b. 'Ammār asked Imam al-Kāzim whether it is permissible or not for a woman who feared pregnancy to drink some liquid to abort what was in her uterus. The Imam replied: 'No.' Isḥāq said: 'That is the zygote *(nutfah)*.' Imam replied: 'Verily the first thing to be created is the zygote.'[17] However, it is only later when the spirit is created that it becomes a real human. For this reason Shi'a jurists, like the late Ayatollah Khomeini, Ayatollah Khamenei, Ayatollah Lankarani and Ayatollah Sistani, declare that it is allowed to abort the foetus to save the life of the mother before the spirit of the foetus is created. But after the spirit is created, it is not allowed to sacrifice the foetus for the sake of the mother.[18]

Abortion

As suggested above, Islam prohibits abortion unless there is an exceptional situation in which case the *Sharī'ah* permits it as a lesser evil.[19] Abortion after the spirit is blown is a case of infanticide and the Qur'anic

---

[15] *Ibid.*, cited from al-Gharawi, Mirza 'Ali, *Al-Tanqī' fī Shar'-i al-'Urwat al-Wuthqā* (notes of the *fiqh* lectures of Ayatollah al-Khu'i), vol. 7, 206 (Al-Adab Press, Najaf, 1988). S M Rizvi adds that in 1987 he wrote to Ayatollah al-Khu'i asking him whether it is permissible to use a medicine or a device which prevents the fertilized ovum from implanting itself onto the wall of the uterus. The Ayatollah replied that it is forbidden to abort the zygote after its settling down, whereas [to prevent pregnancy] before that, is alright. *(Ibid.)*

[16] As we saw earlier in the discussion about animal life, the necessity of respect for life is not limited to human life.

[17] *Wasā'il al-Shī'ah*, vol. 19, 15.

[18] *Aḥkām-i Pizishkī*, compiled by M Ruhani and F Noghani, 107-125.

[19] For example, see Article 1.e of OIC (Organization of Islamic Conference) Declaration on Islamic Human Rights, 1990.

condemnation of killing one's children applies to it. On infanticide, the Qur'an says:

'Kill not your children for fear of want. We shall provide sustenance for them as well as for you. Verily the killing of them is a great sin.' (17: 31)

'Kill not your children on a plea of want. We will provide sustenance for you and for them. Come not near shameful deeds whether open or secret. Take not life which God has made sacred except by way of justice and law. Thus He commands you that you may learn wisdom.' (6: 151)

'The pledge of the believing women that they shall not kill their children.' (60: 02)

'And when the female infant who was buried alive is asked for what crime she was killed?' (81: 2)

Islam severely condemned the practice of the pagans who killed their children because of poverty or out of shame at the birth of a girl. Unfortunately we see that today millions of abortions take place every year. Most of these abortions take place because the 'liberated' people of our age would like to enjoy a life of sexual freedom. These are the people 'who have taken their religion [way of life] to be mere amusement and play and were deceived by the worldly life.' (7: 51)

The end of life

Islam places great emphasis on the sanctity of life and at the same time on the reality of death. Indeed, to have a better appreciation of life one needs to remember death and that there is no way to escape from it. It is only then that one realizes that it must benefit from one's life optimally. Thus, unlike what many people feel today, Islam considers the remembrance of death to be a source of vitality and spiritual power. About one third of the Qur'an talks about the Resurrection, death and life after death. For example, we read:

Every soul shall have a taste of death. (2: 35)

No soul can die except by God's permission. (3: 185)

'Everyone is created for a life span and dying is a part of the contract [with God] and the final decision [of term] is up to God. The quality of life is equally or more important than the duration of living.'[20] In his supplication for noble individuals *(Makārim al-Akhlāq)* Imam Sajjād, the fourth Imam of the Shi'a, asks God:

> Let me live as long as my life is used is serving Thee. When my life becomes a pasture for Satan, be pleased to call me back to Thee before Thy wrath advances towards me or Thy anger be fixed upon me.

It seems to me that one can distinguish between saving a respected life (which is compulsory in Islam) through medical treatment, financial support or otherwise, and prolonging life artificially.[21] For example, someone is dying because of an advanced cancer and there is no treatment for him. The most that can be done is to use medicine just to keep him alive for few days. The cost of this medicine is so high that the whole family will be greatly troubled. Is it necessary for the patient himself or for his relatives or for others to take this measure? Or if this can be done by a very painful operation, is it necessary for the patient to undergo such an operation while there is no possibility of a cure? It seems reasonable to suggest that 'the physician and the family should realize their limitations and not attempt heroic measures for a terminally ill patient or to prolong artificially the life (or misery). The heroic measures taken at the beginning of life (i.e. saving a premature baby) may be more justified than at the end of a life span, though each case has to be treated individually.'[22]

Euthanasia: Islam is against euthanasia (mercy killing). Muslim jurists regard euthanasia as an act of murder. Murder can be committed with a

---

[20] Dr Shahid Athar, 'Islamic Perspectives in Medical Ethics' at http://islam-usa.com/im18html.

[21] This is the author's humble view which he takes to be in compliance with the views of Muslim jurists. However, the issue needs further investigation.

[22] *Ibid.*

gun or with a syringe by a serial killer or by a physician or even by the murdered man himself. For example, Ayatollah Khomeini declared that any measure for hastening the death of someone is considered as a murder.[23] Or as Ayatollah Makarim Shirazi declares:

> Killing a human being even out of mercy (euthanasia) or with the consent of the patient is not allowed. He argues that the main argument for such prohibition is that the verses and the *hadiths* which indicate the prohibition of murder *(qatl)* apply to such cases. The philosophy beyond this prohibition may be the fact that permitting such acts leads to many misuses and for any weak and trivial excuses acts of euthanasia or suicide may take place. Moreover, medical judgements usually are not certain and there have been cases in which people who had no hope for life were mysteriously saved from death.[24]

Suicide: If we have not created our life and it is just a gift of God for which we are held responsible, it is obvious that we have no absolute power over our lives. We have our life in trust from God and we must take care of it to the best of our ability. This is the case with all blessings of God, whether they are physical or spiritual. We can benefit from them, but we cannot destroy them or waste them. No one should say I want to burn my property or harm my health or damage my reputation. Our situation in this world is like a guest who is invited to someone's house. Whatever is there in the house is put out by the host for the benefit of the guest. However, the guest cannot burn himself inside the house or destroy the house or the things put there. This comparison becomes more interesting if we add that our body is also like a guestroom for our spirit and we must observe regulations for using this room set out by God. We must try to please God by preserving life and health, by promoting the quality of life and alleviating suffering.

---

[23] *Aḥkām-i Pizishkī*, 180.
[24] *Ibid.*

RELIGIOUS SOCIALIZATION IN CONTEMPORARY IRAN

Mahmood Taghizadeh Davari

This paper consists of three parts. In the first part, I shall provide a brief explanation of some key elementary concepts, i.e., family, religion, socialization, religious socialization, and on the importance of family and offspring in the Islamic texts. In the second part, I deal with a philosophical question: 'Do our children have the right to be religious?' In response to the question, I provide a comparative theoretical discussion about two opposite educational theories: that of liberal fostering and that of religious training. While criticizing the liberal argument, I strongly support the religious training of children by their families and other educational institutions. And in the third part, which is devoted to the process of religious socialization in contemporary Iran, I shall describe in some detail the processes and procedures which help Iranian children to become religious.

Explaining some key concepts
Family

Family is generally regarded as a group of male and female individuals directly linked by kin connections, who support each other economically and emotionally, and whose adult members assume responsibility for caring for children. Kinship ties are connections between individuals, established either through marriage, or through the lines of descent that connect blood relatives (mothers, fathers, other offspring, grandparents, etc).

Human historiography in all three monotheist scriptures—the Old and New Testaments and the Qur'an—begins with the story of a couple, Adam and Eve, who were husband and wife, even in Paradise. (2: 35; 7: 19, 27; 20: 117) This interesting, meaningful story has, at the same time, a clear message for our present family supporters: the family legally consisting of male and female (and not of two males or two females) is the only authentic form in history. This natural form of family must be protected, and the other deviant types must be rejected for the sake of human health and survival.

Sociologically, the family is considered as one of the primordial social institutions in human history. Since the existence of man, the family unit has manifested itself throughout all civilizations, be they of a religious or irreligious constitution. All people have been nurtured within a family setting, albeit different in structure (e.g. extended, nuclear, lone-parent, etc), and the majority of adults in most societies, have participated in wedlock.[1]

Religion

It is often said that religion is something so individual, so elusive and diverse that it defies definition. It can mean almost anything to just about anyone. That is not the view of theorists like the American contemporary anthropologist, Clifford Geertz. In his widely recognized essay, 'Religion as a Cultural System', Geertz offers his most sophisticated definition of religion as 'a system of symbols which acts to establish powerful, pervasive, and long-lasting moods and motivations in men by formulating conceptions of a general order of existence and clothing these conceptions with such an aura of factuality that the moods and motivations seem uniquely realistic.'[2]

However, religion can be, in a less complicated sense, considered as a set of beliefs, creeds, behaviours, rituals, values, norms, and symbols which are connected to the Divine realm, transcendent /supernatural matter, and spiritual beings. It too has co-habited with man throughout all societies—civilized and primitive—sustaining his/her sublime needs. Religiosity is even observed in contemporary secular and communist states whereby political governing forces have eradicated or suppressed religious customs/practices, eliminating them from the social scene. However socially-deprived it may have been, religion has continuously endured within people's private lives and has survived throughout their daily literature. Hence, after the collapse of the Soviet block and other communist states, one witnessed, for example in Poland and Russia, the

---

[1] A Giddens, *Sociology*, Polity Press, Cambridge, 1996, 390 and 391.

[2] C Geertz, 'Religion as a Cultural System' in C Geertz, *The Interpretation of Cultures: Selected Essays*, Basic Books, New York, 2000, 90.

revival of religious establishments and the restoration of religious customs into society. Therefore, it is apparent now, as Geertz pointed out, that as functionalists claim, a religion is always shaped by its society; it is no less true that a society is also shaped by its religion.

Socialization

At birth, children have few of the qualities, apart from the physical ones, that we expect of human beings. They have no opinions about religion, politics, or science. Human beings are not just created in a physical manner, but also in a social manner. If people were left on their own after birth, merely being fed and physically cared for, they would not develop into recognizable human beings. They would not be able to talk, perhaps even to walk, or to understand others. In effect, they would merely be animals. What changes human beings from animals into the social beings we recognize as members of a given society, is the process of socialization. It is the process whereby the helpless infant gradually becomes a self-aware, knowledgeable person, skilled in the ways of the culture into which he/she is born. The learning process begins in childhood from those closest to them, such as family and friends (primary socialization), but continues throughout life by learning social rules (secondary socialization). This takes place in school, at the mosque or church, at university, at work, through the mass media (television, radio, newspapers). The growing child, through contact with other members of his society, gradually learns the language, beliefs and behaviour, including religious belief and practice, of his own community in which he/she is brought up.[3]

Religious socialization

Religious socialization comes to mean a process whereby the people of a given society gradually become aware of their religious system, and establish their understanding and perception of the spiritual matters. Children begin to make themselves familiar, through formal and informal,

---

[3] Giddens, *Sociology*, 60; S Moore, *Sociology Alive*, Stanley Thornes Ltd, Cheltenham, 1992, 1.

systematic and unsystematic, planned as well as unplanned instructions, with religious authorities and conform themselves to religious rules. They may progressively develop their intellectual and emotional faculties towards entities and personalities so that they will grow in faith towards them. Therefore, religious socialization is regarded as the process of training one's spiritual conscience, i.e. his/her consciousness, understanding, awareness, knowledge, judgment, feelings, emotions, and motives related to the divine realm. As the child gets older, he/she expresses himself/herself as a religious person and experiences spirituality. However, some may not find an interest in religion, and may develop an atheistic worldview and ideology. They may pursue a free life and appeal to hedonism. Nevertheless, they become, to some extent, through this process, aware of the religious beliefs, rituals, ordinances, values, norms, and symbols respected in their society.

As a result of this process, a child's knowledge and information about God, prophets, religious authorities, spiritual leaders, the connection between the supernatural realm and natural universe, the mechanism of the circulation of the cosmos, the connection between the human and the divine realms, and so on are normally expanded, as their feelings, emotions, and spiritual motivations towards God and His saints are promoted. The practitioner of this area gradually learns the examples of God's love and affection towards His creatures, and becomes familiar with the patterns of His resentment, anger and power. He/she learns, little by little, how and by which mechanism, he/she can promote his/her faith and religiosity, and achieve God's satisfaction. At the same time, he/she may develop a self-confidence and inward-consent, and represent him/herself as a true, honest, and sincere believer. In short, religious socialization may be explained as 'the simultaneous gradual (formal and informal) educating of one's rational and emotional capacities towards divine and spiritual matters.'

Religious education may also be used in another context. It may come to mean 'approaching the many religions of the world with an attitude of understanding and trying to convey that attitude to children'.[4] However, it is necessary to recognize a distinction between the two meanings, for both these types can be classified under the term 'religious education'. While the first meaning is the dominant form of

---

[4] G Moran, 'Religious Education', ed. M Eliade, *The Encyclopaedia of Religion*, Simon and Schuster, London, 1995, vol. 11, 319.

religious education in all parts of the world, the second use is a relatively recent development, with the teacher describing various religions rather than seeking to convert learners to a particular faith.[5]

Criticizing the second meaning, it can be argued that children are children and should not be treated like the mature persons. Religion is generally a multi-dimensional and a very complicated system. It includes many theoretical issues and questions which are not easily understood by children, and also cannot be tackled by an ordinary teacher. It is for the good of the children that this type of education awaits the age of intellectual maturity.

The importance of family and offspring in the Islamic texts

A significant portion of the Islamic texts (the Qu'ran and the *Hadiths*) deals with the concept of family and family issues. These texts are generally in three forms: one form is historical, explaining the family life of the Divine Prophets, i.e. the moral situation of their parents, wives and children, and also their societal environments. Another form which is of a philosophical nature, offers arguments for the necessity of marriage, the positive functions of family, the harmfulness of free sexual relations, the right of children to have a clear and clean descent, male and female socialization, and so on. The third form is normative, exploring the religious rules about marriage, the mutual duties of marriage partners and children toward each other, and the legal issues relating to family life and so on.

Regarding the first form, the Qur'an explains the dispute between Cane and Abel (the sons of Adam and Eve) over a certain religious issue, sacrifice. It should be noted that they were both brought up in a similar family background, and shared a similar family training, and were naturally religious. Nevertheless, one of them committed a crime and killed his brother, perhaps for his evil psychological motives. (5: 27-31)

The story of Noah and his son is another Qur'anic story. Although Noah's son grew up in a religious family environment and had benefited from the ethical/religious instructions of a great, pious father

---

[5] R M Thomas, 'Religious Education' in eds. T Husen and T N Postlethwaite, *The International Encyclopaedia of Education*, Elsevier Science, Oxford, 1994, vol. 9, 4996.

such as Noah, the effects of his social environment, i.e. friendship with peer groups, had overcome his family education and had made him an irreligious, deviant, and refractory youth who affiliated with transgressors. (11: 42-6)

Abraham's story in the Qur'an is related to our subject in two ways: 1) the debate with his father (or uncle) over the obscenity of atheism and idolatry; his support of faith in God and theism; the severe difficulties he faced for his faith which, in turn, demonstrate the mutual positive role of children in modifying their parents' attitudes and behaviour (6: 74; 21: 51-71; 27: 84-94); 2) the strong influence he had on his children especially on Ishmael and Isaac and on his grandson, Jacob, in such a way that they were fascinated by the sheer charisma of his personality, and were all ears to his orders. However, they became the spiritual leaders of their own branch after their Abraham. (27: 101-13; 2: 124-33)

The story of Moses is, without exaggeration, the longest historiography of a divine prophet in the Qur'an. Although he was born in the religious family of 'Imrān, Moses was brought up in Pharaoh's aristocratic, corrupted royal palace. However, he benefited from his mother's care and also his mother-in-law's protection, 'Āsiyah, the pious believing wife of Pharaoh. Then he developed in himself through divine guidance and strong will, faith in God and struggled against corruption when he was considered too young to combat his seemingly well-established ruling family. He shaped a new religious society as well as a religious family of his own, thus ultimately becoming a role model for his nation and thereafter. (28: 7-14; 20: 38-40)

The story of Mary and the roles of her parents and her preceptor Zachariah in her religious fostering are clearly explained in the Qur'an. It is from this well-educated, pious mother that Jesus Christ, the Great Prophet of Allah was born and fully trained under her supervision. According to the Qur'an, he was, even in his childhood, saying words of wisdom and vision, and had the message of the Divine for his people. (3: 35-52; 19: 16-35)

However, there exists almost no Qur'anic report about the Prophet Mohammad's family events, i.e. his parents, childhood and his children. Only in one verse, is it mentioned that he was an orphan and received divine care and shelter (93: 6). But these issues were specifically reported in Islamic historical sources. In fostering his sense of morality and religiosity, the roles of his pious mother, Āminah, his grandfather,

411

'Abd al-Muṭṭalib, his uncle, Abu Ṭālib, his nurse, Ḥalīmah Sa'dīyah, have been explained in detail in these sources. The social environment of Mecca was corrupted and idolatry was widely practised; nevertheless, his extended family environment was monotheistic and humanitarian. They were the only followers of Abraham.[6]

However, a relatively minor part of the Islamic family sources deals with the philosophical issues of the family. For instance, a number of Qur'anic verses state that marriage partners are created from one soul, and each party (according to the Islamic ideal type of family) completes the other. (4: 1; 7: 189; 39: 6) A family is planned by God to provide peace and tranquillity (30: 21). It is also reported by the Prophet Muhammad that in Islam no construction has been built dearer to God than marriage; it is the most precious thing to Allah. Marriage is a sanctuary that protects half the religiosity of a person; the majority of the people in hell consists of unmarried people who have not been able to safeguard their piety.[7] However, it is also reported that Imam Ali b. Mūsā al-Riḍā (the eighth Imam of the twelver Shī'a) said that free sexual relations and adultery lead to corruption, interruption and disorder in the family institutional structure, i.e. destroy family ties, create difficulties in children's regular fostering, and cause problems over inheritance.[8]

Almost the overwhelming part of the Islamic family texts have a normative structure, and each includes a moral rule or a legal ordinance. They are considered the authentic sources for Islamic jurisprudence and ethics, and are, in fact, the ultimate references of the Islamic jurists and moralists.

According to a Qur'anic verse, marriage is generally recommended, even if the couple are in poverty and seemingly not able to earn their livings. Allah will give them the means out of His grace (24: 32). Marriage is regarded as a tradition *(Sunnah)* of the Prophet Muhammad. Therefore, Muslims are asked to follow the Prophet's tradition, i.e. they are recommended to marry at a young age in order to protect their faith and to have children.[9] The children must be fully nourished: 'The mothers shall suckle their children for two whole years;

---

[6] Ibn Hisham, *Al-Sīrah al-Nabawīyah*, Dār Iḥyā' al-Turāth al-'Arabī, Beirut, nd., vol. 1, 165-204.

[7] Ḥurr al-'Ā'milī, *Wasā'il al-Shī'ah*, Dār Iḥyā' al-Turāth al-'Arabī, Beirut, n.d., 3, 5,8;

[8] Ṣadūq, M, *'Ilal al-Sharā'i'*, Dār Iḥyā' al-Turāth al-'Arabī, Beirut, 1385/1966,479.

[9] Ḥurr al-'Āmilī, *Wasā'il al-Shī'ah*, vol. 1, 2-6.

if the mother desires to complete the term of suckling herself, on the father shall be the cost of her food and clothing in fairness'. (2: 233) Although divorce is permitted in Islamic law, it is regarded as the most unfavoured matter before God. The Divine throne *('Arsh)* would be shaken by divorce.[10] Therefore, it must be left only for a time of necessity.

In short, family life and child rearing have a clear origin in Islamic sources. It has been strongly supported by the Prophet, by the Imams, and by the Muslim communities throughout Islamic history. Sociologically, it has played a positive role for the strength, health and continuity of human civilization. Therefore, it must be protected from the recent destructive waves of homosexuality and feminism, which affects all types of religious family structure.

Do our children have the right to be religious?

Does a child have a right to receive religious instructions and to be fostered as a religious person? In other words, do the parents (at the first step, and the school and the government, at the next step) have a responsibility towards the religiosity of our children, and therefore, do they have to facilitate matters to promote the religious talent and spiritual inclination of our children?

According to Principle 2 of the 'Declaration of the Rights of the Child' (proclaimed by UN General Assembly Resolution 1386 (XIV) of 20 November 1959), 'the child shall enjoy special protection, and shall be given opportunities and facilities, by law and by other means, to enable him to develop physically, mentally, morally, spiritually and socially in a healthy and normal manner and in conditions of freedom and dignity. In the enactment of laws for this purpose, the best interests of the child shall be the paramount consideration.' Principle 7 declares that 'the child is entitled to receive education, which shall be free and compulsory, at least in the elementary stages. He shall be given an education which will promote his general culture and enable him, on a basis of equal opportunity, to develop his abilities, his individual judgement, and his sense of moral and social responsibility, and to become a useful member of society. The

---

[10] *Ibid.*, vol. 15, 266–68.

best interests of the child shall be the guiding principle of those responsible for his education and guidance: that responsibility lies in the first place with his parents.' Clarifying this principle, however, Principle 10 advocates that 'the child shall be protected from practices which may foster racial, religious and any other form of discrimination. He shall be brought up in a spirit of understanding, tolerance, friendship among peoples, peace and universal brotherhood, and in full consciousness that his energy and talents should be devoted to the service of his fellow men.'

In his well-known essay, 'Liberal Values and Liberal Education', Mark Halstead,[11] a contemporary philosopher of education, supports the liberal fostering, training and education of children. He argues that liberalism provides the theoretical framework of values that comes closest to the actual political and economic circumstances that prevail in Western societies generally. He also argues that there are three fundamental liberal values which influenced the dominant concept of education in the West. These are as follows:

> 1) individual liberty (i.e. freedom of action and freedom from constraint in the pursuit of one's own needs and interests);
> 2) equality of respect for all individuals within the structures and practices of society (i.e. non-discrimination on irrelevant grounds);
> 3) consistent rationality (i.e. basing decisions and actions on logically consistent rational justifications).

He then continues that the central strands of liberal education may be best understood in terms of the liberal framework of values outlined above. The vision of education which these values encompass has come to dominate Western educational thinking. All the values typically associated with liberal education—including personal autonomy, critical openness, the autonomy of academic disciplines, equality of opportunity, rational morality, the celebration of diversity, the avoidance of indoctrination, and the refusal to take side with any definitive conception of the good—are clearly based on the three fundamental liberal values of

---

[11] J M Halstead, 'Liberal Values and Liberal Education', eds. J M Halstead and M J Taylor, *Values in Education and Education in Values*, The Falmer Press, London, 1996.

freedom, equality and rationality, as, indeed, is the more recent emphasis in liberal educational thought on democratic values, citizenship and children's rights. Halstead has gone so far as to suggest that liberal education is the only justifiable form of education. In the final section of his essay, which is devoted to the challenges to liberal education, Halstead illustrates the most fundamental challenge to liberal education. It comes from those who do not share the above mentioned basic values. The values of liberalism and liberal education, as he illustrates, are broadly incompatible with Marxism, radical feminism, postmodernism, and various religious worldviews, including the Roman Catholic and the Islamic, which claim that liberalism lacks a moral and spiritual foundation.

Almost all Islamic thinkers, as well as other monotheistic thinkers who support religious education, share a common view about the human nature. They agree that human beings are uniquely in possession of a divine innate nature—*fiṭrah* (a unique type of creation)—which may guide and lead, inwardly, human beings in a search for God and righteousness. It is appropriate, therefore, that children's fostering, training and education should be based upon principles that would be in accordance with their divine nature and could actualize their spiritual personality. Otherwise, it could damage their sense of spirituality and produce a barrier to their religiosity. It is reported of the Prophet Muhammad that he said 'all children are born in accordance with their divine nature, though they might be misguided by their parents.'[12]

Muslim philosophers assume that human beings are not an accidental or thrown-away uncared for creature, existing on earth; rather, they are both internally (esoterically) and externally (exoterically) sustained and cherished by the Lord's grace. It is reported from Mūsā b. Ja'far (the Seventh Imam of the Twelver Shi'a) that 'Allah has two types of proofs/ authorities *(ḥujjah)* for man; one at outside, that are his apostles and prophets, and the other at inside, that is Man's wisdom/intellect *(al-'aql).*'[13]

It must be noted here that although the children have the right to receive religious instruction, they should be totally free to develop by themselves their sense of morality and spirituality. They must be informed and not indoctrinated, encouraged and not punished, guided and not mandated, motivated and not forced.

---

[12] M B Majlisī, *Biḥār al-Anwār*, Mu'assisat al-Wafā', Beirut, vol. 2, 1403/1983, 88.
[13] M Kulaynī, *Al-Kāfī*, Dār al-Kutub al-Islāmīyah, Tehran, 1388/1969, vol. 1, 16.

Muslim scholars also support the idea that children have been entitled to particular rights in Islamic sources. According to a report from 'Alī b. Ḥusayn l-Sajjād, the Fourth Imam of the Twelver Shi'a) 'It is a right of your child to know that he/she is from you and related to you; you are responsible for what you have taken in charge, i.e. his/her sense of morality *(ḥusn al-adab)*; to lead him/her towards the Lord and to help him/her to be obedient to Him. In respect to him/her, behave like a person who knows that he will be rewarded if he does good for him/her, and will be punished if he mistreats him/her.'[14]

Referring to this type of report, the Islamic theorists come to a conclusion that it is also a duty of the parents to provide a ground for the promotion of the morality and religiosity of their children, in the same way as they should try to improve the material conditions of their life. While there is no mention of the right of having a clear family descent in the Declaration of the Rights of the Child, it is regarded as a right of children in Islamic sources. According to several Islamic traditions, children have the right to be brought up in a legally established family. It is told of the Prophet Muhammad that he said 'Marry (a woman) from your own status *(kufw)*, and choose a proper/pious location for your genes.'[15] According to Principle 3 of the Declaration, the child is entitled to have a name, regardless of it being worthy or unworthy. However, according to the Islamic family texts, it is a right of a child to have a worthy name. It is reported of Imam 'Ali (the first Imam of the Shi'a) that he said 'The first good thing that a person does for his/her child is to call him with a decent name.'[16] It is also narrated that a man asked the Prophet Muhammad 'What is the right of my child over me? The Prophet replied: 'Call him with an appropriate name, train him properly, and settle him at his proper social position.'[17]

Religious socialization in contemporary Iran

It might be useful, first of all, to clarify, in more detail, the term religious socialization. As mentioned before, almost all children spend the initial

[14] M Ṣadūq, *Al-Khiṣāl*, Mu'assisat al-Nashr al-Islāmī, Qum, nd., 568. H b. Shu'bah al-Ḥarrānī, *Tuḥaf al-'Uqūl 'an Āl al-Rasūl*, Mu'assisat al-Nashr al-Islāmī, Qum, 1363/1984, 263.
[15] Ḥurr al-'Āmilī, *Wasā'il al-Shī'ah*, vol. 14, 28.
[16] Al-Kulaynī, *Al-Kāfī*, vol. 6, 18.
[17] *Ibid.*, 48.

years of their lives with their families. They are strongly under the influence of their parents, relatives, and friends, ethically and psychologically as well as socially. They learn their language, become aware of their beliefs, and imitate their behaviour and conduct. If their family environment is of a religious constitution, the children will, accordingly, begin to repeat religious words and expressions, to simulate the religious deeds and actions of their family. They may attend ceremonies (in churches/mosques) with their parents; they may sing, pray and supplicate in ways similar to their parents. In short, they copy their family's religious behaviour. In contrast, if the parents and the family environment are not religious they do not find, at this initial stage, the opportunity to establish their mental religious foundation. The family is the primary socializing agency of the child during infancy, and plays a definite and irreplaceable role towards establishing the child's first positive or negative outlook towards the religious system. But at later stages of their life, many other socializing agencies come into play. Children will receive formal and informal religious instruction at school, in the library, with their peer group, in the mosque/ church, at work, even in sport, on television, on the radio, in the newspapers, in the cinema and the theatre. In other words, society fosters, educates and teaches its religious doctrines to its members through these agencies.

The process of religious socialization in Iran through the above mentioned agencies includes the following activities.

Family

—Provision of a decent name for the newborn. Indecent names are formally rejected.

—Recitation of the *Adhān* (first call to prayer) and *Iqāmah* (final call to salvation) in the right and left ear of the newborn baby, respectively.

—*Taḥnīk*: the process of gently applying the soil of Karbalā' upon the lips of the newborn.

—*'Aqīqah*: offering the sacrifice of a sheep (or a cow) after the birth of a child.

—Circumcision of boys.

—*Ta'wīdh*: attaching a sheet of the Qur'an to the baby's clothes to protect him from possible dangers.

—Shaving the head of newborns and then donating gold or silver equal to the weight of the hair of the child for charitable purposes.

417

—Dressing newborn babies with special clothes resembling Ali Aṣghar (the infant son of Imam Husayn, the second Imam of the Shi'a) during the mourning days of Muḥarram.

—Training children to kiss sacred things such as the Qur'an, the holy shrines, the soil of Karbalā' and so on.

—Training children to participate in charitable activities.

—Training children to take part in religious feasts and ceremonies held for *Nadhr* (special prayer on special occasions including reciting the Qur'an, supplications and offering food).

—Children's imitation of their parents' prayers, fasts and other religious practices.

—Training small girls to wear *ḥijāb* (the Islamic veil).

—Children's participation in mosques accompanied with their parents for daily and Friday prayers.

—Headbands worn by children during the mourning ceremonies held in Muḥarram.

—Learning of male socialization of boys and female socialization of girls.

—Playing the role of *Mukabbir* (a guide for the prayer congregations).

Nursery schools, elementary schools, high schools and colleges

—Teaching of the Qur'an, prayers, and religious ordinances to the children at different levels.

—Participation in morning formal rituals and communal prayers.

—Taking courses in theology and religious dogmas.

—Going on pilgrimage; visiting the holy shrines, religious places etc.

—Participation in school/college religious programmes held on various religious occasions.

Peer groups

—Observing religious rites performed by youths themselves.

—Taking part in religious ceremonies (rites) held in mosques, religious centres, etc. in the neighbourhood.

—Participation in decorating mosques, religious centres, etc. during the special religious occasions.

—Offering services to the public in tents during the special religious ceremonies (of the month of Muḥarram, Sha'bān and so on).

Workplace (occupational group)

—Performing ritual prayers in the prayer rooms of factories and workshops.
—Taking part in feasts and religious ceremonies usually followed by serving meals.
—Going on pilgrimage and religious tours.
—Taking part in occasional religious competitions followed by the awarding of prizes.
—Establishing a group bank for charity works and offering loans to the needy without usury.

Mosques, Ḥusaynīyahs, Takīyahs and other religious centres.

—Taking part in ritual prayer, Friday prayer, supplication, and religious ceremonies.
—Charity works.
—Offering services to the public including financial and medical assistance, food, etc.
—Taking part in Basīj to learn how to defend the country.

Mass media: radio, television, journals and newspapers

—Providing articles, programmes, films, interviews and so on about religious doctrines, dogmas, beliefs, rituals, values, norms, symbols, religious authorities, scholars, pious people, holy shrines, religious places, religious history and so on.

Conclusion

Although the mass media has played a significant role in recent years as regards the religiosity or non-religiosity of Iranian youth and children, the family is still considered the most influential agency for the religious socialization in this country. Through their family, Iranian children become familiar with Islamic beliefs, rituals and ordinances, and are encouraged to comply with the Islamic rules, norms and values. They gradually express themselves as religious boys and girls and participate in religious areas.

A CULTURE OF PEACE AND DIALOGUE: REFLECTIONS ON THE CONCEPT OF PEACE IN ISLAM

Mahmud Mohammadi Araghi

I would like to start my paper by greeting all readers of this volume by saying: *'Salam-un 'Alaykum'* ('Peace be upon you!'). The word *salam* has a special affinity with the word 'Islam'. It is interesting that Islam, that is, the religion which brings about peace *(silm)*, by surrendering and submitting one's soul to God *(taslim)* asks people to open their conversations with others with *salam*, i.e. a request for their peace, both internally and externally.

This greeting of peace is not just a worldly form of greeting. This is the way that the inhabitants of Heaven and the angels greet the people of good will. The Qur'an says:

> Those who believe and work righteousness their Lord will guide them because of their faith: beneath them will flow rivers in Gardens of Bliss. [This will be] their cry therein: 'Glory to Thee O Allah!' and 'Peace' will be their greeting therein! And the close of their cry will be: 'Praise be to Allah the Cherisher and Sustainer of the Worlds!' (10: 9 and 10)

Commenting on the above verses, A Yusuf Ali writes: 'A beautiful piece of spiritual melody! They sing and shout with joy, but their joy is in the Glory of Allah! The greetings they receive and the greetings they give are of Peace and Harmony! From first to last they realize that it is Allah Who cherished them and made them grow, and His rays are their Light.'
Elsewhere, the Qur'an again refers to the greetings of the people of Heaven:

> But those who believe and work righteousness will be admitted to Gardens beneath which rivers flow to dwell therein for aye with the leave of their Lord: their greeting therein will be: 'Peace!' (14: 23)

Regarding greetings of the angels, the Qur'an says:

> There came Our Messengers to Abraham with glad tidings.
> They said 'Peace!' He answered 'Peace!' and hastened to
> entertain them with a roasted calf. (11: 69)
> Gardens of perpetual bliss: they shall enter there as well as the
> righteous among their fathers their spouses and their offspring:
> and angels shall enter unto them from every gate [with the
> salutation]:'Peace unto you for that ye persevered in patience!
> Now how excellent is the final Home!' (13: 23 and 24)

Moreover, God the Almighty greets the pious with salutation of
peace: 'Peace! a Word [of salutation] from a Lord Most Merciful!' (36:
58)

Interestingly, the Qur'an not only tells us that believers are greeted
with 'Peace!' in this world and in Heaven, but also that in the state of
transition from this world to the other, that is death, the angels greet
them with 'Peace!':

> Those whose lives the angels take in a state of purity saying
> [to them] 'Peace be on you; enter ye the Garden because of
> the good which ye did [in the world].' (16: 32)

Thus, those who die in a state of purity will be received into
happiness with a salutation of Peace. The angels greet them with the
salutation of Peace; they congratulate them; and they welcome them in.
(See also 39: 73)

The Qur'an teaches us that a salutation of peace has been the
greeting and slogan of Divine Prophets and is not exclusive to Islam. For
example, Moses and Aaron said to Pharaoh:

> So go ye both to him and say 'Verily we are apostles sent
> by thy Lord: send forth therefore the Children of Israel
> with us and afflict them not: with a Sign indeed have we
> come from thy Lord! And peace *(salām)* to all who follow
> guidance! (20: 47)

Jesus shortly after his birth said:

I am indeed a servant of God: He hath given me revelation
and made me a prophet;
And He hath made me Blessed whersoever I be and hath
enjoined on me Prayer and Charity as long as I live;
[He] hath made me kind to my mother and not overbearing
or miserable;
So Peace *(salām)* is on me the day I was born the day that
I die and the Day that I shall be raised up to life [again]!
(19: 33)

The very fact that peace has been the slogan of the Prophets,
angels and believers can still be witnessed in different cultures and among
people of different faiths. For example, Jews greet each other by saying:
'*Shalom*' and Christians call Jesus 'Prince of Peace' and chant in their
places of worship '*Pacem, pacem, pacem*'[1]

It has been suggested that the oldest passage in the Qur'an that
contains *salām* is the verse 97: 5 which states: 'It [Night of Measure; *laylat
al-qadr*] is peace until the coming of the dawn'. This verse characterizes
the Night of Measure which is the most important night for Muslims in
the whole year, which is 'better than 1000 months' and 'the blessed night',
'in which the Qur'an was revealed' as *salām,* peace. The Night of Measure
is a heavenly night in which Muslims try not to sleep and worship God
throughout the night so that they can witness and feel this peace.

Of course, a permanent and universal state of peace can be
witnessed in Heaven itself which is also called 'Abode of Peace' (*Dār al-
Salām*). The Qur'an says:

This is the way of thy Lord leading straight: We have detailed
the Signs for those who receive admonition.
For them will be the Abode of Peace in the presence of
their Lord: He will be their Friend because they practised
[righteousness]. (6: 126 and 127)

---

[1] Goldzieher believed and quoted passages from poets in support of the view that *salām* was
already in use as a greeting before Islam. The corresponding Hebrew and Aramaic
expressions, which go back to Old Testament usage (cf. Judges xix, 20, 2 Sam. xviii, 28, Dan.
x, 19, 1 Chron. xii, 19), were also in use as greetings among the Jews and Christians. A very
great number of Nabataean inscriptions further show the use of *s-l-m* to express good
wishes in northwestern Arabia and the Sinai Peninsula. (Extract from the *Encyclopaedia of
Islam,* CD-ROM Edition v. 1.0 © 1999 Koninklijke Brill NV, Leiden, The Netherlands)

Now the question arises why this much emphasis has been put on peace. And secondly how it is possible to acquire and prolong peace in this world. Indeed, these two questions are interrelated and finding the answer for each helps to answer the other.

Human beings are created in the way that they do not feel fully satisfied in this material life. There are many desires deep inside us that find no satisfaction in this world unless one is able to understand one's position in relation to one's Lord. The desire for absolute and infinite beauty, power and love can only be satisfied with knowledge of and approximation to God, the Absolute, the Infinite. The Qur'an says:

> O thou man! Verily thou art ever toiling on towards the Lord painfully toiling but thou shalt meet Him. (84: 6)[2]
> Those who believe and whose hearts find satisfaction in the remembrance of God: for without doubt in the remembrance of God do hearts find satisfaction. (13: 28)

The very idea that man strives for approximation to God and that without this he will not be at ease is also well-manifested in Islamic supplications. For example, praying to God Imam 'Ali b. Husayn says:

> Nothing will cool my burning thirst but reaching You, quench my ardour but meeting you, damp my yearning but gazing upon Your face, settle my settling place without closeness to you.[3]

Thus, man's yearning for peace is a yearning for God. It is ultimately amazing that one of the names of God in Islamic literature, including the Qur'an itself, is PEACE *(al-Salām)*. We read in the Qur'an:

> Allah is He than whom there is no other god, the Sovereign, the Holy One, the Peace, the Giver of Safety, the Guardian,

---

2   Commenting on the above verses, A Yusuf Ali writes: 'This life is ever full of toil and misery, if looked at as empty of the Eternal Hope which Revelation gives us. Hence the literature of pessimism in poetry and philosophy which thinking minds have poured forth in all ages, when that Hope was obscured to them'.

3   *The Psalms of Islam*, 251 and 252.

the Majestic, the Irresistible, the Supreme: Glory to Allah!
[high is He] above the partners they attribute to Him. (59: 23)

The real peace that man seeks and aspires to is peace of heart.
This peace can and should be maintained under all circumstances. The
Qur'an praises a group of people 'whom neither business nor trading
distract from remembering God, keeping up prayer, and paying the
welfare tax'. (24: 37) Imam Ali and other members of the household of
the Prophet call upon God:

> My God! Make me completely cut off from all else but You
> and enlighten the vision of our hearts with the radiance of
> looking at You until the vision of our hearts penetrates the
> veils of light and reaches the Source of Grandeur and set
> our spirit to be suspended at the glory of Your sanctity.[4]

To be cut off from anything other than God means to be free
from any reliance on things other than God, and to see everything as His
sign and the manifestation of His power and grace. True servants of God,
whether they are rich or poor, powerful or weak, famous or unknown, in
ease or in adversity and whether they live alone or inside society and
within a crowd, are totally mindful of God and remember Him always
and therefore they have an ultimate peace.

However, to create a pleasant and helpful atmosphere in which a
greater number of people and the masses can have enduring peace and a
better chance to take care of their spirituality and improve themselves,
all people of good faith must struggle for the establishment of a just
society with a fair distribution of welfare and without any sort of injustice,
oppression, discrimination, invasion and aggression. This is why Islam
calls for the prosperity of human beings both in this world and the
Hereafter and asks its followers to strike a balance between the material
and the spiritual and to work for a peaceful and prosperous world.

Now it is the time to turn to the second question and that is
how it is possible to acquire and prolong peace in this world. Addressing
the People of the Book (including the Christians and Jews) the Qur'an
introduces itself as follows:

---

[4] 'Al-Munajat al-Sha'baniyah' in *Mafatih al-Jinan*.

There hath come to you from Allah a (new) Light and a perspicuous Book. Wherewith Allah guideth all who seek His good pleasure to ways of peace and leadeth them out of darkness by His Will unto the light guideth them to a Path that is Straight. (5: 15 and 16)

So what are 'the ways of peace' that the Qur'an has undertaken to show? To study the Qur'anic ways of peace we need a detailed discussion about the Qur'anic plan for human life which is beyond the limits of this paper. Here I would like to focus just on one of those 'ways of peace', that is, a sincere dialogue. This point is also mentioned in an address to the People of the Book:

Say: 'O People of the Book! Come to common terms as between us and you: that we worship none but Allah; that we associate no partners with Him; that we erect not from among ourselves Lords and patrons other than Allah.' If then they turn back say: 'Bear witness that we [at least] are Muslims [bowing to Allah's will].' (3: 64)

The Qur'an itself has taken practical steps towards the unity of the believers in God by asking Muslims to declare their faith in the previous prophets and revelations:

Say: 'We believe in God and in what has been revealed to us and what was revealed to Abraham, Ishmael, Isaac, Jacob and the Tribes and in [Books] given to Moses, Jesus and the Prophets from their Lord; we make no distinction between one and another among them and to Allah do we bow our will [in Islam].' (3: 83)

The Qur'an also teaches us to be open to others and to see the gifts in their hands. For example, the Qur'an praises Christians (5: 82 and 83) and introduces Mary as an exemplar human being (66: 12). Indeed, the Qur'an introduces Islam as the religion of all prophets and considers all the Abrahamic faiths as one family. A Muslim is not obliged to deny or fight against other religions. In fact, to be a Muslim depends on believing in all previous revelations.

In view of the above mentioned points, the necessity of a dialogue of all believers becomes very clear. Religious leaders must not look at each others as rivals or enemies; rather they should consider each other as colleagues and aids in facing the contemporary challenges that threaten mankind.

In accordance with what has been said above, it is hoped that this volume will prove to be a start for subsequent exchanges and pave the way for further dialogue, co-operation and collaboration in a practical and serious manner. No doubt, this will lead to an enduring peace and the comprehensive happiness of man.

I finish my paper by asking peace for all dear participants of this dialogue and for all mankind:

Peace be upon you and the mercy of God!

REFLECTIONS FOR A FUTURE AGENDA
Timothy Wright

The problem now is, 'What next?' Hopefully you have found these papers so informative, readable and stimulating that you will encourage us to continue this work of dialogue, but 'How?'

My purpose in this 'Afterword' is to propose items for a future agenda. Ambitious? Of course! Realistic? Hopefully. Discussions will continue in the universities; they have been going on for some time and there is still much to develop. In our monasteries, seminaries and local communities there is scope for doing more; we can be more open to exchanges and build local friendships through meetings.

The first question we pose, a little gently, is, 'How important is dialogue between Catholic Christians and Shi'a Muslims, compared to dialogue among Christians?' Some might say it is not either/or, but both/and. Let us be realistic: resources are limited; significant progress has been made among the Churches and the time has come to give the Catholic Christian–Shi'a dialogue priority. The reason for this is that there is so much more to cover, the need is great, and increased mutual understanding and respect are essential if we are to build peace into our communities.

Breaking down fear and prejudice is a priority for Catholic Christians and Shi'a Muslims in Britain, Iran and elsewhere. Even if we only remove a few bricks from the wall, we have done enough for some of us to leap over. First hand experience is the proper basis for building trust and love.

Looking forward

The political scene in Europe, the USA and the Middle East is confusing, dangerously so; it is a short step from confusion to chaos, a route certainly marked by violence. Today violence is fostered by extremism, whether from the political extremes or the religious fanatic. As Cardinal Francis

Arinze, the then President of the Pontifical Council for Interreligious Dialogue, put it in his paper at the Catholic Chaplaincy of the University of Oxford in January 2002:

> Some religious fundamentalists knowingly or unknowingly adopt political positions which would justify violence and even terrorism, and some go so far as to suggest that they are waging a religious war for God ... Care has to be taken that religious fundamentalism and extremism do not slide down to terrorism.[1]

Building peace is only possible if we speak to each other, share our lives, forgive each other, support and love each other in times of need. That is not just a matter of words, but requires a style of living, a style of living deeply in conformity with the inspired Word of God, the basis of our faiths. Top of the agenda is the creation of spaces and time to increase contact, to exchange stories, to build friendship.

We are encouraged to proceed with this because, despite our obvious differences, we can recognise in Christianity and affirm a number of values held dear by Muslims, as expressed by one of our conference organisers, Mohammad Ali Shomali:

> No school of thought has emphasized the nobility and value of humanity to the extent that ours has. In our faith, man has the highest possibilities for perfection and closeness to Allah (God). The divine spirit is breathed into him and he is the representative of Allah (God) on earth. Man will be satisfied with nothing short of closeness to Allah (God) and His pleasure ... We can find no rest, but in meeting Allah (God). The value of man is due to his voluntary relationship to the absolute Truth.[2]

The recognition of our place before the Divine is the sure foundation for faith in face of the challenges posed by our contemporary

---

[1] Cardinal Francis Arinze, 'The University as a Promoter of Interreligious Dialogue'. A lecture given at the Oxford University Catholic Chaplaincy, 26 January 2002.

[2] M A Shomali, *Self Knowledge*, Tehran, 1976, vii.

world, in whose philosophy and values humankind has the answer to all needs and does not need to be subservient to an all-powerful God.

Before the Divine, Christians and Muslims share a deep respect for human life, every human life at whatever stage of its existence. Each is valued as a gift of God's love. That value successfully undermines any idea that any person could be the mere pawn of another. Human life and love cannot be reduced to items on the scientific or consumer agendas. Our agreement on this strengthens our challenge to those who hold such anti-human values. Pope John Paul II expressed it thus:

> Beloved young people, I want to exhort you to work to build peace and be artisans of peace. Respond to blind violence and inhuman hatred with the fascinating power of love. Overcome enmity with the force of forgiveness. Keep far away from any form of exasperated nationalism, racism and intolerance. Witness with your life that ideas are not imposed but proposed. Never let yourselves be discouraged by evil! For this you will need the help of prayer and the consolation that is born from an intimate friendship with Christ.[3]

The contemporary world

Together, Christians and Muslims are powerful in facing the destructive liberalism of post-modern society. To be more effective we need greater mutual understanding, and we must make time for that.

Together, Christians and Muslims face the contemporary mistrust of authority (often misconstrued as 'authoritarianism'), whether located in inspired teachings, holy people or the leaders of our respective religions. The removal of constraints has created a world more dangerous than liberals like to admit. Relativism has undermined moral truth, given 'authority' to the powerful and removed it from the weak. The rich can do what they like and justify it; the poor and the weak have to live with suffering and pain.

---

[3] Pope John Paul II, 'Address to Young People', Madrid, 6 May 2003.

Our stance against this has to be solid and convincing: solid in its recognition of the rights of each individual, to life, health, education, home, job. Convincing in the way we present it to our own communities. Lack of consistency gives the post-modern spokesperson the chance to dismiss religious faith as medieval, manipulative and immature. To disarm that we must live transparently by the values we profess.

Might the consumer-led world implode on itself? The signs of decay are there for those with eyes to see; self-centred living has increased in the affluent world and fear has encouraged higher and higher security fences. Whichever side of this fence we find ourselves on, we must work for its destruction. Security fences do not bring protection. They offer a challenge to the thief or the terrorist.

Family life

During the Ampleforth stage of the conference, we heard papers on family life from both the Catholic and the Shi'a perspectives. We shared each other's concerns about bringing up children in an environment hostile to our values, both of marriage and family life. We shared the stance that each child, a special gift of God's love, bestows on its parents a responsibility for stability at home, for challenge in education, and for formation in our respective faiths.

Our shared monotheistic faith gives Catholic Christians and Shi'a Muslims the scope for a greater sharing at the local level, especially where families live side by side. In Western countries, all parents face the same pressures, are asked the same questions and have to find a way forward, faithful to their beliefs, convincing to the young, and sufficiently coherent to withstand criticism from the non-believing neighbour or classmate.

Caroline Dollard's paper to the conference shows how complex modern family life can be:

> From a very young age, the complexities of the contemporary culture come into play. Fashion—Nike trainers for 4 year-olds; the power of money—who has it and who has not; the subtle power of the media and advertizing making empty promises to meet genuine human

needs; choices to believe in God or not, to belong to a Church or not—and in this area the parents have the task of interpreting the culture, harnessing what is good, and not being afraid to be in conversation with their children about all these influences. The challenges to the Church in this period are great—to support and affirm families, and help them make connections between their faith and the reality of their lives and the choices they make.[4]

There is plenty of experience in both our faiths; there is much to be shared; we can learn what works and what does not. We face the same pressures from contemporary culture to abandon family values in favour of a freewheeling consumerism and self-interest. Caroline Dollard again:

> The hectic pace of modern life, and time-pressures created by the many demands on each member of the family meant that we were in danger of losing close touch with one another. We decided to have a 'family meeting' once a week on a Sunday evening, simply to talk about life, make plans discuss concerns, and have some form of recreation together. Anybody could contribute to the agenda—subjects varied from pocket money levels, jobs at home, problems at school, peer pressure, family/other relationships, to major decisions about moving house and changing lifestyle. Attendance was voluntary. God, faith and Church as specific topics were not raised—they simply underpinned the way we tried to live out this commitment to one another in the family, how we communicated with one another, and learnt to make decisions together about important issues, and also had fun and celebrated life together too. ... These conversations changed us—they changed feelings and ideas, they changed the ways we looked at things, they involved searching and honesty and made demands.[5]

---

[4] C Dollard, 'Family Life'. A paper given at Ampleforth Abbey as a part of the conference entitled, 'A Catholic-Shia Engagement: Sharing our Spiritual and Theological Resources in the Face of Contemporary Challenges', July 2003. This paper is not published in this volume.

[5] C Dollard, 'Family Life'.

That is one mother and family's way of facing the problems of bringing up children in the middle of hectic lives, a family meeting once a week. Perhaps that is something others might take up? Catholic Christian and Shi'a Muslim families in the UK could have fruitful discussions about the particular problems posed by today's culture.

Religious schools

Abbas Jaffer in his conference paper on education said:

> Islam considers education to be the acquisition of knowledge that penetrates into the heart of a person, giving him an increased awareness and realization and transforming his thoughts and actions. ... The Prophet Muhammad (God's peace be upon him) instructed the Muslims, 'Seek knowledge from the cradle to the grave.' With this instruction, the Muslim considers the pursuit of all education, whether secular or religious, to be a sacred duty and one that ultimately leads him to achieving God's proximity and pleasure.[6]

Christians agree that the way to God has to include education. Religion needs education just as much as education needs religion. In believing societies, whether Muslim or Christian, our schools fit neatly into that framework. Today, most countries are not religious, and the religious culture has all but disappeared. Education is now focussed on knowledge, skills, and community living. An increasingly heavy curriculum squeezes out 'extra-curricular' activities.

To survive, religious schools have had to improve the quality of their religious teaching (religious studies) ensuring it has proper standing as an academic subject alongside other subjects. Religious education has been more clearly defined. Headteachers and governors focus on the school's ethos, reflecting the faith. This is especially important where the school enrols members of other faiths.

---

[6] A Jaffar, 'Religion and Education: A Presentation of a Shia Perspective'. A paper given at Ampleforth Abbey as a part of the conference entitled, 'A Catholic-Shia Engagement: Sharing our Spiritual and Theological Resources in the Face of Contemporary Challenges', July 2003. This paper is not published in this volume.

Christians in Britain live in a multi-religious society. These words of Cardinal Arinze at the end of Ramadan in 2000 were particularly heartening:

> All who are concerned with the education of youth are certainly conscious of the need of educating for dialogue. In accompanying young people along the highways of life, attention has to be given to the preparation required for living in a society marked by ethnic, cultural and religious plurality. Such education implies, first of all, that we broaden our vision to an ever wider horizon, become capable of looking beyond our own country, our own ethnic group, our own cultural tradition, so that we can see humanity as a single family in both its diversity and its common aspirations. This is education in the fundamental values of human dignity, peace, freedom and solidarity. It evokes the desire to know other people, to be able to share their sorrows and to understand their deepest feelings. Education for dialogue means nurturing the hope that conflict situations can be resolved through personal and collective commitment.[7]

Such a statement might pose problems for some of our Shi'a friends. During our conference Abbas Jaffer said, 'we are more concerned with the aspect of nurturing and education.'[8]

The cardinal makes the point: we cannot truly 'nurture' faith in a multicultural society without being aware of, indeed, without showing some understanding of, the faiths alongside us. How does a religious family nurture its children in its own faith, the Truth, while at the same time showing respect to the faith of our neighbour, without suggesting it is not the Truth? That question can only be answered by one schooled in tolerance and appreciative of the many diverse ways to God.

In school we provide serious academic study of other religions in religious studies. In Britain such courses are academically rigorous, and allow space for those looking from the outside in, as well as challenging those within. The commitment is to train the mind to reason carefully

---

[7] F Arinze, 'Message for the End of Ramadan', 2000.

[8] A Jaffar, 'Religion and Education'.

and to encourage pupils to think 'theologically'. The standard and methods employed in the classroom further encourage young people to take such studies further at university.

There is another important dimension in our schools: to develop the inner soul where faith is but needs strength. That strength comes from prayer and contemplation. Pope John Paul in his address to young people spoke of it like this:

> The drama of contemporary culture is the lack of interiority, the absence of contemplation. Without interiority culture has no content; it is like a body that has not yet found its soul. What can humanity do without interiority? Unfortunately we know the answer very well. When the contemplative spirit is missing, life is not protected and all that is human is denigrated. Without interiority, modern man puts his own integrity at risk. Never separate action from contemplation.[9]

This is perhaps the biggest challenge for our schools: how do we strengthen that inner life? It cannot be forced, but it needs time and space. We need teachers who can lead by example. They need to be not only men and women of faith, but also of prayer.

The challenge of freedom

By 'freedom' I do not mean 'independence from God', but rather 'freedom for excellence', the freedom necessary for us to choose to become what God has created us to be, to be truly and fully human. Such freedom lies at the heart of effective education. For our contemporaries, and following the teaching of the Second Vatican Council, neither faith nor values nor respect can be imposed.[10] 'Indoctrination' used to be a neutral word describing the process by which the young were taught. 'Learn the teachings and think about them later', it was said. But that method is no longer effective: forced religion breeds rebellion

---

[9] Pope John Paul II, 'Address to Young People', Madrid, 6 May 2003.

[10] See Vatican II's, 'Declaration on Religious Liberty, *Dignitatis Humanae*, 7 December 1965.

and hurt. The acceptance of faith has to be freely given. We must respect the freedom of the young to question, to reject, but also to accept.

We know that in the early years the young are told what to do and how to do it. They are taught to pray, and learn the stories of faith and what it involves, in ways they can appreciate. As Abbas Jaffer told us:

> By providing an encouraging, loving and pressure-free environment in the child's formative years, the parents allow the natural curiosity and tendency of children to experiment, to flourish. They allow the inquisitive child to explore and discover the world around him. Harshness is disapproved of, tolerance is encouraged.[11]

As children grow older and start to think for themselves, we respect their independence, but challenge them to think and justify, while stressing their responsibility to own their own beliefs and behaviour. They have to answer before God for their own lives. In the words of John Paul II cited earlier, we propose the faith; theirs is the task of responding.

In an atmosphere freed from constraint, the young see religion taught and lived by their teachers in a true light, not distorted by being imposed. Even so the results can alarm. Yet this quotation from the Second Vatican Council offers some reassurance:

> In the depths of his conscience man detects a law which he does not impose upon himself, but which holds him to obedience ... For man has in his heart a law written by God. To obey it is the very dignity of man; according to it he will be judged. Conscience is the most secret core and sanctuary of a man. There he is along with God, whose voice echoes in his depths.[12]

Within each human being there is the 'presence' of the divine guide from within. This presence is effective, and though not immediately so, the knowledge that it is there can reduce the worry of parents, teachers,

---

[11] A Jaffar, 'Religion and Education'.

[12] 'The Pastoral Constitution on the Church in the Modern World', *Gaudium et Spes*, 7 December 1965, 16.

or friends. The inner voice of God is more powerful than any arguments by teachers or guidance from parents. Freedom allows the voice of God to be heard, without it being deafened by other noises.

As educators we live with open minds, listening to what the young are saying, listening too to the contemporary post-modern world which surrounds them. The more we listen together, the more effective we will be as teachers. The better able we are to stand outside our faith and see it from the other side, the more effective we will be. We kill interest if we use the language of faith to those who have no understanding of it.

By giving space to the young for discussion, experimentation, anger, humour, rebellion and testing, we allow them to be themselves, to grow into who God intends them to be. We go on affirming and encouraging them, sure that in the end they will reach the Truth. By contrast, in my experience it is more dangerous to have a calm, obedient, conforming adolescent; the rebellious phase has not passed, it has been postponed.

Co-operating in schools

In Britain Christian and Muslim schools share much. Now is the moment to take initiatives to bring closer co-operation. Each will benefit from discussion with the other. Issues of common interest like rites of passage, moral issues, coping with failure, disaster, and tragedy, and celebrating occasions of joy. Such co-operation and sharing at school can do much to bring understanding, tolerance and respect.

A last word

The discussions both in Iran and the UK must continue. Our 'Catholic-Shi'a Engagement' could not have happened had it not been for the joint work of Heythrop College in the University of London, Ampleforth Abbey, and the Imam Khomeini Institute for Education and Research working together. Dialogue on this scale can only be fostered when institutions such as these work together, and I am sure that these bodies will continue to support this work.

We hope that you, the reader, have found these essays as fascinating and enlightening as we, the participatants, in the conference did. We arrived at the meetings at Heythrop and Ampleforth just a little apprehensive, but, as we got to know each other better, that apprehension melted away. Within the monastic environment, we were able to put prayer at the centre of each day. That set the priorities, the rest followed, almost naturally.

I applaud the clarity of the presentations; that helped the process. Points of divergence emerged clearly, but without threat. This was truly a divine gift; we give thanks for it. This book bears witness to mutual good will, inspired by the presence of the Divine, enriched by sound scholarship alongside a firm desire to promote the God to whom each of us is accountable. In His Name we give thanks.